POSTMODERN MANAGEMENT AND ORGANIZATION THEORY

POSTMODERN MANAGEMENT AND ORGANIZATION THEORY

David M. Boje
Robert P. Gephart, Jr.
Tojo Joseph Thatchenkery
editors

SAGE Publications
International Educational and Professional Publisher
Thousand Oaks   London   New Delhi

For information address:

SAGE Publications, Inc.
2455 Teller Road
Thousand Oaks, California 91320
E-mail: order@sagepub.com

SAGE Publications Ltd.
6 Bonhill Street
London EC2A 4PU
United Kingdom

SAGE Publications India Pvt. Ltd.
M-32 Market
Greater Kailash I
New Delhi 110 048 India

Printed in the United States of America

Library of Congress Cataloging-in-Publication Data

Main entry under title:

Postmodern management and organization theory/edited by David M.
  Boje, Robert P. Gephart, Jr., Tojo Joseph Thatchenkery.
      p. cm.
    Includes bibliographical references and index.
    ISBN 0-8039-7004-8 (cloth: acid-free paper).—ISBN
  0-8039-7005-6 (pbk.: acid-free paper)
      1. Management—Congresses. 2. Organizational sociology—
  Congresses. 3. Postmodern—Congresses. I. Boje, David M.
  II. Gephart, Robert P., Jr. III. Thatchenkery, Joseph Tojo.
  HD29.P67 1995
  658—dc20   95-32503

96 97 98 99 10 9 8 7 6 5 4 3 2

This book is printed on acid-free paper.

Sage Production Editor: Gillian Dickens

Contents

Preface

Postmodern Management and Organization Theory was written with a wide audience in mind. We believe that it provides a broad critique of modern management, organizations, and related theories, thus offering a brief introduction to the critical analysis of organizations and management. It also provides a useful introduction to postmodern views, concepts, themes, and topics emerging from the critique of management and organization theory and hence provides a rough map of the terrain of postmodern organization theory.

The book should be of interest to readers interested in the nature and meaning of postmodernism and its relevance to organizations and management. It should be of particular relevance to sociologists, anthropologists, and management and organization theory scholars. The book is intended for use by scholars who wish to become familiar with the issues and prospects in the field of postmodern management and organization theory, as well as scholars attempting to do cutting-edge research in the area. However, the book is written to be comprehensible to scholars and students with only a limited prior knowledge of postmodernism. We think that the book should also be especially interesting to graduate students and advanced undergraduate students with an interest in current trends and challenges facing management and organizations. Students are going to have to deal with the postmodern world, and we hope that this book will be an especially useful resource to them in this regard. However, the book has been written in an academic style using many academic terms. We have avoided the use of jargon where possible, but given the emphasis in postmodernism on language and language use, readers and particularly student readers might well expect to find novel, complex, or unusual terms and ideas that require some thought and consideration. Managers will also find the book to be of interest because it outlines the current and future challenges facing management and provides innovative, nontraditional suggestions and approaches to these issues. Indeed, it is the "thinking manager" concerned with future organizational and management challenges who may benefit most from the new foundations for management practice that emerge from the applications of ideas in this book.

The genesis of this book was the All Academy Showcase Symposium on Postmodern Management: Diversity and Change, which was presented to the 1992 Academy of Management Meetings in Las Vegas, Nevada. The symposium was organized by David Boje and Robert P. Gephart, Jr., accepted by the 1992 Academy of Management Vice President and Program Chair Greg Oldham, and jointly supported by the Organization and Management Theory, Organization Development and Change, and Research Methods Divisions of the Academy of Management. Symposium presenters included Stewart Clegg, William Hetrick, Hector Lozada, Patricia Bradshaw, David Boje, and Robert P. Gephart, Jr., with Joanne Martin acting as discussant. We wish to thank these scholars and the three supportive Academy divisions. We were gratified by the success of the symposium and so also wish to thank all those who attended the symposium and who participated in the dynamic discussions that occurred then, particularly the enthusiastic Ph.D. students from the University of California, Irvine. In addition, another postmodern symposium, Postmodernist Readings on Managerial Abilities, Learning Organizations, and Information Systems, was presented to the Managerial and Organizational Cognition Interest Group at the 1992 Academy meetings. This symposium, organized by Tojo Joseph Thatchenkery and Eric Neilsen, added impetus to our ideas for a book. Participants in that symposium were William Pasmore, Richard J. Boland, and Ramkrishnan Tenkasi, with Ronald Purser and Frank Barrett as discussants. We wish to thank these scholars and the MOC interest group for supporting this postmodern venture.

The book itself was launched with the support of Marquita Flemming, editor at Sage, and we wish to thank Marquita and Sage Publications for supporting this project. Furthermore, the book is the outcome of a rich and enjoyable interchange among the editors and authors, and we wish to thank the authors for their extensive work and timely responses to our queries and requests. The editors themselves were responsible for providing all the comments and reviews of the chapters that appear in this volume. The editors' names are listed alphabetically to indicate the collective nature of our efforts and the equivalent participation and responsibility for the final product that each editor assumes. We were assisted in this editorial effort by Punya Upadhyaya and Catherine Cramton, whose ideas, enthusiasm, and insights were greatly appreciated. Many of the ideas in the book, and the book itself, also received support from the Postmodern Organization Theory Track of the International Academy of Business Disciplines, and we wish to thank our "POMO" colleagues and others at IABD for their generous support and enthusiasm and for providing a warm home for postmodern studies at IABD.

We dedicate this book to our children Keith, Laura, Raymond, and Sruthi, whose fate is to inherit a postmodern world we can only attempt to describe.

David M. Boje
Robert P. Gephart, Jr.
Tojo Joseph Thatchenkery

1

Postmodern Management and
the Coming Crises of Organizational Analysis

ROBERT P. GEPHART, JR.

DAVID M. BOJE

TOJO JOSEPH THATCHENKERY

This book advances an agenda for postmodern scholarship in management, organization theory, and organizational analysis. The task is challenging. The relative success of the term *postmodernism* as a popularized, iconic representation of a "new age" (Jameson, 1991, p. xiii) and the multiplicity of meanings of postmodernism have made the range of phenomena to which the term attaches somewhat immense, suggesting the need for a lengthy best-seller on the concept of postmodernism itself. There are scholarly and political factions espousing both favorable (affirmative) and critical (skeptical) assessments of postmodernism (Rosenau, 1992, pp. 14-17), and different terms are used by different groups to depict the phenomenon. For example, the hyphenated term *post-modernism* is often used to indicate a "critical posture" toward the phenomenon, whereas postmodernism is often employed by those who are sympathetic to the phenomenon and recognize its legitimacy (Rosenau, 1992, p. 18). Thus, it is difficult to even describe or define the term without encountering competing and perhaps incommensurate opinions of what the term means, and without entering some political debate on the nature and merits of postmodernism.

1

In this introduction, we seek to outline the general purposes of the book and to provide some background on the emergence, nature, and implications of postmodernism for organization and management theory. Three themes guide our investigation of postmodernism here. First, we conceive postmodernism as the social era immediately after *modernism* (Rosenau, 1992). Postmodernism is a new and distinct social order (Giddens, 1990, p. 46) that involves something different, a break with the past. This is not necessarily "progress" nor a step forward. Even the chronological aspect of postmodernism as a period subsequent to modernism is suspect for Lyotard (1979/1984), who argues that "a work can only be modern if it is first postmodern" (p. 79). A second way we conceive postmodernism is that it is a cultural movement or worldview that is reconceptualizing how we experience and explain our world (Rosenau, 1992, p. 4). Third, postmodernism is an artistic or cultural style that provides an aesthetic reflection on the nature of modernism (Giddens, 1990, p. 45; Lyotard, 1979/1984, p. 81) and that emphasizes "an incredulity toward metanarratives" (Lyotard, 1979/ 1984, p. xxiv).

The relevance of postmodernism to management and organization theory is the specific concern of this chapter. We define management as the activities of social actors and their interventions into organized human processes, particularly actors with discrete formal statuses that provide the legitimate authority to direct and coordinate the behavior of other social actors. Organizations are generally conceived by social actors as relatively reified and concrete features of the social world— aggregations of social actors, meanings, and physical artifacts integrated for purposes of achieving some set of goals. For us, the meaning of organization is problematic. Rather than conceiving of organizations substantively as a concrete facticities embedded in artifacts such as policies and buildings, we regard organization relationally (Mauws, 1995; Morrow, 1994) as a concept of social actors that is produced in contextually embedded social discourse and used to interpret the social world (Bittner, 1974; Gephart, 1978). The meaning of organization thus resides in the contexts and occasions where it is created and used by members, rather than in a specific fixed substantive form. This is important because a paramount feature of postmodernism appears to be radically and rapidly changing conceptions of organizations and a movement away from substantive conceptions among social actors themselves. Finally, we regard organization theory as constituted in and by reflective and reflexive analyses (Pollner, 1991) of organizations and organizing and by the abstract descriptions and interpretations of these processes. Thus, we do not argue that there is a single or "best" form of theory or organization theory but, rather, that there are many possible theories of organization. We use the term *organization theory* in singular form for simplicity, but we envisage and seek to advance a field in which many theories and perspectives exist to inform our understanding of organized phenomena in contemporary society.

Societal Crises
of Late Capitalism

The three general postmodern themes that we address here—era, movement, and style—direct our attention to three sets of crises of late modernity. Here, we discuss these crises and the forms and features of the crises as instantiated in managerial action and organizations. A key purpose of this volume is to develop insights into management and organization that can help us understand the ways in which postmodern management and organization theory can address these crises.

Habermas (1973) is a critic of postmodernism who provides a critical analysis of the crises of late modern society, addressing his analysis to the societal level. His analysis of the crises of capitalism presages the emergence of postmodernism and directs attention to key processes and challenges faced in the transition from modernism to postmodernism. Late capitalist society is conceived to be a contradictory, entropic system composed of four sectors or subsystems: the economic subsystem, the political or administrative subsystem, the sociocultural subsystem, and the legitimation system (Habermas, 1973, following Offe, 1984). The entropic or self-destructive contradictory tendencies arise from the very bases of the system. For example, in advanced capitalism, the inherently exploitative mode of production tends to destroy the very preconditions on which the system depends (Offe, 1984, p. 132; see also Gephart & Pitter, 1993). In particular, there is a desire to accumulate economic surplus and yet a tendency of profit to fall and thereby limit capital accumulation. In this context, a crisis cycle emerges as deficits in rationality in one sector accumulate and spill over into other sectors. Economic exploitation of Nature occurs as natural phenomena are commodified, and economic crises can emerge when increases of technical rationality fail to offset competitive economic forces in the market, and/or when real ecosystemic limits are encountered (Habermas, 1973, pp. 41-42). Where members of society lack the motivation to uphold societal values and roles, the most significant form of crisis—a legitimation crisis—can arise. Legitimation crises occur where the state apparatus fails to secure mass loyalty, and this can lead to disintegration of the state, changes in the basic organizing principles of the state, or social control through authoritarian repression. Economic and motivational crises that can lead to legitimation crises are prevented or delayed by government programs that seek to provide social welfare and thereby overcome the deficits in economic and government rationality that adversely affect social sectors. Yet in the long term, Habermas argues that legitimation crises can be avoided in advanced capitalism only by changing the class structures of societies or by removing the pressures for legitimation that are placed on the political administration.

Current trends in society and organization reflect these emerging potential crises. As the economy and capitalist organizations encounter limits to the growth of profits, there is a tendency for economic endeavors to seek to colonize new sectors of the state, in particular the government and sociocultural sectors. Thus, there is an erosion of the "welfare state" (Offe, 1984) principles basic to the modern state—that is, an erosion of institutions of social redistribution within the government (Peukert, 1987/1989). This occurs through the process of *privatization*—the transfer of services for citizens that the government provided free to the private or market sector and the transformation of these free services into commodities, that is, services for which one must pay a fee. Members of society are thereafter required to perform as consumers of these services, and the services are offered by corporations and businesses and are no longer provided by government. This erosion also occurs where the state retains production and distribution rights to these services but commodifies them by charging user fees. Therefore, previously noncommodified and decommodified (Offe, 1984) public goods and services become economic goods produced and administered by the economic sector.

Although other transformations of capital are occurring, privatization is noteworthy because it involves an erosion and extensive displacement of governmental and sociocultural sectors, and this extensive displacement undermines not only the benefits that members of society receive but also their sense of fairness of the distribution of these benefits. Commodification of social services and benefits clearly privileges the economically advantaged. Thus, the transfer of state functions to the market economy and the colonization of nonmarket sectors by market forces problematizes the legitimacy of the modern state because the state thereby abandons its role as a mediator of the interests of the various social sectors (Habermas, 1973; Weber, 1947), which ensured a just distribution of the resources of society. These crises arising from the displacement of the state by the economic sectors can be seen in the dissolution of social welfare agencies, threats to tenure and job security at universities, the erosion of access to health care, and other social trends that constitute the privatization and commodification of the public sector.

Legitimation crises may thus emerge and other crises are likely to escalate as we reap the benefits of years of concern over enhancing organizational productivity. The result of increased productivity in a constrained ecosystem is simply the production of greater volumes of goods using fewer inputs, including laborers and managers; hence the extensive downsizing, reengineering, and displacement of labor and managerial labor in recent years. We now have the potential for "human-free products" and an economy without labor. One fundamental contradiction of capitalism—the tendency to reduce wages to enhance profits simultaneous with the tendency of reduced wages to undermine markets and production—thus sets internal limits on the legitimatory apparatus of the state, limits that are currently being approached. These social crises emerge and are played out at the organizational level and involve management and managerial decision making. Thus, the societal crises of modernism are basic to challenges facing contemporary organizational and managerial crises.

Cultural Crises and Social Movements

The second set of crises facing organization and management theory relates to postmodernism as a social movement. The challenges, crises, and limits of modernism have led to the emergence of postmodernism as a cultural or social movement that critiques modernism and

offers alternative institutional and aesthetic forms. These social movements can themselves produce crises by challenging the status quo of
cultural processes and institutional forms and by seeking radical,
disjunctive, social and organizational changes. The postmodern social
movements are addressed by Hollinger (1994) in terms of three essentially modernist forms: antimodernist, balanced modernist, and pro-
modernist. Antimodernists (Hollinger, 1994, pp. 31-32) are critical of
industrialization, bureaucracy, and the privileging of technology—
modernist forms. Antimodernists thus offer a critique of the inhuman
aspects of modernity and articulate the shadow side of modernism.
Essential to the antimodernist view is an "incredulity towards metanarratives" (Lyotard, 1979/1984, p. xxiv). Balanced modernists acknowledge both a shadow side and a hopeful side to modernism, thus
embracing both anti- and promodern views. Promodernists, as the
term suggests, are supportive of modernism, celebrate its potential and
successes, and seek to preserve and reproduce modernism. As these
three movements indicate, there is a potential basis for political conflict surrounding the nature and meaning of modernism and its moral
and ethical propriety. This potential arises at the organizational level
where supporters of different movements articulate their views in
organizational policies.

   One important issue central to the debates among these movements
is the commodification of education and knowledge (Lyotard, 1979/
1984). Science has been one of the major social or cultural movements
of modernism. Science embraces a totalizing perspective on knowledge and accepts the metanarratives of the Enlightenment, which
assume the universal progress of society. As late modernism implodes
(Baudrillard, 1983), the world of the "grand narrative" becomes im-
probable; hence the legitimacy of science is eroded. Culture becomes
composed of an indefinite number of relatively autonomous worldviews and meaning-generating agencies. Science is then transformed
from the master legitimation of modernism into yet another sector of
commodified production, with knowledge becoming both a product
to be sold and a good to be consumed. This commodification is resisted
by antimodernists but supported by promodernists for whom "the
market" is the driving and ultimately divine force for positive social
change.

The Crises of Representation

The third set of crises involves crises of representation, that is, crises regarding the nature of images and the manner in which images are produced. The delegitimation of science as a totalizing knowledge or grand narrative has been associated with the emergence of views in which scientific methods are problematized. That is, there has been a loss of grand theory in all disciplines (Marcus & Fischer, 1986). For modernism, there is "a" scientific method, and this is arguably the best way to produce valid knowledge. The method leads, in organizational science, to forms of positivism that focus on the statistically quantifiable relationships among variables (Gephart, 1988a). Alternative views challenge not only the superiority of the scientific method but also the claim that there is a single scientific method (Gephart, 1988a). This produces a crisis in science, as it seeks new grounds to legitimate the validity of scientific knowledge. Crises emerge in society as science is displaced as a primary legitimatory force and as a monopoly producer of "true" or valid knowledge.

The emergence of alternatives to the totalizing views of science suspend rather than reject positivistic scientific frameworks (Marcus & Fischer, 1986, p. 10). The task of alternative frameworks is to use ironic modes of writing to produce realist descriptions of society (Marcus & Fischer, 1986, p. 14) and organizations (Gephart, 1993), which describe "at a microscopic level the process of change itself" (Marcus & Fischer, 1986, p. 15). Ethnographic genres of writing (Van Maanen, 1988) offer alternatives to modernist scientific modes of representation. A number of other alternative representational modes have been explored (Calas & Smircich, 1991; Jameson, 1991; Rosenau, 1992).

The emergence of representational alternatives in social and administrative sciences and studies commonly has been associated with various controversies regarding the dominance of positivist or quantitative methods and the validity of knowledge emerging from qualitative methods or modes of research, although this quantitative/qualitative dichotomy is currently viewed by many as problematic (Gephart, 1988a). We consider the persistence of representational controversies in organizational analysis as symptomatic of the broader ontological and methodological crisis potential of contemporary management studies.

Scientific knowledge and its legitimacy are based in scientific modes of representing the world, and as traditional scientific representational modes are challenged, the managerial and social value of the scholarly field of management studies is itself brought into question. Where some might argue for restoration of scientific legitimacy by return or reversion to a more strictly articulated and regulated scientific positivism, the chapters in this volume argue for development of alternative representations that challenge the dehumanized representations that emerge from objectivist science (Gephart, 1988a). The stage is thus set for methodological, aesthetic, and political controversies and crises within the very field of management and organization theory.

Overview of the Book

The book contains new and original essays on topics in postmodern management and organization theory. The intent was to advance the field of postmodern management and organization studies by offering essays that developed ideas fully within the postmodern domain. We sought essays that review and explain postmodern perspectives and concepts, including ideas developed in the works of postmodern writers, such as Baudrillard and Foucault. The chapters seek to develop the relevance of postmodern ideas to management and organization theory issues by actually undertaking critical investigations and discussions of organizational issues, to demonstrate how postmodern perspectives and concepts can be used in management and organizational theorizing. Thus, we sought to distinguish the book from the first wave of postmodern intrusions into organizational analysis, which involved reflective essays on the potential of postmodernist thought for reconceptualizing management theory. In the current book, we try to advance the field by offering essays that not only review and explain postmodern perspectives and concepts but that also actually apply these postmodern concepts and ideas to emerging managerial and organizational issues that characterize the postmodern era. The chapters frame and illustrate the new and emerging field of postmodern management and organization studies. Thus the chapters summarize prior work in postmodernism and in management and organization theory, but the goal is not to offer comprehensive reviews of these concepts. The chapters selectively use the concepts and ideas directly relevant to the organizational and managerial topics at hand, operationalize them in the context of specific inquiries into important topics in the field, and then carry out these inquiries. We thus prefer to demonstrate postmodern management and organization theory by doing it, rather than limit our attention to reflections on possibilities for doing it. The consequence is that the key concepts and ideas from postmodernism are introduced in the context of topically focused chapters rather than in a general overview of the "great man" theorists of postmodernism.

The book is organized into several parts that reflect important topics and trends in postmodern management and organization theory. Part I, "Deconstructing Organizational Analysis: Critique, Reflections, and Alternatives," offers broad-ranging essays on the state of postmodern management and organization theory. These chapters discuss the features of modernism, modern management and organizations, and modernist organizational scholarship. The challenges facing modernism are addressed, and the chapters seek to posit the features of distinctly postmodern management, organizations, and theories.

Chapter 2, "Management, Social Issues, and the Postmodern Era," by Robert P. Gephart, Jr., provides a historical overview of the rise and decline of the modern bureaucratic state and its relationship to modern organizations. Gephart argues that the changing nature of the capitalist, bureaucratic ethic is basic to the transition from one historical era to another. Gephart uses postmodern concepts from Fredric Jameson and insights from the management scholars W. G. Scott, D. Hart, and Robert Jackall to develop a view of late modernist organizations as "fiefdoms" with a new, postbureaucratic ethic. Gephart then discusses potential future postmodern transformations in society and organizations, using postmodern science fiction to offer futuristic scenarios that represent such transformations. He concludes by arguing that management is being transformed as a fundamental cultural category and by discussing theoretical and methodological perspectives that may help us understand the nature and consequences of this transformation.

Chapter 3, "Exploring the Terrain of Modernism and Postmodernism in Organization Theory" by John Hassard, continues the exploration of postmodernism as an epoch and as a style. Hassard compares

and contrasts modernist and postmodernist concepts and explains
how these concepts can be used to provide insights into management
and organization theory. Hassard is concerned with describing the
state of the art of postmodern management theory and offering suggestions for future applications and extensions of the postmodern
literature into the management domain. He discusses three primary
styles of postmodernism that are emerging in organizational analysis—
ethnoindustrial, sociophilosophical, and synthetic—and he discusses
differences among these positions in terms of the analyses of organizations and organizing. Chapter 4, "Storytelling at *Administrative Science Quarterly:* Warding off the Postmodern Barbarians" by David M.
Boje, Dale E. Fitzgibbons, and David S. Steingard, is distinctly critical
of the current state of critical management studies. Boje, Fitzgibbons,
and Steingard undertake a systemic deconstruction of articles published in *Administrative Science Quarterly,* one of the leading journals in the
field of organizational and administrative studies. The authors find
that although postmodern issues and challenges were noted early in
the life of *Administrative Science Quarterly,* these challenges have been
denied, ignored, and sublimated in an attempt to ensure that they
remain exogenous to the field of administrative studies as an institu-
tionally supported discipline. The implication is that the conservative
bias of managerial ideologies is reproduced in these supposedly value-
free scientific texts concerning organizations. This reproduction of
administrative studies as "science" also silences and precludes taking a
critical voice or role in assessing management and organizations.

The second part, "Beyond MAN-AGE-ment: Gender, Discourse, and
Organizational Voices," addresses the fundamental postmodern concern of opening the field of management to diverse and formerly silent
voices. The term *management* itself invokes and privileges "man" and
"age"; hence the chapters here show alternatives to older male views
of the world. The first essay in this section is "Women as Constituent
Directors: Re-Reading Current Texts Using a Feminist-Postmodernist
Approach" by Patricia Bradshaw. In Chapter 5, Bradshaw addresses the
supposed "boardroom renaissance," wherein boards of directors are
thought to be addressing a much greater range of issues and constituencies than before. Although Bradshaw initially sought to examine
how women directors represent the voices and concerns of women in
general, she found that women directors did not in fact regard them-

selves as representing women's views. Thus, in her chapter, Bradshaw seeks to investigate the inclusion of marginalized voices in board decision making by addressing the role of "constituent directors": board roles designed specifically to bring alternative perspectives—typically those of labor—into corporate governance. The chapter outlines in detail the important elements of a feminist/postmodern deconstructive approach and then applies this approach in the deconstruction of three recent and important texts concerning the corporate boardroom and organizational governance. The chapter argues that despite the evident concern in the texts about how organizational power is distributed, the textual discussions related to constituent directors devolve into claims that continue to exclude women and other (non-MAN-AGE-d) groups from positions of power. Bradshaw then explores a possible strategy to encourage the inclusion and effective participation of diverse stakeholder groups in corporate governance.

Chapter 6, "Liberation From Within: Organizational Implications of Irigaray's Concept of 'Residue,'" by Ian Atkin and John Hassard, takes a somewhat more philosophical approach to the inclusion of gendered voices in organizational analysis. The essay contributes to postmodern management and organization theory by applying ideas from the important feminist scholar, Luce Irigaray, to management and organization theory concerns. Atkin and Hassard address the self-enforced separation of orthodox and radical management theories. The authors note that the fruitlessness of attempts to achieve this radical separatism arises because of the failure of the radical view to break with systems-based organizational analysis. The authors then deconstruct this orthodoxy, using Irigaray's (1985, 1991) concept of *residue* to recover the "other" in organizational life. Mimicry of a dominant theory's representation of subordinate theories can provide the bases for the subordinate theory to escape textual imprisonment. This mimicry can be accomplished by using the residue of the flow of meanings to problematize the dominant discourse. This thesis is illustrated by textual analysis of a systems-based text and a radical separatist text (Burrell, 1980). The problematic theoretical status of radical theorists is explored and a strategy for developing an emancipatory theory of organizations is offered, based on the concept of "residue of flow," which is developed from within the conventions of systems-based analysis.

Chapter 7, "Do You Take Your Body to Work?" by David Barry and Mary Ann Hazen, builds on the postmodern premise that deconstructing dualisms is essential for the reconstruction of postmodern management and organization theory. For postmodernism, the human body is not a dichotomous other to the human mind; rather, it holds that as humans, we must conceive ourselves as composite and nondifferentiable physiological/psychological creatures. Barry and Hazen address the implications of our failure to transcend mind/body dualism, a failure that is represented in organizational life through the ongoing suppression and deprivileging of bodily functions, needs, and feelings. Barry and Hazen argue that modernist organizations seek control over the body for purposes of enhancing performativity.[1] Thus, although organizations have tended to shape how we attend to our bodies, a postmodern perspective might invert this to ask how it is that our bodies shape organizational and management theories, as well as investigating the problematics of the organizational control of bodies. The authors offer elements for developing a perspective on the body in organizations and organizational theory—that is, for treating the body as an organizational stakeholder. The important implication of their chapter is that control over physiological aspects of people is an important feature of organizations and that a postmodern management and organization theory must address and more adequately incorporate the body into organizational theories. It seems evident that such theories must also provide for a better accommodation of the body and its needs within organizational frameworks and structures, that is, for a conception of the organizational manager and member as an integrated psychological/physiological entity. Chapter 8, the fourth essay in the part, "A Theory of Stakeholder Enabling: Giving Voice to an Emerging Postmodern Praxis of Organizational Discourse" by Jerry M. Calton and Nancy B. Kurland, provides a general discussion of the problem of multiple stakeholders and the challenges of formulating a theory that "enables" diverse stakeholders and that contributes normatively to changes in contemporary firms. The chapter begins by critiquing the stakeholder concept and stakeholder theories of the firm in the contexts of strategic management, agency theory, and transaction cost economics. The authors note that a fundamental stakeholder paradox arises because the theory indicates that managers should exercise fiduciary responsibility to all stakeholders and yet the financial interests of these stakeholders diverge substantially. Meeting the interests of one stakeholder can mean undermining the interests of other stakeholders. Calton and Kurland thus propose a theory for enabling the joint expression of diverse stakeholder concerns and collective control, which can be used to transcend the stakeholder paradox that rests on a conception of management as controlling the views of stakeholders. Their theory critiques masculine metaphors basic to modernist stakeholder theory and offers an alternative epistemology and ontology and also alternative forms of praxis founded on a feminist metaphor. The new theory calls for corporations to be conceptualized as webs of relations among stakeholders, integrated by communication and collective action in a radically decentralized context where the different stakeholders are empowered.

The title of Part III is "From Techno-logy to Eco-logy: Epistemological Issues in Environmental Management." This section addresses the role of Nature, ecology, and the natural environment in organization and management theory. Jameson (1991) defines postmodernism as an era in which technology has substituted for Nature as the "other" or mystery to society. Thus, in postmodernism, there is a retreat from Nature, as the logic of technique substitutes for the logic of Nature. Paradoxically, ecological issues and the preservation of Nature are important social issues to postmodernists (Rosenau, 1992) who wish to reprivilege the logic of Nature and to ensure that this dominates or constrains the logic of technique. Part III addresses the paradox. The first essay, "Ecological Futures: Systems Theory, Postmodernism, and Participative Learning in an Age of Uncertainty" by Alfonso Montuori and Ronald E. Purser, addresses the uneasy relationship between postmodernist concerns for the natural environment and postmodern skepticism concerning systems theory, which is basic to any understanding of the environment as ecosystem. Given this antipathy, the authors ask, Can we legitimately think systematically, ecologically, in a postmodern context? The authors thus seek a theoretical context in which this antipathy can be transcended, using an "epistemology of complexity" to develop a form of systems analysis that is inherently pluralist rather than totalizing. They explore the implications of the new competencies this epistemology requires and address participative scenarios that incorporate cybernetic processes in organizational discourses and learning.

Chapter 10, "Simulacral Environments: Reflexivity and the Natural Ecology of Organizations" by Robert P. Gephart, Jr., seeks to reconceptualize the concepts of Nature, environment, and ecology in radically postmodern terms. Gephart uses ethnomethodological conceptualizations of reflection and reflexivity to investigate the textual practices that compose Nature, environment, and ecology in management, scientific, and naturalist writing. He argues essentially that the naturally occurring displacement of Nature in the postmodern era and the concomitant rise of concern for Nature in the postmodern movement can be conceptually integrated by using radical reflexivity to apply Baudrillard's concepts of simulation and simulacra to understand the ontological status of Nature, environment, and ecology. He argues that management theory, science, and naturalist writing all compose images of Nature, environment, and ecology that increasingly become distant from the underlying reality these images are thought to represent. Ultimately, Nature and environment are transformed by science into ecology, a scientific concept and representation that is itself a model based on other scientific models—that is, a simulacrum. Similarly, Nature emerges as "voices of Nature" in naturalist writings, and these are also simulacral—representations of phenomena for which no real originals exist, because Nature does not use human voices. Rather, the natural voices are in fact the voices of humans representing Nature. Nature, the environment, and ecology are thus reconceptualized as socially constructed phenomena, that is, as representations of a reality that can be known only through human images and representations. The consequences of this reconceptualization for management and organization theory are explored.

Part IV, "Postmodern Pedagogy," addresses the challenges of teaching and learning postmodernism in contemporary faculties of business and management. Many disciplines within the business school, such as accounting, management science, and marketing, offer training in quantitative, technical skills. That is, students are taught how to "manage by the numbers." Although departments of management offer training in scientific techniques for control of human and organizational behavior (Scott & Hart, 1989), these techniques are at best rather amorphous, as reflected in the phrase "soft skills." An alternative to technique-oriented teaching is to provide instruction and support in learning critical thinking. However, management as a discipline has resisted this role of cultural critique, choosing instead to seek to emulate the technical offerings and orientations of the quantitative disciplines. The result is a significant problem in the legitimation of management theory, teaching and learning, and management departments themselves. Management courses are viewed by many academics, business students, and business practitioners as arts-oriented courses that provide technical training in soft skills and thereby offer only a weak form of competition to so-called hard disciplines of management that offer hard skills, constituted by the ability to use quantitative decision tools, tight scientific codes, and clear algorithms for management decision making. The assumed lack of hard knowledge and skills in management has led to frequent calls for the field of management and organization theory to become more scientific. However, becoming more scientific means focusing on reproducible, measurable, quantitative phenomena with statistically specifiable relationships among them. Thus, in our view, an emphasis on becoming more scientific means that management theory will become less relevant to the concerns and issues that organizational members experience. The attempt to be more scientific limits the ability of management theory to demonstrate real-world relevance and hence legitimacy based in this practical relevance. On the other hand, an attempt to transform management into a discipline focused on cultural critique means that management theory must abandon its claims to scientific status; hence management is also delegitimated in this scenario. The chapters in this part relate to this paradox; they all propose strategies for teaching postmodernism and management in ways that reflect and attempt to balance the dual forces threatening to delegitimize university-level management education.

The first, Chapter 11, "Pedagogy for the Postmodern Management Classroom: Greenback Company," by Grace Ann Rosile and David M. Boje, addresses this paradox in the context of the authors' own life experiences as university management teachers. The authors review the history of teaching and learning in premodern, modern, and postmodern eras, and they summarize the postmodern and other critiques of modern education. They then offer elements of a postmodern pedagogy for management education and guidelines for readers to create their own pedagogical tools. An important topic in this chapter is the Greenback Company, a class exercise in which students create their own corporation to raise funds for socially responsible purposes and then critique and reflect on the organization and their own behavior in constructing it. Rosile and Boje offer Greenback

Company as one strategy for creating a postmodern learning organization that can facilitate postmodern teaching/learning about management and organization. They conclude with cautionary notes reminding us that not all students are ready—nor willing—to experience postmodern management education.

Chapter 12, "Reconstructions of Choice: Advocating a Constructivist Approach to Postmodern Management Education" by Ghazi F. Binzagr and Michael R. Manning, discusses how constructivism can be used to fashion an approach that reorients management education to postmodern concerns and issues. The authors discuss ontological and epistemological assumptions of constructivism and connect these assumptions to postmodernism. They then discuss how the assumptions can be used to fashion a participative pedagogy wherein students deconstruct classic, modernist management ideas and reconstruct them based on the concept of choice, which the authors view as central to a postmodern, constructivist epistemology. Binzagr and Manning illustrate this pedagogical process through a case description of a doctoral course wherein students deconstructed Fayol's principles of management and reconstructed them to incorporate choice.

The third essay in the section, Chapter 13, "Modernism, Postmodernism, and Managerial Competencies: A Multidiscourse Reading," by Eric H. Neilsen, investigates managerial assessment and competence training. Neilsen subjects the field of competence training and assessment to a postmodern critique, noting that it is thoroughly modernist in positing a set of competencies that can be operationalized, measured, coded, and reproduced through technical training. Neilsen then provides a case description of a course designed to teach the managerial competencies that are represented in a model by Boyatzis (1982). The case description illustrates how postmodern features of discourse emerged in the class to supplement the modernist discourses based in the model of managerial competencies. This supplementation was basic to the success of the modernist aspects of the course, that is, understanding, coding, and learning the competencies as objectified features of behavior. Neilsen notes problems that students and instructors experience in teaching modernist knowledge when supplementing modernist insights with postmodern discourses that abandon a grand narrative and transform the competencies into local knowledge. He notes that the transition to postmodern teaching will include difficulties, yet studies such as this elucidate features of pedagogy necessary for overcoming these difficulties and integrating postmodernism into business school curricula.

The fifth part is titled "Critical Issues in Global Organizational Studies," and it addresses globalization as an important feature of postmodernization. Chapter 14, "Metaphors of Globalization" by Stewart R. Clegg and John T. Gray, investigates the metaphors used in understanding the globalization of organizations. They find that globalization is itself a metaphor that rests on prior metaphors used in the neoclassical economics paradigm and that this theoretical and metaphorical base forecloses all questions of identity in postmodernism. The authors seek alternative metaphors that transcend this economistic bias and find that compression and relativism of experiences, coupled with a conception of conduits of power, offer bases on which to open these questions of identity. They explore the issues for postmodern management and organization theory that emerge from this revised metaphorical framework.

In Chapter 15, "Organizations as a Play of Multiple and Dynamic Discourses: An Example From a Global Social Change Organization," Tojo Joseph Thatchenkery and Punya Upadhyaya argue that the socially constructed reality in organizations is shaped by discourses that are themselves transformed during the natural evolution of organizations. Based on a case study of a large international private voluntary organization, they show that a cyclical phase of privileging, deprivileging, and reprivileging of discourses may be observed in organizations, as they attempt to adapt to changes. What is privileged, deprivileged, and reprivileged is almost always preferred ways of engaging in the world, such as the core values or processes of organizing.

Chapter 16, "Technologies of Representation in the Global Corporation: Power and Polyphony" by Kenneth J. Gergen and Diana Whitney, extends discussion of the issues of identity and metaphor that Clegg and Gray view as central to the problematics of postmodernism and globalization. Gergen and Whitney explore the problem of power in the global organization and the relationship of this problem to technologies of representation. They address the important role of technologies of communication in the process of globalization and note that the shift from direct to electronically disseminated discourses produces a diversity of voices or views, as well as a loss of top management control over local forms of life. These points are illustrated by examples drawn from the experiences of a global organization that sought to create a unified corporate culture. The effort was self-limiting because of a combination of the basic features of communication and features inherent in communications technologies. Gergen and Whitney suggest that a new metaphor is necessary to understand organizational representation in the era of electronic conversations, and they offer the concept of polyphony in this regard. Polyphonic dialogue places local languages in a beneficial relationship with centralized power. This may yield new forms of organizing that are more viable in the global context, and it may serve as the most effective technology of representation for postmodern organizations.

The final brief chapter in the book is "Conclusion: Reconstructing Organizations for Future Survival" by Robert P. Gephart, Jr., Tojo Joseph Thatchenkery, and David M. Boje. Here, we briefly review important themes that emerge from the present work and suggest future issues in postmodern management and organizational analysis. We believe that our species faces important challenges at this point in history and that radical reconceptualizations of society, organizations, and management are necessary to ensure the viability of our species, other species, and our planet as we know it. The ideas in this book and future explorations of these issues can thus become the basis for reconstructing organizations for future survival.

Note

1. Performativity is the performance of an individual or entity as judged based on pragmatic criteria or outcomes, particularly the productive capacity and efficiency of the person or entity (Rosenau, 1992, p. xiii).

PART I

Deconstructing Organizational Analysis: Critique, Reflections, and Alternatives

2

Management, Social Issues, and the Postmodern Era

ROBERT P. GEPHART, JR.

This chapter explores the social and organizational changes management may encounter during the passage from modernism to postmodernism. I define *postmodernism* as a form of society or social era and as a style of cultural production and focus on the "era" approach to postmodernism. Thus, I review the history and features of traditionalism and modernism as a basis for understanding the features of postmodern organizations and society. Next, important features of postmodernism as a social form are discussed. The chapter concludes by reviewing contours of the postmodern organization and theoretical frameworks that may provide insights into postmodern management and society.

Postmodernism: An Overview

It is essential to indicate the nature of postmodernism at the outset so as to clarify the goal, the focus, and the intent of our journey here.

AUTHOR'S NOTE: This chapter is a greatly revised version of a paper presented to the First Biannual International Conference on Advances in Management, Orlando, Florida, March 27, 1992. I wish to thank Walter Nord, W. G. Scott, and Punya Upadhyaya for their comments on the ideas in this chapter. I also wish to thank Robert Hogner for inviting me to organize the symposium on postmodern management at the conference from which this chapter emerged. Finally, special thanks to the faculty and Ph.D. students at the Graduate School of Management, University of California, Irvine, for encouraging my commitment to postmodern scholarship.

Definition here is provisional because as Weber (1958) noted, attempts to define an era "cannot start at the beginning, but must come at the end" of descriptions of the era (p. 47) and must thus be worked out in the course of the description.

I initially discuss postmodernism as having two meanings. First, postmodernism is a cultural form or social era that follows modernism (Giddens, 1990; Rosenau, 1992). Postmodernism is a new and distinct form of society with a unique form of cultural logic (Giddens, 1990, p. 46), which involves a break with the past: "Postmodernism is what you have when the modernization process is complete and nature is gone for good" (Jameson, 1991, p. ix). Second, postmodernism is an epistemology, a method or style of cultural production that is reconceptualizing how we experience and explain our world (Rosenau, 1992, p. 4). Postmodernism is a worldview "outside the modern paradigm" (Rosenau, 1992, p. 5) that is attempting to "think the present historically in an age that has forgotten how to think historically in the first place" (Jameson, 1991, p. ix). Postmodernism is also a style of artistic production that reflects this cultural movement, provides an aesthetic reflection on the nature of modernism (Giddens, 1990, p. 45; Lyotard, 1979/1984, p. 81), and emphasizes "an incredulity toward metanarratives" (Lyotard, 1979/1984, p. xxiv). Postmodernism challenges the very foundations of knowledge, including the teleology of history and the myth that history reflects constant progress (Giddens, 1990, p. 46).

Clegg (1990, p. 15) articulates the distinction between postmodern styles and social forms by differentiating between "postmodern sociology," which uses a particular style or worldview, and "a sociology of postmodernity," which addresses postmodern society as the object or subject of analysis. The analysis of postmodern social forms or eras can be conducted with or without postmodern methods (Clegg, 1990). As a consequence, analysis of postmodernity as a social form need not "be notably different in its approach, nor perhaps in its methods, from more orthodox conceptions" (p. 21). The four possible foci that emerge are modernist studies of postmodern styles, modernist studies of postmodern society, postmodern studies of postmodern styles, and postmodern studies of postmodern society. The variations in focus that emerge are exemplified by Clegg (1990), who uses modernist methods to study postmodern society and organizations, in contrast to Jameson

(1991), who uses postmodern methods to study postmodern styles and society.

The study of postmodern social forms is important to organizational analysis because these include and are associated with new forms of business and corporate organization and other issues of central concern to organization and management theories. Furthermore, there is an interrelationship between postmodernism as a social form and emergent postmodern styles that demarcate the new social forms. The new styles emerge from and constitute important features of the postmodern era. Thus, the examination of postmodern social forms requires an examination of styles, and vice versa. These two aspects of postmodernism—cultural form and style—are addressed in this chapter. The era view of postmodernism leads one to investigate the historical emergence of modernism and postmodernism, whereas the style view of postmodernism offers management scholars a means to identify postmodern features, as well as providing "new" ways of addressing postmodern phenomena and ones different from those available within the modernist perspective.

In this chapter, I wish to encourage and provide a more substantial basis for future postmodern research on postmodern society, organizations, and management. To this end, I address how postmodern styles and forms provide insights into organizations, management, and society. My task thus differs from that of Clegg (1990), who examines a largely modernist literature as a basis from which to induce features of postmodernism. Here I seek to develop a postmodernist perspective on postmodern management, to elucidate distinctive trends and processes in postmodern management, and to distinguish the postmodern perspective from modernist perspectives and concerns.

Traditional Society, Classical Modernism, and Bureaucracy

An examination of features of modernism and its emergence from traditional society can clarify the nature of postmodernism. Traditional society was characterized by patriarchal, patrimonial domination of subjects based on "traditionally transmitted" patterns of usage of authority (Weber, 1947, p. 340), often based in rules of inheritance (Bendix, 1960, pp. 329-337; Weber, 1947, p. 341). Government administration was based in the household of the ruler, who engaged in trade as a personal prerogative. The conduct of official business in traditional society was a matter of the ruler's discretion; rule-based limits of authority were resisted by the ruler; the ruler determined delegation and allocation of authority as a matter of personal preference and loyalty; administrative offices were part of the property of the ruler, and costs were met through payments out of the ruler's treasury; and business was conducted in personal encounters, not on the basis of documents (Bendix, 1960, p. 425). Essentially, rulers exercised authority as an aspect of personal property, and this authority was constrained by what one might "normally permit," based on prior patterns of subjects' resistance to authority (Weber, 1947, p. 242). In traditionalism, less work was preferred to more pay: "A man does not 'by nature' wish to earn more money, but simply to live as he is accustomed to live and earn as much as is necessary for that purpose" (Weber, 1958, p. 60).

The transformation from traditional to rational/legal (modernist) domination was associated with the rise of a capitalist ethic, although some aspects of capitalism were present before the modern capitalist order (Weber, 1958, p. 55). The capitalist ethic involves the secularization of a Protestant religious (Calvinist) worldview that presumes hard work is both a moral virtue and an obligation (Bendix, 1960, pp. 52-53), coupled with secular ideas and habits that favor rational economic pursuits (Bendix, 1960, p. 54). This ethic is "that attitude which seeks profit rationally and systematically" (Weber, 1958, p. 64).[1]

The economic organization of the modern capitalist state has several specific features. First, the legal order provides for the legal form of the business corporation and for related institutions, including commodities and securities exchanges. Second, there is a voluntary supply of labor. Third, there is a planned division of labor within enterprises, and fourth, production functions are allocated to enterprises through the operation of a market economy. Modernism is thus based in the formal rationality of the law (Bendix, 1960) and the use of technical knowledge by a bureaucratic governmental administration. A fundamental belief in modernism is that all social problems can be solved rationally by state intervention and the application of scientific and social theory (Peukert, 1989, p. 134). Traditional society thus

contrasts sharply with modernism, or modern society based on technical rationality, the Protestant ethic, and the "Spirit of Capitalism"
(Weber, 1958).

The Weimar Republic:
The Rise of the Modern State

The Weimar Republic in Germany (1919-1933) was the first experiment in the creation of a fully "modern" state (Peukert, 1989), with
the legitimacy of the state based on democratic decision making,
constitutionality, and a welfare system (Peukert, 1989, p. 132). Virtually
all the initiatives associated with the modern state were formulated and
put into practice in the Weimar Republic (Peukert, 1989, p. 266). Thus,
a discussion of the features of modernism enshrined in the Weimar
Constitution provides an overview of the distinctive features of classical
modernism and the challenges it faced.[2]

Classical modernism is a welfare state, where the state administration has the goal or duty to provide for general social welfare through
the establishment of government-supported social programs and institutions. The Weimar Constitution focused on marriage as the foundation of the state (Peukert, 1989, p. 131). It provided for equality of the
sexes and the protection of motherhood. Second, it provided both the
freedom to own property and the obligations of property ownership
(Peukert, 1989, p. 132). Third, it included labor laws and extended the
right to productive work to all members of society. Where work could
not be obtained, the constitution provided for a comprehensive unem-
ployment insurance plan and state welfare subsidies. Fourth, the constitution provided for public health, including health insurance and
housing (Peukert, 1989, p. 138). Fifth, following the passage of the
Reich Youth Welfare Law of 1922, education became an important
focus: Children were given the right to a "good upbringing"; public,
nondenominational schools were established (Peukert, 1989, p. 141);
and teaching was professionalized. Key aspects of Weimar and hence
modernist social policy thus include the development of unemploy-
ment insurance, concern for public welfare, financial policy that is
interrelated with social policy, public health provisions, and provision
of public education. Other noteworthy features of the Weimar Republic

included new employment status for women in modern sectors of the economy; a superfluous younger generation, with few prospects for employment; and the rise of mass culture and market society based on mass production and communication technologies, including cinema and news media (Peukert, 1989).

The Weimar Republic was destroyed by several historical processes (Peukert, 1989, p. 279). First, the economy was shrinking, making state provision of welfare difficult. Second, the state lost legitimacy because it retreated from the original post-World War I financial settlement for war reparations. Third, there was a reversion to authoritarianism—a "conservative revolution" that prefigured the postmodern critique of modernism (Peukert, 1989, pp. 277-278)—and a movement away from democratization. And finally, the rise of the National Socialist (Nazi) movement displaced the democratic process. It is important to consider these crises of classical modernity, because they demonstrate how easily the process of modernization can be harnessed by autocratic regimes and turned into a catastrophe (Peukert, 1989, p. 281). A similar risk may well be present in current transformation processes of late modernization.

Modern Bureaucracy

The modern organization is a managerial system using behavioral science and technology to integrate people into "mutually reinforcing, cooperative relationships" (Scott & Hart, 1989, p. 2). Bureaucracy is basic to the modernist form of organization (Clegg, 1990; Weber, 1947): "The development of the modern form of the organization of corporate groups in all fields is nothing less than identical with the development and continual spread of bureaucratic administration" (Weber, 1947, p. 337).

The general features of bureaucracy and bureaucratic positions are the continuous and ongoing nature of administrative activities, rule-based specification of authority and its limits, supervision of the exercise of authority, specification of a hierarchy of authority, separation of the office from the incumbent, and the use of documents as bases for official business (cf. Bendix, 1960, pp. 424, 426; Weber, 1947, pp. 329-341). Many features of bureaucracy could be found in traditional systems of administration under patrimonial rule; hence modernism was distinguished by the substitution of rational/legal authority for traditional authority and by the extensive technical rationalization of work and work activities. Thus, in contrast to premodern forms, the modernist bureaucracy is characterized by a hierarchy of authority for officials; specialization and delimitation of work activities of these officials, based on their expertise; rules and regulations (documents) that specify bases of work activities; and independence of the officials from ownership of the resources of the enterprise or government, based on free contractual appointments of officials and fixed salaries. Following from these features, key attributes of the modern organization or bureaucracy thus include the following:

1. The rational calculability of decision making, that is, the fact that decisions are logical consequences of the rule of law (Weber, 1946, p. 215)
2. Concentration of the means of administration and separation of the agent or member from the institution (Weber, 1946, pp. 221-224)
3. Leveling of social and economic differences; that is, authority is based on rules applied equally to everyone (Bendix, 1960, p. 429; Weber, 1946, pp. 224-228)
4. A system of authority relations that is enduring, that is, indestructible or relatively permanent (Bendix, 1960, p. 430; Weber, 1946, pp. 228-230)

The modern bureaucracy is viewed as technically superior to other forms of organization because officials execute their tasks in a dispassionate or depersonalized manner, based on the application of impersonal rules applied using their technical knowledge and expertise (Bendix, 1960, p. 428). Although it is common to view bureaucratic structures as being localized in government organizations, bureaucratic characteristics are also distinctive features of modern corporations basic to their success.

Late Modernism:
The Rise of the Organizational Imperative

The modern management paradigm assumes that the basic purpose of management is to increase the efficiency of organizational production

(Scott, 1974) and to enhance growth and adaptability (Scott & Hart, 1989, p. 34). These values of modern organization—growth, abundance, and consensus (Scott, 1974, p. 245)—lead to an emphasis on technical aspects of increasing productivity and hence replace and thereby undermine the "founding values" of the United States of America. The result is new goals and values based on the organizational imperative, which posits that (a) good for the individual can only arise from the modern organization (Scott & Hart, 1989, p. 30) and (b) all behavior of individuals and organizational members must thus be directed to enhancing organizational health. In the organizational society, managerial power is legitimated not by rational/legal aspects as in early modernity, but by the assumed relationship between managerial power and organizational health. Managers are legitimate authority figures who require power to take actions to maintain organizational well-being (Scott & Hart, 1989, p. 6) and to produce a just distribution of organizational and social benefits.

The legitimation of managerial authority in modernism requires one to secure the organization for management and then to serve constituents. This legitimation is driven by a sense of determinism that treats the imperatives of effective management as unquestionable givens; it is based on social Darwinist premises and no longer on technical rationality. Social Darwinism assumes that managerial status is based on the superior competitive qualities of people, including technical knowledge; hence managerial elites are the fittest people and have risen, quite rightly, to the top of the organization. A new morality thus emerges in late modernism. Managers are morally superior and are encouraged on this basis to do whatever the scientific "facts" of organic systems management require to enhance organizational efficiency and effectiveness. Managers have no moral concerns beyond enhancing the functionality (Scott & Hart, 1989, p. 33) or "performativity" (Lyotard, 1979/1984) of the organizational system. Organizational decisions must thus be organizationally just, even if they are morally indefensible (Scott & Hart, 1989, p. 35). Hence, managers are amoral; so long as they act expediently with regard to the organization's interests, the organization will shield them from accountability.[3]

New rules of organization derive from the organizational imperative (Scott & Hart, 1989, pp. 31-33).

1. There is an emphasis on (upward) hierarchical obedience, thereby disrupting the two-way flow of authority and responsibility.
2. Technical rationality, concerned with optimizing efficiency as a function of inputs and outputs, is basic to decisions.
3. Stewardship is emphasized with regard to husbanding organizational resources for the interests of hierarchical elites.
4. There is pragmatism in decision making, that is, a devotion to expediency guided by the organizational imperative.

The organizational imperative and bureaucratic ethic in late modernism differ from the imperatives of earlier modernist forms. First, obedience is now worth more than individuality (Scott & Hart, 1989, p. 50). Second, the individual is dispensable (Scott & Hart, 1989, pp. 53-54). Third, the individual specializes so as to fit the organization and its needs (Scott & Hart, 1989, p. 55). Fourth, all organizational acts are planned where possible, and spontaneity is avoided because it reflects a loss of control (Scott & Hart, 1989, p. 57). Fifth, there is a move from voluntarism to paternalism. Sixth, late modernism is characterized by the rise of feudal or fiefdom-style organizations and management (Scott & Hart, 1989, p. 125).

Fiefdom-Style Management

Jackall (1988) argues that fiefdom-style management emerges in the hybrid bureaucracy that is characteristic of late modernism. This a combination of bureaucratic values and patrimonial values common to the U.S. cultural setting, including loyalty, favoritism, informality, and nonlegality (Jackall, 1988, p. 11). The hybrid bureaucracy and fiefdom management arise because managers are the principal carriers of the bureaucratic ethic (Jackall, 1988, p. 12) or organizational imperative, which emphasizes hierarchical compliance and the duty to provide for organizational health. The ethic, as operationalized, leads to expectations of employee fidelity to hierarchical superiors. Essentially, employees take an "oath of fealty" (Scott & Hart, 1989, p. 125) to their supervisors, in exchange for certain privileges and protections, thereby producing an organization or bureaucracy (Jackall, 1988, pp. 17-57) where the hierarchical structure is the basis of individual identity and this hierarchical structure is informally constituted in terms of fiefs or territories of control by given managers, which are based on alliances among managers. Employees' effective power in the organization is based on their position within a fiefdom, particularly their identity in the eyes of their supervisors. Subordinates must respect their obligations of fealty to their supervisors. Mistakes, in particular breaches of the oath of fealty, lead the supervisor to abandon the subordinate to organizational forces. Details are pushed down the hierarchy, and credit is pushed up, such that the credit for any success is appropriated by the highest-ranking official involved as a decision maker. In this manner, the successes of subordinates are appropriated by managers.

Political struggles are constant in such settings. Success and failure are more directly related to supporting the fealty and alliance structure, to the ethos and style of the corporation, and to luck and fortune, than they are to work efforts and professional or technical success. Another important aspect of success is "face," including external appearance, behavior, and image in the eyes of others. The ability to be (seen as) a team player is also important. Team players are interchangeable with others, do not hold strong convictions, and are flexible in taking perspectives. Furthermore, team players put in long hours at work, are "good members," align with the dominant ideology of the moment, and display a happy, upbeat, can-do attitude—the "right" style. "Making one's numbers" is basic to exhibiting proper style. For employees, success is constituted by being seen as promotable, whereas failure is the perception they are not promotable, based on their supervisor's assessments. To be labeled not promotable is cause to leave the organization. An employee's task is thus to ensure that events occur as the supervisor wishes. In this regard, employees have to understand and monitor institutional logic—the way a particular social world works—because the fate of the manager is based on accomplishing goals in accord with the prevailing institutional logic of the organization.

Moral Dilemmas

The organizational imperative (Scott & Hart, 1989) and its concomitant managerial code (Jackall, 1988) produce an ongoing series of

largely intractable moral contradictions and dilemmas for management. These arise as a result of the disjunctive nature of social, organizational, and technical rationalities. Legitimation of modern management
rests on the ability of managers to comply with the organizational
imperative to provide general social welfare. However, the instantia-
tion of the organizational imperative in the context of fiefdom-style
management is based on a narrow and distinct rationality embedded
in the management code. Many actions governed by the management
code are inconsistent with general social and even organizational
welfare. Furthermore, the managerial code or ethic is generally not
visible and may seem irrational to nonmanagerial social actors. Hence,
the organizational imperative and managerial code lead to intractable
dilemmas that "demand compromises with traditional moral beliefs"
(Jackall, 1988, p. 12). The common solution to these dilemmas is to
give precedence to the managerial code, to the exclusion of other
codes or ethics (Scott & Hart, 1989, p. 113). This is accomplished only
at significant psychic cost: "a curious sense of guilt, heightened as it
happens by narcissistic self-preoccupation," that is, "the pain of self-
repression" (Jackall, 1988, p. 204).

The Transformation of Modernism

Changes in the environment have challenged the early modernist
management paradigm by eroding older growth-oriented values (Scott,
1974). Instead of an era of growth and prosperity, society faces a period
of social decay, resource scarcity, and social conflict because of declining reserves of natural resources, resistance to environmental pollution,
changing work expectations, and declining confidence in established
institutions. The result is "a rising confidence in the individual's
dispensability" and "a rising nihilism" (Scott, 1974, p. 249), both of
which challenge the assumption that organizational leadership will
provide solutions to social problems or will enhance individuals' goodwill (Scott, 1974, p. 250).
    At the organizational level, the transformation from classical to late
modernism is evident in the displacement of generalized technical
rationality as a basis for organizational actions and the substitution of
"local" institutional and organizational logics and rationalities as bases

for action and legitimation. These local logics are evidenced in the partial reversion to traditional aspects of authority that occur in fiefdom-style organizations. Clearly specified bureaucratic positions with a restricted range of competence and authority are being eroded by the need to meet the performative commands of organizational elites, which require members to do whatever is necessary to achieve management's operative goals, even if this means undertaking activities outside of their formal position or authority. Technical training as the basis for promotion, advancement, and success is thus eroded and supplanted with alternative criteria such as loyalty, style, and fit with organizational logics and style. Fixed salaries are supplemented with performance pay, stock bonuses, and other rewards that reinforce the fealty structure of the organization. Corporate officials are no longer independent but are (part) owners of the corporation; hence, they have a vested interest in its success. The control of behavior by rules is supplanted by discretionary behavior, which is allowed for fiefdom rulers or leaders. Furthermore, the equal application of authority based on rules is undermined, and rules are differentially applied (or ignored) so as to reinforce the status differentiation that constitutes the fiefdom. Thus, the hybrid bureaucracy of late modernism incorporates a political differentiation that was denied or sublimated in classical modernism. The focus is no longer producing technical rationality but rather producing and maintaining local political rationalities that support and protect one's fief and team.

These changes in organizational environments and structures challenge organizational legitimation and reflect the emergent crises of late capitalism, which include economic, political, motivational, and legitimation crises (Habermas, 1973; Offe, 1984). The crises of late modernity may result in several possible future social and organizational scenarios: revolution, restoration of traditional values, moral drift, and totalitarianism (Scott & Hart, 1989). A "managementocracy" is likely to emerge: "The locus of sovereignty has shifted away from traditional forms of government and property. The result is to create a managerial society in which primary modules of government and economic management are administrative in nature" (Scott, 1974, p. 250).

Scott and Hart (1989) call for moral courage necessary to restore the founding values (p. 177) and thereby avoid the less desirable alternatives. Through acts of moral reasoning and courage, managers can enlarge the domain of reason, explore and determine the conditions for improving managerial and social life, and thereby "pioneer a new path into a lovely and gentle future" (Scott & Hart, 1989, p. 178). The development of moral courage requires rebuilding "the sagging moral texture of business and society" (Ryan & Scott, 1995, p. 457).

The Emergence of Postmodernism

We arrive then at the brink of postmodernism. Authority based on rational/legal grounds is supplemented by traditional authority based in organizational fiefdoms. The myths of the organizational imperative are becoming difficult to legitimate because individual good is often obtained through organizational activities that undermine general organizational and social welfare. And the changing moral commitments of management threaten social totalitarianism and encourage the emergence of a simulacral management meritocracy, based not on true merit but on representations or simulations of superiority that arise from the fiefdom-based status frameworks. Society thus faces the potential crises that may arise with the dissolution of the vestiges of modernism. A clearer conception of postmodernism now emerges. Postmodernism supersedes or follows modernism, but it does not constitute "progress" or advancement over modernism. Postmodernism embraces distinctive forms of "commodification" (Offe, 1984), the processes by which phenomena outside the market are brought into the economy and acquire economic-use values. An example of commodification is the sale of public lands for timber leases, which moves Nature from the noncommodified sphere of "public property" into the economic realm. In postmodernism, we encounter the second-order commodification of previously commodified phenomena, as well as the commodification of previously noncommodifiable phenomena. Postmodernism thus extends commodification to new social spheres. For example, through privatization of public goods and services, goods and services that previously were noncommodified are commodified and transferred from the government sphere into the economic sphere. Indeed, in postmodernism the consumption of sheer commodification has become the evident process and end in itself. Hence, it is no longer possible to critique commodification; in modernism, the critique of commodification was still possible and was driven by efforts to make commodification transcend itself. Thus, in postmodernism, there is a tacit surrender to the market ideology itself. The market becomes essentially a metaphysical entity, a feature of human nature, and a model of social totality (Jameson, 1991, p. 272). The market has become the utopian vision and form for postmodern society.

Postmodernism thus involves a profound transformation in the logic of modern, industrial society, based on changes in the processes of commodification. Postmodernism involves a "specifically North American" world or global capitalist system distinct from the earlier forms of imperialism (Jameson, 1991, p. xix). Postmodernism is thus a form of society wherein culture has greatly expanded and Nature has been replaced with technology as the "other" of our society (Jameson, p. 35). Technology thus comes to play a significant role as a privileged means of understanding postmodern power and control.

Other distinct features of postmodernism —transnational business, a new international division of labor, computers and automation—reflect new forms of commodification and business organization. In particular, organizational hierarchies have dissolved, in part through extensive corporate downsizing, restructuring, and reengineering (Keidel, 1994; O'Neill, 1994) even during a "jobless recovery." Whereas modernist downsizing was a strategy to deal with financial crises and potential insolvency, the dissolution of hierarchies in postmodernism is done to enhance organizational profits and performativity and for ideological reasons; hierarchies are now being challenged as organizational forms by proponents of market forces. Coincident with dissolution of self-contained hierarchies is the emergence of network organizations (Powell, 1991) and contractually based hierarchies (Stinchcombe, 1985).

Postmodern Perspectives

Postmodern worldviews, styles, and methods also provide insights into possible features of the postmodern order. The postmodern nature of cultural productions lies in their essential break from the past and their abandonment of meaning, interpretation, and sensibility as tacit goals or a priori accomplishments. In moving from the work of art to "the installation" (Jameson, 1991, p. 168), for example, one finds the world itself opposed to its own representation (Jameson, 1991, p. 169). Interpretation and sense making thus give rise to a nostalgic feeling for the real object that lies behind the representation of the world, and yet this real object itself is imaginary—a simulacral entity (Baudrillard, 1983), that is, a perfect copy for which there is no original. The process of postmodern analysis (Habermas, 1987) is exemplified by Michel Foucault's investigations of the historical emergence of important social categories such as *man* and *value.* Foucault's analysis (1965, 1970b, 1973) defeats the tacit absoluteness or inevitability of social facts and meanings (social typifications) by demonstrating the historical specificity and uniqueness of the meanings, by illustrating the ongoing evolution of these meanings and interpretations, and by demonstrating the social implications of different meanings or worldviews.

Video Texts

Postmodernism styles of cultural production are reflected by "video texts," highly material high technology that captures and reifies the flow of life in a depersonalized and depersonalizing, objectifying manner. Video is postmodern when it defeats modernist thematic questions and answers, such as "What is this about?" Thus, a fully postmodern video text can be defined as "a structure or sign flow which resists meaning, whose fundamental inner logic is the exclusion of the emergence of themes as such in that sense" (Jameson, 1991, pp. 91-92). For example, the experimental video, *AlienNATION,* presents a series of collages that systematically prevent traditional interpretive acts and allow new aesthetic values to emerge. The "fully" postmodern text is flawed where it allows interpretation or meaning, and it is successful where it prevents or defeats meaningful interpretations. The postmodern text is thus a "pure and random play of signifiers" (Jameson, 1991, p. 96) that does not invent nor create new themes or ideas. Rather, the "new" postmodern cultural forms are parasitized, simulacral, fragmented, nostalgic reproductions of "prior" cultural objects, which did not really exist.

Postmodern texts use extended descriptions of space or place to replace themes and plots. Minute descriptions of situational details become central features of the text, in contrast to modernist texts where such descriptions are secondary to plots. The text attains a new kind of depthlessness, a level of superficiality (Jameson, 1991, p. 9) in which interpretation is repudiated. Therefore, the "subjects" are no longer alienated but are now schizophrenically fragmented (Jameson, pp. 14, 28). The "world" itself becomes fragmented by a plethora of worldviews too numerous and varied to be comprehended or taken seriously. The "right" interpretation is superseded by movement away from interpretation itself, and a new, hegemonic structure of feeling emerges (Jameson, 1991, p. xiv)—the postmodern sublime. This involves a detached feeling in which the many difficulties and horrors of postmodern society—murders, violence, major industrial accidents—generate bemusement and cynical disinterest rather than concern or disdain.

Envisioning the Postmodern: Organizational Science/Fiction

Fictional descriptions of postmodern organizational and social scenarios can be found in contemporary works of science fiction, in particular, the postmodern science fiction of William Gibson (Jameson, 1991).[4] This fictional postmodern society (Gibson, 1984, 1986, 1988, 1993; Sterling, 1988) is integrated into and based in the new electronic spatial frontier: an elaborate computer matrix or network one can "travel through," termed *cyberspace*. Cyberspace can be accessed through a "cyberspace deck," which is a device much like a CD player crossed with a computer terminal. Cyberdeck operators have specially implanted electrodes to connect their brain functions to the deck, and through this, the operator can "jack in" to the computer network.

Postmodern science fiction depicts the activities of corporate personnel (Sterling, 1988) bound for life to large-scale organizational fiefdoms, as well as computer criminals (Gibson, 1984) hired on a contractual basis to undertake clandestine but common corporate tasks. Common work activities include the theft of corporate data from other organizations (Gibson, 1984). The "techno-criminal" contract employees are physically altered "posthumans." Consider Molly, a trained assassin and heroine of *Neuromancer* (Gibson, 1984). Strikingly beautiful, she warns her newly assigned work partner not to take any stupid chances with her and demonstrates why: "She held out her hands, palms up, the white fingers slightly spread, and with a barely audible click, ten double-edged, four centimetre scalpel blades slid from their housings beneath the burgundy nails. She smiled" (p. 6).

In this fictional postmodern society, "permanent" corporate personnel are indentured or bound to the corporation for life, and they may be subject to execution if they seek an alternative employer (Gibson, 1986). The allegiance of corporate employees is secured by various means, including financial rewards; toxic implants in their bodies, which can be released should they fail to complete their task; and murder when their usefulness is ended.

Spatially, the world is fragmented. Most of it is collapsing in decay, composed of huge megalopolises, such as "the Sprawl," which stretches for hundreds of miles and is composed of collapsing megashopping malls, burned-out factories, massive slums, and the decadent abodes of the still rich and wealthy. Environmental degradation has proceeded unhindered, such that no "Nature" is left or even conceivable to the characters. An important example of the new spatiality is the transformation of usage of abandoned structures from the modernist era. For example, one setting in Gibson's (1993) novel *Virtual Light* is the Golden Gate Bridge. Abandoned because of structural problems, the bridge became a secondary habitation when it was taken over and settled during a mass action among disadvantaged and homeless persons.

In this new spatiality of postmodernism, political systems have been displaced by Zaibatsu—Japanese criminal conglomerates that wield effective political power for their own interests, using any means available, including violence, to gather knowledge and human resources and to preserve their businesses. Senseless violence is everywhere, a simple tool for simple crimes such as stealing expensive brain implants from people. For example, one character in *Neuromancer* (Gibson, 1984) steals brain implants from another character and is followed. The followers find the thief has been killed by other criminals because this was the cheapest way to obtain the implants from her (p. 39). The narrative is often senseless, composed of fragmentary dialogues dense with jargon and the names of technological objects that do not exist. And the world itself is senseless to the characters. For example, in *Count Zero* (Gibson, 1986), one character tells another about a visage he might encounter in the computer matrix and notes that many of the things that occur in the matrix lack names and are not identified by concepts (p. 76).

In this world of corporate violence, decay, and squalor, survival is a matter of parasitic existence. The spatial abodes are parasitic, and even the characters themselves are parasitic—computer images that "reflect" formerly real people are now images contained in the matrix and exist only there. There is also a depthlessness here, a lack of emotionality, a deadened sense of horror, a slippage into the postmodern sublime. It is a fragmented world. Nations have collapsed, organizations seek their interests in criminal ways, and people are fragmented and commodified in the extreme.

Discussion:
Contours of Postmodern Organization

Postmodern science fiction suggests possible contours of postmodern social organization. These contours emerge from the logic of an advanced and collapsing capitalism, an inverted force of nonnature where reality can no longer be grasped as the primary object: Rather, the sign, the symbol, and the representation substitute for reality, capture it as simulacral in nature, and repress it so that reality is displaced by the image. All "humans" become merely interesting adjuncts, superfluous images of commodification. The value of life becomes the least value of all, to everyone except the one whose life is at stake.

There is no overriding "rationality" guiding the postmodern system, only the logic of commodification reproduced in situational forms that themselves are often contradictory. There can be no appeal to powers beyond the organization because even "government" control is vanishing. Increasingly, managers and employees may ask "What's in it for me?" and within the situational controls of their life space, this may be the driving rationality for action. Hence, social actors are likely to settle into the postmodern sublime. Commitment and motivation will likely be transformed into quasi-contractual commitments to particular projects undertaken by transient work teams composing temporary organizational fiefdoms (Jackall, 1988). Postmodern fiefdom-style organizations may come to reflect and reproduce an increasing fragmentation of the social world and of organizations. Each fiefdom may develop its own commitments, interests, and members, and increasingly its own linguistic codes, values, and culture. Organizations will then become clustered political coalitions linked by self-interest and threats of violence. This violence itself may become institutionalized and increasingly legitimate, particularly as privatized security forces substitute for public-funded police.

The fragmentation of society, coupled with the globalization of business, may accentuate the politicization of the organization and the disintegratedness of organizational forms. Meaningless communications may increase and become the integration mode of organizations. For example, the restricted codes of multiple fiefdoms may proliferate, given the "need" to communicate with others while protecting one's own interests and views. Restricted codes could be transmitted to other fiefdoms in expressly undecodable forms such that the representation of communication could substitute for "real," meaningful communication and undecipherable sign flows could be transmitted and re-coded into "acceptable" messages by their recipients. The production of new information may decrease as corporate communications become increasingly parasitic and reuse old ideas and reports to produce new solutions to problems that never existed. Indeed, attempts to solve new, real problems may become rare, as autocratic pressures on organizational action ensure that the only acceptable problems for solution are those that are already solved or that never existed in the first place. Solutions will thus become simulacra, as will decisions: They will become representations of problems that never existed.

The role of technology may also undergo transformation, as technology replaces Nature as the other of society. There may be greater concerns and fears about technology and a greater number of "mysteries" to be encountered in the technological domain than in others. For management, this means some people will accept new technology at the same time others greet it with extensive challenges—an ambivalence about technology coexistent with increasing deification of it. Cults of technology and antitechnology may well emerge, both inside and outside organizations. The built environment (rather than Nature) could become the setting for "escapes" from the built environment. And leisure industries may become simulated forms of activity because of ease and because of declining quality of the real experience. For example, golf courses may become electronic phenomena that replace "outdoor golf." The management of technological experts—including "illegal" or technocriminal professionals—would then become increasingly important; this would occur where managers lack the technological expertise to control the technology or the technological experts. Managers may find themselves "controlling" processes they do not understand and cannot control. Organizational communication and integration may increasingly become spatialized in computer networks. As global, computer-mediated forms of organization grow in preponderance, management may increasingly involve human-machine interactions, and this management will occur at a distance. Entire organizations could become spatially fragmented and linked via machine-mediated communication, with limited human contact among the members of the organization. A postmodern organization can be envisioned where human-machine interactions replace human-human interactions and where these are ultimately replaced by machine-machine interactions.

Political struggles and the use of any and all means of control are likely to become increasingly prominent; thus the use of illegitimate professional practices may also increase. This would affect any new organizational values. As decay, scarcity, and conflict become the "stable" features of society, value inversions emerge. In the past, the whole organization was more valuable than the part, a living person was more valuable than a dead one, and rationality was more valued than irrational, senseless action. In postmodernism, the parts of the organization may be more valuable than the whole, as indicated by leveraged buyouts and subsequent asset auctions. People may be worth more dead than alive, and the resources that once were directed toward health and safety are likely now to be used to dispense with people. A premium could be placed on senseless communications and actions that fulfill external demands for communication while denying external groups any useful information. In a brief phrase, meaningless flows of signs may come to dominate communication because they constitute messages but deny the recipient any useful information.

Conclusion:
Postmodern Methods
and the Postmanagement Era

And what about management? In the postmodern era, management as a category of human existence and sense making is destined to become a fleeting image of order and control. As teams substitute for leaders, the myth of human agency is eroded and the value of significant people is challenged. Indeed, management has been a fundamental form of the myth of human agency, the postulate and assumption that individual humans can and do act so as to control the direction and nature of the social system and the organizations therein. But with the erosion in value of human life and the politicization of organization, the logic of the system (itself a contradictory incoherence) displaces individual human actors, who are themselves replaced when they disrupt systemic logic. This is the commodification of the process of commodification of management—the commodified substitution of alternative values for the value of human control over commodification. In a sense, the system will be anarchistically out of control by humans.

In postmodernism, management is withered into vestigial form. Management is merely a transparent image, an arbitrary interpretive constraint on free-flowing commodification. That is, it is an elusive if reified, meaningless sense-making device in a world that is impervious to control by (sensible) agents. Management is technology, the computer matrix a human product with a life of its own. Management is Molly, a posthuman subject, ripping at flesh as part of her job.

Thus, management vanishes with the myth of human agency, the death of belief that individuals have power, that they can control "the system," and that the system exists and acts for humans. It is the logic of the system that transcends postmodern people, detaching their lives from meaningful purpose. The logic persists; people—managers— do not.

Modernist (positivist) theories or methods cannot capture the variegated forms of postmodern existence and are bound to reproduce, represent, or value the very rational, modernist structures and values that we argue are in retreat. Thus, we now examine postmodern alternatives that lie in ethnography, semiotics, deconstructionism, ethnomethodology, postmodern cultural critique, and "relationalist" theories of organizations.

Postmodern Perspectives

Ethnography is the thick description of organizational culture (Geertz, 1973; Spradley, 1979), focusing on actual people or behavior in specific settings. Ethnography is used to describe the actual situated behaviors composing the everyday features of organization, behaviors that are often displaced in formalist, modernist descriptions (Van Maanen, 1988). Ethnography has been used to study social deviance and to penetrate and describe the "underlife" of organizations (Goffman, 1961). If postmodern organizational activity intensifies within the underground or deviant side of conduct and in the "backstage" areas of organization (Goffman, 1959), then careful, insightful ethnographies will be necessary to penetrate and uncover the real but hidden life of organizations, which is unknown to outsiders and to modernist theories of organization. Semiotics—the theory of signs (Culler, 1981)—can be used to address changes in organizational signs and symbols. In particular, the deformation of signs and symbols (Douglas, 1970) through inversion is an important topic for postmodern management theory. However, postmodern theory must transcend the surface level of signs and symbols to penetrate the hidden political interests and tacit features of social power that symbol systems contain. In this regard, deconstructionism (Bradshaw, Chapter 5, this volume; Calas & Smircich, 1992; Culler, 1982; Gephart, 1986, 1988a; Martin, 1990) will be useful for penetrating the surface of symbols—for silencing symbols to reveal their detached and hidden implications.

Ethnomethodology (Garfinkel, 1967) is a science of sense making that assumes that shared meanings do not exist. Members work to maintain a "sense" of shared meanings, and this sense is always fragmentary, historical, and situationally accomplished (Garfinkel, 1967). Ethnomethodology provides an elaborate and systematic theory of sense making that addresses local logics, because it assumes there is no grand narrative. Ethnomethodology thus offers a theory of meaning that defeats meaning. Ethnomethodology is a truly postmodern theory of culture, one that embeds a theory of interpretation in a spatial theory of meaning (Heritage, 1984).

Postmodern cultural critique and "relationalist" theories of organizations are two additional strategies for reconstruction of organization and management theory. Postmodern cultural critique refers to efforts by Calas (1987) to reposition organizational inquiry as a form of cultural analysis and criticism. Calas argues that organizational inquiry has legitimated itself by appealing to an empiricist, positivist, "scientific" discipline that produces definite knowledge; this allows prediction and control over organizations. Thus, organizational analysis is a set of hegemonic discourses that require deconstruction. Reconstructing organizational analysis as a critical discourse requires organizational scholars to reflexively investigate the naturally occurring discourses of members, managers, and organizational scholars. This can be accomplished by "joining other disciplines" (Calas, 1987, p. 254), reducing the separation between scholarly enclaves and other areas of society (p. 255), and bringing excluded, marginal voices into organizational representations and theories (p. 255).

Relationalist theory (Mauws, 1995) offers a potentially useful theoretical basis for postmodern theorizing in organizational analysis. Organization theory has been tyrannized by a focus on the substance of organization, and an alternative metatheoretical framework founded on "relations of organization" would be more consistent with the postmodern worldview (Mauws, 1995). Relationality assumes that form is an aggregation of relationships among forces; hence, the investigation of forms limits the nature and kind of knowledge we can develop about organizations and society. By conceiving of organizations as relations among forces (Mauws, 1995), the organization is conceptualized as a "constellation" wherein structure is not substantively fixed but rather is a shifting cluster of variable aspects or elements. Relationality provides a decentered perspective to organization because the forces are dispersed and any view of the organization itself requires one to take a spatiotemporal position and hence to invoke yet another set of relations. A relationalist perspective on organizations overcomes many problems and limits of a substantialist perspective, including reification, the tendency to center analysis on certain substantive features or structures, and the exclusion of the observer from the system of organizational relations. A relationalist position uses a methodological strategy that aims at understanding conditions of possibility, rather than describing cause/effect mechanisms, in organizations. From a relationalist perspective, change is endemic and the problem is to conceptualize stability. From the modernist/substantialist view of lifeless objects, the problem has been to determine how and when change might occur. The relationalist perspective is clearly an important and comprehensive attempt to disrupt the prevailing metatheory of organizational analysis and to reconstruct it on assumptions consistent with postmodern perspectives.

In conclusion, a postmodern theory of management implies a postmanagement theory of organization and a "postorganization" theory of management. As management control becomes a transparent myth, the myth of organization (Gephart, 1988b, 1993) itself becomes a transparent ideological tool, an opiate of the masses who yearn for a lost sense of human agency and control. Postmodern organization and management theory begins with the dissolution of organizational substance, the death of the myths of management control. What it offers is yet unclear. Where it ends, we do not now know.

Notes

1. Besides the capitalist ethic, the other conditions related to the emergence of the modern capitalist state (Bendix, 1960, pp. 383-389) were the following: state monopoly power over the means of domination and administration, a central tax system and centralized military force, a state apparatus that monopolized legal enactments and the legitimate use of force, and a rationally organized officialdom. The modern capitalist state that emerges has an administrative apparatus that conducts official business in accord with administrative regulation. Administration and the legal order are subject to change by legislation. The state also exercises binding authority over all people, and the state alone has the legitimate right to use force (Bendix, 1960, pp. 417-418).

2. Weber's well-known ideas about the attributes of the modern state were theoretical descriptions of unfolding historical processes that he observed during his lifetime. These ideas were given substantive form in the Weimar Constitution developed in post-World War I Germany. Although Weber himself participated as a consultant to the commission charged with drafting the constitution (Bendix, 1960), he died of pneumonia in June 1920 and therefore was not alive to witness the successes and failures of the Weimar Republic.

3. This shielding can occur through three modernist means: reification of the organization as an actor, which disrupts the allocation of agency to specific human actors; measurement of managerial performances by purely operative criteria; and the organizational value system that guides managerial activities but that is not generally publicly visible (Scott & Hart, 1989).

4. Jameson (1991) regrets the absence of a discussion of Gibson's work in the context of postmodern literature. Here we redress this lacuna to some extent.

3

Exploring the Terrain of Modernism and Postmodernism in Organization Theory

JOHN HASSARD

This chapter offers a brief exploration of the terrain of postmodern social theory as it relates to that branch of analysis concerned with organizations. In so doing, it contrasts modern and postmodern forms of explanation and examines a range of concepts derived from these two generic approaches. Initially, I assess some of the chief theoretical positions of modernism and review different approaches to the modernist trajectory in organizational analysis. Subsequently, through reference to the works of key writers, I explore a range of postmodern concepts in social theory and trace how they have been used as tools in organization theory. The culmination of the chapter sees this exploration of key concepts and trajectories form the basis for determining three main styles of postmodern organizational analysis, which I call the ethnoindustrial, sociophilosophical, and synthetic. The chapter concludes by noting the different ways in which these positions make sense of organizations and organizing.

The Postmodern Mood

One of the main reasons that postmodernism is of interest is because it focuses our attention on a topic currently considered important for organizational analysis: culture. Although once of peripheral interest to organization theorists, during the past decade or so, work on culture has come to the fore. Evidence of this lies in the increasing number of articles and books on the subject and in new academic journals with the word *culture* in the title. Above all, it is the way in which modern societies appear to be experiencing a number of major cultural transformations that has made postmodernism an important issue for writers on social and organizational analysis.

If we explore deeper to consider the philosophical basis of postmodernism, we find a key characteristic is that the postmodern approach rejects the concept of a univocal relation between forms of representation (words, images, etc.) and an objective, external world. At the postmodern level of analysis, the focus is upon "the rules grounded in practices which precede subjectivity" (Power, 1992, p. 111), which is essentially the structuralist attack upon the philosophy of consciousness. There is no real space for the voluntary actor as, instead, the actor's space is found in the notion of action as *play* rather than as *agency* (see Lyotard & Thébaud, 1985). Postmodern analysis succeeds in distancing itself from the assumptions of unity implicit in the Enlightenment notion of reason. Unlike modernism, where there is faith in the recovery of a relationship with Nature, postmodernism gives rise simultaneously to "increasing liberation from the natural world and to the splintering of culture into discrete spheres" (Power, 1992, p. 111).

Writers often define the modern or postmodern by contrasting associated sets of antinomies (cf. Clegg, 1990; Featherstone, 1988). Featherstone, for example, expands upon a family of terms derived from these two generic concepts. Specifically, he contrasts modernity and postmodernity, modernization and postmodernization, and modernism and postmodernism. On deploying these terms, Featherstone notes how the prefix *post* seems to signify "that which comes after." The postmodern appears to represent a break with the modern, which is defined in contrast to it. Like Power (1992), however, Featherstone suggests that the situation is more complex than this, for the term *postmodernism* is also used to denote not so much a rupture with, as a negation of, the modern. Although in one sense the postmodern is what comes after the modern, in another it is an abandonment of the modern, with the emphasis being placed on a relational move away.

A subsequent distinction is that between postmodernism as the signifier of a historical periodization or as a theoretical perspective. This underpins both Bauman's (1988a, 1988b) demarcation of *post-modern sociology* and a *sociology of postmodernity* and Parker's (1992) splitting of post-modernism (with a hyphen) from postmodernism (without a hyphen). Both writers use their first term to signal a new epoch of sociological inquiry and the second to suggest a new form of epistemology.

For postmodernism as an epoch, the goal is to identify features of the external world supporting the hypothesis that society is moving toward a new postmodern era. The practice is based on the realist notion that we simply need to find the right way of describing the world "out there." Parker (1992) notes how the "post" prefix is related to a number of other concepts that reflect specific features of post-modern society. Although the most common of these are post-Fordism, post-capitalism, and post-industrialism (Bell, 1973; Harvey, 1989; Piore & Sabel, 1984), he notes, following Callinicos (1989), how at least 15 other post-prefixed terms share this naming of a new historical period. A theme associated with many of these post-prefixed concepts is that the social and economic structures reproduced since the Industrial Revolution are now fragmenting into diverse networks held together by information technology and underpinned by what Lash and Urry (1987) call a *postmodernist sensibility*.

Alternatively, the notion of postmodernism as an epistemology reflects developments in poststructuralist philosophy. Postmodern epistemology suggests that the world is constituted by our shared language and that we can only "know the world" through the particular forms of discourse our language creates. It is argued, however, that as our language games are continually in flux, meaning is constantly slipping beyond our grasp and can thus never be lodged within one term. The task of postmodern writing, therefore, is to recognize this elusive nature of language, but never with the aim of creating a metadiscourse to explain all language forms. We must beware of trying to explain formal structuring, for this is impossible. The myth of structure is just one of the processes through which social action is reproduced. The postmodern theorist should instead seek to uncover "the messy edges of mythical structure, the places where the [structuring] process becomes confused and defies definition by the discourses that are used within it" (Parker, 1992, p. 13).

The Terrain of Modernism

In order to comprehend the terrain of postmodernism, we must also understand the terrain of modernism. To achieve this, we will define the main theoretical positions within the modernism debate and clarify what is meant by the modernist approach to organizational analysis.

Cooper and Burrell (1988) suggest that modernism is "that moment when man invented himself; when he no longer saw himself as a reflection of God or Nature" (p. 94). Like Power (1992) and Featherstone (1988), Cooper and Burrell trace the origins of the modernist trajectory to the Enlightenment notion of reason, which is held to be the highest of human attributes. Similarly they point to the influence of Kant, and centrally to his suggestion that we discover reason when we cease to depend on any external authority as the basis of belief. Kant's idea of "dare to know" (*aude sapere*) offers a critical posture in which we not only display powers of rational discrimination but also have the courage to express them.

For Cooper and Burrell, however, reason was also appropriated by writers on society. Notable were works by Saint-Simon and Comte on the particular problems of government and administration brought about by increasing industrialization. In these writings, we find elements of organizational thinking. Cooper and Burrell (1988) suggest that at this historical point, reason was appropriated by "an early form of systems thinking which subverts its critical edge to the functional demands of large systems" (pp. 94-95). While Saint-Simon's followers were drawing up a blueprint for the système de la Mediterranée (a projected association of peoples of Europe and the Orient through a network of railways, rivers, and canals), Comte was similarly defining industrial organization as the foundation for community and progress. Modernization became represented by the organization of knowledge as expressed in the development of macrolevel technological systems.

In sum, we find two theories of modernism emerging here. On one hand, we have a systemic modernism, which reflects "the instrumentation of reason envisioned by Saint-Simon and Comte," and on the other a critical modernism, which offers "a reanimation of Kant's programme of enlightenment" (Cooper & Burrell, 1988, p. 95).

Modernist Organization Theory

The modernist trajectory of organization theory is described by both K. Gergen (1992) and Clegg (1990). Gergen contrasts an advancing postmodern period for organizational analysis with a retreating modern one. He suggests that modernism has advanced in concert with faith in the notion of progress and our absorption in the machine metaphor. These various assumptions remain central to Western culture and have left a lasting impression on our theories of organization. Not only have modernist principles granted the professional investigator a privileged position in the domain of organizational inquiry, but they have also promised that progress can be attained in our understanding of organizational life.

Gergen feels, however, that the paradigm of modernist organization theory may be in decline. Although the modernist discourse is far from exhausted, for a great deal of research is still carried out in its name, Gergen feels that it has lost its sense of "lived validity." Organization theory has so far drawn its inspiration predominantly from the modernist leitmotif; Gergen suggests that the gains to be acquired from this tradition are diminishing. There is generally a "yearning for alternatives," the modernist discourse having almost become a "formalism" or, worse, an "ideological mystification." For Gergen, this sense of unease has prompted a growing interest in the "postmodern turn" in organization studies.

Clegg (1990), in contrast, suggests that rather than notions from the Enlightenment, the concept of structural differentiation represents the motive force behind the modernist theory of organizations. A key part of the sociological enterprise has been the emphasis on processes of differentiation as a basic element of the modern experience. In particular, the division of labor is one of the core concerns of both classical sociology and political economy. In documenting this trajectory, Clegg (1990) argues that the key modernist thesis on organizations is found in Max Weber's work. Indeed, the modernness of modern organizations stems from the way they are appreciated "within a genre of more or less harmonious variations on the theme of Weber's composition of bureaucracy" (Clegg, 1990, p. 176). Clegg suggests that Weber's work on bureaucracy ranks alongside, if not above, Smith's pin factory and Marx's conception of the labor process. Weber and his followers personify organizations as one of the great achievements of modernity.

For Clegg, therefore, modernity is premised on processes of differentiation. In particular, task differentiation denotes the crucial separation of occupation from organization, or, as Offe (1976) describes it, the move from task-continuous to task-discontinuous operations. When organizations become more complex in their task structures, it is increasingly unlikely that any one person can have sufficient knowledge to control all practice adequately. This process sees the mapping of people onto types of jobs and the control of their discretion once they are in place. Task divisions are no longer related by any normative community; instead, organizational relations become constituted in hierarchical forms.

Knowing the Postmodern

If a modernist epistemology reflects assumptions of progress, absolutism, and differentiation, what are the key characteristics of a postmodern epistemology? A first theme of the postmodern approach to knowledge is the notion of the replacement of the factual by the representational (see also K. Gergen, 1992; Linstead & Grafton-Small, 1991). This suggests that attempts to discover the genuine order of things are both naive and mistaken. In particular, the modernist objective of determining factual relationships through the empirical method is considered problematic. In the modernist view, the empirical method reflects the assumption that language is a slave to observation and reason. The logic is that through rigorous research, we will continuously improve language through a more accurate correspondence with Nature.

Under a postmodern approach, however, the empirical process is redefined. The language produced by the empirical process does not equate with an increasingly accurate correspondence with Nature. Instead, it represents a process of professional self-justification. Research proceeds on the basis of discourses that are already shared within a particular scientific community. The evidence produced is interpreted and justified within a restricted linguistic domain. As the empirical process starts with its theoretical assumptions intact, data produced through experimentation are defined by reference to an existing theoretical spectrum (K. Gergen, 1992). Findings produced through empirical science reflect preexisting intellectual categories.

In a postmodern approach to knowledge, we must also possess the ability to be critical or suspicious of our own intellectual assumptions (Lawson, 1985). This is achieved through the notion of reflexivity (see Platt, 1989). The rationale for reflexivity is that propositions that remove representation from the grasp of the factual are themselves representations. In other words, they treat as real both language and a universe divorced from language. The result is that they beget their own critical analyses.

The reactions of postmodernists to this irony have been varied. Derrida has pursued intentionally ambiguous and self-negating practices in seeking to deconstruct his own propositions. In contrast, Julia Kristeva (1980) has created forms of expression that appear nonsensical within traditional conventions but are, she argues, sensible within a primordial semiotic. Others have proposed the less heady alternative of the intellectual playing the fool (K. Gergen, 1992). Uniting all these approaches, however, is the view that we should not portray knowledge as a prestigious and objective estate divorced from the mundane activities of everyday life. Instead, the forms of language we call knowledge should be viewed in a more humble way. Knowledge bases are things that are either more or less interesting to us, but no more than that. They are not the stuff of which ultimate commitments are made. In Lyotard's (1979/1984) terms, we should beware of subscribing to the grand narrative of progress, for the prime purpose of this discourse is to justify our actions. Above all, we should not subscribe to the seriousness of the progress narrative, for its assumption of unitary and linear progression only serves to suppress the possibility of a multitude of alternative voices.

Derrida's notions of deconstruction and writing rely on a denial of conceptual mastery and definition. It is necessary, therefore, for Derrida to develop a strategy of thought that reflects but does not capture this process. He achieves this through the notion of *differance*. In defining differance (with an a), we see the extension of Derrida's wish to express writing as a self-deferring process of *difference* (Cooper, 1989).

Cooper (1987) suggests that the concept of difference can be compared to the concept of *information* in information theory, where it takes the form of a binary structure based on the idea of division. There are two ways of considering division (or difference): by focusing on the two forms that have been separated or by focusing on the actual process of separating. Whereas the former suggests logocentrism, through emphasizing hierarchical binary oppositions, the latter suggests that division is not simply a static act of separation but can also represent an undifferentiated state where terms are conjoined (Cooper, 1990). Division thus both separates and joins: The act of separation also creates the image of something that is whole.

The second sense of the term reflects Derrida's notion of undecidability in which terms inhabit each other. To counter the static logocentrism of hierarchical binary oppositions and to activate the processual sense of difference, Derrida invents the term differance, which is derived, in part, from Saussure's (1974) conception of language as a system of differences (Cooper, 1990). In developing the term differance, Derrida incorporates two senses of the French verb *différer*—to differ (in space) and to defer (in time)—into one designation that both subverts and produces the illusion of presence and consciousness (Johnson, 1980). To explain the concept, Derrida outlines how our traditional understanding of the sign is what we substitute for the absent thing we wish to present. The sign represents the present in its absence—it is "deferred presence." Derrida argues against the notion of a fully present reality that is directly available to our understanding. Instead he posits a world that is continually deferred both in space and in time.

Our final concept develops Derrida's analysis of the deconstruction of presence in terms of its implications for human agency. This is achieved through the notion of decentering the subject as the locus of understanding. From the logocentric view, the human agent represents a holistic and clearly bounded cognitive universe. Human agency is founded on a personal, subjective core of awareness in which actions and emotions are coordinated from a knowing self. The agent acts within the context of its own dynamic presence. In contrast, we have seen in Derrida's work that presence is always already mediated by absence. We noted earlier how consciousness is never a direct and unmediated experience but rather comes to us in an indirect way. In this view, agency is an artifact and subjectivity is a process of locating identity in the language of the "other" (Harland, 1987). Agents are constituted through a symbol system that locates them while remaining outside of their awareness (Linstead & Grafton-Small, 1991).

The process that establishes agency, therefore, is one that takes recourse to the concept of the other (Cooper, 1983). The subject is decentered and thus bereft of the logocentric authority it possessed when self-aware and present. The self-conscious agent of modern psychology becomes an image that is no longer sustainable. Derrida (1978) replaces the grand isolation of the modern subject with the notion of agency as a system of relations between strata. The subject is no longer self-directing but is instead a convenient location for the throughput of discourses. As Linstead and Grafton-Small (1991) suggest, subjectivity becomes "a weave, a texture, fragmented but intertwined rather than hierarchical and integrated, a process and a paradox having neither beginning nor end" (p. 39).

The Terrain of
Postmodern Organization Theory

Having noted earlier the tendency to define postmodernism as representing either a historical periodization (an epoch) or a theoretical perspective (an epistemology), and having identified elements of a postmodern approach to knowledge, we now consider how these lines of analysis offer conceptual tools for assessing the postmodern approach to organization studies. In particular, through viewing their landscapes, or prospects, we suggest that in their "strong form," both the historical/ethnoindustrial and the theoretical/sociophilosophical positions can appear to inhibit theory building for postmodern organizational analysis. We note, in addition, that a synthetic position that develops ground between these extremes may offer a more robust basis for organization theorizing.

THE ETHNOINDUSTRIAL PROSPECT

A work that reflects the ethnoindustrial perspective of the historical (or epoch) orientation is Clegg's (1990) *Modern Organisations: Organisation Studies in the Postmodern World*. In this work, Clegg advances the historical periodization position by citing detailed empirical examples of postmodern organizational forms. Declaring his objectivist intentions from the start, Clegg remarks, "empirical realities are neither imaginary nor whimsical: they cannot be side-stepped" (p. 5). Indeed, the tangible description of postmodern organization structures—ones that can be distinguished from the classical modernist form of the bureaucracy—defines this work. Clegg documents the structural properties of postmodern organizations from a review of comparative data. He argues that unlike the highly differentiated and modernist bureaucracy, the postmodern organization is based on a "de-differentiated" form.

From this perspective, the postmodern organization has structural characteristics that reflect the socioeconomic philosophies of *flexible specialization* and *post-Fordism* (see Hirst & Zeitlin, 1991; Piore & Sabel, 1984; Pollert, 1988; Smith, 1989). Clegg (1990) argues that examples of the postmodern form are found in the business enterprises of Japan, Sweden, East Asia, and the Third Italy. The suggestion is that these are organizational structures in which we find, inter alia, a niche-based marketing strategy, a craft-oriented or multiskilled workforce, and a technical core of flexible manufacturing. Although postmodern organizational forms are as yet relatively ill-defined, Clegg suggests they may encourage, as in Sweden, progressive developments in industrial democracy and improvements in the skill levels of labor. He reminds us, however, that the postmodern form, although in certain respects appealing, may also rely upon repressive and elitist industrial practices. Such organizations may be based on a segmented labor force with a clear stratification of privilege, as in Japan.

THE SOCIOPHILOSOPHICAL PROSPECT

Alternatively, an example of the strong epistemological position is found in the sociophilosophical work of Cooper and Burrell (1988; see also Burrell, 1988; Cooper, 1989). Although, like Clegg (1990), Cooper and Burrell address the modernist assumptions that underpin Weber's work on bureaucracy, they argue that postmodern concepts are appropriate to an antifoundationalist rather than empirical understanding of organizations.

Instead of privileging the functionality associated with increasing levels of differentiation, Cooper and Burrell (1988) seek a more abstract understanding of the principles of bureaucratic organization. Their discussion of Weberian modernism centers on the alienating forces of bureaucracy and, in particular, on the notion of bureaucracy as the "iron cage" that imprisons modern consciousness. Instead of Weber's analysis representing a functional assessment of organizational design, for Cooper and Burrell it is a grand narrative of administrative progress. Although Weber's work emphasizes the processual character of organizational life, modern organizational analysis has seen it decontextualized and rewritten to stress static issues of efficiency and administrative control.

Cooper and Burrell (1988) argue that the postmodern project emphasizes the futility of such totalizing tendencies. The idea of a superior, objective standpoint is completely rejected, emphasis being placed on the inherent instability of organization. The discourses of organization are no more than changing moves within a game that is never completed. Cooper and Burrell suggest that under postmodernism, we should seek to disrupt continuously our normative structures about the organized world. Above all, we should seek to explode the myth of robust structural relations through establishing the fragile character of organizational life. For Cooper and Burrell, a postmodern analysis should focus on "the production of organization rather than the organization of production" (p. 106). Under this strategy, we must eschew the idea that organizations are formed and then act themselves to structure relations. We realize, instead, that it is the analysis alone that creates a discourse on organization. The constructs we employ to make sense of organization are moral imperatives that serve to presuppose certain features of organization while excluding the possibility for others. The academic study of organizations is reduced to nothing more than a series of discourses that have no prior claim to an understanding of organizational affairs.

CRITIQUE

A major problem with the sociophilosophical prospect, however, is that it often remains difficult to discern any significant movement beyond a perspective on postmodern organization, especially in the direction of a conceptual framework. Although they offer a deeper level of conceptual reflection than, for example, writers who associate postmodern organization with flexible specialization or post-Fordism, it can be argued that writers such as Cooper and Burrell have, nevertheless, "consciously avoided being programmatic" (Parker, 1992, p. 9) in their theorizing.

When faced with the problem of constructing a postmodern conceptual model at the institutional level, we have few exemplars to consult (see Kreiner, 1989, on this point). An obvious reason for this difficulty stems from the assumptions of rationality and purpose that underpin the enterprise. Traditional theory construction is founded on belief in the factual nature of a knowable universe. The dominant knowledge bases of social theory rest on logocentric foundations. Given these assumptions, it seems that postmodernism must reject the very idea of theory construction at the institutional level. If a factual world is beyond our grasp, what are the grounds for developing such static formulations? Why should we seek to develop formal schemes if the method of deconstruction shows them to be objects for our amusement, elements of "serious play" at best? As Kreiner (1989) argues,

> It would be futile for an organization theory to propose new and alternative reifications of a "reality" which is probably complex, paradoxical, ambiguous, and superficial, and which thus escapes ultimate reification. If we succeed in marketing such alternative reifications, they would only be new costumes for the masquerade of knowledge. (p. 6)

The main postmodern positions in organizational analysis thus appear to be successful in inhibiting formal theory building, albeit in an unconscious way. On one hand, the ethnoindustrial position provides positivist descriptions that are developed with scant reflection on the philosophy of postmodern analysis. On the other hand, the sociophilosophical position explodes the myth of the structural form but fails to account for the everyday experiences of social actors. As such, neither develops a framework in which formal organization is acknowledged as a phenomenon that is accessible to postmodern deconstruction.

THE SYNTHETIC PROSPECT

What could be described as a more robust framework for postmodern organizational analysis is offered by K. Gergen (1992), who argues that postmodern statements do not necessarily leave us bereft of the potential for theory building. Gergen suggests that the discourses that have historically shaped organization theory—romanticism and modernism—are beginning to lose their luster, especially when compared with the emergent discourse of postmodernism. Although he does not wish to suggest that postmodernism has greater explanatory power than these older discourses, he feels that it is more closely attuned to the spirit of the times.

K. Gergen (1992) argues that the hallmark of an organization theory should be whether or not it supports patterns of relationships we feel have positive rather than negative consequences for social life. He feels that "if the function of theories is not derived from their truth value, but from their pragmatic implications, then theoretical voice is restored to significance" (p. 217). The successful communication of this intelligibility provides the grounds for its usefulness. Theory and practice are inseparable: There is "no language of understanding placed beyond the boundaries of potential" (p. 217). We should be continuously in the process of absorbing other cultural intelligibilities into our own. As postmodernists, we are concerned not only with the social relationships championed or discredited by particular theories, but also with the potential for theories to offer new possibilities for our culture.

In this analysis, it can be argued that Gergen develops a synthetic position, or at least one that explores the intellectual space between the strong ethnoindustrial and sociophilosophical positions. One possible advantage is that this position maintains the tension between the empirical reality of organizations and the fragile nature of their reproduction. Gergen argues that the concept of postmodern writing can offer new options for organization theory. Indeed, it directs him to go beyond speculation about a substantive contribution to postmodern organization theory and to offer one himself, in the form of a relational theory of organizational power. In accepting that a tangible aspect of organization can be addressed from a deconstructionist position, it can be argued, the work achieves a tension between the ethnoindustrial and sociophilosophical approaches to postmodern analysis.

For analyzing organizational power, Gergen argues that the post-modern drama begins with the realization that the rational sayings available to the manager are in fact of indeterminate meaning. It is here that the concept of differance comes into play for, as Derrida suggests, the meaning of any word is derived from a process of "defer-ral" to other words that "differ" from itself. The strength of the single concept of differance is that it reflects both the simultaneous and conflated processes at work in organizational power.

The postmodern plot thickens as it becomes clear that there are multiple meanings for the everyday terms used in organizational power networks. Such terms are polysemous: They have been used in many contexts and thus bear "the trace," as Derrida says, of many other terms. The position becomes more complicated still when we discover that each term employed for clarifying an original one is itself ob-scured, until the process of differance is once again set in motion. We also know that these terms subsequently bear the traces of others in an expanding network of significations (see Lash, 1988, on this point). Thus, statements that appear to be but simple pieces of organizational rationality "on closer inspection can mean virtually anything" (Gergen, 1992).

This postmodern theory of organizational power demonstrates that we are empowered only through the actions of others—through *social supplementarity.* This suggests that textbook theories locating power in individual discretion or the structural properties of organization should be abandoned. Relational theory suggests that managers do not control the fate of their decrees. Instead, power is a matter of social interdependence; it is effected through the coordination of actions around specified definitions.

Conclusions

This chapter has explored the intellectual terrain of modernism and postmodernism as applied to organization theory. Initially, the concept of postmodernism was defined and contrasted with its sister term, modernism. I suggested that currently we possess no firm consensus on the meaning of the concepts of modernism and postmodernism. Instead we find a range of meanings associated with these generic terms.

To place structure on the debate, I identified two main orientations within the literature: postmodernism as either a historical periodization or a theoretical position. The former approach suggests that postmodernism is an epoch of ethnoindustrial life, the latter that it is an epistemology. In the former, we can explain cultural change by reference to empirical examples. In the latter, we counter the totalizing tendencies of empiricism by presenting a conceptual alternative.

Exploring the literature further, I joined the epoch-epistemology distinction with themes from a postmodern approach to knowledge. This was developed by extracting key concepts from the works of leading writers on postmodernism. Drawing upon Derrida and Lyotard in particular, I identified themes of postmodern knowledge relevant to social theory, especially representation, reflexivity, differance, and decentering.

These themes and distinctions then provided the structure for a discussion of postmodern organization. Contrasting the main intellectual positions on postmodernism, I argued that in their present form, neither the ethnoindustrial nor the sociophilosophical prospect offers a robust basis for developing postmodern organization theory. Instead, we suggested that the synthetic perspective appears to offer a more promising location for theory building.

4

Storytelling at
Administrative Science Quarterly
Warding off the Postmodern Barbarians

DAVID M. BOJE

DALE E. FITZGIBBONS

DAVID S. STEINGARD

> There is great comfort to be derived from following the
> well-trodden paths; hypothesis testing is an activity open to all;
> there are numerous outlets for its expression, and abundant
> promises of professional advancement. As many fear, when
> one sits smugly beside warm fires, the murmurs of cold winds
> only increase one's comfort. Others believe that professional
> gatekeepers will stifle the interests of the beginning
> professional in "new paradigm" inquiry. Such inquiry may
> seem merely an irritant to be eradicated.
>
> (Gergen, 1982, p. 208)

It is postmodern to observe that science is storytelling (Lyotard, 1979/
1984) and postmodernism is returning to storytelling (Boje, 1995;

AUTHORS' NOTE: Direct all correspondence to Dale E. Fitzgibbons, Department of
Management and Quantitative Methods, Illinois State University, 329 Williams Hall,
Normal, Illinois, 61761

Jameson, 1991, p. 367). Gephart (1988a) suggests that researchers undertake ethnographies of (modernist) organizational theorists to investigate their knowledge claims in situ. This, along with a deconstruction reading of their storytelling practices, might make their knowledge claims more apparent. Such is the purpose of this study: to do a deconstructive re-reading of the resistance stories of *Administrative Science Quarterly* (ASQ) to the postmodern, as well as critical theory critique-stories of orthodox organization theory. Our thesis is that the orthodox administrative science subcommunity, as exemplified in ASQ, has succeeded in using storytelling to ward off writings in critical postmodernism for the past four decades.

Both postmodernism and critical modernism (i.e., critical theory) are being adopted by organizational theorists to critique orthodox administrative science for its empiricism, positivism, and gatekeeping. We include defenses of administrative positivism by Donaldson and others. Our chapter explores the backlash to critical postmodernism, including stories of editorial gatekeeping, with a critical analysis of the editorial rhetoric in ASQ, which publishes essentially orthodox administrative science discourse, while steadfastly resisting the introduction of critical postmodernism. In particular, the value of the latter is the focus on discursive analysis (hermeneutics and deconstruction) and the fact that it reveals organizations, including ASQ, to be engaged in knowledge production embedded in a hegemonic political struggle among remarkable storytellers.[1] This is followed by a different postmodernism, which borrows from critical modernism, as well as epoch and epistemological postmodernism.

A variety of modernisms and postmodernisms constitute what Jameson (1991, p. 342) describes as a "play of differences" (Hetrick & Lozada, 1992). Jameson (1991) defines modernism as "the result of incomplete modernization" (p. 366). Cooper and Burrell (1988, pp. 95-98) begin the play by differentiating two versions of modernism: systemic and critical. Systemic modernism would be an "instrumental rationality," as exemplified in Bell's (1973) postindustrial thesis that seeks to "finish" us with even more rational systems. Systemic modernism links science and technology together to promote a unity of knowledge in large-scale functional systems with many interacting variables to yield progress via rationally preferred outcomes, such as higher productive performance with a more economical deployment of resources.

Systemic modernism promotes a machinelike system of social functionality or what Lyotard (1979/1984, p. 11) refers to as programs for
"performativity." Examples of organizational theories include structural functionalism, interorganizational networks, population ecology,
transaction costs, and contingency theory.

There have been four radical organizational theory alternatives to
move beyond orthodox (systemic modernism) organizational theory:

1. The critical modernism of Clegg and Dunkerley (1980b) following a
   critical theory/neo-Marxist perspective
2. The epoch postmodernism of Drucker (1957) and Clegg (1989, 1990,
   1994a)
3. The epistemological postmodernism of Burrell and Morgan (1979),
   which subscribes to what Rosenau (1992) terms a skeptical postmodern
   perspective
4. The perspective of this review, the critical postmodernism of Boje and
   Dennehy (1994), which takes an affirmative postmodern position
   (Rosenau, 1992) and a modified epoch perspective (see K. Gergen,
   1992; Hussard, 1993; Morrow, 1994, p. 7)

We turn now to the radical discourses.

The second form of modernism is *critical modernism,* which is critical
of the rational-functionalist-cybernetic-systems discourse of systemic
modernism. Its unfinished business is to rescue the Enlightenment
from systemic modernism. Critical modernism is based on the work of
the Frankfurt School (Critical Theory) and is staunchly defended by
Habermas (1987), for example, who seeks to rescue "bourgeois" Enlightenment from the repressive discourse of capitalism's systemic
modernism (an instrumental domination over Nature defended as
"scientific") by constructing rational procedures for consensus (Jameson,
1991, pp. 58-59). Giddens (1991b, p. 207), like Habermas, seeks to
radicalize modernism by pursuing postempirical inquiry with critical hermeneutic methods and an interpretive foundation of inquiry
suggested by early Marx (Morrow, 1994, p. 158). Critical modernists
have done a critique of positivism from the 1930s onward (Morrow,
1994, p. 142), favoring postempiricist theories of science. Critical
modernism also critiques scientific efforts to rationalize productive
performance and administrative "authority" by exposing the connection between knowledge creation and politics/values (Alvesson &

Willmott, 1990, p. 24). Early critical modernism work by Clegg (1975, 1979), Clegg and Dunkerley (1980b), Benson (1977), and Frost (1980) extended traditional Marxist critiques to organization theory. Politics and knowledge are bedfellows that fashion clever cover stories to appear to be "objective" scientific knowledge without politics or stories.

Epoch Postmodernism. A complete review of types of postmodernisms is beyond the scope of this chapter (see, for example, Hetrick & Lozada, 1992; Rosenau, 1992, and chapters in this book).[2] However, we do need to briefly review differences between the epoch and epistemological approaches. The most fully developed epoch organization theory is Clegg's (1990) book, *Modern Organisations: Organisation Studies in the Postmodern World.* Clegg's empirical work identifies emerging organizations in Japan, Sweden, East Asia, and the Third Italy that are de-differentiated, flexible, and niche-driven, with craft-oriented or multi-skilled workforces operating in information technology networks and subcontracting (p. 181). However, the earliest formulation of a post-modern alternative was Drucker's (1957) Cartesian paradigm-shift approach (Boje & Dennehy, 1994, pp. 14-15). Drucker has subsequently written about the "post-business" (1990) and "post-capitalist" (1992) era. Clegg and Rouleau (1992) and Boje and Dennehy (1994) are far less convinced that a grand paradigm shift has occurred in which modern has been replaced by postmodern. Rather, whatever postmodernism is, it struggles in an age of modernity. Jameson (1991), on the other hand, in his periodization of late capitalism, capital, and multinational capitalism has expanded into previously uncommodified areas of Nature (the Green Revolution; e.g., Devall & Sessions, 1985; Purser, 1994), the unconscious, and consumer culture.

Epistemological Postmodernism. Organizational examples of a strong epistemological postmodernism (often referred to as poststructuralism) can be found in the work of Cooper and Burrell (Burrell, 1988; Cooper, 1989; Cooper & Burrell, 1988). The epistemology approach centers Derrida's deconstruction methods to "deconstruct" organizational discourse. It relies mainly on the work of Lyotard (dissensus, local narratives, and performativity), Derrida (difference and undecidability), Foucault (censoring function of discourse and his adaptation of Nietzsche's method of genealogy), and Deleuze and Guattari (active-reactive representation of Nietzsche) to differentiate a postmodern organizational discourse (Cooper & Burrell, 1988, pp. 91-110). "Postmodernism reveals formal organization to be the ever-present expression of an autonomous power that masquerades as the supposedly rational constructions of modern institutions" (Cooper & Burrell, 1988, p. 110).[3]

Critical Postmodernism: A Mid-Range Position. We are labeling the mid-range position *critical postmodernism* (Morrow, 1994, pp. 29, 79). Critical postmodernism dances between epoch postmodernism, epistemological postmodernism, and critical modernism. From a critical postmodernism position, environmental sustainability is superior to nonsustainability, participation is better than nonparticipation, and although everything is related to everything else, some relationships have more hegemony than others. This mid-range position is typified in work by K. Gergen (1982, 1991, 1992), Hussard (1993), and Boje and Dennehy (1994). Gergen, for example, "appears not to recognize a difference. He moves seamlessly between applying postmodernism to suggesting that organizations need to find new ways of working in the postmodern age" (Parker, 1992, p. 12). Critical postmodernism is epochal in the sense that there is a transition from modern to postmodern, but it is in its infancy. Modernism, modernist organization, and positivist science rule the day. There are, as yet, no postmodern organizations. Empirical analysis is possible from a postmodern perspective. For example, Boje (1995) analyzes Walt Disney and the Magic Kingdom and concludes that the organization Baudrillard defined as postmodern was still a very modern organization, with only very limited pockets of postmodern discourse. Boje uses a "play of differences" (*Tamara*) metaphor to explain the contention among premodern, (systemic) modern, and postmodern discourses at Disney. For every postmodern turn, there is a modernist reaction. Boje and Dennehy (1994, p. 22), for example, point out that once a postmodern construction becomes a formula that organizations implement, it is transformed by modernist discourse into a pattern for exploitation. For example, the corporate culture movement has become another tool to control how employees think and what they value in order to improve administrative control over productivity and quality (Alvesson & Willmott, 1990; Willmott, 1992). There is a downside to postmodern organization: "labeling dimensions of organization as postmodern does not remove the specter of exploitative control of humans by technical, cultural, and administrative fibers" (Boje & Dennehy, 1994, p. 25). In sum, critical postmodernism has roots in epoch and epistemological postmodernism, as well as in critical modernism.

Having briefly identified modernisms and postmodernisms, our purpose is to review the backlash as critical postmodernism moves out of the margins and identify some possible features of a critical postmodernism.

The Systemic Modernism Backlash. Donaldson, in a series of writings (1985, 1987, 1988), defended positivist organizational theory against epistemological postmodern critiques presented by Burrell and Morgan (1979, p. 398) and against the critical modernism of Clegg and Dunkerley (1980b, pp. 257-262). Donaldson's defense against postmodern attacks on positivist organizational science, particularly on contingency theory, was joined by Hinings (1988). Donaldson (1988, p. 28) even claims to have "routed" the critics. Marsden (1993), however, believes that Donaldson's defense of positivist organizational theory is flawed on at least three counts:

1. He dualizes theory and practice, ignoring that ordinary people (including academics) theorize and develop categories based upon the practices of their network of social/power relationships (Marsden, 1993, p. 97).
2. Donaldson (1988, p. 31) misses Burrell and Morgan's (1979, pp. 398-399) "point about the emasculation and incorporation of rival paradigms by the positivist techniques of functionalist organization theory—widening organization theory by assimilating its rivals so as to incorporate their criticisms."
3. Donaldson (1985, p. 8; 1988) and Hinings (1988, p. 3) reverse "the popular impression: critics become conservative custodians of an old orthodoxy, and Donaldson's defense of what has been practice in North American business schools for the best part of fifty years becomes the 'brilliant' midwife of a new discipline" (Marsden, 1993, p. 101).

With this map of the field and its controversies as a backdrop, we turn now to an empirical exploration of resistance to critical postmodernism.

Reading *Administrative Science Quarterly*: "Don't Publish Postmodern Studies Here!"

One place to examine the reactive trends in administrative organization theory is in the theorizing and empirical work done at so-called top-tier journals such as *Academy of Management Journal, Academy of Management Review, Organization Studies,* and ASQ. Journals are artifacts of subcultures or speech communities within academia (Barley, Meyer, & Gash, 1988). ASQ is the most cited organizational journal of what has been defined as the systemic modernism speech community (Stablein, 1993, p. 5). *Organization Studies,* for example, publishes far more (epistemological) postmodern, as well as critical modernism, articles than do any of the top-tier American organizational theory journals (e.g., Burrell, 1988; Cooper, 1989; Cooper & Burrell, 1988; Parker, 1992, to cite a few). At the other extreme, ASQ has not published much (that we could find) with postmodern/critical modernism as its primary focus, except for Benson (1977) and Barker (1993). In our commentary on published studies, we distinguish between authors who make postmodern/critical perspectives their primary theory and investigative framework and a second group of authors who only include these perspectives in a tangential and marginal way in their literature review or implications. As examples of the second group, we include semiotic analyses (Barley, 1983; Sutton, 1991), social construction studies (Astley, 1985; Boje, 1991), and an occasional ethnomethodology article (Gephart, 1978). In our re-reading of ASQ neither group succeeded in developing the kind of dialogue and debate that has gone on in *Organization Studies, Journal of Organizational Change Management, Organizations,* or even *Academy of Management Review* (e.g., Smircich, Calas, & Morgan, 1992).

One might assume that because ASQ, as we shall argue, is dominated by a sociological perspective, critical/postmodern discourse would have migrated from journals such as *Sociological Theory* (see special issues "Symposium on Postmodernism" and "Debate on Postmodernism," as well as Brown, 1990; Denzin, 1986); *Sociological Focus* (Richardson, 1988); *Annual Review of Sociology* (e.g., Agger, 1991), *Canadian Journal of Sociology* (e.g., Cheal, 1990); *Theory, Culture, and Society* (e.g., Bauman, 1988a); *Sociology* (Smart, 1990), and other sociology journals that have written on, debated, reviewed, and critiqued the critical perspective over the past decade. We also find it disturbing that ASQ, a leading organizational theory journal among respected organizational theorists, seems mired in the traditional scientistic orthodoxy of systemic modernism. Radical modernist and postmodernist theories of organization provide important critiques of systemic modernist organizational theory, including theories of progress, enlightenment, rationality, objectivity, male dominance, racial dominance, and environmentally unsustainable business practices.[4] We propose therefore to further examine and re-read the resistance of ASQ by analyzing some of the editors' discourse published in ASQ between 1956 and 1994, as well as the reviews they published with stories of ASQ's interdisciplinary diversity and the state of organization theory knowledge as a normal progress of the application of empirical science to organizations.

Rather than a march of science thesis, Frost and Taylor (1985), for example, theorize that editors and reviewers are in a hierarchical relation to authors and can block other paradigms from entering the community's discourse (Stablein, 1993, p. 3). ASQ editors occupy such a position of authority by selecting editorial boards and outside reviewers and thereby effectively concentrate their power. But they also have power to define top-tier publishing in their discipline. The tenure trap does not give authors outside this elite much power to resist. In sum, we question the story of interdisciplinary openness, which the editors of ASQ have steadfastly claimed in their editorials from 1956 onward. Rather, we hypothesize that persistent knowledge boundaries that either exclude or co-opt the critical/postmodern positions have been kept intact for four decades by this storytelling. Below we detail specific historical and contemporary examples of how the ontological and epistemological policing of our field is being conducted at ASQ.

The very foundation of ASQ is resistant to the kinds of arguments presented by critical postmodernism. James D. Thompson, the first ASQ editor, set the foundation for a noble new social science. The journal's mission was to use a variety of social sciences as models to differentiate an organizational science from management science. He set the stage for four decades of structural functionalist, rationalist theory, and empirical scholarship on administrative organization theory. In his editorial, Thompson (1956) states that the first and last articles define more than the physical boundaries of this issue. . . . Litchfield's essay outlines the scope of present editorial policy of *Administrative Science Quarterly.* . . . The final article, by the editor, sets forth methodological objectives. (p. 1)

In this first article of the first issue, Litchfield (1956) called for a general theory of administration that would have universal aspects of administrative science based upon a Parsonian functionalist framework.

As other disciplines were illuminating selected portions of the administrative process, Talcott Parsons and others were elaborating at least the beginnings of a comprehensive theory of social action which might provide an over-all framework within which to develop a more specific theory of administration. (p. 5)

Thompson's and Litchfield's manifestos for administrative organization theory envisioned a focus on abstract concepts borrowed from the "basic social sciences," operational definition of same, empirical measurement, testable hypotheses, and generalizations that could be verified by other researchers. In short, our definition of systemic modernism:

An administrative science will be an applied science, standing approximately in relation to the basic social sciences as engineering stands with respect to the physical sciences, or as medicine to the biological. (Thompson, 1956, p. 103)

In issues one and two, Talcott Parsons (1956a, 1956b) laid out a structural functionalist theory for what we have termed systemic modernist organizational theory. In March 1958, Thompson and the other editors wrote a joint reappraisal of the first ASQ volume that invites us to question ASQ's bias:

Turning now to the types of articles needed, first priority should be reserved for pioneering, synthesizing articles which apply theoretical analysis to empirical materials. Such operations will most advance an administrative science (as we have defined it).

Finally, it is pertinent to ask whether the gaps in this volume reflect a neglect, by students of administration, of certain variables and relationships and a preoccupation with a limited range of problems, or

TABLE 4.1 Comparison of Subject Content, *Administrative Science Quarterly*

	Subject	Pages, Volume 1	Pages, Volume 2
I	Theory and philosophy	102	126
II	Methodology and pragmatics	90	6
III	History and description	154	88
IV	Research: Quantitative and empirical	98	219

Source: Boulding, 1958. © 1958 by *Administrative Science Quarterly*. Reprinted by permission.

whether the gaps reveal a biasing factor in obtaining articles. The answer to this question will become clearer in the future.
—J.D.T., W.J.M., R.V.P., F.L.B., J.S.D. (p. 532)

At the end of its first 2 years, ASQ editors also did something very daring. In 1958, they invited Kenneth Boulding (1958) to do a critical reading of the journal to ensure there was no bias against particular theoretical analyses or various social sciences.

Boulding (1958, p. 3) saw administrative organization theory as a spin-off from economics and as a revolt against Taylor's "scientific management" and the public administration theories of Gulick and Urwick. Boulding empirically tested the editor's vision of a new social science that would separate itself from its parent-disciplines by appropriating theories and methods from "all" social sciences (p. 3). He concluded that, in its first two years, ASQ had already begun to marginalize some social sciences, theories, and methods. For example, between Volumes 1 and 2, the number of pages devoted to historical studies was cut in half, whereas the attention to quantitative/empirical studies more than doubled (see Table 4.1).

Boulding (1958), mourning the decline of historical analysis, commented, "It would be a great pity if a morbid fear of being 'unscientific' were ever to lead to a suppression of this type of writing" (p. 14). He added,

Administrative science particularly needs good studies of exceptional individuals. . . . Biography is therefore an essential part of the raw material of administrative science. We still need to do much more thinking on how to integrate the knowledge gained from descriptive and historical case studies into the knowledge gained from empirical and quantitative research. (p. 15)

ASQ's retreat from historical case studies and management science was coupled with an exclusion of several academic disciplines.

Boulding (1958) revealed yet another split when he classified articles according to his estimate of the field of competence of the author(s). Sociology had the most space, 139 of 444 pages in Volume 1, jumping to 288 of 439 pages in Volume 2. The growth was from less than a third of the first volume to almost two thirds of the second volume. In the meantime, other social sciences disappeared altogether (e.g., psychology went from 21 pages to 0, social anthropology from 15 pages to 0, and social psychology from 37 pages to 0). These disciplines would not reemerge until Weick and Pondy became editor and associate editor in the late 1970s.

In addition to these splits, yet another was identified. The academic writers had began excluding practitioners (articles by authors practicing administration went from 53 to 9 pages). Boulding (1958) concluded that by ASQ's second year, sociologists were already dominating the interdisciplinary origins of administrative science discourses in ASQ. He warned that

it would not be difficult for administrative science . . . to become a sort of imperialistic foray on the part of sociologists

that

there is more to administrative science than the statistical analysis of questionnaires

and that

the only "controversy" in the Quarterly . . . has been between administrators in the hurly-burly of the practice of administration, not between academics who might supposedly have more time for it! (pp. 9-10)

Boulding (1956) also thought that basing administrative organization theory on a Parsonian framework would lead to purely mechanical systems theories with lots of variables and concepts. More cybernetic or control systems would be ignored, as would Boulding's preference, language-based systems. For example, he critiqued Litchfield's (1956) more cybernetic formulation for not addressing the more complex system levels of reality of organizations in theories that account for humans as communicators of symbolic and semantic values. It would be 20 years before Louis Pondy (1976) would revisit Boulding's theory of a hierarchy of system complexity and critique Thompson's (1967) input-output machine model of organizations. Preferring Boulding's level 7 or 8 system formulations (Pondy, 1976, p. 36), Pondy, in several other papers, advocated theories that viewed organizations as socially constructed, language using, language creating, and sense making cultures (Pondy, 1978; Pondy & Boje, 1980). Pondy, an associate editor of ASQ, and Weick, its editor, would shift the journal discourse to include more social construction and ethnomethodology articles in the late 1970s and early 1980s. However, as we shall see, this realignment of ASQ was short-lived.

In sum, Boulding (1958) concluded that as early as 1956, ASQ had initiated "rituals of science" in which, because of a lack of critical conversation among multiple fields of organization inquiry, nonquantifiable aspects of the social situation were being systematically excluded. The resulting theories were too mechanical, and analyses were beginning to ignore history, the symbolic, practitioner-authors, and a variety of social science disciplines (pp. 14-16). He labeled this situation data fixation. Boulding cautioned that statistical rituals, such as sandwiching commentary between tables with lots of correlation coefficients and tests of significance, was a "spurious" form of social science research.

> I must confess that I regard the invention of statistical pseudo-quantities like the coefficient of correlation as one of the minor intellectual disasters of our time; it has profoced legions of students and investigators with opportunities to substitute arithmetic for thought on a grand scale. (p. 16)

"Data fixation" and the marginalization of historical case studies of individuals and organizations seriously exclude postpositivist approaches. Boulding ends by summarizing his understanding of the challenge for ASQ that invites the birth of critical postmodernism.

The importance of the problem can hardly be exaggerated: how can organizations be built, and by what principles shall they be conducted, which will serve to free and not to enslave the individual and which shall be protected against the gangrene of corruption which besets all human institutions? (p. 19)

By the time Boulding's critique appeared, Robert V. Presthus was editor of ASQ, a post he held from 1957 to 1963. He chose to ignore Boulding's warnings and "stay the course!" In his Editor's Commentary (Presthus, 1959), he said, "The need for empirical research remains great, and the number of Quarterly articles based upon such research has been substantially increased during the past year" (p. iv).

In 1961, Presthus's associate editor, William Delany, confirmed Boulding's most skeptical predictions when he conveyed an even more fundamentally positivistic scientific philosophy of ASQ in discussing preferences for "systematic" (modernist) analyses in the Research Notes and Comments section:

[ASQ] aims to produce knowledge of complex human organizations that, insofar as possible, meets the usual scientific canons of validity, reliability, generality, parsimony, explanatory power, and usefulness for purposive control. . . . *Historical research, while not ruled out, is given second-level priority and rigorous comparative studies substituted at the first-priority level.* [italics added] (p. 449)

Giving second-level priority is a significant marginalization. Thomas Lodahl (1963-1968 first term; 1972-1977 second term) became editor for the first time in 1963. In Volume 8, the stage was set for the first of the Aston group articles (Pugh et al., 1963, pp. 289-315). Their systemic modernist formulation indicted the field for using "one-case" studies that ignored systematic relationships between organization structure and environmental context (p. 289). The authors proposed a profile of abstract variables capable of empirical verification in comparative, structural studies.

Lodahl's editorial board was reconstructed with the addition of Warren Bennis, Amitai Etzioni, W. Richard Scott, and Stanley Udy. The first editorial commentary of note from this new team did not appear until Volume 10 (No. 1, June 1965). By December, Jay Schulman had become associate editor, and Robert Kahn and Charles Perrow were added to the editorial board. Yet the direction of ASQ, in its insistence upon positivistic discourse while professing an interdisciplinary focus "without dilution," was unabated. As Lodahl (1965) proclaimed in his Editor's Note,

> As we look forward to the next decade of the Quarterly, we anticipate no major changes in editorial policy. We will continue to encourage contributions . . . from any academic discipline—contributions which are presented without dilution and which are theoretical, empirical, or (preferably) both. (p. iv)

The discourse, however, was full of dilution. In 1966, William Starbuck (who would serve as editor, 1969-1971) was added to the editorial board. Starbuck had a rather interesting exchange with an author who tried to intensify what Boulding had termed the "data fixation" theme (Price, 1966). First, Price proposed that ASQ would improve if authors increased their sample size of organizations in all comparative studies. Second, in studies of single or just a few organizations, researchers should inventory *all* major organizational variables, using standard terminology and standardized measurement techniques. Starbuck (1966) wrote a response that did not dispute Price's positivistic notions but argued about the magnitude of their calibration: "The effort required for a case study would increase to, say, twenty man-years, and the effort needed for a small-sample study would be proportionately greater" (p. 156).

What is interesting in this exchange is that ASQ editors had become so fixated on the rational, structural functionalist, survey method that no one was looking at alternatives to positivist organizational science. Starbuck added a reading of administrative organization theory that mythologizes the role of editors, review boards, and the rank and tenure hierarchy: "Organization theory has no central authority structure with the power to punish nonconformity or to reward compliance" (p. 156).

From a postmodern/critical theory perspective, we obviously disagree with this rationalization. Starbuck, to his credit, does glimpse a part of the nonself-reflexive forest.

> Organization theory is one of the least cooperative research societies,
> and we rarely analyze our own behavior. We divide into subcultures on
> the basis of academic traditions and methodological biases. (p. 157)

But, on the other hand, from a historical perspective, the discourse of
the editors, editorial board, and authors is a powerful control over
traditions and methodological biases.

Having found a way to defend the citadel from intensifying the
rational positivistic-panopticon of "systemic modernism," Starbuck
succeeded Lodahl as ASQ editor. Lodahl, however, returned in 1972
and continued to be a champion of positivistic discourse until 1977,
when Karl Weick became editor. The Weick editorial team would
actively open ASQ to alternatives to the structural/functionalist/
rationalist/positivist paradigm. Lodahl (1976, p. 715) announced Weick's
selection as the new editor as of January 1. Weick (1977, pp. 138-139)
appointed Lou Pondy and Howard Aldrich as associate editors, with
Sam Bacharach as book review editor. The new editorial board was
smaller. Weick reasserted that "ASQ remains an interdisciplinary journal with soul," but then added a curious statement:

> ASQ is not the house organ for any particular level of analysis, it is not
> a sanctuary for the "cute school" of organizational analysis (as one
> referee put it), any more than it is a sheltered workshop for the
> "opposite" group which presumably must be called the "brute school."
> (pp. 138-139)

Once again Weick, like his predecessors, defends the story of the
interdisciplinary role of ASQ but drops the "without dilution" phrase
from the editorial policy. Weick's editorial influence is obvious from
the start. Volume 22's first issue looks substantively different from what
had been published over the previous decade. It began with Kenneth
Benson's critical theory/critical Marxism analysis of organizational
science, which was followed by a controversy between Pondy and
Dogramasi over methodological points. The issue included Quinn's
(1977) article about romance in the workplace "Coping with Cupid."
A look at the Benson (1977) article will help us understand the rivalry
between the systemic modernism and the emergent critical theory/
postmodernism positions in organization theory.

Benson (1977) cites Habermas frequently in the text, and he concludes effectively what we have noted earlier. What Boulding had prophesied in his 1958 review of ASQ is confirmed by Benson (1977): "The study of complex organizations has been guided by a succession of rational and functional theories and by positivist methodology" (p. 1). Systemic modernism organization theory had failed to adopt a critical or a self-reflexive posture. Instead, what Benson calls alternatively the "rational selection model," "goal paradigm," or "tool view" had been

> coupled with a methodological stance which accepts the conventionally understood components of the organization as scientific categories . . . [organizational theorists] uncritically accepted existing organizational arrangements and adapted [their studies] to the interests of administrative elites. (p. 2)

Benson's rendition of a dialectical view of critical modernism has four principles. First, in "social construction/production," relationships, roles, and institutions are produced via power holders who defend their interests within an established order. Second, in "totality," people produce their relationships within unique, partially autonomous contexts with relations of dominance between sectors or layers in relation to emergent processes. Third, the social constructions contain "contradictions," as well as seemingly autonomous, determinate structures. The structures can be studied and observed as if not a human product. "Hence, conventional, theoretical approaches and positivistic methodologies may contribute to the description of these orderly patterns" but fail to challenge their historical/political context (Benson, 1977, p. 5). Fourth, praxis, the free and creative reconstruction of social arrangements using rational and/or ethical commitment limits how the social situation is appreciated.

Like Burrell and Morgan (1979), as opposed to Clegg and Dunkerley (1980), Benson (1977) cleverly writes his challenges to the field by paying respect to, and even including a role for, the dominant paradigms. Benson's (1977) account confirms a march of positivist science myth. Referring, for example, to Hickson, Hinings, Lee, Schneck, and Pennings (1971), Hinings, Hickson, Pennings, and Schneck (1974), and others, Benson says,

> [They] have provided important beginnings. . . . Yet, these insightful analyses must be placed within a more encompassing framework with a critical-reflexive component, otherwise, this line of investigation breaks down easily into a technocratic effort to reduce irrational bases of resistance to authority. (p. 8)

Benson's (1977) main conclusion, once again, parallels Boulding's earlier prophecy concerning the impact of marginalizing historical studies in ASQ:

> Thus, the entire explanatory effort remains within the confines of an abstracted organization ripped from its historical roots and societal context and innocent of its deeper-lying power struggles and negotiations. Thus, the research itself is drawn into the presuppositions of the order under study. (p. 11)

Again, like Hamlet's ghost, Boulding's ghost, although not referenced, is present in this final quote:

> The proponents of political economy, resource dependence, strategic contingencies, and the like remain committed to a basically positivist methodology. They have adopted an uncritical, unreflexive stance toward organizational realities. (p. 13)

With Karl Weick as editor and Louis Pondy as associate editor (1977-1979), there were growing expectations (at least from young scholars) that the journal would become more open to social construction and even critical theory analyses (although neither Weick nor Pondy was a critical theorist). The only critical theory article was Benson's (1977) critical-Marxist analysis of organization theory (until Barker's 1993 study). However, rather than opening the door to critical theory, Benson's (1977) critique was just as ignored as Boulding's (1958) critique. Both articles had challenged the cybernetic, positivistic, antihistorical assumptions of the journal (Boulding directly, and Benson very indirectly). The dominant paradigm began to reassert itself before any substantive debate between the old and new paradigms could commence.

A short story will help clarify this last point. In 1976, future associate editor Pondy attempted to transform the knowledge-making system of administrative science. Largely based on Boulding's (1956, 1968) construction of a nine-tiered model of systems, and revised in Pondy and Mitroff (1979), his papers extolled the virtues of elevating mainstream administrative science "beyond open systems" and into higher, more loosely coupled, and less rationalized levels of analysis. In a very caustic rejection of the Pondy article by ASQ, one particularly staunch defender of scientific orthodoxy had this to say about Pondy's visionary work (cited in an unpublished editorial response to Pondy's submission). We do not know the identity of this staunch defender, but references to the "cute school" did appear in Weick's (1977) opening editorial:

> This paper is representative of what I would label the "cute" school of organizational research, which makes it substantially less boring to read than most of the papers I have to review, but I am not sure that this quality alone makes it more of a scientific contribution. The "cute" school believes that mired in present modes of thinking and analysis, the study of organizations will progress only if the scholars engage as much in playful, or foolish activities as they recommend for the organizations they are studying. In part, the "cute" school is on the right track, but in part, it is not. It is certainly clear that this field can stand new models, new perspectives, and new insights into organizational functioning, and in this respect, these people are quite correct. The problem is, however, that these insights, perspectives, approaches must serve the scientific goals of understanding, explaining, and finally, being able to predict organizational functioning, at some level. The problem with the cute school is that it becomes lost in its own cuteness, captivated by novelty for its own sake, cuteness for its own sake, and at the end, begins to play language games with itself which, while interesting to read, do not add much to the study of organizations.

By labeling the article as a representative of the "cute school," the anonymous reviewer marginalized this important intellectual step in organizational thinking. Although it was eventually published in a highly respected research annual (Pondy & Mitroff, 1979), this important article arguably did not receive the acclaim it deserved. The dominant systemic modernism speech community of organizational science remained secure.

Every crisis of legitimation of the status quo necessitates a cover story that explains away an institution's vulnerabilities, for example, the stories of Boulding, Benson, and the cute school. In 1980, Dick Daft (a future ASQ associate editor) published a 20-year (1959-1979) analysis of the journal. It is curious to us that Daft elects to use Boulding's (1956) levels of system hierarchy and complexity framework (discussed earlier), while electing not even to cite or otherwise mention Boulding's (1958) study of ASQ's first two volumes. Furthermore, as an exclusionary, rhetorical move, Daft concludes that the first 2 to 3 years of publication are not sufficient time for its editors to effect an editorial grip on the types of articles being published. Boulding had argued just the opposite. In addition, the Daft (1980) study does not evaluate each year of the journal. Rather only five particular years (1959, 1964, 1969, 1974, and 1979) are actually "read" and classified. These omissions allow Daft to tell his legitimating story of ASQ. According to Daft, "low-variety statistical languages" being used in article after article are an "organizational mapping phase" or "trend" or "important phase in organization theory" in which simple, quantifiable, relationships get defined and measured using very "low-variety languages" (pp. 623-631). The low-variety language of choice is linear statistics, which with practice could extend to new variables and more difficult problems in the mapping phase of defining and measuring formal characteristics of organizations (p. 631). This was a necessary (evil) in order to derive a "comparative view of organizations."

By not including the first few years of ASQ in the study, as Boulding had done, Daft (1980) could defend the story/thesis that the field of administrative science had matured and was in 1979 shifting to higher levels of analyses on Boulding's scale. This story appropriated Boulding's seemingly scientific jargon (1956, 1968): that is, using level 1, mechanical system frameworks of arrays of variables was a necessary first step in building an organizational science, before more complex types of studies that theorized people as language users and meaning shapers could be profitably attempted. Including Boulding's 1958 study, published in the third volume of ASQ, would have completely muddied Daft's story plot: organizational science as the long steady march of progress with empirical science as its major foot soldier. Postmodernists label this plot the "progress myth." In addition, including the volume for 1979 skewed the results to fit the story because this volume included a special issue on qualitative methodologies considered appropriate to the study of organizations. Had the study stopped at 1978, an entirely different story would have been required. Finally, Daft is able to ignore the politics of publishing and affirm that the kinds of articles published in ASQ reflect changes in the progress of science as its community discovers refinements in methods. Although noting that editors and editorial board composition influence the types of articles published, he conveniently concludes that in reporting "new knowledge," editors and boards from 1959 to 1979 did not control what got submitted. Rather, the "discipline-wide" changes taking place in the research methods and theories of organizations explain his empirical evidence.

> A possible alternate explanation might be ASQ editorial policy, implicit or explicit. For example, new editors took over before 1969 and 1979, and their views might have influenced the type of articles published. (Daft, 1980, p. 631)

In other words, those at the "forefront of a discipline" do not reflect "the diversity within the discipline," but these "editors and board members do not control the type of papers submitted for publication, and their goal is to publish articles that report new knowledge" (p. 631).

It is mind-boggling how Daft (1980) could conclude that an editor and editorial board (who are at the forefront of their discipline) do not control the kinds of knowledge and methods, let alone the authors, that are published in their journal. One of his suggestions for improving scholarship is precisely the same conclusion reached by Boulding (1958) in the earlier study of ASQ, published in ASQ, but conveniently, his ghost is not referenced: "Maybe we can avoid accepting a level of theoretical analysis too far below the complexity of the empirical world we are investigating" (Daft, 1980, pp. 633-634).

There are other cover stories. For example, in her introduction to the special issue "Part I: The Utilization of Organizational Research," Janice M. Beyer (1982, pp. 588-590), one of only two females on the board of ASQ prior to Weick's administration, partially reintroduces debate between the existing paradigm and alternatives when she summarizes concern over ASQ relevance: "Recently, increasing numbers of organizational scholars have begun to express concern that organizational/administrative science has had little effect on life in organizations" (p. 588). However, she quickly covers over the differences and differentiations ASQ has made from Management Science and practitioners (managers are the practical-other who lacks our rigor) by invoking an interesting rhetorical move, a privilege to nostalgia for the past, and also a second move, recasting Thompson, the first editor of the journal, as a heroic idol:

> After the field of organizational studies crystallized into a distinct field in the mid-1950s, researchers became oriented toward producing basic research. The first editor of ASQ, James Thompson, either foresaw or greatly influenced the direction in which the field evolved. In the first issue of ASQ (Thompson, 1956), he argued for less pressure for immediately applicable results and for more emphasis on relationships, measurement, conceptualization, abstract thinking, new systems of logic, and in general, research that would build and test theory. Subsequently, theoretical or empirical rigor came to distinguish members of the fledgling "organizational" field from their colleagues who studied "management" in more practical and less scientific ways. (p. 588)

At the other end of the spectrum from Daft's and Beyer's cover stories, in 1983, Astley and Van de Ven published an article titled "Central Perspectives and Debates in Organization Theory." They see a growing theoretical pluralism in the organizational literature and try to provide a cross-integration model. However, the integration misses the main point that the assemblage of models does not include a critical perspective and does not deal with the models and voices (e.g., practitioners and historians) already excluded. Editors control discourse by the inclusion and exclusion of editorial board members.

This relates to issues of gender. In its first two decades, all of the editors and editorial board members of ASQ were men. Before Weick, only Beyer had made it past this glass ceiling. By 1983, Weick, as editor, had added more women to the mostly male board than any previous editor, including Karen Cook, Rosabeth Moss Kanter, Meryl Louis, and Lynne Zucker. In Volume 30 (No. 3, September 1985), Weick stepped down and John Freeman of Cornell University became the editor-elect. By the time he left, Weick had added Jean Bartunek, Joanne Martin, Janet Near, C. Kaye Schoonhoven, and Lee Sproull. Out of 40 editorial board members plus Dick Daft and Gerald Salancik as associate editors, Weick (outgoing editor), and Freeman (incoming editor), there are now 10 women on the editorial board. However, the feminist critique of organization theory has yet to be published in ASQ. Some debate relevant to our systemic modernism thesis did manage to surface on the pages of ASQ.

Every few years the nonmodern or nontraditional organizational theory literature is reinvented by yet another call for revolutionary change in the administrative science model. However, each successive call for revolutionary change is a reinvention, not different in kind from the ghost of Boulding.

For example, Astley (1985) wrote another article using social construction theory that would seem to invite a postmodern/critical theory submission to this administrative science. Astley viewed administrative science as a "socially constructed product" where "definitions of truth" became invested with "the stamp of scientific authenticity" (p. 497). The ASQ model "assumes that knowledge grows linearly" by "adding to the existing data base," but, "the lack of standardized measures and variables . . . greatly impedes scientific progress" (p. 497).

Astley (1985) pointed out that administrative scientists sought "preeminence for their chosen paradigm as an end in itself" (pp. 497-498). The hegemony of knowledge came from attracting support for a theory, not because one theory was better than another (p. 505), but because there was a "rapid rise of business schools" during the 1950s and 1960s, along with management doctoral programs in search of emancipation "from its origins in managerial practice" (p. 508). Astley also asserted the gatekeeping thesis of this article. "Key figures" in this "hierarchical evaluation system" are "those gatekeepers who determine which articles will be accepted by prestigious journals" by defining what "good science" is (p. 508). The "judgments made by these gatekeepers" are defined as the "discipline's formal evaluation system," which is also "what good science is" and "what constitutes valid knowledge" (p. 509). Thus, Astley's rendition of social construction theory parallels our critical modernism/postmodernism perspective of a hegemonic power/knowledge relationship.

Despite this obvious invitation, no modern or postmodern submissions seemed to be making it through the formal evaluation system that constituted valid knowledge. Contrary to official stories (editorials and sanctioned studies), it is our story that Weick and Pondy did (temporarily) alter the direction of ASQ fixation on the sociological, empirical, rational, systemic modernism position set in motion in the first issues of ASQ. However, after Weick's editorship, the dominant systemic modernism paradigm reasserted its dominance during the early years of the Freeman editorship.

Stablein's (1993) study of publishing trends in ASQ, AMJ, AMR, and OS between 1985 and 1989 corresponds to Freeman's (1985-1993) period of editorship at ASQ. Stablein confirms Boulding's (1958) and Astley's (1985) political/social construction perspective: Knowledge published in each of the journals is a socially (and politically) constructed product of a (sub)community of elite scholars. Stablein's work, for example, documented that a few universities enjoy privileged access to journal publication. He examined where authors published in these journals received their university training:

> ASQ is again the most concentrated by far when considering the concentration ratios. Fully one-third of all authorships received their training in just three universities [Stanford, University of Illinois, University of California, Berkeley]. Stanford alone accounts for 17% of [the doctoral training of the] authorships. (p. 9)

We can get some sense of Freeman's (1986) systemic modernist philosophy of science and how similar it is to Thompson (i.e., his original editorial manifesto), Litchfield (1956), Starbuck (1966) and his debate with Price (1966), and Lodahl (before and after Starbuck's administration) by looking at Freeman's manifesto on how to build administrative science, published as part of his editorial essay. Freeman's thesis is that the organizational literature is too frequently based on "small samples of opportunity," which results in a "lack of comparability" across studies and limits "legitimate generalizations. "This is a pitiful state of affairs for any group of scholars laying claim to scientific standards" (p. 298). Therefore, he urges authors to do "centrally funded," large-sample studies from "theoretically meaningful populations" (p. 298). Freeman cautions that his project is not an "ambitious" or "an omnibus organizational research venture" trying to answer all questions with all variables (pp. 298-299).

> Such an ambition could not possibly be realized. The field is too diverse and too much in flux for this to be practicable.

Freeman recommends that organizational researchers prioritize the quantities of organizations and variables sampled across levels and over time; given "limited resources, compromises will be necessary." However, the "possibilities for advancing social science research on organizations are staggering" (p. 303).

As the backlash to such staggering empirical positivist/systemic modernist storytelling of the march of science, in which the gatekeepers defended their good science, interdisciplinary voices got louder. The pages of the journal began to be opened to just a few scholars, who having graduated from the "right" (ASQ) institutions (most of them), could be trusted to publish qualitative, social construction, attribution, and semiotic articles (Barley, 1983, 1990; Bettman & Weitz, 1983; Boje, 1991; Fiol, 1989; Larson, 1992; Sackmann, 1992; Salancik & Meinl, 1984; Sutton, 1991). However, there were very few person studies (except Chen & Meindl, 1991) or historical analyses (except Kieser, 1989) published during this period, unless they dealt with a population ecology model of history (Stablein, 1993, p. 14). However, as our sample of observations across time reveals, in the main, the kind of critical modernist theory perspective advocated by Benson (1977) and the social/political construction of Astley (1985) has yet to reassert itself in ASQ (except Barker, 1993). This, as mentioned earlier, is despite the fact that in *Organization Studies* (perhaps because of its more international editorial board), these critical perspectives get significantly more page space.

In 1992, Barley and Kunda published a historical analysis of management and organizational science discourses. Barley would succeed Freeman as editor of ASQ in 1995. He and Kunda concluded that managerial discourse alternated repeatedly between ideologies of normative and rational control. With respect to the periods covered by ASQ journal publishing, Barley and Kunda's reading of management discourse supports some trends discussed in our own reading. ASQ, for example, was launched in the "rational control" period of 1955 to 1980, which we call systemic modernism. However, unlike Barley and Kunda (1992), we do not read, at least as far as ASQ discourse is concerned, a continuous "normative" discourse dominated by the organizational culture movement from 1980 to the present. Instead we see, with limited exceptions, a continued resistance, even with the rise of the culture articles, to a postmodern/critical theory perspective in ASQ. Furthermore, as postmodernists, we are uncomfortable with the totalizing narrative, which collapses the play of differences into a cycle of alternating paradigms. Rather, we see that in the systems rationalism of 1955 to 1980, ASQ sought to differentiate itself from the Operations Research Society of America and the Institute of Management Science, which formed in 1952 and 1953 respectively. ASQ's original editors formed the journal to capture the quantitative orientation in elite business schools, while differentiating themselves from the discipline of Management Science. The sociologists needed to deny their Taylorite origins in engineering and scientific management. Barley and Kunda do, in fact, point out that a second differentiation occurred in the 1960s as administrative organization theory began to differentiate from organizational behavior (p. 377). These two differentiations served to remove consideration of the individual as a language user and language maker. "In some areas of organizational theory, it even became popular to write as if the actions of employees and the decisions of managers were irrelevant to an organization's fate (e.g., Aldrich, 1979)" (Barley & Kunda, 1992, p. 380).

The next cycle, a culture/quality alternative discourse after 1980 according to Barley and Kunda (1992), challenged organizational theory and management on two fronts. First, more theorists argued that organizations should be viewed as socially constructed systems to counteract the rationalist systems paradigm for organizational analysis. In terms of scholars editing and writing for ASQ, Barley and Kunda mention that Karl Weick, Louis Pondy, Joanne Martin, Graham Astley, Alan Wilkins, and Andrew Van Maanen asserted such a position. Second, the other culture/quality discourse came from the writings of consultants and practitioners, or from those who wrote primarily for these audiences (p. 381). As we argued earlier, both groups had been dismissed from ASQ after the first volume and redismissed with the "cute school" language game. Culture was seen in ASQ as a better way to control individual behavior, and culture was postulated as another variable that could be manipulated by management to effect said control (pp. 382-383).

From a postmodern perspective, one problem we see in Barley and Kunda's (1992) cycle of knowledge theory is the assumption that one wave of discourse roots out and replaces or succeeds another discourse. This, admittedly, is also the flaw of epoch postmodernism. Culture, as written about in ASQ, is also the kind of discourse that is critiqued in postmodern/critical theory for its focus on performativity and the grand narrative (Lyotard, 1979/1984) and on similar grounds in critical modernism by Willmott (1992) and Alvesson and Willmott (1990). In short, because of performativity and progress assumptions, both the rationalist systems and the organizational culture/quality discourses are antithetical to a critical modernism or critical postmodern organizational science. The culture/quality discourse is a reinvention of systemic modernism by the system rationalists to preserve Daft's and other editors' myth of interdisciplinary scholarship. The Barley and Kunda formulation also ignores the differences and political action among multiple discourses within these time periods, such as the marginalization of the cute school even during the reappropriation of the culture/quality discourse from practitioners to organizational theory academics. Total Quality Management (TQM), for example, is included as an example of Organizational Culture and Quality (1980 to present), but TQM is also a way to monitor and rationalize the technical processes through techniques that are grounded in Tayloristic (i.e., systemic-rationalist) discourse (Boje & Winsor, 1993, 1994). The only difference is that now consultants, instead of engineers (although many are in fact engineers), do the time and motion studies. Rather than one discourse leaving the stage for another, Boje and Dennehy (1994), along with other postmodern writers in the epistemological tradition, have argued that discourses compete and appropriate one another. The historical elements are shifted about, but the storyline is the same. Postmodernists in general critique evolutionary grand and metanarratives.

Finally, at issue 4 of 1994, Steven Barley became ASQ editor, having provided a cover story that defended the ASQ citadel of modernism and the status quo of evolutionary science (as simply cycles of the discipline) from attacks by critical modernism and critical postmodernism (just evolutionary fads). Robert Sutton, Marshall Meyer, and Christine Oliver were named as associate editors. Finally, a woman had broken the glass ceiling. Barley, like Weick before him, represents a shift from a focus on totally positivist-rational science, by holding out the promise of expanding ASQ to include more qualitative, social construction, and possibly, even postmodern/critical theory analyses. In fact, a 1993 article by James Barker, using ethnographic methodology, did cite Foucault, Coombs, Knight, Willmott, and Giddens— authors that had been only very sparingly mentioned in ASQ.

What is the evidence that the postmodern infusion into the organizational discourse of ASQ is being subtly thwarted? Postmodernism is getting the same treatment that the cute school of social construction and symbolic theory received in the mid-1970s. Social constructionist work, for example, by Gephart (1978) and Pondy (1976, 1978) with foundations of ethnomethodology, and reinterpretive work in Van Maanen, along with postmodern organizational theory, have been kept on the margins of modernist organizational science, especially in ASQ. This has been accomplished by using appeals to the story of interdisciplinary objectivity, combined with an appeal to disciplinary trends and the demands of good empirical science.

Two final short stories. Two recent rejections from ASQ demonstrate the current exclusion of anything postmodern (Gergen & Thatchenkery, 1993; Fitzgibbons, Steingard, & Boje, 1993). The following excerpt was drawn from a rejection letter to these two postmodern submissions:

> The manuscript will not be sent out to our Editorial Board for review because, as we read the paper, it became clear that this article is not suited to this journal. Please examine the "Notice to Contributors" which appears at the end of each issue. It states our editorial policies and defines the kind of work we publish.

Who is "we"? How did this "we" read the paper if it was never sent out for review? This is typical of the mysterious nature of the review process used by orthodox professional journals. We ask, how can two articles explicitly written about administrative science not be "suited" to the journal? How do these editorial policies get formulated? Whose voices are included/silenced in the formulation of these editorial policies? Given that the articles were not even distributed for review, it is clear that anything postmodern or nonstructural functionalist/logical positivist is unwelcome. Reflecting on Pondy's (1976) attempt, we sardonically wonder how far the field has come.

Summary

In sum, our re-reading of ASQ official stories (the epistemological history of ASQ editorial discourse) and our inclusion of marginal stories suggest strongly that in the first two decades, its editors used their powers to establish and enforce a structural/functional/rational or systemic modernist knowledge of administrative science. Systemic modernism in ASQ began as a differentiation from empirical and historical science, followed by differentiations with Management Science, then from practitioners, then in the 1960s from Organizational Behavior, and in the 1970s from the cute school, and most recently from the postmodern science school. These stalwart scientific and logical-positivist, knowledge-making practices socially construct a story of ASQ's progress through the discipline of science in ways that echo the 18th century Enlightenment project, a cornerstone of systemic modernity (Habermas, 1987). ASQ, for example, publishes a program of emancipation through empirical science that will discipline administrative practice while sustaining a cover story that the ASQ discourse community has no control over what gets submitted or the interdisciplinary nature of the field. ASQ is a tool in the hands of editors operating in the context of a political economic knowledge industry of higher education. In particular, in the 1950s, newly formed colleges of business and public administration, including Cornell, Stanford, Carnegie, Pittsburgh, and the University of Illinois needed a journal to summarize and symbolize their communal discourse. Although some of us assume that MBA students do not read such journals, the impact of ASQ has been hypothesized by Fox (1989) to affect Western management education through a Foucaultian panoptic discipline: "Administrative studies themselves gradually became a social science (for example, the *Administrative Science Quarterly*) and specialized masters courses were developed to teach aspirant administrators (most notably the MBA)" (pp. 727-728). Fox (1989, pp. 730-733) suggests that three panoptic mechanisms are disciplining ASQ: unilateral hierarchical observation, normalizing judgment, and the examination. These mechanisms operate to produce an administrative elite that preaches the discourse of elite decision makers ruling nation states, as well as multinational and national corporations.

This elite community of scholars then helps administrators perpetuate a field of administration shaped in that image in MBA and doctoral
education. To the extent that ASQ is an appropriated symbol of
organizational theory excellence ("the rigor we need for accredita-
tion") by business schools, the hegemony of systemic modernism has
also affected the career path of younger intellectuals, who might have
otherwise pursued studies using deconstruction, postmodern, or hermeneutic approaches. This thesis has been developed by Aronowitz
and Giroux (1991, p. 149). They argue that young scholars are coerced
into holding the line "against the invasions of the new 'barbarians.'"
Those who resist the elite are even choosing to "work in second- or
third-rank institutions rather than wait for the front-rank universities
to make room for the new" (p. 149). We would add that some are
electing to attend alternative conferences, such as the European
Group of Organizational Scholars (EGOS is also an elite group) and
the International Academy of Business Disciplines (IABD has a postmodern organizational theory track). These scholars are also publishing journals, such as *Journal of Organizational Change Management* and
Organizations, to promote a more critical and postmodern science.

Our concern in this chapter is that the recent burgeoning of postmodernism, which promises a fundamental rupture (Hall, 1986, 1992)
of these hegemonic knowledge-making practices, is being subverted by
the gatekeepers of the dominant systemic modernist school, so deeply
entrenched in ASQ. Our critique challenges ASQ's organization theory disciplinary boundaries as conveniently arbitrary. It parallels a
similar critique of sociology, in general. Cheal (1990), for example,
views sociology as bound up with the project of modernity as referred
to by Habermas (1987). ASQ, except for a very few critiques, is also a
"totalizing metanarrative" of a unified knowledge brought about by
the progressive application of a positivist methodology (Cheal, 1990,
p. 133). Waves of new concepts included in ASQ from decade to decade
have not altered this overall project. If anything, the original Boulding
(1958) critique becomes partially reinvented every few years, but in
more watered-down forms. Cheal (1990) suggests that the high point
of the metanarrative of unification was Parsonian functionalist systems
theory, which privileges male hegemony and neglects difference as
well as pluralism. Boulding identified this at the start of ASQ. Finally,
Cheal (1990), picking up on Lyotard (1979/1984, p. 8) supports our

premise that journal editors are legislators of knowledge, prescribing the conditions under which statements are admitted into the discourse: in other words, gatekeeping (Cheal, 1990, p. 134). We have tried to argue that ASQ is an example of paradigm politics: "The very act of selecting particular paradigms from a broad range of possibilities is a political act" (Cheal, p. 137). In ASQ, as the gatekeepers changed, what was included and excluded in the positivist pasture also changed. The editorial hierarchy marginalizes authors and perspectives that do not support the aspirations and goals of the reigning speech community. To its credit, the editorial board has in the past two editorships significantly expanded the number of women on the board, but few, if any, articles have presented a feminist critique. We advocate a pluralistic organizational science, with a more diverse constituency that would examine the shortcomings of positivism. Positivist Organization Theory, in its current form, is a kind of discourse that the community of ASQ editors judge to be rational in relation to their set of methodological rules for the verification and falsification of ideas.

A critical postmodern perspective, Boje and Dennehy (1994, pp. 17-21), suggests a skeptical critique of ASQ. First, referring to the progress myth: "Why should we assume that as time marches forward, [administrative science] has gotten better?" (p. 17). Second, rather than a cycle or a displacement of discourses, the study of organizations is a dialectic among modernists (systemic and critical) and postmodernists (epoch and epistemological) that needs to be explored (pp. 18, 40-46, 107-114, 163-169). Third, history has many oppressed voices with many marginalized sides of a story to be unraveled in any single-voiced statement of history such as ASQ (p. 18). Boje and Dennehy point out that the problem with Drucker's (1957, 1990, 1992) epoch approach, as well as the cycle theory of knowledge of Barley and Kunda (1992), is that the areas are constructed as a two-act play from the privileged and elite viewpoint of the administrative industrialist. Fourth, organizational theory texts de-select alternative explanations and theory, while shrouding the control and exploitations in the mystic rhetoric of scientific-sounding principles. Fifth, we fear that when ASQ gatekeepers allow for the word *postmodern,* it may be more in the sense of Bell and Toffler's systemic modernism or a postindustrial thesis. The postindustrial paradigm was developed in the late 1950s through the early 1970s in work by Bell (1973) and Toffler (1970, 1980, 1990).

> The postindustrial story is organized around the theme that prosperity
> will come from becoming an information age service economy as we
> work in our "electronic cottages." . . . Following the prescriptions of
> Third Wave-Postindustrialism, America and other advanced capitalist
> economies began by dumping manufacturing industries in favor of
> service and high-tech industries. As the electronic industry and recently
> the computer parts and aerospace industries also started their decline,
> we were told not to worry, prosperity is around the corner. (Winsor,
> 1992, in Boje & Dennehy, 1994, p. 19)

As populations of organizations downsize, their administrative elite
needs good scientific rationalizations of their practices. Sixth, Boje and
Dennehy (1994) conclude that there is nothing sacred about the
postmodern epoch approach. From an epistemological perspective,
the epoch/cycle model hides the fragmented, disintegrated, alienating, meaningless, vague, devoid of ethical standards, chaotic, and
controlling and torturous aspects of the current era by invoking the
progress of science thesis.

A Critical Postmodernism Manifesto. We suggest that a more critical
postmodernism is a radical disjunction from the systemic modernism
discourse we have examined in ASQ. Critical postmodernism could be
a play of differences of the micropolitical movements and impulses of
ecology, feminism, multiculturalism, and spirituality without any unifying demand for theoretical integration or methodological consistency. Critical postmodernism could include several elements:
self-reflection on how we do our science discourse within the context
of late capitalism, populist-activism to decenter administrative knowl-
edge/domination, a focus on creating environmentally sustainable
enterprise, and valuing the person instead of privileging, reproducing,
and legitimizing administrative control.

Critical Postmodern Methods. Morrow (1994) and Alvesson and Willmott
(1990) have done an outstanding job of compiling methodologies that
can inform not only critical theory but also critical postmodernism.
Instead of a worship of abstraction (totalisms, universalisms, grand narratives), antihistoricism (no case studies), the objective observer, and
generality (logocentrism or logical essentialism), as postempiricists and
as critical postmodernists, we would like to suggest the deconstruction

methods of Derrida (1982), as well as critical hermeneutics (Gadamer, 1975; Thatchenkery, 1992), critical feminism (Farganis, 1994, p. 47; Holvino, 1993; Iannello, 1992), critical ethnography perspective (Barker, 1993; Boje, 1991; Clifford & Marcus, 1986; Clough, 1992; Conquerwood, 1991), ethnomethodology (Garfinkel, 1967), ethnostatistics (Gephart, 1988a), power/knowledge discourse analysis (Boje, 1995; Foucault, 1980b), and the methods of ecological science (Purser, 1994).

In conclusion, critical postmodernism will revitalize the organizational disciplines by reconnecting them to their pluralistic roots. Following Calas and Smircich (1991), we re-read the foundation of administrative science etymologically. Endemic to a re-reading is exposing tacit assumptions or worldviews. Every body of knowledge has some particular epistemological and ontological assumptions that ultimately shape our existential, social, political, and economic relations. A postmodern re-reading aims to expose these unchallenged assumptions and to submit them to a critical analysis in order to expose the putative facticity or "naturalness" of administrative science as timeless and universal truths. Therein lies our (postmodern) work.

Notes

1. The relevance and irrelevance of postmodern/critical modernism theory (the radical school) have received more comprehensive review in sociological circles (Agger, 1991; Brown, 1990, 1992; Calas & Smircich, 1991, 1992; Cheal, 1990; Clegg, 1990, 1992; Denzin, 1986; Richardson, 1988; Smart, 1990) than it has in organization theory (Alvesson & Willmott, 1990, 1992; Boje, 1992a; Burrell, 1988; Burrell & Morgan, 1979; Cooper, 1989; Cooper & Burrell, 1988; K. Gergen, 1992; Gergen & Thatchenkery, 1993; Hetrick & Lozada, 1992; Hussard, 1993; Marsden, 1993; Martin, 1990; Parker, 1992; Smircich, Calas, & Morgan, 1992; Thatchenkery, 1992; Thatchenkery & Pasmore, 1992). Radical organizational theory is further developed in two special issues of *Journal of Organizational Change Management* (Boje, 1992a; Hetrick & Lozada, 1992), in a special issue of *Academy of Management Review* (Smircich, Calas, & Morgan, 1992), and in empirical studies rooted in the critical postmodernism perspective that is our focus here (Boje, 1995; Boje & Dennehy, 1994; Gephart, 1991). Yet, despite this growing organizational literature, the orthodox school remains entrenched and resistant.

2. For example, Derrida's postmodernism is a search for differences and indeterminacy using his deconstructive method; Lyotard's is a search for local narratives, instabilities, and dissensus; Baudrillard's is a search for simulations and hyperreality; Nietzsche's is a will to know, because people cannot tolerate not knowing; and Foucault's uses genealogy to oppose essential truths as expressions of discursive power and domination. In addition, Foucault and Derrida are often labeled poststructuralists

instead of postmodernists, and there is talk of a middle ground between postmodernism and critical modernism: critical postmodernism (Morrow, 1994, p. 79). Further, Lyotard, Baudrillard, and Foucault are critical of Habermas's attempt to develop a rational approach to consensus and communication. Among all these differences, there is agreement that it is time to be critical of empiricism, the progress myth that science and technology improves the social condition year after year, and the systemic modernity project (excluding the critical modernism defended by Habermas and Giddens, and critiqued by most postmodernists).

3. Administrative science has ignored a debate among the epoch and epistemological postmodern theory formulations (Boje & Dennehy, 1992, pp. 442-448; 1994, pp. 12-25; Clegg, 1994a, p. viii; Hassard, 1993, pp. 31-36; Parker, 1992, pp. 2-7). "The problems are not just external to the postmodernists but are compounded by differences within the postmodern camp: a key question is whether the postmodern is an era or a style of theorizing" (Clegg, 1994a, p. viii). Epistemological postmodernism has been criticized for being too relativistic (Boje & Dennehy, 1994; Hassard, 1993; Marsden, 1993; Parker, 1992; Rosenau, 1992). The epistemological position holds that there are multiple, socially (and politically) constructed discourses, but none is better than another.

4. See, for example, special issues in *Journal of Organizational Change Management,* on the Green movement (Purser, 1994); diversity (Cheng, 1994); spirituality (Boje, 1994d); and anti-TQM (Boje, 1993).

PART II

Beyond MAN-AGE-ment:
Gender, Discourse, and
Organizational Voices

5

Women as Constituent Directors
Re-Reading Current Texts Using a Feminist-Postmodernist Approach

PATRICIA BRADSHAW

Corporate boardrooms are increasingly the focus of much debate. Trends such as the growing threat of takeovers, mergers, and buyouts, increasing power from institutional investors, and new definitions of fiduciary responsibility and globalization are reported to be causing a fundamental shift in power away from professional managers to corporate directors or, as Fleischer, Hazard, and Klipper (1988, p. 189) call them, to the "new princes of industry." Within the context of what Gillies (1992) calls a boardroom "renaissance," a greater range of issues is being questioned, including the role and selection of directors (Dunn, 1987; Earle, 1990; Geneen, 1984; Griffin, 1985; MacDonald, 1990), society's expectations of boards (Hatton, 1990; Thain & Leighton, 1988), legal liability of directors (Glaberson & Powell, 1985; Kesner & Johnson, 1990; Krasa, 1987; Perkins, 1986) and the actual composition of boards (Longair, 1990; Mimick, 1985). It is suggested that boards have frequently failed in their governance role and that it is time for them to be more than a "rubber stamp" or "the parsley on the fish" (Fleischer et al., 1988, p. 3).

AUTHOR'S NOTE: The author gratefully acknowledges helpful comments from Robert Gephart, Neil Shankman, Tamara Johnson, Karen Clarke, Stephanie Newell, Eileen Fisher, and Vic Murray on earlier drafts of this chapter. Also thanks to Hannah Mestel.

95

The current trends have been described as creating "ferment" or "crisis" in the boardroom, and it appears that a great deal is changing, and many dimensions of corporate governance are now open to debate. Despite the range of the current discussions, other issues are being silenced. This chapter uses a feminist/postmodernist perspective to deconstruct these silences and to critically examine what has been said about constituent directors in three recent books on boards (Fleischer et al., 1988; Gillies, 1992; Lorsch with MacIver, 1989). This re-reading will demonstrate how the texts, by privileging discourses of change, actually support the status quo and the continued marginalization of women. The goal of this chapter is to go beyond surface explanations of why women are not on boards and reveal the deep structures of power that are being replicated and left unchallenged despite the apparent changes in the boardroom. First, however, I will briefly review the literature on women and boards and the related issue of constituent directors and then outline the feminist/postmodern deconstructive approach.

Literature Review

I have been interested in women on boards for some time. In particular I am intrigued with questions of power, and I thought that boards might represent a domain in which women could have more influence and could begin to bring different subjectivities into the discourses of business. In the not-for-profit sector, Vic Murray and I have statistically shown that boards with a higher proportion of female directors are significantly different on a number of dimensions from boards with a lower proportion of female directors or boards with a female chief executive officer (CEO) (Bradshaw, Murray, & Wolpin, in press). For example, a higher proportion of women on the board is significantly associated with less board prestige, greater board formalization, smaller organizational size, a higher proportion of government funding, and a "power-sharing" board governance model.

To explore these issues on corporate boards, I interviewed 20 Canadian female directors and, although I was not surprised, I was disappointed to find that these women did not see their role as representing the interests or perspectives of women or other marginalized groups (Bradshaw-Camball, 1990). The majority of the women interviewed did not see themselves as feminists, and they spoke in voices that I concluded were like the voices of the dominant, white, male power holders. Mattis (1993), similarly, reports that female directors in the United States want to be primarily recognized for their general (not specifically female) qualities and expertise and that they fear being stereotyped as having a "single issue" agenda. Despite this, Mattis does report some shift among these women toward more feelings of responsibility to address issues related to women's recruitment, retention, development, and advancement in corporations. Part of the problem may be that women only represent 6% of Canadian corporate directors and only hold 4% of directorships on *Fortune* 1000 companies in the United States (Burke, 1994; Mattis, 1993).

THE ROLE OF CONSTITUENT DIRECTORS

Because women on boards typically do not see themselves as responsible for or able to advocate for women, I decided to explore the role of representative or constituent directors. These are explicit roles, most commonly filled by representatives of labor, designed to bring alternative perspectives into corporate governance. Thus, it is argued, representatives of different stakeholder groups can formally ensure that the interests of their groups are taken into account in boardroom decision making. I believe that a formal role can legitimate the voice and perspective of women and other stakeholder groups. Currently directors in North America have fiduciary responsibility to all the shareholders who own the corporation, and governance of the corporation is not seen as involving lobbying or advocating for one particular set of interests (Tricker, 1984). Directors are legally guided by the duties of care (using due diligence) and loyalty (Lorsch with MacIver, 1989). Thus, it is argued, all directors regardless of perspective, background, or sex have the same responsibility to look after the best interests of the corporation and must not favor one perspective or interest group.

The academic literature on representative or constituent directors in the boardroom is not well developed (Stone, 1985). Mintzberg (1983) has asked:

1. Who can be a member of the board, given no legal specifications?

2. Whose interests does the board represent and, once appointed, do directors have external constituencies?

3. How does the board exercise its power and control?

He does not, however, answer these questions, other than to say that "the directors can protect whomever they choose to—organization or external constituency—depending on their own needs and the pressures to which they are subjected" (p. 69).

Baldwin (1984) points out that the "idea behind the constituency board is not to reduce conflicts of interest, it is to institutionalize conflicts of interest of which its proponents approve" (p. 141). In an interview study with directors from 11 international companies headquartered in eight different countries, Demb and Neubauer (1992) found a "commitment to avoid a 'representational' board where members spoke for constituents—like consumers or environmentalists" (p. 150).

This topic, however, is expected to become more prevalent in North America. In Europe, labor participation on boards is common (Tricker, 1984). For example, in Germany there is a mandatory two-tiered board system that has been in place since the end of World War II. It is anticipated that the European Economic Community will require labor membership, and perhaps broader stakeholder representation, on boards for all firms operating in the European Common Market (Gillies, 1992). North American corporations will thus be exposed to this model when establishing subsidiaries in Europe. Although I did not find extensive consideration of constituent directors in the North American literature, I did find some brief reference to this alternative in several recent books on boards. After briefly reviewing feminist/postmodern deconstruction, I will present several of these commentaries on constituent directors.

A Feminist/Postmodern
Deconstructive Approach

Deconstruction is an analytic approach that originated in philosophy and literary critiques (Derrida, 1976; Norris, 1991) and is based on a postmodern perspective (Clegg, 1990; Habermas, 1981; Lyotard, 1979/1984; Turner, 1990). Focusing on the multiple meanings embedded in every text, deconstruction moves us away from universal truth claims and a belief in a metanarrative toward a mode of engagement that uses play, fragmentation, and differentiation in order to disrupt and erode "normalizing" discourses. In this approach, subjectivity and consciousness are seen to be socially produced in language, and meanings do not exist prior to being articulated in language. Discourse is seen as a structuring principle of society, and thus through detailed deconstruction, we can examine the working of power on behalf of specific interests and analyze the opportunities for resistance to it (Weedon, 1987). Deconstruction largely relies on a recognition of the oppositions inherent in all texts, identification of the ways in which one term in the opposition or dichotomy is presented as hierarchically superior, and then a movement to reverse the opposition. In this way, suppressed conflicts and devalued "others" are exposed, and silences and gaps in texts are identified. Deconstructing binary opposites also challenges existing knowledge claims and allows us to examine the links between discourse and institutional forms that create relations of power.

In organizational behavior, postmodernist theorists have raised questions about many inherent and usually unrecognized oppositions or differences in our theories. For example, oppositions such as the following have been identified as neglected in current theories: rationality and irrationality, consensus and dissensus, determinacy and indeterminacy, stability and instability (Power, 1990), order and disorder, equilibrium and disequilibrium, and organization and disorganization (Cooper, 1990). Increasingly deconstruction of organizational texts is being done to reveal these and other dichotomies (e.g., Gephart, 1986; Kilduff, 1993).

A feminist/postmodern deconstruction enables us to become resisting rather than assenting readers of a text (Culler, 1982). Using this approach we can reveal the ideological assumptions underlying texts and show how they suppress gender conflicts. As Fetterley (1978) says: "Feminist criticism is a political act whose aim is not simply to interpret the world but to change it by changing the consciousness of those who read and their relationship to what they read" (p. viii). For many feminist theorists, although the modernist-postmodernist debates have some unique problems (Di Stefano, 1990; Flax, 1990; Richters,

1991), the use of poststructuralist deconstruction has yielded powerful critiques of organizational texts.

For example, Mumby and Putman (1992) deconstruct Herbert Simon's concept of bounded rationality and present bounded emotionality as an alternative. Martin (1990) deconstructs the text of a story given by a corporate president about "helping" female employees and reveals the way the text reifies false dichotomies between the public and private and suppresses gender conflicts. In an elegant, elaborate, and systematic article and using a combination of Foucault's genealogies, Derrida's deconstruction, and poststructuralist strategies, Calas and Smircich (1991) show how the rhetoric on leadership creates a seductive game. Their focus on the leadership/seduction opposition exposes how the discourses on organizational leadership are polysemous, containing multiple meanings.

DECONSTRUCTIVE STRATEGIES
USED IN THIS CHAPTER

I attempt to use a number of different deconstructive approaches in order to denaturalize or to call into question the knowledge claims of the texts and to reveal how they present as inherently neutral the ways things are always done on boards (Ferguson, 1994). First, by exposing the gaps or silences in the texts, I can examine what is said and, more important, what is not said. It is in the significant silences in a text and what is left absent that the "presence of ideology can be most positively felt" (Eagleton, 1976, p. 34). For example, the use of pronouns such as *we* or *them* reveals who is considered to belong in the boardroom and which groups are excluded. The creation of the category of *other* reflects how women and other groups are marginalized and excluded from the discourse and subsequently from institutional power. Other signals of a silence in the texts are the use of parentheses, quotation marks, metaphors, or asides. Derrida has powerfully demonstrated how to pick out loaded metaphors and "show how they work to support a powerful structure of presuppositions" (Norris, 1991, p. 27), in this case about the role of women.

By exploring the use of language and metaphor, we can also see how these texts create myths about harmony, homogeneity, unity, and rationality and thus deny the existence of other viewpoints or inherent conflicts of interest. Exposing how the texts create the impression of one, unitary, and objective reality through reliance on historical convention, the legal system, or apparently neutral practices allows me to reveal the multiple realities contained in the texts and to show how they privilege the existing power holders. Gendered language and terms such as *princes, potentates,* or *chairman* are discussed to support the argument that the texts privilege the masculine and correspondingly devalue the feminine.

In a similar way, I dismantle hierarchical dichotomies and show how a valued opposition is privileged in the text while the *other* is simultaneously devalued and excluded. Oppositions such as public/private, change/nonchange, and male/female are explored. I draw on the work of feminist scholars who have effectively exposed how such foundational and hierarchical oppositions in Western philosophy in many ways work to the detriment of women (Nye, 1989; Richters, 1991).

Extensive etymological analysis using the *Concise Oxford Dictionary* (1983)[1] is done in an effort to explore multiple meanings embedded in the texts. As Calas and Smircich (1991) say, such strategies are

> intended to enhance the doubleness in every discourse . . . [and to show] that the standard interpretation of those meaning systems within a particular community of knowledge, e.g., organizational scholars, is just an arbitrary limit imposed on such writings, which does not always succeed in limiting the meanings. (p. 569)

In addition to such detailed deconstruction of specific words, phrases, and metaphors, I also explore sentence structures and the overall rhetorical style (McCloskey, 1983; van Dijk, 1993), examining the texts' use of irony, mockery, and hyperbole. The use of the imperative voice or an implied threat are examined in order to see how the status quo is preserved in the texts.

Rewriting of one of the original texts as a performance management problem for the directors of a morality play is presented as yet another way to subvert the text and reveal an unintended or unconscious subtext. Calas and Smircich (1991) say iteration "explicitly removes the 'original text' by displacing its context. Using the multiple meanings available, the rearticulation 'uncovers' another plausible text inscribed

TABLE 5.1 The Texts

Authors	Title	Approach
Jay W. Lorsch with Elizabeth MacIver	*Pawns or Potentates: The Reality of America's Corporate Boards* (1989)	• Study based on mail survey and 80 interviews with directors in the United States and Europe • Four case studies of boards in crisis
Arthur Fleischer, Jr., Geoffrey C. Hazard, Jr., Miriam Z. Klipper	*Board Games: The Changing Shape of Corporate Power* (1988)	• Stories of eight of the most significant corporate transactions of the 1980s and court decisions relating to them; impact on directors explored
James Gillies	*Boardroom Renaissance: Power, Morality, and Performance in the Modern Corporation* (1992)	• Historical contexts • Comparative analysis • Case examples • Literature review • Summary statistics

in the apparently straightforward and unequivocal description" (p. 575). The chapter ends with a re-reading of the dominant metaphor of the *board*. Instead of the board being a game with winners and losers or a stage with prescripted performances and directors, I play with the board as a round table with diversity re-present-ed.

THE TEXTS

The texts that I selected (see Table 5.1) are all public documents. Although I do not intend this critique to be seen as a personal attack on the authors of the books, I do understand that they may not be comfortable with this type of approach. In the spirit of deconstruction I also know that my text is equally open to other interpretations and readings. I am not claiming to have found any kind of objective truth or the correct interpretation, or to have reflected what the authors intended to say. I also recognize my own subjectivities, and this chapter reveals what Martin (1990) describes as my "I/eye/ideology." These interpretations are clearly colored by my position as a white, Canadian, female business school professor who has close family ties to corporate Canada and a change agenda. My own position of privilege shapes my reading of these texts.

The texts I have selected to deconstruct are all from relatively recent books on corporate governance. As reflected in Table 5.1, they are based on extensive research and/or on case studies of actual legal situations involving corporate boards. Each explores the significant changes directors are currently facing, and each addresses the need for corporate boards to be more powerful and influential in corporate governance. The authors write based on their experiences as directors, researchers, and corporate lawyers, and all are well-respected in their fields. These texts, in my opinion, reflect the current thinking about boards, and the quotations selected represent the dominant discourse on the topics of constituent directors and corporate governance.

Deconstructing the Texts

A: TEXT FROM LORSCH WITH
MACIVER'S *PAWNS OR POTENTATES*

The first text I would like to engage comes from a book by Jay Lorsch "with" Elizabeth MacIver (1989),[2] titled *Pawns or Potentates: The Reality of America's Corporate Boards.*

Lorsch with MacIver, working also with input from their colleagues at Harvard, claim to have found "the reality of America's corporate boards." They argue that the "changes in the corporate portrait are significant, some might say staggering" (Lorsch with MacIver, 1989, p. 2) and propose several improvements in the boardroom, for example, separating the positions of chairman and CEO and making directors accountable to constituencies beyond the shareholders through broader constituency laws. On page 189 of the book, they address the issue of constituent directors directly (see Figure 5.1). It is important to understand that this is the only section of the 200-page book where

Text	*Dictionary Definitions*
01. We considered, and reject other possible	**constituent**—1. composing or
02. changes in board composition. For	making up a whole;
03. example, several European Countries,	appointing, electing; able to
04. including Germany and the Netherlands,	frame or alter a (political)
05. have labor representation on the board.	constitution (constituent
06. We also considered the idea discussed by	assembly, power);
07. Senator Howard Metzenbaum and Ralph	2. component part, member
08. Nader in 1978, that there should be	of a constituency; one who
09. constituent representation on the board	appoints another his agent
10. (that is, women, consumers, or	
11. minorities). While recognizing the	**pawn**—a chess piece of
12. importance of the other stakeholders, we	smallest size and value;
13. don't see how including them would	unimportant person
14. contribute to the governance process.	subservient to others' plans, a
15. Many such representatives would be	thing left in another's keeping
16. unlikely to have the breadth of experience	as security, pledge; a state of
17. a director needs. In addition, directors	being pledged
18. representing the viewpoint of one	
19. constituency or another could fractionalize	**potentate**—root is *potent*,
20. the board and impede decision making.	meaning cogent (of drug
	etc.), strong (of male), not
	impotent; powerful, mighty

Figure 5.1. Text From *Pawns or Potentates*
Source: Lorsch with MacIver, 1989, p. 189.

the issue of constituent directors is raised, which itself reveals something about the authors' perceptions of the importance of the issue.
Women (or other stakeholders such as environmentalists) as a topic is
not in the book's index, and issues related to a feminist agenda are not
raised in the book. The language of the book is not gender inclusive, as
the repeated use of the word *chairman* reflects. The book is presented as
gender neutral but, as this re-reading will demonstrate, the ways in
which the ideas are developed is not neutral and in fact they promote
and perpetuate male dominance in management and governance.

Creation of Dichotomies and the Category of Others

I would like to address several dynamics in this text, and by deconstructing the paragraph in Figure 5.1, reveal a different way of reading
Lorsch with MacIver's suggestions. Reading the text, we see the crea-

tion of a category of *others* and the marginalization and exclusion of these groups from consideration of "board composition" (line 2). The use of parentheses (lines 10-11), in particular, draws our attention to the groups that the text defines as other or as eligible for "constituent representation": "that is, women, consumers, or minorities." Thus, these groups are outside the constituent assembly and the powerful and are seen as marginal. Different interest groups, such as environmentalists and employees, are not included within the parentheses. Does this imply that their interests are already being adequately addressed or that they are not even important enough to be defined as relevant constituents?

The parentheses, coupled with the phrase, "While recognizing the importance of the other stakeholders" (lines 11-12), again emphasizes the otherness and the excluded status of women, consumers, and minorities, and simultaneously the privileging of the "we" who "don't see how including them would contribute to the governance process" (lines 13-14). These others are not a part of the implied important groups and the existing power structure. They are positioned outside the current boardroom activities. Structured as a dichotomy or opposition, this us versus them relationship implies that the power to decide who is included rests with the us, those who dominate the top of the corporation. This us has the power to include or exclude the others, and it is clearly implied that the choice rests with the us. The domain of the boardroom is in the possession of the current members, and they have the implied right to decide whose voices will be represented at the boardroom table.

This distinction takes me back to the title of the book, *Pawns or Potentates*. This construction sets up another dichotomy or opposition and constructs board members as either powerless and insignificant pawns or as potentates (by definition, monarchs or rulers who have dominion). The picture on the book jacket reinforces this distinction and has the blurred shapes of two chess pieces; one is the king (not the queen), and the much smaller pawn sits to its left, again signaling that the potentate is a male king or ruler. This clearly maintains the message that the boardroom is a male domain or kingdom and to be impotent is to be a pawn, female, and powerless. The others/them must be excluded in order to maintain the us. The alternative is to become a pawn, a helpless thing left in the hands of a pawnbroker. The pawnbroker in this analogy could be management or constituent groups. It is revealing that just as more women are breaking through to the position of CEO, the call is being made by Lorsch with MacIver to separate the positions of CEO and board chair*man* and to ensure that the power shifts to the potentates on the board.

Maintaining Harmony, Rationality, and Unity

The statement that relevant stakeholder groups are "unlikely to have the breadth of experience" (line 16) seems to imply that these others' experience is not like ours (the current power holders) and that it therefore does not count as relevant experience. The concept *experience* becomes reified and linked to expertise gained only in limited settings. It also implies that other constituents have nothing important to contribute to the governance process. The word *breadth* implies a valuing of a certain type of experience in the domain of business, and it is not broad if it is experience in a different (i.e., private) domain. While implying that directors need a breadth of experience, this comment actually puts value on a narrow definition of experience that is more typical of men in corporate contexts. For example, the experiences of different women in the women's movement or in community or voluntary organizations is not considered as broad as the experiences of men in "big business." This reinforces the dichotomy between public and private and once again privileges that which is associated with the male/public domain while devaluing the female/private (Martin, 1990).

The comment that directors representing constituency viewpoints could "fractionalize the board" (lines 19-20) reveals a desire for harmony, unity, and homogeneity. It suggests that conflict is currently not present on boards and that such conflict would be a negative influence. This comment denies the existence of heterogeneity and conflicting interests. The implied assumption of harmony and unity at the board level creates and perpetuates myths about unity, rationality, and objectivity in organizations (Ferguson, 1984). This perspective is reinforced earlier in the book when the authors indicate that one of the only sources of power for directors is group cohesion when challenging management decisions, saying that "united we stand; divided we fall" is an apt motto for American directors (p. 96). This type of normative and unitary view of boards rules out the possibility of a sociopolitical or more pluralistic perspective that would validate the claims of multiple interest groups (Tricker, 1984, p. 103). Lorsch with MacIver subtitle their book *The Reality of America's Corporate Boards,* and they try to position a unitary view of governance as the one objective, concrete reality. This argument works to naturalize the status quo and reduces the legitimacy of other perspectives or definitions of reality.

Likewise, the comment that constituent directors could "impede decision making" (line 20) again suggests that current decision-making processes are rational and currently unimpeded by contrary opinions. Thus, the conflicting interests of the marginalized groups are suppressed and devalued in the myth of a harmonious board that makes "effective" decisions.

Thus, the oversimplified and overgeneralized comments in the text reveal attempts to present as natural and obvious the current structure of inclusion and exclusion of the board. Why is the current situation so obvious and natural? Why is the myth of harmony reinforced and taken as necessary for effective decision making? Even in the literature on decision making, it is widely accepted that "group think," which is characterized by a lack of conflict and avoidance of disagreement, is a contributor to poor decision making (Janis, 1971). The text suggests that constituent directors could fractionalize the board and impede decision making, but it appears that this can be re-read as saying that such conflict will impede "us" from making our decisions at your expense.

Taking into account other points of view and interests by having constituent directors on boards would primarily be disruptive, not to effective decision making, but to the existing male-dominated power structures. Having women and representatives of other groups sitting as constituent directors could lead to challenges to the fundamental structure of the organization and the distribution of power enshrined in patriarchal structures.

B: TEXT FROM GILLIES'S *BOARDROOM RENAISSANCE*

Jim Gillies is an influential person in Canadian business circles. As the first dean and still active colleague of the Faculty of Administrative Studies at my own university, York in Toronto, former member of parliament, adviser to the Canadian prime minister, and director of many corporations, he is well respected by his peers. Gillies (1992), in his preface, somewhat defensively acknowledges that *Boardroom Renaissance: Power, Morality, and Performance in the Modern Corporation* is not written in a gender-neutral style, and although he says he is making strides in using the term *chairperson,* he finds the use of "he/she awkward." He goes on to say that

> this should not be interpreted by my many women friends in business or professional education as an ingrained prejudice against women in senior executive positions and on boards of directors. To the contrary I strongly and actively support the appointment of able women to such positions. (p. xii)

Gillies's book focuses on the need for significant changes on boards, and he calls what he sees as the required move from the "old board" to the "new," a "renaissance." The Concise Oxford Dictionary defines the Renaissance as "the revival of art and letters under the influence of classical models in the 14th-16th centuries." Burke (1987) says the Renaissance (with a capital R) meant modernity, and the imagery of renewal used by the scholars and writers of the time reflected their sense of living in a new age, reawakening into the light after what they called the "dark ages" (p. 2). *Naissance,* meaning birth, is related to the word *nascent,* meaning "in the act of being born, just beginning to be, not yet mature." Gillies subtitles the book *Power, Morality, and Performance in the Modern Corporation,* and he seems to be reflectively flagging his position in the modernist worldview. His book would seem to be a call for rebirth of the board within and constrained by classical models of modernity.

Gillies's (1992) book gives a relatively lengthy description of constituent directors and the history of labor representation in Germany (pp. 58-61). In Figure 5.2, I quote some of what he says about the alternative of constituent directors.

Hyperbole and Mockery as the "Insiders" Joke

In addition to deconstructing the various words and phrases in this text, I think its overall structure and framing can be explored. The text

01. In recent years there has also been a call for the election of various constituencies of the
02. corporation to the board. Corporations, of course have many more stakeholders than shareholders
03. and the case is made that if directors are expected to take into account the interests of all the
04. stakeholders when they are making decisions, then it is only common sense to have representatives
05. of all stakeholder groups on the board. From this point of view (a) a board of a large public
06. corporation should include women, minorities, consumer advocates, government representatives,
07. community representatives, regional representatives, and environmentalists; (b) board members
08. should be academics, scientists, professional directors, and homemakers, and (c) the only inside
09. director should be the CEO. Proponents of these changes also believe that no director should be
10. permitted to serve on the board of another company, terms of office should be limited and that the
11. guiding factor in putting together a board should be obtaining the maximum possible diversity of
12. views (p. 58). . . . When a board is made up of representatives of the various stakeholders of the
13. corporation it operates quite differently from the traditional board. Indeed, it basically becomes
14. a political institution with the members negotiating with each other to obtain a larger share of
15. rewards for their constituents. Under such circumstances, the traditional activities of a board—
16. assessing management, preparing strategic plans, dealing with social and ethical issues—in the
17. hope of maximizing the value of the assets of the enterprise for all quickly becomes redundant. Not
18. astonishingly there is limited support among chief executive officers, directors, and even
19. stakeholders in Canada and the United States for the representational board, although
20. astonishingly a survey of Canadian CEOs found that only half were opposed, at least in principle,
21. to the idea of some stakeholder directors (p. 60).

Figure 5.2. Text From *Boardroom Renaissance*
Source: Gillies, 1992, pp. 58, 60.

seems to be using a form of irony based on hyperbole or exaggeration, and it is not expected that the informed reader will take the text seriously. In the rhetorical style of irony, the language of the text contains a type of double entendre (see Calas & Smircich, 1991, p. 580) in which there is an inner meaning intended for the privileged audience and an outer meaning for the persons addressed (the general readers). Thus, it is anticipated that uninformed readers will read the text literally and will conclude that the idea of having constituent directors has been fully studied. However, the tongue-in-cheek presentation of a set of apparently extreme and ridiculous ideas seems to me to be designed to enjoin the knowing reader to share in an "insiders" joke. The dichotomy between the insider (line 8) and outsider seems to play to the implicit understanding that some of the readers are insiders and will get this inside joke, written for those in the know or with the privileged knowledge. Inside directors on Canadian boards are a part of the "old boys' club" (Leighton, 1993) and of the Canadian establishment and upper class. Presumably they will know that the suggestion of having all these constituent directors is really an ironic joke, and they can together share the humor implied in this exaggeration.

The implication that insiders are the privileged ones is reinforced by the use of the term *common sense* (see line 4) right after the exaggerated suggestion that directors will have to take into account "all" stakeholders' interests and have them "all" represented on the board. The word *common* has many meanings including "1. belonging equally to, coming from, or done by, more than one. 2. ordinary, of ordinary qualities, without rank or position. 3. of inferior quality, of low-class, vulgar." It seems to me that the text is suggesting that if it is "common sense," then it may be a vulgar idea of lower-class and ordinary people, as opposed to a first-class idea of an insider of the boardroom, who would obviously know that such exaggerated and extreme proposals are impossible to implement and frankly funny.

The outcome of this humorous suggestion of having "all" (see lines 3 and 5 for repetition of the word all) the stakeholder groups on the board is the conclusion: "Not astonishingly there is limited support" for representational boards (lines 17-18). The repetition of the word *astonishingly* (lines 18 and 20) indicates that this conclusion is not amazing or surprising; it is obvious to those who know. If it goes without saying or surprise, then the paragraphs are written so as to eliminate the possibility of representational boards without discussion. The status quo is reinforced and taken as natural, obvious, and beyond debate. The exaggeration seems to rest on what the text presents as a number of ridiculous and extreme (presumably radical) suggestions:

1. Directors should take into account the perspectives of all stakeholders and have "women, minorities, consumer advocates, government representatives, community representatives, regional representatives, and environmentalists" (lines 6 and 7) on the board. That would mean at least seven different groups. It seems to me the text is making a mockery (mockery meaning "to deride, a ludicrously or insultingly futile action") of the list by including representatives of government, community, and region. These are hard to define and differentiate as stakeholders, and such definitional problems would make selection and appointment difficult. The list once again defines who is considered to have a claim against the organization and who is not.

2. This mockery is extended by then saying that the list would also have to include "academics, scientists, professional directors, and homemakers" (line 8). This list seems to go back to Lorsch with MacIver's complaint that representative directors would not have the necessary breadth of experience. The devaluing of the work done by women in the private realm of their homes, by absent-minded academics in ivory towers, and by white-coated (mad?) scientists in their labs would presumably not have a place in the boardroom. One might almost have been able to take this suggestion seriously until the idea of homemaker is added to the list. This statement goes back to the quotation given from the preface to the book, where Gillies says he supports the appointment of "able" women to the boards.[3] Could a homemaker, academic, or scientist be able? If able is defined as "having the means or power," then they currently do not have the power and are not, therefore, able. Professional directors who are paid for their time doing board work are tarnished by the association with these *other* categories. The category of professional director is out of place in this list and has been proposed as an alternative to constituent directors by several authors (e.g., Stone, 1985, p. 139); thus this alternative is subtly eliminated from consideration along with the others.

3. "The only inside director should be the CEO" (lines 8 and 9), and "no director should be permitted to serve on the board of another company, terms of office should be limited" (lines 9 and 10). The text again presents exaggerated and extremely limiting rules, which are then implied as being demanded by outside stakeholder groups. Words such as *permitted* and *should* set up an implicit and undefined power bloc that wants to define and constrain the boardroom. *Permit* means "to give consent or opportunity," and this can only be granted by someone with power. The word *should* "forms a statement of question involving the notion of command and future of conditional duty, obligation, likelihood, etc." The message seems to me to be that the inside directors and current power holders had better get ready to defend themselves against the unreasonable demands of these *others,* who outnumber even the shareholders who currently demand accountability from directors. (See line 2, "Corporations, of course have many more stakeholders than shareholders.") Within the textual structure of hyperbole, there seems to be a developing subtext of implicit threat from other power holders.

4. The implied threat to the power of the director is further developed when the text predicts that the board would operate "quite
differently" and "basically becomes a political institution with the
members negotiating with each other to obtain a larger share of
rewards for their constituents" (lines 13-15). The result of the political
struggles will be the end of the "traditional activities of the board" (line
15), and the goal of "maximizing the value of the assets of the enterprise for all quickly becomes redundant" (line 17). Again the opposi-
tional structures implied in the text such as between *theirs* and *ours,*
between *traditional* and *nontraditional, shareholder* and *stakeholder, political* and *rational,* and between *difference* and *sameness* can be seen to be
underlying the construction of the text. There seems to be a privileging
of the status quo, with a board containing only a rational, homogenous,
traditional group who work for the shareholders.

The threat here is that the board could become a site of struggle,
resistance, and political conflicts characterized by negotiation over
scarce resources for various groups. Like the Lorsch with MacIver text,
which warned against fractionalization, this text similarly privileges
harmony and unity on the board.

The outcome of a change to constituent directors is for the traditional to become "redundant" (line 17). Turning again to the dictionary, the fear of redundancy becomes clearer because it means to
become "superfluous (of industrial worker); liable to dismissal as being
no longer needed for any available job; excessive, pleonastic; that can
be omitted without loss of significance; copious, luxuriant." The threat
to current directors is to be found to be superfluous or perhaps to be
"downsized" or laid off as so many workers and middle managers have
been. The implicit humor of the mockery and exaggeration hides a
warning that is not addressed or discussed directly but that makes it
not astonishing that the changes will be resisted.

RE-READING THE TEXT

Again drawing on the *Concise Oxford Dictionary,* I would like to
re-read Gillies's text and rewrite it in order to reveal a possible subtext
embedded within the original text (see Table 5.2).

One way of re-reading this text is to explore a subtext of a stage performance, reminiscent of Shakespeare's *As You Like It*: "All the world's a stage, And all the men and women merely players" (see also Goffman, 1959). As can be seen in the definitions presented in Table 5.2, many of the words used in Gillies's text have meanings associated with the stage. For example, the *board* itself has the meaning of stage. *Directors,* of course, direct the *performance.* The word *morality* in the book's title drew me to explore the genre of the morality play, anonymous, Christian plays written in English to be performed to the general population in medieval England (Potter, 1975). The pattern of these plays is a sequence of innocence/fall/redemption. The human drama of a morality play involves a person who begins life in innocence and falls by exercise of free will. From these depths, however, he or she is delivered by divine grace and "the end is regeneration, never death, always a rebirth" (Potter, 1975, p. 10).

Gillies's use of the word *renaissance* with its links to rebirth, as well as his choice of the words *morality* and *performance* in the title of the book, lead me to the re-reading of the text presented in the third column of Table 5.2.

The choice to re-write this small section of the book to play up the metaphor of board as stage is only one option. The next text, like Lorsch with MacIver's, plays on the metaphor of board game (i.e., chess). The use of the stage metaphor, however, highlights the en-acted nature of the boardroom and the struggle of the patriarchs or directors to preserve their roles and maintain the status quo. The frustration of women and other stakeholders who feel they do not have a "voice" comes to make more sense when it is reflected that they are not scripted into the play and are designated the audience to the performance. It was all scripted long ago when the corporation was created by charter as a "fictitious person."[4]

C: TEXT FROM FLEISCHER, HAZARD, AND KLIPPER'S *BOARD GAMES*

The last paragraph of a book by Fleischer et al. (1988), entitled *Board Games: The Changing Shape of Corporate Power,* is presented in Figure 5.3.

TABLE 5.2 Re-Reading Gillies's Text

Original Text	Dictionary	Re-Written Text
Boardroom Renaissance: Power, Morality and Performance in the Modern Corporation	**Board:** means stage; tread the boards means to be an actor in the theater **Morality:** points of ethics, degree of conformity to moral principles; moralizing **Power:** particular faculty of mind or body (man of varied powers), vigor, energy, [having a powerful voice] **Performance:** execution (of command), performing a play, action resembling a public exhibition **Recent:** not long past, modern	In modern times there have been threats to the script we had written for our morality plays. We have always known that to control the commoners, we needed to give them the message about the dangers of extravagance and also the hope for deliverance and redemption through wise repentance. Thus, we arranged for these scripts to be written (but didn't claim authorship) and created these fictitious characters. It was, of course, all set up in the time of the renaissance; in a time of renewal after the dark ages. Up until now we have had curtain calls from our audiences after each performance. We made sure that the performances kept their attention. Now these watchers want to select performers from their own body of supporters to play parts on the stage. Can you imagine how
In recent years there has also been a call for the election of various constituencies of the corporation to the board.	**Call:** a cry or shout, a brief visit, order, demand, appeal, request or summon; i.e., curtain call is to summon actor after the curtain **Constituency:** body of customers, supporters etc. [audience] **Election:** being elected; chosen, selected **Corporation:** fictitious person created by charter, prescription, or act of legislation	
Corporations, of course, have many more stakeholders than shareholders and the case is made that if directors are expected to take into account the interests of all the stakeholders when they are making decisions, then it is only common sense to have representatives of all stakeholder groups on the board.	**Share-holder:** share—a part one gets; Holder—possessor of title **Stake-holder:** stake— surveillance, wager, risk; Holder—contrivance for holding something **Case:** (colloq.) comical person **Director:** person who directs a play **Expect:** look forward to (from spectare, look) **Account:** narration, report, performance (of piece of music, etc.)	

114

From this point of view (a) a board of a large public corporation should include women, minorities, consumer advocates, government representatives, community representatives, regional representatives, and environmentalists; (b) board members should be academics, scientists, professional directors, and homemakers, and (c) the only inside director should be the CEO. Proponents of these changes also believe that no director should be permitted to serve on the board of another company, terms of office should be limited and that the guiding factor in putting together a board should be obtaining the maximum possible diversity of views

Interest: quality exciting these or holding one's attention, curiosity
Make: perform, execute
Decision: settlement, resoluteness, decided character
Common: open to, affecting the public, without rank, ordinary, low-class, vulgar
Re-present-ative: represent—act (play etc.), play part on stage
Group: a number of persons or things standing near together
Public: open to or shared by all the people

Point of view: standpoint, survey with eyes
Insider: one who is in on the secret, especially so as to gain unfair advantage
Include: embrace as part of the whole, treat or regard as so comprised; shut in, enclosed
Proponent: (person) that puts forward a proposal; from Propound: offer for consideration, produce before proper authority so as to establish its legality
View: what is seen, scene

ridiculous it will be if they all get a part? Should we really be expected to embrace, as part of us, all these outsiders: women, consumers, environmentalists, minorities, academics, scientists, and even homemakers! They even want to set rules about how many stage companies we can work for and how long we can direct. Ridiculous! They threaten to stage performances with a maximum of different scenes. We have given parts to those who possess a title. We will continue to give those who stand together a good place from which to see the plays and with their standpoint they ought to feel a part of the whole. But those of us who are in on the secret really know that all those groups who are proposing changes cannot share with us the job of directing.

Note: Text is from Gillies, 1992, p. 58. Definitions are from the *Concise Oxford Dictionary.*

01. Directors, shareholders, and management know that the one constant in the economy is change.
02. But directors know also that their accountability to shareholders reaches back to eighteenth-
03. century legal standards still being adapted to today's realities. The new princes of industry must
04. be careful, methodical, thorough, critical, responsible, and, above all, accountable to shareholders.
05. It is expected. It is demanded by the free market. And it is the law.

Figure 5.3. Text From *Board Games*
Source: Fleischer et al., 1988, p. 199.

Change—"But"

This last paragraph in the book's last chapter, "The New Princes of Industry," again reveals a number of dynamics, the most obvious being a reinforcement of the status quo. The book is explicitly about change (the subtitle, for example, is the changing shape of corporate power), "but" (line 2) when re-read can be seen to be resisting change. The word *but* means "except; an objection." Positioned at the start of the second sentence it works to negate the first sentence, which says that the "one constant in the economy is change" (line 1). Instead of change are 18th-century legal standards that are "still being adapted to today's realities" (line 3). Again we see the claim to understand today's "realities," which are positioned as concrete, objective, and "know"-able.

The paragraph starts with a definition of the relevant players: "directors, shareholders, and management" (line 1), a group that, it is implied, is complete in and of itself. Other stakeholders or players in the "game" are defined out of the equation. The word *know* (lines 1 and 2) reflects the implicit belief that the knowledge of this group is the definition of reality. It denies or denigrates other definitions of reality and ways of knowing. The work of Foucault (1970a), for example, highlights the process of reality construction through which the knowledge of the powerful becomes the only legitimate and valid knowledge that is articulated or spoken. The knowledge of others, such as women, becomes a form of "subjugated knowledge." The dominant modes of discourse, which reflect the knowledge and biases of the powerful, become the only modes of discourse used. If the "directors, shareholders, and management know" (line 1), then the knowledge or realities of others groups, such as women, are excluded and not articulated (Ferguson, 1984).

A system of "accountability to shareholders" (line 2) that dates back, as the authors say, to the "eighteenth-century" (lines 2 and 3) is implied as being one that is not open to change. The "accountability to shareholders" explicitly precludes accountability to other stakeholders. Being accountable means being "bound to give account; responsible; explicable." Account means a "reckoning of debit and credit, in money or service." This implies that transactions must be quantified or counted, and thus this text privileges the quantitative and quantifiable over the qualitative and nonquantifiable or soft.

The short, choppy sentences at the end of the paragraph are very emphatic and again serve to reinforce the message that the current system is not open to change. . . . After all it is "expected. . . demanded. . . . It is the law (line 5). This style of writing reinforces the existing reality, making a challenge very difficult to even contemplate. The imperatives, as presented in the text, build on one another in a way that appears cohesive and inevitable. "But" because something is "expected," it does not necessarily follow that it is "demanded," and something that is "demanded" is very different from "the law." Somehow it is ultimately being suggested that the roots or foundation of the whole legal system are behind the current system and are not open to change without possible damage to the whole edifice.

One could ask who expects and demands the current system and whose needs are being met by the law as currently defined. Other stakeholders may have totally different expectations and demands. Fleischer et al. in this text suggest that the "free market" (line 5) is making the demand. The concept of "free market" is associated with an objective, rational system that operates without bias or distortion. This supports the implicit conceptualization of the current structure and composition of the board as rational and unbiased. Tricker (1984) identifies five different frameworks for understanding board activities (legal, normative/descriptive, rational/economic, organizational, socio/political). What Fleischer et al.'s text does is call upon only three of these perspectives—the legal, normative, and economic—to justify the current system.

These three models are all based on assumptions of harmony, objectivity, and rationality. As Tricker (1984) says, "the prerogative to direct the enterprise, whether as an entrepreneur or as a member of the top management peer group is unquestioned" (p. 100), and a unitary chain of command is assumed.

Privileging of the Masculine

The message is clear in this concluding paragraph that the board-room is the domain of men. The use of the masculine-gendered word *princes* is the most obvious manifestation of this. The word princes also harks back to directors' roles originating in the 18th century. The term princes again works to forge a mental link between directors and royalty or potentates. Dethroning a prince is a radical or rebellious act because princes are seen as having legitimate power.

The metaphor of princes bestows the legitimate or divine right of kings/princes on the ruling elite of business and implies that power rightfully rests with these men. The board is also positioned as the natural and unquestioned domain of men also by presenting the string of adjectives that follow the word princes: "careful, methodical, thorough, critical, responsible, and . . . accountable" (line 4). The location of these words immediately after the word princes leads to the interpretation that men are the ones who are in possession of these desirable traits (see Table 5.3). These semantic structures or "couples" mimic the institution of the male/female couple and correspond to the accepted power relations implied in this pairing (Nye, 1989).

The message is that the masculine traits are the desirable ones, and the dichotomy works to privilege the strong/male over the weak/female. The "new princes of industry must" (line 3) have these traits. The word *must* means "obliged to," and I get the image of these princes being trapped in their roles, just as the princesses were trapped in their chastity belts. The alternative is to be associated with the female qualities and not be a man (impotent). One can also question whether the adjectives that Fleischer et al.'s text privileges are reflections of the attributes that the directors of the future should ideally possess. What about innovativeness and the ability to integrate, or traits such as vision, courage, insight, caring, nurturing, grace, and progressiveness? The connection between patriarchy and the privileging of the rational, the abstract, and the intellectual needs to be resisted by the reader (Culler, 1982, p. 58).

TABLE 5.3 Comparison of Male and Female Traits

Male/Director/Prince	Female/Not a Director
Careful	Impetuous
Methodical	Intuitive
Thorough	Emotional
Critical	Subjective
Responsible	Irresponsible
Accountable	Personal

Historical Convention

Within this one paragraph, there are two references to the legal system: "eighteenth-century legal standards" (lines 2-3) and "it is the law" (line 5). These references are interesting for a number of reasons. The status quo is currently captured in the legally defined roles and responsibilities of directors. Again, calling on the apparently objective, neutral, and stable legal system, the text works to exclude change. This line of argument serves to obscure the socially constructed nature of law; after all, the legal system is "man made." Smart (1986) describes "the role of law in creating, reproducing, or mitigating forms of oppression" (p. 109). In the context of the boardroom, such an analysis seems important, not only because changes in the laws to require constituent directors would challenge patriarchal systems, but also because such analysis might allow other voices to be heard in the decision-making context of the boardroom.

Implicit in the text is a call for a return to traditional premodern authority relations. Weber defined three ideal types of authority (traditional, charismatic, and rational/legal). Traditional authority, dominant in premodern societies, is based in belief in the sanctity of tradition. It is not codified in impersonal rules, like in the rational-legal authority, but inheres in particular persons who may inherit or be invested with it by higher authority (Coser, 1977). Thus, calling for the return of the authority of princes is a call for a return to premodern authority relations and enhanced, not reduced, dependence of the subjects on traditional "authority."[5]

The text's reference to the legal system of the 18th century encouraged me to explore the historically embedded nature of the relations of power reflected in boardrooms. For example, Gillies (1992) suggests that to have legitimacy, the corporation has always looked to the state or other ruling bodies. He says that the code of Hammurabi in 2083 B.C. was the first set of codified laws that allowed the organization of entities with the goal of carrying out commercial transactions (p. 28). Furthermore, he says,

> By the thirteenth century, legitimacy for organizations was obtained in many instances from the Roman church. Indeed, Pope Innocent IV at that time gave papal blessing, and authority, to the corporation. Consequently, business enterprises began to organize around areas and institutions, such as papal districts and monasteries and convents, over which the pope had power. (p. 29)

From the pope, authority for forming organizations moved to monarchs who granted charters, often to their friends and followers. By the end of the 20th century, the concept of the corporation became a legal one, and the way the courts interpret the law has a great impact on the ways in which companies act (see Hatton, 1990). The references in the above texts to kings, Christian morality plays, and legal systems are a reflection of the long history of legitimating activities that provided individuals with the opportunity to associate and organize. The texts call on these historical roots as an ongoing legitimating device, and they also work to limit our perceptions of the possibility of change.

Conclusions

In this deconstruction, I have attempted to problematize the discourses of change in corporate boardrooms and expose some gaps and silences. It appears from a quick reading of recent publications on corporate governance that there is a great deal of ongoing ferment and crisis about the future of boards and how power should be redistributed. When the question of constituent directors is raised, however, the nature of the discussion about change is very different. The texts discussed here are not advocating change but appear to me to be calls for a reinforcement of the status quo and the continued exclusion of women and other stakeholder groups from positions of power.

This deconstruction has suggested how each of the texts can be re-read as containing a subtext that creates a category of *other* in order to marginalize and exclude groups such as women.

Through privileging of only one part of dichotomies such as pawns and potentates, public and private, and masculine and feminine, the texts promote an inherently gendered view of corporations and work to make it appear neutral and natural. The privileging of a unitary, harmonious, and rational worldview subjugates certain knowledge claims and makes them appear to be disruptive to the smooth operation of the boardroom. Suggestions in the text that certain groups know the reality of the boardroom are reinforced through suggestions that the status quo is supported by historical convention, premodern forms of authority, and the market and legal systems. This objectification and concretization of "man"-made processes again reflects a set of power/knowledge relations that suppress gender conflicts. The failures of women to have a greater voice, to gain more power, or to even gain a seat at the boardroom table are more understandable given the biased and self-serving subtexts of the dominant discourses of business. The ways in which the patriarchal worldview and the status quo are normalized make it essential for women to become resisting readers of these texts and to challenge the deep structures of power that they perpetuate and reinforce.

TOWARD AN ALTERNATIVE READING

In the spirit of offering an alternative to reading boards as games with dichotomous winners (powerful/potent/male) or losers (pawns/impotent/female) or as stages for prescripted performances controlled by the directors, perhaps we can read a board as a table. How about a-round table? Going back to my dictionary, we find "round" meaning "1. spherical or circular or cylindrical; plump, not hollow; 2. done with or involving a circular motion; 3. entire, continuous, all together, not broken or defective or scanty, sound, smooth, plain, genuine, candid, outspoken." A *round table conference* is one at which "all present are on equal footing." Looking first to the idea of "all present," I am reminded of a public corporation (public means open to or shared by all people) where all constituents (constituent meaning composing or making up a whole) are re-present-ed. Present means "being dealt with, discussed; existing, occurring, being such, now." If all are present at a-round-table, the diversity of the whole could be re-present-ed. This is of course impossible; not all groups, voices and perspectives can be a-round simultaneously. No table can contain it "all," as Gillies (1992) pointed out.

But what if every conversation at the round table were then assessed to reflectively identify what and who the ongoing discussion was privileging and what silences and gaps were being created? The table could then genuinely attempt to include other voices. Every table could be critiqued and every discussion deconstructed from other perspectives, including academics, scientists, people from other countries and cultures, historians, working-class people, entrepreneurs, government representatives, homemakers, religious group members, conservationists, homeless people, feminists, gays and lesbians, people with disabilities, elderly, youth, aboriginal peoples, French- and Spanish-speaking people, Third World women, and many other knowledge groups. Multiple, contested readings of the same "reality" from a variety of locations and positions would be explicitly sought (Radhakrishnan, 1994). And it would be understood that every inclusion would create another exclusion. Every conversation would create another silence. Every empowerment would create another disempowerment. Every change would create another stability. Every circle would create another gap. Every whole would create another hole. And a-round and a-round and a-round the table would go, reflectively knowing that a-round-table must be built simultaneously on paradox, reflection, and dissent (Clegg, 1994b). And a-round table would be plump, tentative, and nonprivileging of anything, for long, not even itself.

LIMITATIONS OF THE CHAPTER

The objective of this re-reading is to problematize the discussion of boardroom change from a feminist/postmodern perspective. By indicating some silences in these texts, I hope to help expose the gendered nature of the assumptions that continue to dominate the discourse on boards. Becoming a resisting reader is, however, only a first step. Culler

(1982) suggests that the final step in such a critique is to investigate the assumptions and procedures of the criticism to see if they are in complicity with the preservation of male authority and to explore alternatives (Culler, 1982, p. 61).

In taking this final step, I recognize that the focus of this chapter on constituent directors does not challenge the dominant relations of power in organizations and women's roles and places in it. I have not questioned bureaucracy and organizational hierarchy based on patriarchal assumptions. I have left unquestioned the existence of a boardroom at the "top" of an organizational hierarchy. I am also fully aware that my re-reading needs to be seen as only one possible way of interpreting the texts. Readings that more fully expose the inherently classist, elitist, and racist assumptions of the original texts are equally important. My deconstruction must be deconstructed again to reveal the gaps that exist in what has been presented. In attempting to introduce a more reflexive approach to these texts, I hope to stimulate thinking about what changes can be made to en-"able" other, different perspectives and constituents to be re-presented in governance. Having re-presentative or constituent directors a-round the table may yet be possible. But it will be necessary to challenge power relations currently sustained by the routines, practices, and structures of the discourses on governance; to oppose the biased language and metaphor used in the literature; and to resist the dominance of rational, unitary worldviews. More deconstruction and re-construction of the theories of governance are needed.

Notes

1. All references to dictionary meanings are from the *Concise Oxford Dictionary*, 1983 edition.

2. The *Concise Oxford Dictionary* defines the word *with* in 11 different ways, but the first four are: 1. in antagonism to, against (fight, quarrel, struggle, dispute, argue, compete, vie with). 2. in or into company of or relation to, among, beside (come, go, walk, eat, live, spend the day or night with; king is expected with or together with queen or court; numbered with the transgressors, (un)connected with; associate oneself with). 3. agreeably or in harmonious relations to (I feel, think, sympathize with you; am with you on that point), one-, part of same whole as. 4. in care or charge or possession of (have no money with me, leave child with nurse). Which of these meanings the term *Lorsch with MacIver* is intended to portray is unclear. The book jacket says Lorsch is

director of research, Louis E. Kirstein is Professor of Human Relations at Harvard Business School, and Elizabeth MacIver is a former research associate there. MacIver is said to have conducted most of the interviews, supervised the collection and analysis of the questionnaires, and prepared the cases.

3. Able. 1. talented, clever, competent, having the means or power (to) (esp. used w. parts of *be* to supply the deficiencies of can, e.g., shall be able to as fut. of can); legally qualified. 2. -bodied, fit, skilled.

4. Fictitious: counterfeit, not genuine, assumed, imaginary, unreal, regarded as what it is by legal or conventional fiction.

5. Thanks to Robert Gephart for clarifying this point.

6

Liberation From Within?
Organizational Implications of Irigaray's Concept of "Residue"

IAN ATKIN

JOHN HASSARD

Developed in three stages, this theoretical chapter argues that the textual representation of organization theory reflects a system of intellectual self-imprisonment. In Part 1 (Context), we suggest that within organization theory, attempts by the proponents of radical separatism to release themselves from such confinement have resulted only in their conceptual recapture. Drawing upon Cooper's (1990) development of the notions of undecidability and zero degree—from his thesis on organization/disorganization—we contend that this was inevitable, given that radical separatism failed to break with the conventions of representation within orthodox, systems-based organizational analysis.

Given this situation, in Part 2 (Theory), we offer a theoretical strategy for deconstructing organizational orthodoxy, one that operates unusually from within the conventions of systems-based analysis. This sees Irigaray's (1985, 1991) concept of "residue," from her thesis on mimicry, deployed to recover the *extra-* of organizational life; that which is situated outside, the space beyond, otherness. At the conceptual

AUTHORS' NOTE: The authors would like to thank Kate Deverell and Martin Parker (both Keele University) for their comments on an earlier draft of this chapter.

level, it is argued that the mimicking of a superordinate theory's representation of a subordinate (e.g., systems theory's representation of radical organization theory) may provide the conditions to effect an escape from textual imprisonment. The route for this escape is via the residue of the flow of meaning to the discourse of the other in organization theory.

Finally, in Part 3 (Application), we return to our concern with the relationship between systems theory and radical separatism to explore how the poststructural concepts developed in the middle reaches of the chapter can be used to deconstruct particular forms of textual representation. This section is given over largely to an exploration of the writings of two key authors associated with the systems versus separatism debate, namely Donaldson (1985) and his attempt to subsume radical structuralism within structural functionalism and Burrell (1980) and his attempt to develop a distinct theoretical voice for radical organization theory. Reasons for the failure not only of the radical separatists to establish a distinct theoretical voice but also of system theorists to incorporate radical theory within functionalism are given through denoting the logical undecidability that characterizes such attempts.

Part 1: Context

It is difficult to escape the authoritative discourse of organization theory. This is the outcome of the theorist-author being confined within a chain of statements that represent the concept *organization*. Given that the predominant definition of organization is "a circumscribed administrative-economic function" (Cooper & Burrell, 1988, p. 92), postmodern analysis informs us that the textual topography of organization theory is a confined "inside," a boundary of exclusion.

As intellectual capital, the concept of organization has similarly been described as a "psychic prison" (Morgan, 1986, p. 199). This prison is constructed and guarded by members of the academy of science, in this case administrative science (Clegg & Dunkerley, 1980b). It is founded on the notion that the formal organization is a confined and disciplined space, with the term *formal* being an imperative that privileges order. One of the predominant ways in which this order is reproduced is through the theories and methods of functionalist organizational analysis (Cooper & Burrell, 1988, p. 109).

Reviews of the history of organization theory (e.g., Alvesson, 1987; Grint, 1991; Reed, 1992) tell us, however, that, shackled to the hegemonic discourse of organization theory, certain theory groups have attempted to pursue a policy of intellectual separatism. A well-known expression is the work of the radical organization theory movement of the 1970s and 1980s (see Benson, 1977; Burrell, 1980; Burrell & Morgan, 1979; Clegg & Dunkerley, 1980b; Goldman & Van Houten, 1977), which sought emancipation through developing an intellectual voice qualitatively different from sociological functionalism. For the proponents of radical organization theory, emancipation would be the outcome of an escape from powerful institutional consensus; as such: "the immediate need is for 'paradigmatic closure'—a clear-cut separation of radical organization theory from its orthodox functionalist counterpoint" (Burrell, 1980, p. 92).

The motivation to establish such a separate voice arose from the apparent underdevelopment of radical, predominantly Marxian theories of organization (Burrell, 1980). This lack of a self-sustaining capacity was based upon the tendency for radical theorists to become ensnared by the very concepts they sought to reject. As the metaphors of orthodox theory remained the agency of mediation (see Morgan, 1980, 1986), radical theorists apparently became influenced by the writings of "a community of scholars to whom [they were] in many ways fundamentally opposed" (Burrell, 1980, p. 91). Although these theoretical metaphors were rarely identified, they were indicative of modes of thought that enabled the conventions of the orthodoxy to "govern the terms of all debate" (Burrell, 1980, p. 91). Without sectarianism, it was felt, the metaphoric conventions of conservative systems thinking would continue to govern the radical theorist's self-concepts.

Although it is possible to characterize radical organization theory as a movement that failed to establish an alternative voice for organization theory, it can be argued that, given the intellectual premises on which the movement was founded, any such attempt would have inevitably run up against the "theorizing power" (Clegg, 1979, p. 13) of organizational science's textual representations. Taken to its logical conclusion, this would make the development of an alterative, emancipatory discourse difficult, if not impossible, given that radical critiques invariably find themselves defined as orderly. This orderliness is perhaps itself inevitable, given that the authenticity of accounting signifies the power of the tradition of thought within the academy over the theorist.

Although this may appear a mischievous claim—for during the past 20 years the hegemony of functionalist theory has been challenged by several alternative agendas (Burrell & Morgan, 1979; Hassard & Pym, 1990; Reed, 1985; Silverman, 1970)—we will argue that it can be justified by reference to poststructuralist strategies of reading. To explain the logical problems faced by those wishing to escape from the confines of textual representation, we begin by introducing concepts developed in concert with Derrida's notion of *undecidability*.

An introduction to the process of textual undecidability is provided by Derrida (1981) in *Dissemination*, where he, like Irigaray (1985) below, deploys the concept of mime to frame the analysis. Derrida, for example, offers a reading of Mallarmé's *Mimique*, which concerns a mime whose gestures imitate no tradition of mime, and whose performance (of a pierrot who murders his unfaithful wife by tickling her to death) appears to be unscripted: in sum, an original mime. Derrida's reading, however, accounts for certain "self-deceptions" that have been hidden within the text of this unscripted mime. This reading finds that at the moment Mallarmé begins his story, it is already caught up within a chain of supplementary inscriptions. To give but one example, Mallarmé bases his story on a second edition of a pamphlet. The author of the pamphlet, Beissier, had been a witness to the mime of the murder 5 years previously. The reader of Mallarmé's text is now confronted by a story that is already composed of multiple writings and readings. Mallarmé's mime artist is not inventing the script but is rather a phase in a chain of textual representation and transmission. Although Mallarmé's story concerns an original mime, it must admit to the lack of an original foundation or logos. Derrida's reading of *Mimique* thus invokes the notion of a chain of representations that contextualize authoritative statements.

An explanation of the inherent undecidability of organization is provided by Cooper (1990), who argues that texts on that discourse called organization theory represent the supplementary "organization of organization" (p. 197). He notes that often texts on organization are themselves organized according to a set of normalized scientific and/or academic criteria. As the content of a study of organization and the theoretical context that frames the text are indistinguishable, it follows that a text does not strictly add information on the study of organization, for it produces statements on that which it designates to be organization. In this way, the text as supplementary "includes itself in the structure it seeks to analyze and understand, therefore creating undecidability" (Cooper, 1990, p. 197). The inclusion of organization theory texts as a focus for study restricts representation to the protocols demanded by the authority of the academy.

Through a reading of Lévi-Strauss (1950, 1978), Simmel (1968, 1980) and Derrida (1978), Cooper develops this analysis through the notion of the "zero degree" (1990, pp. 182-183). The zero degree amounts to pervading undecidability: an excess "of no specific order, organization, or direction" (Cooper, 1990, p. 182). Cooper draws upon Derrida's (1978, pp. 278-293) notion that structure—and Cooper adds organization—is conceived by tradition and in a limited form, this being the presence of a "fixed centre or point of origin" (Cooper, 1990, p. 183). In Cooper's reading of Derrida, this center has two functions: One is to orient and balance the structure in a coherent way; the other, and more important, function, is for the principle of the structure to limit "the play of the structure" (Derrida, 1978, pp. 278-279, quoted in Cooper, 1990, p. 183). The center's ability to organize the structure allows for the play of elements inside the "structurality of the structure" (Derrida, 1978, p. 278).

The process of centering, however, both opens up and closes off play, in that to close off play, it must exile from itself the play that is more than the structurality of structure, or the zero degree. As the means of a responsibility to act, the flows of otherness are played to excess as a responsibility to otherness. That is, the flow of change as a matter of degree is always, inasmuch as it is perceptible, an excess: the zero degree. Put simply, not everything is carried along with the flow, for a residue or excess always remains outside the bounded frame of the inside of organization, to the exclusion of disorganization.

Cooper suggests that the frame differentiates between an ordered inside and a disordered outside. The former corresponds to organization and the latter to disorganization. Cooper's specific working through of the framing of the boundary between the binary pairing system and environment takes place within a clearly defined framework. The function of the frame is to privilege the system: "the boundary belongs to the system and not to the environment" (Cooper, 1990, p. 170). Indeed "in its most fundamental sense, organization is the appropriation of order out of disorder" (p. 172). Cooper's reading of Derrida suggests that the order of the inside of the boundary is attainable only if the outside or disorganization is an excess or a supplement. In its desire to be complete, the order of organization discards the surplus. But this cannot be complete, for without the surplus of disorder it has a lacuna. This lacuna can only be filled by the disorder of the undesired supplement necessarily constituting the meaning of the inside. Without the disorder of the outside, the order of the inside is meaningless.

In seeking to develop an emancipatory alternative for organization analysis, our theorizing will take recourse to this strategy of textual undecidability. It can be argued that the way to disclose the conventions of an orthodoxy in organization theory is through a close reading of its narrative boundary characteristics. Such liminal phenomena are important for they make known the undecidable moment between what a text permits in meaning and what it constrains.

To explore the possibilities for a postmodern emancipatory analysis, our strategy will be to invert the incommensurability thesis of radical separatism and work from within the conventions of orthodox organization theory. As the discourse of organization theory inhibits a separatist analysis, we argue that the liberation of the radical theorist's selfhood may arise from within its mirror image, as represented by systems analysis. We will now articulate these self-images through developing our exploration of undecidability by way of a poststructuralist writer who has, thus far, been relatively neglected in organization theory, namely Irigaray (1985, 1991), her work on mimicry, and in particular her notion of residue.

Part 2: Theory

The main concern of Luce Irigaray's poststructuralism is to liberate the feminine from phallocentric structures of discourse. To do this, Irigaray deliberately mimics the oppressive symbolic representation of the female body to excess so as to make explicit, by playful repetition, women's exploitation through the representation of the feminine by masculine discourse. The function of Irigaray's mimical gestures is not, however, to overthrow the phallocentric order, nor to elaborate a new theory of which women would be the subject or the object: Less ambitiously, it is to emphasize the theoretical self-disruptions "of suspending [the phallocentric discourse's] pretension to the production of a truth and of a meaning that are excessively univocal" (Irigaray, 1991, p. 126). By disrupting the phallocentric discourse, Irigaray feels we create some of the conditions for altering women's status in society (Whitford, 1988, p. 110).

The scene from which mimicry emerges is the sexualization of discourse. For Irigaray (1991), Freud's work portrays "the sexual indifference that underlies the truth of any science, the logic of every discourse" (p. 118). Although sexual indifference has always existed, its effects are hidden. In Irigaray's reading of Freud, this covert indifference becomes apparent in the way female sexuality is defined in masculine terms. The feminine is always described in terms of "lack" or "deficiency," for instance in the theory of penis envy. The statements of Freud that describe feminine sexuality fail to note that the feminine might have its own specificity. Freud does not identify two sexes whose differences are articulated in the act of intercourse, or more generally speaking, in the imaginary and symbolic processes that regulate the workings of society and culture. Rather, the feminine is defined as either a complement to the operation of male sexuality or, more commonly, as a negative image that provides male sexuality with an unfailing phallic self-representation.

Irigaray (1991) suggests that Freud, rather than making original statements about male or female sexuality, is merely describing an actual state of affairs. Freud accounts for sexuality without examining the contextualizing historical factors (p. 119). In other words, he takes female sexuality as he sees it and accepts this as normative. Women's dissatisfactions are artifacts of individual histories whose resolution is achieved through women's submission to a rapport with the father figure. The pathology of these cases is not questioned in relation to differing styles of society or culture. The specific demands of women are thus silenced.

Freud's account of this actual state of affairs, however, itself emerges from the sexualization of discourse, for it is caught up within the presuppositions of the production of discourse— presuppositions that Freud does not fully analyze. This demands a challenge to philosophical discourse "inasmuch as it constitutes the discourse on discourse" (Irigaray, 1991, p. 122). The domination of this discourse derives, to a large extent, from its power to reduce all other discourses to the economy of the "Same" (Irigaray, 1991, p. 119). Its greatest power of domination is to eradicate the differences between the sexes in systems that are self-representative of the masculine subject.

Irigaray intends to disrupt philosophical discourse by opening up the figures of philosophical discourse—substance, subject, absolute knowledge, and so on—in order to make visible what they have borrowed: "that is feminine, from the feminine, to make them 'render up' and give back what they owe the feminine" (Irigaray, 1991, p. 123). To do this, the feminine must disrupt the coherence of discursive statements whose very coherence hides the conditions of their production. Coherence can only be maintained so long as it is not interrogated through the process of interpretive re-reading. In order to open up the economy of the Same, Irigaray (1985) calls for a reenactment of each figure of discourse. She argues that although woman as a residue (p. 114) is beyond a conceptual grasp, because she is defined as feminine by the masculine subject, she nevertheless possesses the facility—"of the 'perceptible' of 'matter' " (Irigaray, 1991, p. 124)—to recover ideas about herself that are elaborated in and by masculine logic. This responsibility to "otherness" is accessed through playing the mime of the historically assigned feminine.

The mime of the historically assigned feminine sees the feminine role assumed deliberately so as to make visible, by an effect of playful repetition, that which is supposed to remain outside. By excessively interpreting and repeating the way in which the feminine finds itself defined as lack, as deficient, or as the imitation of the masculine subject, this gesture converts a form of exploitation into one of affirmation of the feminine subject. For woman to play a mime is to try to recover the place of her exploitation by discourse, while challenging the authority of discourse to be reproduced by it. Such a challenge makes visible a disrupting of residues, or excess on the feminine side (Irigaray, 1991).

In concert with the largely Derridian analysis presented earlier, Irigaray's work presents an opportunity to pursue an alternative textual representation of organization. This alternative sees mimicry employed as a reading strategy for recovering the extra- of organization—those senses situated outside, the space beyond, the other. We have taken as the stimulus for this alternative Irigaray's theory of exploitation through the discourse of political economy. Irigaray (1991) asks how women can analyze their own exploitation and inscribe their own demands within an order prescribed by the masculine. For Irigaray, the demand for women's equality and difference cannot be articulated by the acceptance of a choice between class struggle and sexual warfare. This alternative serves only to minimize the question of the exploitation of women through a definition of power of the masculine type.

Expanding this theme, Irigaray argues that the relationship between economic class oppression and patriarchy has not been subject to sufficient dialectical analysis. She claims that the origins of class opposition lie in the economic relationship between men and women in monogamous marriage. This opposition coincided with that of the oppression of the female sex by the male. Although this early antagonism signifies a first movement in class history, its associated oppression still remains normative. Through the established organization and monopolization of private property, patriarchal order functions to the benefit of the head of the family. As a result, women are exploited in most exchange relations, be they sexual, economic, social, or cultural. Irigaray (1991) writes: "The use, consumption, and circulation of their sexualized bodies underwrites the organization and the reproduction of the social order in which they have never taken part as 'subjects.' " (p. 130).

If this general relationship holds, the question arises of how can woman claim the right to speak and participate in nonexploitative exchange? A woman's social inferiority is reinforced and complicated by the fact that she does not have a language except through reference to masculine systems of representation. The feminine is never to be identified except by and for the masculine.

Such oppression does, however, present an opportunity for elaborating a feminist critique of the patriarchal discourse. This is based on the undecidable theory of mime outlined earlier. A radical mime of political economy begins with the concept that women are in a position outside the laws of exchange, even though they are included inside them as commodities. This sets in train a discourse on discourse by a residue, woman, who is ostensibly beyond the conceptual boundary of political economy.

The mime is enacted through an excessive, yet seemingly playful, mimicking of the dominant patriarchal discourse. Otherness is revealed through disrupting the coherence of economic statements whose very coherence hides the condition of their production. A radical mime is accomplished by playing to excess the role of the historically assigned exploitable female. Through excessive gestures of the masculine subject, exploitation is converted into an affirmation of the economic position of the feminine. By mimicking personal economic status, the subject becomes knowing of, but not subjugated by, the objective situation.

Part 3: Application

If this analysis were applied to a similarly inequitable relationship (e.g., systems theory and radical separatism in the field of organizational analysis), it would perhaps serve to chart an undecidable path through the residues of the former's representation of the latter. These residues could be defined by excessively mimicking the systems theorists' critique of radical separatism. As extravagant mimics of themselves, radical separatists could, potentially, become aware of, but not enslaved by, their own subordination. Excessive mimicry could conceivably convert its otherness into an affirmation of intent—within limits. As the radical theorist sets in motion this process of self-radicalization, the authoritative conventions of systems theory are theoretically terrorized.

We can begin to reflect on some of the tangible implications of this form of poststructuralist theorizing for making sense of the textual character of radical organization theory. Initially, we will apply poststructural concepts to assess the work of one of the staunchest critics of radical separatism, Lex Donaldson. Here we will conduct a textual audit of his reply to the attempt by radical separatists to establish an emancipatory voice for organizational analysis. Subsequently, again by applying poststructural concepts to assess the fate of radical separatism, we will highlight the gulf between the theoretical possibilities for

textual emancipation outlined above and the failure of radical organization theory to realize such an emancipatory alterative in practice.

In his book, *In Defence of Organisation Theory: A Reply to the Critics,*
Donaldson (1985) reflects directly on the relationship between systems
theory and two related forms of radical separatism: radical organization
theory and radical structuralism. In this analysis, Donaldson (pp.
40-46) makes the controversial claim that radical organization theory and
radical structuralism are in fact commensurable with the dominant
systems theory position of structural functionalism. This representation
draws on what he reads to be a contrary position within the writings of
the "critics" of organization theory, that factional and catastrophic
models of change are not necessarily incompatible with the functionalist framework.

The critics' own position is basically that radical structuralism and
functional structuralism arise from distinct theories of society. The
former suggests deep connections between social structures and radical change; the latter a relationship between social formations and
regulated order (Burrell & Morgan, 1979, p. 400). Donaldson, however, counterposes these differences with the actual comments made
in the critical literature. Specifically, he cites Burrell and Morgan's
(1979) continuum of change in system theory models, where

> the mechanical, organismic, and morphogenic models are consistent
> with a perspective characteristic of the functionalist paradigm; the . . .
> [factional and catastrophic models] . . . are more characteristic of the
> radical structuralist paradigm. (p. 66)

The definition of factional and catastrophic models provides
Donaldson with the means to dispose of the radical other through a
reconciliation of radical structuralism and structural functionalism.
His vehicle for achieving this is a reading of Merton (1975), who argues
that the concepts of contradiction (from Marxism) and dysfunction
(from structural functionalism) are complementary. To make these
two concepts of change commensurable, and thus to bring change into
the social system, Donaldson (1985) makes similar assertions. He
begins by writing that the outputs of one subsystem may be dysfunctional for other parts. In this way, "the essential notion of conflict has
been *introduced*" (p. 40, emphasis added). Subsequently Donaldson

postulates that such flows of functioning between system parts will increasingly produce dysfunctions that "overstrain" the system, the outcome being that the breakdown of the system is followed by its subsequent reorganization. This allows Donaldson to provide an account of contradiction and crisis in "systems rather than Marxian terms" (p. 41).

A further claim of Donaldson, however, presents an opportunity to open his text by employing the notion of residue. Having reduced contradiction and dysfunction to comparable meanings, Donaldson (1985) ambitiously attempts to subsume radical structuralism within a structural-functionalist framework. For Donaldson, radical structuralism concerns the historically specific structures of feudalism and capitalism and the change from one to the other. As such, "it should be seen as a sub-type of structural-functionalism which deals with those historical issues and which posits crisis and revolutionary change as the mechanisms of transition" (p. 41). Donaldson thus facilitates a masculine incorporation of a feminine radical structuralism, as a subtype, into the structural-functionalist framework, to the very notion of which the critics object.

Following the path laid by Irigaray, however, it is possible to open this text for perceptible residues, so as to enable a responsibility to otherness in a way that disrupts the conventional discourse of systems theory. In our case, that which is perceptible is the conceptual process of the flows between systems parts. Donaldson's elucidation of flow begins with an attempt to make two quotations in Burrell and Morgan (1979) complementary: one by Radcliffe-Brown from the functionalist paradigm, the other by Rex from the radical structuralist paradigm:

> The concept of function as defined thus involves the notion of a structure consisting of a *set of relations* amongst *unit entities,* the *community* of the structure being maintained by a *life process* made up of the *activities* of the constituent units. (Radcliffe-Brown, 1952, p. 180, quoted in Burrell & Morgan, 1979, p. 52)

> Social systems may be thought of as involving conflict situations at central points. . . . The existence of such a situation tends to produce not a unitary but a *plural society,* in which there are two or more classes. . . . The activities of the members [of the classes] . . . must be explained by reference to the group's interests in the conflict situation. (Rex, 1961, p. 129, quoted in Burrell & Morgan, 1979, p. 353)

It would appear that once their terminological differences have been stripped away, the main issue of concern is the pervasiveness of negative flows in the social system. The flows between parts can be positive or negative. Positive flows assist the continuation and development of the recipient unit entity; negative flows impair continuation and development. A negative relationship between two entities amounts to a "situation of conflict" (Donaldson, 1985, p. 42), with the entities involved in a conflict situation being classes.

For Donaldson, the only part of the radical structuralist paradigm that seems inconsistent with structural functionalism is the argument that negative relationships between unit entities (classes) are a pervasive and persistent characteristic of the social system. To overcome this difficulty, Donaldson (1985) suggests that the problem is not a fundamental category difference but rather a "matter of degree" (p. 43). Furthermore, he argues that this degree—the balance of negative or positive flows, the variation between capitalist societies because of this balance, and changes over time—can apparently be tested empirically.

To write, however, that change as flow is a matter of degree is to close off or give value to the level of positive or negative flow. And yet to close off and give coherence to change cannot encapsulate all change; it is a reduction of that which is always a residue or excess. In Donaldson (1985), we are confronted with the blunt, decidable assertion that when radical structuralism is adopted as an organization theory, it avoids any excess in terms of the ideological representation of organization. Although this maneuver appears to allow structural functionalism and radical structuralism to be presented as complementary, such a process only serves to reveal the undecidable moment of their antagonism. This attempt at commensurability or subsumption sets in motion immediately the image of incommensurability, which stems from the differing levels of analysis that each would address. Whereas the theory of radical structuralism ostensibly operates at the societal level, the systems approach to organization analysis is concerned with the characteristics of administrative structures. It relates to "the organization structure and its attendant social system" (Donaldson, 1985, p. 8). As a form of organizational analysis, the dynamic of radical structuralism would be to establish significance in terms of radical change at the societal level. Donaldson's argument falters in that the undecidable character of the reconciliation also requires the subordination of organization theory to the principle of organizational analysis as a means of revealing conflict and change in the wider society. For Donaldson, this is anathema.

In turn, a reading of the attempt by radical separatists to develop an emancipatory organization theory also reveals residual tensions. Burrell (1980) makes a series of exploratory moves in line with advocating radical structuralism as a genuine paradigmatic alternative to the conventional organization theory "which ubiquitously confronts us" (Burrell, 1980, p. 98). He notes that although there is at least a superficial resemblance, there is a fundamental difference between the concept of totality and its associates and that of system. For Burrell, a radical structuralist paradigm has no place for the notion of a social system that is in open relationship with its environment, nor for related discussions of external forces and causal flows. This is because the totality draws the boundary around that which is theoretically relevant. The totality does not take recourse to that form of systems thinking that asserts that the social whole is greater than the sum of its parts. Instead an adequate theory of the part is a theory of the totality, just as a theory of the totality is a theory of the part.

Burrell's text, however, only mimes the ideological conventions of the representation of bounded organization. It is captured within the chain of supplementary inscriptions of the dominant discourse and thus does not escape the grasp of conventional representation. The assumption is that in late capitalism, the mechanism of totality integration is the organization itself, for it is currently found at the point of production where labor and capital meet. This mechanism has in fact taken various forms. Under early capitalism, the role of integrating the social formation or social relations of production was fulfilled by the family. Just as the family was replaced as the primary unit of production, the organization may also be replaced as the mechanism of totality integration at some future time.

Furthermore, as the current mechanism for totality integration, the organization must create an inside-outside boundary of its own. Just as Donaldson's (1985) scripting of the mime of radical structuralism cannot account for the residue of flow, so this boundary cannot account for the excess of exploitation and oppression that radical structuralism attempts to give voice. Exploitation belongs to, and is maintained by, the inside of the organization: through the established social relations of capital and labor. The inside is privileged over the outside or other.

At the conceptual level, it can be argued that radical separatism, in the form of radical structuralism or radical organization theory, thus failed its manifesto, for its rhetoric invokes the image of orthodox social systems notions. Although radical separatists claimed to have developed an autonomous political space, this took recourse ultimately to functionalist conventions. Because its discourse was structured by systems concepts, radical separatism was "intrainstitutional" (Derrida, 1983, p. 16). In sum, although radical separatism sought emancipation and otherness, it remained subject to the institutional protocols and symbolic representations of orthodox organization theory.

Conclusion

At the heart of this chapter has been an attempt to develop the poststructural concepts of undecidability and residue for application in the formal study of organization. The aim has been to deploy these notions in order to assess the failure of radical separatism to develop a distinct voice for organization theory, one insulated from the sociological conservativism of systems theory. By joining the philosophy of Derrida and Irigaray to the organization theory of Cooper, we have attempted to show how theorists who subscribed to radical separatism only succeeded in adding to the orthodox representation of organization theory, for radical separatism failed to disrupt the inside/outside boundary of conventional organization theory. On illustrating the intellectual imprisonment that results from a failure to break with representational conventions, we have offered an alternative route to an emancipatory theory of organization, one developed from within the conventions of systems-based analysis. By deploying the concept of the residue of flow, we have attempted to recover a sense of otherness in organizational analysis. At a prosaic level, we have used the concept to deconstruct particular forms of textual representation. In particular, we have noted the logical undecidability that besets attempts by systems theorists to incorporate radical theory and attempts by radical theorists to establish a distinct intellectual voice.

7

Do You Take Your Body to Work?

DAVID BARRY

MARY ANN HAZEN

D o you take your body to work? If you are a laborer, build houses, or pour concrete, you are probably well aware of your body at work. If you are an artist, a policeman walking a beat, or a professional athlete, you probably listen to your body's voices, are alert to your gut reactions, and respond to variations in vibrations and rhythms. If you are a manager in a corporation, you may attend to these as well. But mainstream management and organization theories tend to ignore such practices and, to the extent that they acknowledge the human body at all, stress conformance to organizational dictates and constraints. Certainly, our theories about organizations influence how we act and perceive ourselves at work. We posit that the way we see our selves/bodies shapes the ways we organize and create theories about organization. As our self-images change, so can our ideas about organizing. In this chapter, we suggest that various energy flow and polyvocal models of the self can help us to revise current organizational models that are predicated on traditional mind/body splitting.

AUTHORS' NOTE: The two authors have contributed equally to this chapter and wish neither to be considered "first" nor "second."

The Embodied Organization

For some time now, modernist management writers have searched for ways by which human performance might be increased, using varied organizational structures, cultural manipulation, ergonomic adjustment, and emotional control. More recently, radical modernists and postmodernists, rejecting performativity concerns, have discussed how organizational forms and practice have regimented and diminished the body. But regardless of the orienting camp consulted, this discourse suggests the presence of a one-way gaze, one that travels from organization to body: Organization and management treat the body as object. Missing have been considerations of how the body constitutes organization and managerial practice.

In this chapter, we seek to invert received thinking on the body and organization by highlighting ways in which our relationship with our bodies shapes organizational and management theories. We begin with a consideration of *body*; this is coupled with a brief review of both modernist and postmodernist discussions of the body in organized contexts. We then attempt to show how controlling organizational forms and practice originate from and are informed by how we relate to our bodies. This thesis is used to suggest ways in which restrictive practices might be challenged. Ideas about human beings taken from discourses rooted in Freud's psychoanalysis offer metaphors for revis(ion)ing models of organizations.

Following Rosenau's (1992) "affirmative" postmodern position, we seek a discourse that is "introspective and anti-objectivist, a form of individualized understanding" (p. 119), one that constitutes "a more subjective, nonrepresentational conception of reality" (p. 97). For us, this means drawing from writers within other discourses and upon our own voices and experiences when formulating and illustrating our ideas. It also means a striving for *evocation* rather than *conclusiveness*, text that requires that you, the reader, chew awhile before swallowing. We ask you to make/remake your own meaning around bodies and organization, even as we make/remake ours.

Finding the Body

What is the human body? This question is central to the project of relating the body to organizational theory. When we asked this of ourselves and of those around us, we got answers such as:

That thing I wake up with each morning, the one with foul breath, aching limbs, and full bladder.

That through which I experience pleasure and pain, desire and satiation.

This flesh, the parts I can see and touch.

That through which I create, express, and reproduce.

Each implies a separation between our mental and physical aspects— "I" and "me" seem distinguishable from our corporeal form. In a Derridian play of opposites, the body is neither mind, nor thought.

By most accounts, this line of thinking has dominated Western history and culture—since the ancient Greeks, the body has been viewed as a sometimes welcome, but often problematized, adjunct to the soul/mind (for a succinct but informative review, see B. S. Turner, 1991). Not only have mind and body been separated, but the mind also has, with few exceptions, been singled out as the body's master and keeper. In fact, it has been argued that the entire project of Western civilization has depended on the mindful control of bodily desires, whether sexual, appetitive, or emotive: "The growth of civilization requires simultaneously the restraint of the body and the cultivation of character in the interests of social stability" (B. S. Turner, 1991, pp. 14-15).

Dividing Bodies

This theme is especially evident in the writings of Foucault, who traced the body's subjugation relative to the crisis of French urbanization. For him, constraint of the body occurred through three interrelated modes of objectification: The first, dividing practices, "combine[s] the mediation of a science (or pseudoscience) and the practice of exclusion—usually in a spatial sense, but always in a social one" (Rabinow, 1984, p. 8), as with slaves, prisoners, and mental patients. In the second mode, scientific classification, the body politic is studied demographically. The category of "normal" is developed. This provides a floating standard by which people are categorized and partitioned. Institutions, such as families, schools, hospitals, and prisons, exist in order to "normalize" people. Scientific classification is used as one way of partitioning people. The third mode concerns self-control or subjectification, the "way a human being turns him or herself into a subject" (Foucault, 1982, p. 208). Foucault examines techniques through which the person initiates an active self-formation, which takes place through a variety of "operations on [people's] own bodies, on their own souls, on their own thoughts, on their own conduct" (Foucault in Rabinow, 1984, p. 11). These operations characteristically entail a process of self-understanding that is mediated by an external authority figure, be that a confessor or psychoanalyst (Foucault, 1984, p. 178; Rabinow, 1984, p. 11). It is through this third mode that people introject what is considered normal and attempt to conform.

These categories of control are applicable to organizational practice and theory: "Historically, and either implicitly or explicitly, the question of control has been a mainstay of interest for social theorists and corporate managers alike" (Hetrick & Boje, 1992, p. 49). These practices occur in work organizations in numerous ways.

Dividing practices or enclosure involve physical separation. Townley (1993) points out that "early work organizations tended to be physically enclosed spaces, often surrounded by high walls and fences" (p. 527). Currently, "the effects of the discourse of enclosure can be seen most dramatically in the separation between paid and unpaid labor, . . . the public and private divisions that feminist discourse is eager to counter" (Townley, 1993, p. 527), the physical separation between devalued "house" work and paid work outside of the home.

People are further divided according to Foucault's second mode of sociological classification, by race, gender, ethnicity, and roles. There are social partitions between part-time and full-time, temporary and permanent, management and hourly, line and staff, and union and nonunion workers, as well as those on the fast track and those in dead-end jobs. People are classified spatially, analytically, politically, and hierarchically (Townley, 1993).

Often, the body is perceived as the source of problems for managers and suggestions for control often constitute bureaucratic partitioning practices: Laws, policies and procedures, and corporate training programs are put forth as solutions for sexual harassment (Title VII, 1964 Civil Rights Act; Fisher, 1993; Lee, 1992, Terpstra & Baker, 1992) and violence in the workplace (Bensimon, 1994). Diet and exercise plans as well as employee assistance programs (Sonnenstuhl, 1986) are offered as organizational stress-management techniques.

People internalize dividing practices and comply with what is normal for their roles through processes of secondary socialization into the organization, including participating in formal education, training, and management development programs; following policies, procedures, and informal norms; and engaging in supervisory practices and mentoring. Townley (1993) describes how the concerns of personnel specialists, particularly in relation to performance appraisal, are included in this category. Most workers, including factory assemblers, hamburger flippers, muffler changers, executives, and flight attendants, are trained to attire, intonate, and move their bodies and control their emotions in certain ways. Common organizational norms, such as sitting for long hours, acting emotionally strong, or being physically fit, are related to self control. Organization members are urged to control their time and emotions as well as their careers (Casey, 1995; Froiland, 1993; Hochschild, 1983; Quinn, Faerman, Thompson, & McGrath, 1990; Sonenclar, 1990).

Organization Theory Gazes on the Body

Such body-centered practices have been informed by waves of management theory. During the awakening of industrialism, microlevel theorists such as Taylor (1911) and Gilbreth (1911) helped bring dividing, normalization, and self-control practices to the shop floor. Through their efforts, a managerial class was created whose primary responsibility was to scientize labor-intensive work, to create production blueprints that any "Schmidt" could follow. The individual, personified body was fashioned into an interchangeable cog as people were reduced to psychomotor skill sets.

Weberian models of bureaucracy were seized upon and expanded by industrialists such as Fayol (1949), who championed the benefits of hierarchy and fixed spans of control as ways of enhancing authority. Human relation theorists such as Mayo (1933) and Roethlisberger and Dickson (1939) supplanted objectivist control with socially and internally based, paternalist control methods. Nascent systems and decision theorists such as March and Simon (1958) and Cyert and March (1963) managed to eliminate the working body altogether, reducing organizational life to the practice of rational, programmatic decision making. Organizational structuralists created frameworks for locating and connecting disembodied roles, based on environmental turbulence (e.g., Lawrence & Lorsch, 1969) or operating technology (Woodward, 1965). Strategic planning theorists promoted highly rationalized, aseptic direction-setting systems that treated human bodies as "implementation problems" (Ansoff, 1965a).

The legacy of these early theorists is readily seen in post-Fordist management theories. Scientific management and human relations theories of control have been recast into dividing practices such as ergonomics, in which the body is considered a machine in relationship to a machine. Self-managed teams and continuous improvement are used to further internalize self-control. Partitioning control formerly exercised through hierarchy has been replaced by empowering and transformational leadership (Bass & Aviolo, 1994; Block, 1987) and electronically mediated panopticism (Poster, 1990). Bodies have become the objects of sophisticated, instrumental watchfulness: It is assumed that people can learn to read others' bodies to secure a job, win an argument, gain compliance, or discern comprehension levels (Bixler, 1984; Elsea, 1985; Feldman, 1992).

Sensory-motor and emotional regulation constitutes an integral facet of designer cultures (e.g., Deal & Kennedy, 1982), as managers are urged to create "work hard/play hard" environments that tantalize workers with delayed emotional and sensory stimulation in return for nose-to-the-grindstone conformance. Emotional bonding and performance are part of the work contract. "It is the total integration of human being and human doing for production, and a further triumph for instrumental rationality" (Casey, 1995, p. 194).

And Then Again . . .

It would seem our bodies have been hopelessly molded, regimented, and made to disappear by managerial and organizational practices, projects that in turn owe their rise to widespread societal and techno-logical movements. But this is only one way of understanding things. Another is to think of these practices as originating from and being informed by our experiences of and ideas about the body. As Frank (1991) states, "The theoretical problem is to show how social systems are built up from the tasks of bodies, which then allows us to under-stand how bodies can experience their tasks as imposed by a system" (p. 48).

Lakoff and Johnson (1980) have persuasively argued that social constructions are metaphoric outgrowths of our corporeal nature. They maintain that "most of our fundamental concepts are organized in terms of one or more spatialization metaphors" (p. 17). Some primary orientations include up-down, front-back, and in-out, all of which emerge when, as infants, we begin to move around in the world and learn to associate these orientations with sociocultural values. For example, in Western societies, the parental "up" tends to be associated with authority, goodness, and security, whereas "down" tends to signify the opposite.

Historically, our body's immediacy helped in developing means of classification: "The body (with its orifices, regular functions, reproduc-tive capacity, environmental adaptation and its organic specificity) proved a 'natural' resource for social metaphor: the head of state, the body politic, and corporate culture" (B. S. Turner, 1991, p. 9). Christ's body served not only as an organizing metaphor for the church but also as a model for early mercantile corporations and political institu-tions (Douglas, 1973; B. S. Turner, 1991, p. 5).

We believe the body continues to operate as a situating, classificatory device in modern organizational life. Up-down is reflected in hierar-chical, pyramidal conceptions of power and authority: "It is evident that the imagery of a pyramidal organization is so widespread that organizational hierarchy tends to be regarded as inevitable" (Evan, 1993, p. 29). Mintzberg's (1979, p. 20) hierarchical template for organization design resembles a robotic humanoid, with a head, neck, collapsed chest, Popeye-like arms, and massive platform where feet would normally be. Within this orientation, the dominant organizational head attempts to mold the rest of the body, to make it more svelte and muscular (Northcraft, Griffith, & Shalley, 1992; Pearson, 1987), or a "lean and mean machine." The corporate body is an instrument controlled by the head, which is also expected to represent the body. Just as we accord identity to photos of faces but not headless bodies, we look to corporate heads to reflect organizational identity.

Whereas an up-down orientation is a hallmark of Weberian organizational models, in-out, forward-back, and reproductive metaphors are more characteristic of open system, institutional, resource dependence, and ecological macrolevel theories of organization. For example, open systems theory (e.g., Miller, 1972) uses a digestive metaphor as it emphasizes the analysis and control of inputs, throughputs, and outputs. Institutional (Parsons, 1960) and resource dependence (Pfeffer & Salancik, 1978) theories regard organizational success as depending on in-out exchange relations with institutional environments. Ecological theories (Hannan & Freeman, 1989) are modeled after the body's development and decay, a forward movement through time: Individual organizations and organization populations are founded, suffer newness liabilities, mature, are afflicted with structural inertia, and incur mortality.

Strategy theory also embraces these dimensions. Strategic planning is an exercise to move an organization from present to future. Companies move forward into new industries; when they get in trouble, they retreat. Organizational environments are divided into internal and external arenas. Strength and weakness are internal attributes, whereas opportunities and threats constitute external environments (Andrews, 1971). A masculine, reproductive gloss is evident in theories of strategic change over time: strategic orientation is described as beginning with penetration, shifting to growth, and concluding with withdrawal (Paine & Anderson, 1983). To keep a market, organizations have "staying power" relative to competing "suitors" (Porter, 1980). Companies become "prospectors" and markets "saturated" (Miles & Snow, 1978).

By now, it should be evident that the body informs organization and management, both in theory and practice. More than we realize, we create organizations in our own image. But a question arises: Why this image and not another? Why are so many modernist organizations characterized by hierarchy and control, acquisitiveness and defensiveness, traits that are essentially egocentric?

Perhaps part of the answer lies with the idea that organizations are solutions to individual problems of continuity. They serve as "something that is potentially immortal whose identity we can adopt. . . . It may be asserted that from the existential point of view, this is their central function" (Schwartz, 1985, p. 37). Our corporeal bodies die, but if the self is construed as mind, not-body, and invested in organizational practice, we might live on in *corpo*rations. From this perspective, individual continuance depends on the collective mind controlling the individual body. Extending this, if we, as corporations, are to survive, we must eliminate weakness, increase endurance, and harness emotionality.

Opposing this egocentric framework are models of the human being that attempt to dissolve mind-body dichotomies. These are informed by Freud's psychoanalytic discourse, as he "eliminated the self-conscious subject and substituted a decentered, fragmented, and heterogeneous subject who was often unaware of his/her unconscious" (Flax, 1990, p. 59, in Rosenau, 1992, p. 45.) Such models portray the body not as part of a "divided self" (Laing, 1965) or a machine to be controlled by the ego, but as one part of a total figure/ground gestalt; an energy flow; or a voice to which we listen and from which we learn. This understanding reflects a shift away from self-control and toward self-expression, away from normalizing thoughts of what we "should" be and toward who and where we are right now.

We briefly describe here the work of several writers who, while rooted in psychoanalytic discourse, have diverged from it in ways compatible with postmodernism's consideration of process, difference, multiplicity, and fragmentation. (For a mapping of more traditional psychoanalytic method and theory to organizations, see Kets de Vries, 1991.) To the extent that organizational practice is informed by how we conceptualize our bodies, these models provide an alternate way to understand current shifts in management and organization. They also serve as vantage points from which to consider future changes.

A Different Body (of) Knowledge

Representing some of the more vigorous critics of mind/body duality, the originators of Gestalt therapy emphatically denied "independent status to 'mind,' 'body,' and 'external world.' What these words apply to are artifacts of a dualistic tradition which has sought to build them right into the functioning of [the human] organism" (Perls, Hefferline, & Goodman, 1951, p. 17).

Gestalt theory is a system of psychology based on perception. Within this framework, theorists believe that when we perceive we are not passive, but rather order perceptions of the incoming stream "into the primary experience of a figure as seen . . . against a background" (Polster & Polster, 1973, p. 29). Examples of this are a melody against a harmonic background or a coherent visual pattern emerging from a grouping of extraneous lines. A figure in the context of ground "compels attention and enhances its qualities of boundedness and clarity. . . . It invites scrutiny, concentration, and even fascination" (Polster & Polster, 1973, p. 29).

So it is the whole, the figure in relationship to the ground, that is significant. Awareness of difference and contact at the boundary that marks differences—the whole picture—are critical for understanding the self-in-the-world (Perls et al., 1951; Polster & Polster, 1973). Difference marks the boundary between figure and ground, and this dynamic, shifting boundary is the locus of energy at any moment. Gestalt theory understands boundary as "not so much as part of the organism as it is essentially the organ of a particular relation of the organism and the environment" (Perls et al., 1951). Energy and attention will remain at the boundary or contact point until there is closure, until there is "enough" contact, at which time awareness shifts and a new figure/ ground configuration emerges. The human being, then, can be understood as part of a total gestalt, with shifting moments of awareness, attention, focus, and contact. This is not incompatible with the emphasis in postmodern thought on context, process, change, multiplicity, and uniqueness.

In another vocabulary that grows from psychoanalysis, Reich (1949) and his protege, Lowen (1958, 1967, 1985, 1990), have developed a bioenergetic model of the human being. They, too, refuse to separate mind and body. Lowen claims that this separation characterizes people who have succumbed to narcissism, who "act without feeling . . . [are] seductive and manipulative, . . . strive for power and control, . . . [and] lack a sense of self derived from bodily feelings. . . . They function more like machines than people" (Lowen, 1985, pp. ix-x).

Instead, both Reich and Lowen characterize the alive person as a flow of energy: one who is truly vital is one who does not impede this flow. Lowen claims that chronic muscular tension resulting from physical or psychological trauma throughout life blocks the full functioning of the person. When chronic tension is released, repressed or suppressed memories of pain are recalled with full emotional release. This emancipation allows energy to flow through the body more freely, resulting in increased physical and emotional flexibility and fuller experiences of pleasure, enhanced awareness, and greater responsiveness. "The more alive the body is, the more vividly does [the person] perceive reality and the more actively does he respond to it" (Lowen, 1967, p. 5). This understanding of the human person as an ongoing pattern of energy flow, part of the life force of the earth, again suggests postmodernism's emphasis on process and change, as well as interconnectivity and intertextuality.

A third group of writers founded in psychoanalysis build on the works of Jung (Hillman, 1983; Moore, 1992; Progoff, 1975). Hillman (1983) says each person is a "Pandaemonium of Images," embodying multiple discourses, perspectives, feeling states, spirits, and ways of knowing and understanding. He urges individuation, "a process of differentiating, of differing, of recognizing the many complexes, voices, and persons that we each are" (Hillman, 1983, p. 66). The process of active imagination is one way, developed by Jung (1965), to become aware of, listen to, and dialogue with the "little people"—archetypes and complexes—that constitute each of us. Moore (1992) suggests that as we individuate through developing our imaginations, what he calls in his title *Care of the Soul,* we also care for the world. Each human person as a pandemonium echoes postmodernism's emphasis on text and multiplicity. That we can care for the world by using our imaginations to discover and cherish the many aspects of ourselves points to interconnectivity and intertextuality, as well as postmodernism's use of imagination as a method of knowing.

These models portray human beings quite differently from the egocentric, rational, goal-directed prototypes of the subject depicted in modernist thought. In the sense of the individual that emerges, there is no separation of mind and body, but rather mind/body/environment are perceived in a figure/ground relationship. Contact occurs at shifting boundaries. Energy flows through the mind/body/environment. Dysfunction is understood to be a lack of good contact at points of difference or a blocking of the flow of energy. Each human being is multiple identities, shifting according to context and relationship.

Shifting Our
Reflections of Organization

These and other postmodern notions of self are part of mainstream culture. Mass media expose us to a continuous, kaleidoscopic stream of self-images; consumerism entreats us to fashion a wardrobe of selves; and rapid transport and communication times propel us toward omnipresence (Gergen, 1991). These forces promote an awareness of and hyperconsciousness about our bodies (Featherstone, Hepworth, & Turner, 1991). Even as these trends cause overload for egos everywhere, they provide an impetus toward less egoic forms of understanding, ones that we believe are beginning to inform organizational practice and theory.

Just as we perceive ourselves in these different images, so too are organizing patterns and practices and our understanding of them shifting. For example, organizations are no longer defined by physical enclosures, because people's ability to interact through electronic communication technologies is not limited by geography. An attorney who lives and works on her 50-foot oceangoing cabin cruiser in Michigan leads a firm made up of six staff members, all of whom live and work elsewhere in the state and are linked by a Centrex telecommunication system (McNichol, 1995). The collaboration required for writing this chapter took place from opposite ends of the earth, through E-mail, telephone, and fax transmissions. Such lack of physical enclosure is not limited to small organizations, as even large corporations rely on electronic communication to link those who are working together from around the globe.

Physical boundaries are not the only kind that disappear or shift. Who is "in" and "out" of an organization is not always constant, but depends on task definition. For example, major automobile manufacturers in the past gave specific directions and blueprints to suppliers for major interior components such as seats. Suppliers now work as long-term partners on projects with manufacturers, participating in team meetings and even using office space at customer facilities. They are responsible not only for producing parts but also for research and design (Winter & Sorge, 1995, p. 49). Parts might be shared among different customers, so that the same components could be used in competitors' cars (Sorge, 1995).

Responsibility and liability are ambiguous when boundaries dissolve or shift. For example, computer on-line companies are grappling with unanswered legal questions about their liability for customers' transmissions related to issues of libel and pornography, copyright violations, and jurisdiction (Yang, 1995).

Although these examples are made possible by changes in communication technologies, the transformations in organizing reflect changes in human self-image that are consistent with the models of mind/body/environment described earlier. Boundaries disappear and shift, contact points become focal then recede into the background, energy flows, time and space collapse, people are interconnected, and varied and multiple aspects of the individual emerge.

Some of these changes are reflected in current theories about organizations. Daft and Lewin (1993) characterize new forms of organization as less hierarchical with decentralized decision making, self-organizing units, self-integrating coordination mechanisms, and a capacity for renewal (in Schwartz, 1995). Stakeholder models of management reflect widened notions about who and what constitutes the organization. Circular (Ackoff, 1989) and distributed (Barry, 1991) models of leadership work to decenter the authoritative executive head. Organizational learning theorists (e.g., Huber, 1991; March, 1991) promote the questioning of organizational identities and boundaries. Many writers in organization culture have abandoned integrationist, prescriptive approaches and favor differentiation or fragmentation perspectives (Martin, 1992). Organizational development theorists are calling for pluralistic, autopoetic, less phonocentric methods of organizational representation (Barry, 1994; Hazen, 1993, 1994; Hazen &

Isbey, 1994). Organizational effectiveness is being reconstructed in terms of aesthetics theory (Strati, 1992).

Conclusion

Even so, these shifts represent only a beginning. As our notions of self change, as we begin to invert the split between (organized) bodies and minds, we invite fundamental revisions to the entire project of organizing.

Alternative models for understanding the human person lead to alternative metaphors for organization. For example, if organization, using Gestalt theory, is understood as a total field in which the emergent boundary and focus of energy between figure and ground is constantly shifting, we will pay attention not to hierarchy and bureaucracy, but to relationship and the fluid boundaries at which energy is focused and contact and withdrawal occurs. If organization is imagined as a flow of energy, using Reich's and Lowen's concepts, we will be mindful of how and where energy flows or is blocked, where movement and life or tension and stagnation occur. If we listen to Hillman and Moore, organization is perceived to be a pandemonium of voices from which pattern emerges, a polyphony in which each person is the center: "the hierarchical pyramid collapses in a circle of sound. . . . The bureaucratic monologue is drowned out by the humming of a living group of people organized to do their work" (Hazen, 1993, p. 23).

We disagree with Rosenau's (1992) claim that "post-modern organization theory [is] almost by definition a contradiction" (p. 131). We suggest, instead, that as we stop seeing our selves in modernist terms, as rational, egocentric, goal-driven creatures, and begin to experience our selves as energy flow, with fluid boundaries and multiple realities, our organizational images and theories can change as well.

8

A Theory of Stakeholder Enabling

Giving Voice to an Emerging
Postmodern Praxis of Organizational Discourse

JERRY M. CALTON

NANCY B. KURLAND

In this chapter, we offer a postmodern theory of stakeholder enabling to help resolve the problematic nature of modern theories of stakeholder management. Modern stakeholder texts "center" managerial authors who adjudicate stakeholder differences by exercising discretion within a hierarchically defined (and hence constrained) organizational space. By comparison, a theory of stakeholder enabling engenders stakeholder-firm interdependence and consists of a postmodern (a) epistemology of interdependent, connected knowing, (b) ontology of interactive organizational forms, and (c) praxis of organizational discourse. Our theory "decenters" organizational discourse by replacing privileged managerial monologues with multilateral stakeholder dialogues. Thus, we explore the normative implications of the stakeholder theory of the firm in a postmodern context.

AUTHORS' NOTE: We would like to thank Terri Egan and Bill Frederick for their comments on an earlier draft.

154

The Problematic History
of the Stakeholder Concept

Since the publication of Freeman's (1984) landmark book, the stakeholder concept has gained widespread currency in the discourse of management theorists and practitioners. Other early efforts to apply the stakeholder concept to strategic management include Mitroff and Emshoff (1979) and Mason and Mitroff (1982). In a recent reprise of the literature, Donaldson and Preston (1995) count a dozen books and more than 100 articles devoted to the subject since Freeman's early effort at synthesis between the stakeholder concept and the assumptions underlying strategic management processes. Freeman (1984) defines stakeholders as "those groups and individuals that can affect, or are affected by, the accomplishment of organizational purpose" (p. 25). A short list of stakeholders would include shareholders, lenders, employees, suppliers, customers, and community groups. The problematic nature of this concept is reflected in a history of efforts, by Freeman and others, to reconcile the conventional assumption of managerial agents' fiduciary responsibility to serve a unitary organizational purpose (i.e., profit maximization) with the expectation of agent responsiveness to the counterclaims of nonowner stakeholder groups.

OTHER CONTRACTUAL THEORIES OF THE FIRM

Freeman (1984) notes that integration of stakeholder concerns requires "a radical rethinking of our model of the firm" (p. 24). Agency theory seeks to constrain the threat of managerial opportunism by designing governance safeguards that link motives and actions of agents with owner-principals' interests (e.g., Alchian & Demsetz, 1972; Jensen & Meckling, 1976). Williamson's (1985, 1991) *efficient contracting model* highlights the role managerial activism plays in lowering the *transaction costs* of doing business within hierarchical exchange relationships. In both of these quintessentially modern contractual theories of the firm, the manager is cast as a "rational actor" (Allison, 1971) who (given the proper diet of incentives and constraints) can be expected to enact a unitary goal-centered organizational script that dictates an "economizing" (Frederick, 1995) pattern of organizational interaction. The stakeholder theory of the firm, as a more complex "nexus of contracts," seeks to have managers encompass a wider range of stakeholders in their decision making.

THE STAKEHOLDER PARADOX

A theoretical extension of contractual relationships and obligations to all stakeholders complicates the economizing "objective function" standard of performance to which agents (presumably) are held: How can managers exercise a fiduciary "duty of care" to multiple stakeholders when different stakeholder interests clash (between reaping short-term profits and spending retained earnings to reduce pollution or to meet affirmative action hiring guidelines, for example). Ansoff (1965b), a seminal strategic management theorist, repudiates the possibility that stakeholder concerns could be integral to the firm's decision-making processes on the grounds that managers cannot be expected to effectively or efficiently balance and reconcile coexisting economic and social organizational objectives. He argues that non-owner stakeholder concerns should be treated as secondary, external constraints upon the managerial pursuit of primary economic objectives. Goodpaster (1991) refers to this overlap of multifiduciary agency responsibilities (or objective functions) as the *stakeholder paradox*. Simply stated, this paradox arises from the appearance of "business without ethics" if managers focus on profit maximization to the exclusion of stakeholder claims and "ethics without business" if managers compromise their allegiance to a unitary objective function by trying to reconcile their ethical responsibilities to nonowner stakeholder groups. In this chapter, we argue that the stakeholder paradox cannot be resolved so long as theory and practice centers managers qua agents who adjudicate stakeholder differences by exercising discretion within a hierarchically scripted organizational text.

In particular, we propose that a postmodern theory of stakeholder enabling is needed to reconstruct current modern theories of stakeholder management. We distinguish the term *enabling* from past conceptualizations of stakeholder theory, which emphasize the term *managing*. Where managing implies that agents exercise control within an institutionalized hierarchy over stakeholders, enabling implies that stakeholders, together with agents, jointly exercise control over shared concerns. This new approach will integrate and, to some extent, reconcile the perspectives of postmodern epistemology, ontology, and praxis within an interactive process of multivoiced stakeholder discourse. In this postmodern context, epistemology refers to ways of knowing within interdependent organizational relationships; ontology refers to ways of being within emerging networks, or interactive organizational forms; and, praxis refers to cooperative ways of doing, via multilateral "action-learning."[1] This praxis of organizational discourse becomes the dynamic core of our theory of stakeholder enabling. It draws attention to the processes of sense making, ethical rule building, and trust formation within an emerging system of collaborative network governance (see Calton & Lad, 1995).

EFFORTS TO RESOLVE THE "PARADOX"

Recent modern treatments of stakeholder theory are problematic to the extent that they fail to integrate voice mechanisms, while implicitly accepting Williamson's (1991) "efficient contracting" justification of managerial activism (i.e., authorship) within hierarchically determined relationships. In particular, Williamson argued that professional managers, as agents of the board of directors, must have the discretionary authority to resolve by fiat the complex relational problems that arise as multiple participants interact within the nexus of contracts that constitutes the firm. This complex, open-ended, often implicit process of rule building has been characterized as *relational contracting* (Macneil, 1981; Williamson, 1985). Managers seek to retain autonomy and control, which is necessary to preserve discretionary action, by mediating stakeholder relationships via separate bilateral contracts with each group.

The Separation Thesis

Goodpaster (1991) adopts Williamson's defense of managerial discretion when he tries to resolve the stakeholder paradox by separating the agent's fiduciary duty to maximize shareholder profits from his or her ethical duty to minimize harm to other stakeholders. Goodpaster argues that any move to institutionalize multifiduciary responsibilities "represents nothing more than the conversion of the modern private corporation into a public institution and probably calls for a corresponding restructuring of corporate governance (e.g., representatives of each stakeholder group on the board of directors)" (p. 66).

This *separation thesis,* criticized by Freeman (1994), would rescue managers from the paradox of conflicting duties by juxtaposing two separate versions of economic and moral rationality. However, the paradox between these different modes of analysis and action remains; Goodpaster is silent on the process by which managers would reconcile their potentially conflicting ethical obligations to multiple stakeholders. He excludes stakeholders from exercising any direct voice in this governance process, and the manager, as ethical hero, has no clothes.

This discussion of the stakeholder paradox exposes the limitations of a perspective that centers management and organizational theory on the exclusive discourse of managerial actors or authors. In the following selective review of recent contributions to the stakeholder theory of the firm, we will highlight the inability of the concept of stakeholder management, expressed as unilateral managerial discourse in a modern context, to reconcile stakeholder interests within a normatively preferable joint pursuit of organizational purposes. Some of these contributions foreshadow our theory of stakeholder enabling. However, all are limited by their neglect of stakeholder voice mechanisms and their dependence on the managerial exercise of economic and moral "rationality," either separately or in combination, to balance or reconcile stakeholder interests. The stakeholder paradox remains unresolved in this modern conceptual context.

The Stakeholder Value Matrix
and the Analytical Hierarchical Process

Brenner and Cochran (1991) propose a *stakeholder value matrix* as a decision-making tool to help managers operationalize the stakeholder theory of the firm. It is designed to help managers sort out their responsibilities in the more complex case of multiple, potentially conflicting, stakes. However, in the absence of a stakeholder voice mechanism, this rational tool serves only to embed unilateral managerial activism. Hosseini and Brenner (1992) partially redress this oversight by incorporating the *analytical hierarchy process* (AHP) as a mathematical, multiattribute decision-making tool for assigning weights to stakeholder values in a given organizational context. They note that value weights in the stakeholder value matrix could be assigned either by an upper management team or "in a group environment consisting of a representative set of each group's stakeholders . . . [so as] to build consensus among the participants" (p. 107).

Hosseini and Brenner (1992) suggest that "by comparing value matrix information with organizational performance information, a normative model can be constructed" (p. 103). This statement, enacted in the analytical hierarchy process, could imply the following: (a) that values consistent with organizationally determined goals (e.g., profit maximizing) should be reinforced and (b) that organizations should be responsive to the needs and/or values of those stakeholders with the most influence. These normative implications are particularly troubling because Hosseini and Brenner (1992) recommend that "individuals in the upper echelon of the organization . . . provide the data to estimate the relative influence of each stakeholder group" (p. 110). Even where stakeholder value weights are determined by input from stakeholder representatives, managerial determination of influence weights can skew "normative" outcomes in two ways. First, social justice may be ignored because concern does not lie in balancing benefits and harms. Although the AHP could be associated with a process of broader stakeholder representation and empowerment, a more likely outcome is to reinforce the dominant coalition, further muffling the voices of the disenfranchised. Second, the privileged authority of managerial authors who use the AHP to sort and prioritize stakeholder values remains centered and unchallenged. As currently proposed, AHP does not promote inclusion within a broader stakeholder dialogue; rather, it empowers patriarchal managers to "refine [their] definition of various clients and incorporate their needs and wishes in [their] decision making" (Hosseini & Brenner, 1992, p. 103).

Instrumental Stakeholder Theory of the Firm

Jones (1995) would resolve the stakeholder paradox within an instrumental, "what would happen if," theoretical perspective. He argues that managers could enhance organizational performance by integrating economic and moral rationality more effectively in their dealings with stakeholder groups. He focuses on the role of trust between agents and stakeholders in promoting efficient contracting (i.e., lower transaction costs) within the nexus of agent-stakeholder relationships. He suggests that cooperative relationships reduce the threat of agent-stakeholder opportunism and generate competitive advantages associated with mobilizing joint learning capabilities. Jones references Frank (1988) on the importance of the emotional or passionate dimension of trust in facilitating cooperation. However, Jones retains the modernist hierarchical assumption that top managers, as agents, are equivalent to the firm and that managers deal with stakeholders through separate bilateral contractual relationships. As such, top managers (as authors) maintain "privileged" control of separate stakeholder dialogue "texts." Moreover, Jones does not explore the possibility that differences in power between managers and stakeholders, objectified in the absence of a stakeholder voice process, can undermine cooperative, mutually beneficial, trust-based stakeholder relationships. Without stakeholder participation in a trust-building process, the prospect of lower transaction or contracting costs remains problematic. This instrumental focus slights the normative requirement of a transformation in agent-stakeholder relationships.

Kantian Capitalism

Similarly, Freeman and Evan develop strategies for incorporating multiple stakeholder voices, but they fail to decenter the manager. For example, in Evan and Freeman's (1988) vision of *Kantian capitalism*, they seek to redefine the firm's purpose by invoking Kant's categorical imperative: that all people should be treated as ends rather than as means. Thus, the "very purpose of the firm is, in our view, to serve as a vehicle for coordinating stakeholder interests" (p. 103). Evan and Freeman (1988) visualize a patriarchal system of stakeholder governance within which moral rationality largely subsumes economic rationality. This vision is embodied in a Stakeholder Board of Directors, comprising representatives of five primary stakeholder groups (employees, customers, suppliers, the local community, and the corporation). Significantly, the corporate representative is termed the *metaphysical director*. Whereas other directors would be elected by each stakeholder group in a "stakeholder assembly," the metaphysical director would be elected unanimously by the stakeholder representatives (p. 104). Thus, Evan and Freeman (1988) visualize the manager's ethical responsibility as "akin to that of King Solomon" (p. 103). The metaphysical director becomes a metaphoric embodiment of the ideal manager-agent who should exercise discretion in balancing conflicting stakeholder claims in a manner consistent with Kantian moral rationality. The requirement of universality in applying ethical principles, derived from Kant's categorical imperative, justifies the unanimous metaphoric stakeholder election of this managerial philosopher king. This elevation of "enlightened" managerial discretion is necessary because the idea of the corporation as a unitary metanarrative, as opposed to a pattern of stakeholder interactions, requires the agent as author. The metaphysical director would be responsible for "convincing both stakeholders and management that a certain course of action was in the best interests of the long-term health of the corporation, especially when that action implies the sacrifice of the interests of all" (Evan & Freeman, 1988, p. 104). Because this normative praxis of stakeholder governance via enlightened philosopher kings retains the modern device of a managerial monologue, it cannot resolve the stakeholder paradox.

Fair Contracting

Somewhat differently, the Freeman and Evan (1990) "fair contracting" stakeholder theory of the firm anticipates our theory of stakeholder enabling. They propose a theory of the firm "which treats the transactions among stakeholders as multilateral contracts with endogenous [i.e., internal governance] safeguards" (p. 349). They emphasize that stakeholders and the firm are interdependent and linked by "reciprocal stakes." Because stakeholders must consent to this reciprocal relationship, they must have the right to exercise voice in the firm's governance process. However, Freeman and Evan develop the governance implications of multilateral interdependence primarily in modern terms; they resort back to the autonomous, rational individual whose coherent bundle of needs and "right to bargain" precedes the process of entering into a contractual relationship. By treating fair contracting as the logical outgrowth of a rational bargaining process, the authors seem to argue that stakeholder voices are needed to fulfill the efficient transaction requirements of modern organizational purposes. They seem to imply that these organizational purposes should encompass the discrete "personal projects" of each stakeholder (see also Freeman & Gilbert, 1988). It is not at all clear, however, how this multitude of stakeholder voices and projects can be reconciled within the agent-mediated hierarchical governance processes of the modern business corporation.

Integrated Social Contracting
Theory of Economic Ethics

Donaldson and Dunfee (1994) offer their integrative social contracts theory (ISCT) as a replacement for stakeholder theory. Yet, it can be understood as an extension of the Freeman and Evan (1990) fair-contracting stakeholder theory of the firm, in which Donaldson and Dunfee offer a more robust epistemology of ethical rule building in the hypothesized process of social contracting. However, like the fair contracting method, the ISCT remains burdened by an implicit ontological assumption of hierarchical decision-making structures and by a patriarchal praxis of managerial adjudication in agent-stakeholder relationships. In particular, the ISCT is positioned as an integrative conceptual tool to help decision-making agents act "fairly" in resolving ethical dilemmas under conditions of "bounded" moral rationality, without the assumption of Rawls's (1971) "veil of ignorance." The authors argue that moral rationality is bounded, particularly in economic communities, because economic institutions, including markets and organizational or interorganizational arrangements, are "artifacts" of human designs and purposes (Donaldson & Dunfee, 1994, p. 257). They hypothesize that a social contracting process at macrosocial (global) and microsocial (community or organizational) levels makes sense (provides an epistemology) and guides action (praxis) within these artifactual arrangements. Yet, this ambitious "thought experiment" is flawed to the extent that it lacks a viable voice mechanism at either the macrosocial or microsocial level.

The ISCT is put forth as a mechanism by which all people whose interests are affected will come together to formulate and consent to the terms of the macrosocial contract. However, it lacks a voice mechanism by which macrosocial contractors actually engage in dialogue to reach consensus. Rather, the two authors engage in a Rawlsian thought experiment to hypothesize rules to which macrosocial contractors presumably would consent. Without a voice mechanism to empower participant interaction, the two authors, sharing relatively similar cultural histories and gender experiences, must break free of their psychic or communal boundaries sufficiently to determine ethical principles acceptable to, and inclusive of, a diverse group of macrosocial contractors.

It follows that the ISCT implies hierarchy, assumes an external moral authority, and fails to detail a process whereby values emerge, consent is offered, and consensus is achieved. It implies hierarchy because it privileges macrosocial contractors by granting them the authority to allow local communities to specify their own ethical norms. It assumes an external moral authority because macrosocial contractors grant local communities only a confined moral space within which they can specify their own ethical norms. By interposing "hypernorms" and "priority rules" to resolve community dissensus over ethical guidelines, it denies that values and ethical norms emerge from social interaction rather than from a praxis of patriarchal deduction and hierarchical determination.

In addition, without Rawls's veil of ignorance device to ensure impartiality, the ISCT fails to consider power differences among and between macro and micro social contractors. As a result, both macro and micro social contractors may act according to their own best interests in crafting and enforcing ethical norms. This is particularly troubling if stakeholders are denied active participation in the social contracting process. The macrosocial principle that microsocial contractors enjoy the right either to exercise informed consent or to exit the relationship is rather hollow in the absence of stakeholder voice mechanisms. As such, Donaldson and Dunfee's ambitious effort to incorporate contextual experience into a process of normative rule building falls short by implying a consent process without enabling participation.

RETROSPECT AND PROSPECT

We conducted our critique of the above theories of stakeholder management in an affirmative spirit of reconstruction, rather than as a skeptical act of deconstruction. Our intent was to reinforce the normative promise of stakeholder theory once the modern presumption of a centered management was challenged. We develop the argument below that the stakeholder paradox, which bifurcates the individual and institutional processes for "doing well" and "doing good" within or among organizations, can be better resolved by our theory of stakeholder enabling.

Reconstructing a Theory
of Stakeholder Enabling

The contribution of our theory of stakeholder enabling resides in its integration of the epistemology, ontology, and praxis elements in emerging postmodern expressions of organizational discourse.

POSTMODERN EPISTEMOLOGY:
COMMUNITY CONVERSATIONS AS CONNECTED KNOWING

Of the epistemology, ontology, and praxis elements, postmodern epistemology is most fully developed. Given its celebration of difference, this epistemology is hardly a monolithic construct. It seeks to decenter the authorship of metanarratives that impose a privileged unitary meaning on organizational relationships and outcomes. This critical act of decentering seeks to empower the "silent voices" of marginal groups by "deconstructing" the hidden meaning within the predominant organizational text (Freeman & Gilbert, 1992; Rosenau, 1992). Thus, decentering enables multiple stakeholder discourses. Critics of postmodern epistemology complain that its methodology of textual deconstruction decenters meaning to such an extent that nothing remains but the ironic "word play" of the disengaged reader (see Parker, 1993; Thompson, 1993; Walton, 1993).

A more integrative, enabling alternative to this skeptical school of postmodernism, grounded in revisionist literary criticism (see Rosenau, 1992, pp. 167-168), may be found in "affirmative" postmodern epistemology, which itself is drawn from the philosophy of liberal pragmatism and, most notably, from the work of Rorty (1989). Rosenau (1992) notes that affirmative postmoderns preserve for the author a role as interpreter of multiple voices in local community dialogues or conversations (pp. 169-173). Thus, authors become storytellers, weaving a linguistic text of shared meanings. In addition, affirmatives focus on the margins, seeking to give voice to those who have been treated as objects in patriarchal, hierarchical monologues. Their political agenda is toward enabling a participatory process that includes and legitimates the community's previously silenced voices.

The Wicks, Gilbert, and Freeman (1994) feminist reading of the stakeholder concept is an example of an affirmative postmodern "community conversation." The authors remind us that we should "remain continually aware of the dominant metaphors we use to describe ourselves and our practices because they often shape us in ways that we don't initially recognize or desire" (p. 475). They identify five masculine metaphors typically associated with the stakeholder concept, noting that these metaphors serve to silence the voices of nonowner stakeholders. Instead, they suggest metaphors, drawn from the feminist "ethic of care" and "connected knowing" theories of Gilligan (1982, 1988) and Belenky, Clinchy, Goldberger, and Tarule (1986), to include and enable voices of multiple stakeholders. Wicks et al. offer these metaphors not so much as replacements for the masculine language game but as ways for authors to "expand the conversation" about the meaning and significance of organizational life. As affirmative postmoderns, they recoil from the prospect of authoring an exclusively feminist theory-centered metanarrative.

Metaphor No. 1: Corporations as autonomous entities are recast as webs of relations among stakeholders. Whereas the masculine metaphor encourages managers to think of nonowner stakeholders as an external cost of doing business, the feminist metaphor includes all participants in the nexus of contracts by embracing Gilbert's (1992) reworking of Rorty's (1989) point that "the social glue holding together the ideal [corporation] . . . consists in little more than a consensus that the point of social organization is to let everybody have a chance at self-creation to the best of his or her abilities" (p. 84; cited by Gilbert, p. xi). Thus, the corporation becomes the collective embodiment of a shared pattern of participant interactions within stakeholder relationships.

Metaphor No. 2: Companies enacting and controlling their environment are transformed into companies that "thrive on chaos" by adapting to the pressures of discontinuous change. Companies like the old AT&T, seeking to enact and control their environment to preserve a stable technological core, become companies like MCI, with fast-cycle product development and targeted micromarketing delivery systems that thrive on the chaos of new technological possibilities for identifying and satisfying customer needs.

Metaphor No. 3: Metaphors of conflict and competition are replaced with those of communication and collective action. The management scenario of becoming "lean and mean" to fight off competitive threats can disrupt long-term relationships with stakeholder groups, such as employees and suppliers, thereby rending the fabric of trust that could bind agents and stakeholders together in a collaborative effort to craft long-term "win-win" solutions to their shared problem. Wicks et al. (1994) note the relational benefits of communication among agents and stakeholders:

> Communication provides a mechanism for persons to interact with and learn from one another, to build trust, to find points of agreement and disagreement, to discover how a relationship can enrich each party involved, and to sculpt a form of interaction that fits them. (p. 487)

Metaphor No. 4: Strategy as "objective" analysis becomes strategy as solidarity in relations between agents and stakeholders. Strategic management embraces the "modern project," which calls upon scholars to objectify phenomena within a social science metanarrative that prescribes value-free means for agency prediction and control. Corporate strategists are counseled that, in order to rationally pursue an organization's unitary objective function, they must strip away the subjective veil of "language, culture and context to reveal real reality in its untutored and true form" (Wicks et al., 1994, p. 481). This modern epistemology of "separate knowing" elevates the author/manager as the final arbiter of economic and moral rationality, even as it silences nonowner stakeholder voices.

Whereas separate knowers play the role of "impartial reasoners," connected knowers in the feminist metaphor "see the other not in their own terms but in the other's terms" (Belenky et al., 1986, p. 113). This managerial capacity for empathy and affection, informed by an "ethic of care" that is expressed in acts of responsibility to particular others, need not be gender specific. This "institutional capacity for intimacy" (Kegan, 1982, p. 244) is essential to the development of a context in which the meaning underlying stakeholder relations is jointly created and periodically renegotiated. Thus the "rules of the game" are not surgically extracted from an objectively "true" natural state; instead, they are politically defined in an interactive process of organizational discourse that is driven by a shared appreciation of participant interdependence in a negotiative context.

The epistemological insights offered by the feminist connected knowing literature could be refined by exploring related organizational discourse models that characterize communicative processes for the cognitive construction of reality. Among these are Habermas's (1990) *discourse ethics,* Kegan's (1982, 1994) *interdependent knowing,* and Deetz's (1995) *communication model.* We will touch upon some of these models below. However, a full discussion is beyond the scope of this chapter.

Metaphor No. 5: Power and authority embedded in hierarchies is supplanted by radical decentralization and empowerment. The relevance of this metaphoric transformation will be discussed below. Indeed, the primary contribution of this chapter is its linkage of the metaphoric insights of affirmative postmodern/pragmatist epistemology with the emerging organizational structures and processes associated with postmodern ontology and praxis.

POSTMODERN ONTOLOGY: EMERGING NETWORK OR INTERACTIVE ORGANIZATIONAL FORMS

Efforts to develop a postmodern organizational theory have been vexed by the tension between the skeptical postmodern epistemology of linguistic deconstruction and the burgeoning stream of ontological literature that purports to see emerging postmodern organizational forms. Parker (1992) poses the interesting question of how an epistemology that debunks all theory could be employed to develop a new theory of organizations. This apparent paradox is resolved by our turn to the affirmative postmodern/pragmatist epistemology of community conversations. Thus, our task is to highlight the relevance of stakeholder voice mechanisms to the ontology of postmodern organizations.

Clegg (1990) was among the first to apply the term *postmodern* to new flexible, adaptive, networklike organizational forms emerging (initially in Japan) from the turbulent stresses of global capitalism. Piore and Sabel (1984) point the way in hypothesizing an "industrial divide" that separates the secure world of hierarchically coordinated mass production from an emerging age of "flexible specialization." Also foretelling the birth of new organizational forms were the evangelical sermons of "transformational gurus," calling upon beleaguered top executives to "flatten" or even "blow up" the hierarchy (Peters, 1986) and to empower employees in "high-involvement," self-managed team processes (Lawler, 1986).

The ontology of postmodern organizational forms encompasses interorganizational arrangements, including Japanese keiretsu[2] (Gerlach & Lincoln, 1992); international strategic alliances (Contractor & Lorange, 1988); public-private social problem-solving alliances (Austrom & Lad, 1989); total quality management (TQM) linkages among employees, suppliers, and customers (Schonberger, 1992); and "virtual organization" relationships (Davidow & Malone, 1992). It also includes intraorganizational networks such as cross-functional product development teams and quality circles (Snow, Miles, & Coleman, 1992).

Developing an ontology of postmodern organizational forms is complicated by the fact that they have not, as yet, fully emerged. Moreover, these nascent forms often coexist with (and may even reinforce) hierarchical arrangements in the near term. Heckscher (1994), among others, deals with this problem by arguing that the rigid bureaucratic structures and routine-based processes are maladaptive to the new "turbulent" competitive environment. He argues that a distinct "ideal type" of postbureaucratic or interactive organization is emerging because the new competitive environment rewards the new form's capabilities for cooperative resource sharing and the leveraging of invisible learning assets. The contrast of General Motors's top-down style and committee-driven, multidivisional structure with its own Saturn Corporation division's collaborative governance system that enables supportive stakeholder relationships captures this process of new wine emerging from old bottles.

Saturn was born of necessity. Earlier GM efforts to build competitive small cars had fallen woefully short of the new Japanese standard. In February 1984, the Group of 99 was formed, representing a broad cross-section of GM managers, professional staffers, and United Auto Workers members. What emerged from the year-long community conversation was a new microsocial contract that combined a collaborative governance system with state-of-the-art manufacturing capabilities. In January 1985, GM's chief executive officer, Roger Smith, announced the formation of Saturn as an autonomous, wholly owned subsidiary. Saturn's precedent-shattering labor contract has been characterized, by both management and union officials, as a "living constitution." Saturn's philosophy identifies responsiveness to stakeholder needs and concerns as the core of the company's values and mission:

> We the Saturn Team, in concert with the UAW and General Motors, believe that meeting the needs of Customers, Saturn Members, Suppliers, Retailers, and Neighbors is fundamental to fulfilling our mission.

The primary partners on the Saturn team are managerial/professional "support" personnel and UAW-affiliated employees. R. T. Epps, vice president for "people systems," characterizes the Saturn approach as not only "to create a culture in which employees accept ownership for the direct labor functions they perform, but to also create a culture that reaches out and helps them understand the system that supports them (Solomon, 1991, p. 72). This clanlike organic system encourages voluntary, learning-oriented commitment to fulfilling Saturn's mission, values, and philosophy. Active participation and shared decision making enact this commitment (see Calton & Lad, 1993, p. 86).

The Saturn example illustrates Heckscher's (1994) point that in the interactive organization "everyone takes responsibility for the success of the whole" (p. 24). Where modern bureaucracies regulate relations among organization members by separating them into predefined functions or tasks, the interactive form is

> a system in which people can enter into relations that are determined by problems rather than predetermined by the structure. Thus, organization control must center not on the management of tasks but the management of relationships; in effect, "politics" must be brought into the open. (Heckscher, 1994, p. 24)

The Saturn example also confirms Heckscher's assertion that interactive organizations must be governed by a consensus-building process of "institutionalized dialogue" (this and quotes that follow from pp. 25-26). He defines dialogue in terms of the use of influence, rather than coercive power. Such influence depends initially on trust, reflecting a "belief by all members that others are seeking mutual benefit rather than maximizing personal gain." A major source of this trust emerges from participants' recognizing their interdependence, based on "an understanding that the fortunes of all depend on combining the performances of all." Participants must share a common vision to know how they can cooperate to realize a shared mission. This focus on mission requires that bureaucratic *rules* defining tasks to be accomplished should be replaced by *principles* that express the "reasons behind the rules." Such principles are necessary to empower and guide participant problem-solving initiatives. These principles must be defined by metadecision-making processes that involve all relevant stakeholders (Heckscher, 1994, pp. 25-26). Saturn's Group of 99 articulated these processes. Heckscher goes on to argue that these metadecision processes reflect the institutionalization of discourse that leads to "consensual legitimation" of organizational purposes and actions (p. 39). Interactive problem-solving organizations are process-oriented, in the sense that the organization becomes a collective process in search of a solution (see Wheatley, 1992, 1994). Organizations become verbs, rather than nouns.

In sum, ontology in a theory of stakeholder enabling involves a way of being that evokes postbureaucratic, network, interactive organizations. There is no clear center of power; rather, power is located in multiple stakeholders and not exclusively in an institutionalized, managerial hierarchy. Stakeholders engage in interactive dialogue for the purposes of achieving shared goals and mutual growth. A metadecision process for achieving consensual legitimation consists of three essential elements: (a) bringing together stakeholders, (b) creating a dialogue, and (c) achieving consensus on a path forward. Although they appear to be simple steps, they are "extremely difficult" to implement (Heckscher, 1994, p. 40; see also Boje & Wolfe, 1987).

Heckscher's "bright side" perspective may be contrasted with some "dark side" ontological possibilities. Thus, Heydebrand (1989) characterizes the emerging postbureaucratic form as "a thoroughly intentional, conscious postmodern strategy of increasing the flexibility of social structures and making them amenable to new forms of indirect and internalized control, including cultural and ideological control" (p. 345). Along a similar dark vein, Deetz (1995) has warned that when organizational discourse retains the unilateral management push to transmit information, the multilateral exchange of views associated with his communication model and our theory of stakeholder enabling opens the way to patriarchal "cultural management" and the "manufacturing of consent" in nominally transformed organizations (p. 118). When managers woo stakeholders as objects in the pursuit of unilaterally defined organizational objectives, consummation of the exploitative relationship suggests a metaphor of *organizational seduction* rather than *organizational marriage*. (See Calton, 1991, for a fuller development of this point.) Thus, employee involvement in a TQM or reengineering process need not imply true empowerment. Stakeholders must have the capacity to "co-determine" their own identity and destiny by exercising the right of voice or exit in the process of organizational discourse. Otherwise, they may fall prey to cultural managers who lure them into complicity with their own victimization.

This contrast of bright and dark ontological possibilities underscores the normative implications for stakeholder enabling of a properly understood and exercised postmodern praxis of organizational discourse.

TOWARD A PRAXIS OF
TRUST-BUILDING COLLABORATIVE
GOVERNANCE VIA STAKEHOLDER DISCOURSE

The elements of epistemology, ontology, and praxis are intertwined in our theory of stakeholder enabling; praxis is concerned with ways of doing to enable jointly created meanings in a shared organizational context. The example of Saturn's trust-building collaborative governance processes illustrates some key features of a normatively preferable postmodern praxis of agent-stakeholder discourse.

Saturn's commitment to serving stakeholder needs and concerns is enacted in a collaborative system of joint decision making by the Saturn team, in association with other stakeholders. The "70% comfortable" rule governs joint decision making. Both UAW and management/professional personnel are represented at every level of the company. No team decision is final until all team members are at least 70%

comfortable with it. Gridlock is avoided by requiring each dissenter to offer a positive alternative and by expecting anyone at least 70% comfortable with a decision to fully support the final team decision. This rule is an excellent example of the metadecision processes for reaching consensus discussed earlier. The rule activates voice processes that respond to a shared problem by search for a basis of collective agreement and mutual consent (see Calton & Lad, 1993, p. 86).

The above example illustrates the intersection of self-determination and interdependence in agent-stakeholder relations. Saturn's living constitution is a jointly created *negotiated order* (Nathan & Mitroff, 1991) in which participants continue to exercise the right to voice, while reserving the right to renegotiate the terms of their membership. Young (1984) defines self-determination as

> a principle that social decisions ought to be made by those most affected by the outcome of the decision, whether in terms of the actions they will have to take or in terms of the effects of the actions on them. (p. 180)

The means for determining who is affected and how, thereby triggering the right to exercise stakeholder voice, needs further exploration. Evidence of participation in efforts to cope with a shared problem seems to be a key element. In particular, Wood and Gray (1991) find that "collaboration occurs when a group of autonomous stakeholders of a problem domain engage in an interactive process, using shared rules, norms, and structures, to act or decide on issues related to that domain" (p. 147).

A brief discussion of how a shared agent-stakeholder problem was resolved at Saturn can illustrate this process. In 1991, top managers at GM pressed Saturn to speed up production to limit losses and begin recouping the high cost of startup. Saturn managers were inclined to acquiesce to pressure from this important stakeholder group. However, workers staged a slowdown to protest the spike in the defect rate associated with management's attempt to introduce new teams lacking the level of training stipulated in the living relational contract. Because 20% of employee compensation was a bonus plan geared to meeting quality, productivity, and training targets, employees responded to contractual safeguards designed to link employee interests to the long-term interest of all stakeholders. Management backed down and subsequently developed an effective ad campaign that stressed the relational benefits to customers of this evidence of the Saturn team's "commitment to quality" (Woodruff, 1991).

This example underscores Gray's (1989, pp. 11-16) five factors critical to collaboration:

1. Stakeholders' concerns must be interdependent.
2. Stakeholders must share responsibility for any future direction.
3. Decisions must be jointly owned.
4. Solutions should emerge by dealing constructively with decision outcomes.
5. Collaboration itself must be an evolving process.

Also critical to a praxis of collaborative governance is the importance of nurturing interpersonal trust within relational networks. Collaborative problem solving requires an "institutional capacity for intimacy" (Kegan, 1982, p. 244) built up over time by a mutual investment in trusting, nonopportunistic interactions. Lewicki and Bunker (1994) propose that trust in relationships develops over time and potentially passes through specific stages. The first stage, *calculus-based trust,* is the interpersonal transaction equivalent of the economic behavior of actors in a market or hierarchy. Continued interaction requires ongoing assessment by each party of the costs and benefits associated with upholding or violating the agreed terms of the relationship. This stage of trust is fragile (Ring, 1994) in the sense that it lasts only as long as the cost of cheating is sufficiently credible to deter potentially opportunistic behavior by either party (Lewicki & Bunker, 1994, p. 15). Jones's (1995) instrumental stakeholder theory of the firm hypothesizes that enhancing the level of trust between agents and stakeholders would lower transaction costs, thereby improving firm performance. Where a relationship rests solely upon calculus-based trust, the costs needed to deter opportunism would be sufficient and yet transaction costs may not have been minimized. Instead, the relationship must enter Lewicki's and Bunker's second stage of *knowledge-based trust.*

This more robust or resilient (Ring, 1994) form of trust develops over time as both parties in the relationship gain confidence in the other's goodwill. Dore (1983) defined goodwill as the "sentiments of friendship and the sense of diffuse personal obligation which accrue between individuals engaged in a recurring contractual economic exchange" (p. 460). Knowledge-based trust develops over time out of regular communication and "courtship" behavior, directed toward relationship building and learning more about the other partner (Lewicki & Bunker, 1994, p. 18). This development recalls Zucker's (1986) "process-based" trust and Axelrod's (1984) "tit-for-tat" strategy for incrementally strengthening the bonds of trust when each party, in repeated prisoner's dilemma games, continued to act (and benefit from behaving) in a nonopportunistic manner. In this manner, a local UAW leader at Saturn recalls "a number of small tests along the way in which he waited to see if the managers would truly share power" (Geber, 1992, p. 29).

It follows, then, that knowledge-based trust, as well as the final stage of *identification-based trust,* is associated with long-term interpersonal relationships in private, as well as organizational, contexts. Identification-based trust involves "a full internalization of the other's desires and intentions to a point where each can effectively act as the agent for the other" (Lewicki & Bunker, 1994, p. 19). This stage of trust is reached only in the best of long-term marriages, where transaction costs would be truly minimized. This affective outcome from a praxis of collaborative governance would be found only in normatively ideal agent-stakeholder relationships.

RECASTING MANAGERIAL
DISCRETION AS MORAL AGENCY

Our proposal for decentering organizational discourse does not dispense with the managerial function. However, it does suggest the need to recast managerial discretion as an enabling force of moral agency within the stakeholder dialogue. Wood and Gray (1991, p. 160) hint at this possibility in their view of the facilitative role of the "convenor" in promoting a move toward "fusion and acceptance" among participants in a collaborative problem-solving process. Lyons (1988) characterizes the new kind of moral agent as "an individual aware, connected, and attending to others"; morality becomes "a 'type of consciousness,' which, although rooted in time, is not bound by a single moment" (pp. 21-22). In applying the ethic of care perspective,

Heimer (1992) argues that managers' responsibility for nurturing trust in ongoing network relationships calls for a more particular application of discretion on behalf of each participant (p. 145). Trusted long-term customers, employees, suppliers, and other network participants expect special consideration and reciprocal treatment, not simply the consistent, unilateral managerial application of abstract principles of justice. Powell (1991) characterizes this form of reciprocity in terms of "indebtedness and conditional action." Thus obligations to give, receive, and return favors within a network define "normative standards that sustain exchange" (pp. 272-273).

The modern manager as leader strives to craft and communicate a coherent vision. He or she is viewed as psychologically complete by him- or herself—autonomous—and as bestowing gifts, wisdom, and leadership on the followers. The ideal postmodern moral agent would focus on "providing a context in which all interested parties, the leader included, can together create a vision, mission, or purpose they can collectively uphold" (Kegan, 1994, p. 322, characterizing the views of Heifitz & Sinder, 1988). Within our theory of stakeholder enabling, the managerial agent is no longer the unilateral author, seeking to objectify stakeholders as means for realizing organizational (i.e., the author's) purposes. Rather, agents and stakeholders become co-authors, voicing and acting out the intertextual "script" that defines each other's responsibilities and expectations within an ongoing, multilateral, interdependent relationship. Thus collaborative, trust-building praxis drives the shared epistemological community conversation that defines meaning within and among emerging organizational forms.

Conclusion

Our theory of stakeholder enabling draws attention to new, exciting possibilities for the study and practice of management and organizational theory.

IMPLICATIONS FOR STAKEHOLDERS

Our theory enables stakeholders by creating a context and rationale for their inclusion as legitimate participants in sense-making, rule-building conversations within and among organizations. In the absence of voice mechanisms and the mutually recognized right to speak, stakeholder theory can never realize its normative potential as a metaphoric framework for cooperative agent-stakeholder problem-solving discourse.

IMPLICATIONS FOR MANAGERS

For managers, our theory draws attention to the possibilities of multilateral organizational discourse as a route to escape the "moral mazes" (Jackall, 1988) thrown up by the apparent contradictions between the agent's fiduciary "duty of care" to serve owner interests and his or her ethical responsibility to minimize harm to nonowner stakeholders. When managerial discretion is conceived as a mandate to define and control bilateral contractual relationships, the agent is tempted into practices that distort the decision-making process, obscure accountability for organizational actions, and deny justice to all relevant stakeholders. More informed decision making will result when diverse voices are heard. Rather than the manager exercising his or her own discretion by anticipating the needs and concerns of stakeholders, stakeholders themselves will express their needs and concerns. The unilateral exercise of discretion prompts managers to "pull up" credit for the good ideas of subordinates and to "push down" blame when stakeholder relationships go awry (Jackall, 1988, pp. 20-21). Pulling up credit and pushing down blame acts to both privilege authority and unlink decisions from accountability for those decisions. Our theory of stakeholder enabling will act to relink decisions with accountability. Decisions will emerge from multiple stakeholder dialogue, facilitated by moral agents. Effective dialogue requires mutual respect, shared goals, and resilient trust. Participants in organizational discourse will jointly take credit or assume responsibility for the decisions made. When decision outcomes go awry, participants will focus not on whom to blame, but on how to fix the problem, as has been the case at Saturn. When stakeholders can affect decisions that affect them, the collaborative, trust-building governance process enables the possibility of jointly enacting "strategy as justice" (Gilbert, 1992).

IMPLICATIONS FOR MANAGEMENT
AND ORGANIZATION THEORY SCHOLARS

When authorship is conceived as participation in organizational discourse, management and organization theorists must rethink the modern notion of scholarship as impartial observation, objective analysis, and scientific prediction. Our theory of stakeholder enabling invites scholars to participate in the design of organizational "podiums" to elevate and magnify stakeholder voices. It also invites scholars to seek out, participate in, and clarify the metaphoric implications of interesting and informative organizational conversations. By far the most effective way for scholars to "predict" a normatively preferable future is for them to join in conversations that seek to resolve the stakeholder paradox by including all who can affect or are affected by organizational outcomes in an engaged praxis of discourse.

Notes

1. See Nielsen (1993), for a discussion of epistemology, ontology, and praxis dimensions of organizational ethics.

2. Some may argue that *keiretsu* is a modern term for control because it emerged in part on the basis of homogeneity and discrimination against women.

—

PART III

From Techno-logy to Eco-logy: Epistemological Issues in Environmental Management

9

Ecological Futures
Systems Theory, Postmodernism, and Participative Learning in an Age of Uncertainty

ALFONSO MONTUORI

RONALD E. PURSER

The approaching millennium finds organizational theory struggling with at least two streams of thought that often seem quite at odds with each other. On one hand, we have the call of the environmentally conscious for an ecological organizational theory, based on the perceived need for a (swift) reaction to, and reconceptualization of, industry's role in light of environmental degradation. We also find a different voice, namely that of postmodernists: This is a voice of profound suspicion in any "project," a voice that deconstructs attempts at developing theories and warns us that the road to hell is paved with good (and bad) intentions.

Some of the unresolved questions that immediately come to mind include the following: How can the urgent call for action of the ecologists be reconciled with the suspicion and *negative dialectics* of postmodernists? How can the penchant for systems thinking in ecological thought (the word *ecosystem* gives it away) be reconciled with the almost visceral distaste for systems theory found in postmodernists?

Furthermore, despite the emerging recognition of the need for a more ecological organizational theory, the implications of such a

wedding are far from clear—about as unclear as a postmodern organizational theory seems at this point. In this chapter, we will attempt a
shotgun wedding of ecology and postmodernism—in reality more like
a menage à trois, because we want to further wed this uneasy couple
with organizational theory.

What we intend to do is not to present an ecological/postmodern
organizational theory, but rather to attempt to develop a theoretical
context for a set of practices with which we believe thinking about this
wedding might be a little less awkward—or at least possible. Crucial
here is the contribution of Morin (1994), whose work is as yet little
known in the United States, suggesting a shift away from what he has
called "simple thought," which is reductive, disjunctive, and founda-
tionalist. Morin's call for a "complex thought" urges the need to
completely and radically revise our ways of thinking. He suggests a shift
from simple thought to complex thought that is systemic, dialogic, and
conjunctive. A complex alternative epistemology is presented, inviting
a form of thought that is systemic, conjunctive, and creative. Complex
thought recognizes that system and environment can be said to exist
in a dialogic, interretroactive relationship.

Complex systemic thought and postmodernism share a lack of faith
in prediction, control, and certainty. This suggests the need to think
differently about the future and engage in an ongoing process of
learning/action that recognizes the incomplete nature of our knowledge. Rather than attempt to predict the future, this view suggests
developing a plurality of scenarios based on uncovering fundamental
values regarding the relationship between specific organizations and
their environment. We will present the following:

1. A necessary but not sufficient set of competencies for a process of
   ecological learning that will provide participants with the appropriate
   knowledge context for a systemic, collaborative/partnership and creative learning process
2. A proposal for the use of scenario planning, participative design, and
   search conferences, which can be extremely useful when applied to
   the process of designing ecologically/economically sustainable futures by developing a systemic, collaborative, and creative set of dis-
   courses/practices

We begin by outlining the differences between modern and postmodern views. Before embarking on the development of a systems

alternative, we will first address the criticisms of systems theory by postmodern thinkers; then we will develop an outline for an epistemology of complexity based on the work of Morin (1994) and Ceruti (1986/1994); finally, we will speculate about its relevance for modern organizational discourse.

Modern/Postmodern

Rossi (1987) outlines the postmodern differentiation between modernity and postmodernity in terms of a number of different propositions. Modernity is seen as an age in which reason creates a unifying structure of thought and knowledge, and modernist knowledge is seen as resting on solid foundations. Reason is worshiped because of its supposed capacity to construct "absolute" or totalizing explanations. The use of reason is connected to the idea of progress, whereby reason leads continuously to ever-greater "enlightenment." There is faith in technology, which is seen as being able to provide ever-greater control and domination over the natural and human environment. Time is linear, and novelty succeeds upon novelty to create an effect of ever-changing, ever-improving newness and originality.

In postmodernity, on the other hand, we find a weakening of reason, a breaking down of homogeneous, unifying models of knowledge, and "a plurality of non-homogeneous models and paradigms of rationality, which cannot be linked, but are tied together only by the specificity of their particular domain of application" (Rossi, 1987, p. 14). In other words, knowledge becomes relative and contextual, any pretense at linear progressive development is removed, and the fascination and faith with the new is replaced by a sense of irony and severe doubt in the ability of science/technology/reason to improve the human condition. Indeed, efforts at improving or controlling the human condition are often viewed with great suspicion.

A modernist approach to the perceived ecological crisis might be "we can rebuild the ecosystem—we have the technology." Postmodernists would immediately reply, "that's the zeal you showed last time, when you got this modern ball rolling: your faith in progress always hides the dark shadow of those who get left behind by your need to control things." A crucial disagreement therefore resides in the nexus of power/knowledge. What is knowledge? Who benefits from it? How are knowledge and power used to create—and/or destroy?

We will begin with one of the main sticking points, namely the systemic nature of much ecological thought. Can we legitimately think systemically, ecologically, in a postmodern context? Do "wholes" and "systems" immediately become part of a "totalizing," oppressive story used for the domination of others? Or can we think systemically, contextually, in a way that is not totalitarian and orienting toward the status quo, as postmodernists have accused systems thinkers of doing? Next, we will summarize a systemic approach to knowledge as developed by the Italian epistemologist and philosopher of science, Mauro Ceruti. The purpose of this section is to show how a systemic approach can in fact be pluralistic rather than homogenizing/totalizing, and how it recognizes both our fundamental ignorance and uncertainty, as opposed to the certainty sought after and claimed by modernist thought. This ignorance, we will later argue, can become a starting point for an inquiry into ecology and organizational theory, a starting point that can potentially generate a plurality of approaches to our problems if it is pursued in the context of relationships of partnership rather than domination.

The Postmodern Critique
of Systems Theory

The postmodern critique of systems theory can be summarized in three parts. According to postmodern thinkers such as Lyotard (1979/1984),

1. Systems theorists operate with a modernist epistemology.
2. Through their emphasis on equilibrium, they reinforce the status quo through the maintenance of power structures that, in deconstructive terms, can be found in hierarchical relations, such as man/woman, humans/Nature, and management/workers, disguised as symmetrical relations devoid of power dynamics and merely embroiled in logical/rational differences.
3. They use the term *system* in a way that becomes a totalizing, homogenizing description; in the case of a human system, it is strictly instrumental and/or functionalist in nature, that is, "this is the system, and all parts must collaborate for the benefit of the system or else." Lyotard calls this the "terror" of "systems performativity."

SYSTEMS EPISTEMOLOGY

We will begin with a discussion of the claim that systems theorists (presumably all of them) operate with a modernist epistemology through a discussion of Italian epistemologist and philosopher of science Mauro Ceruti (1986/1994), who has explained the historical nature of the shift in our conception of knowledge from a systems/ cybernetic perspective by pointing out that the latter has rejected the ideal of a fundamental, objective vantage point, the result of a neutralization of the observer's values and perspectives. Consequently, no neutral language is possible or even desirable, and the observer cannot be considered as somehow standing outside the events that are observed.

The systemic challenge to the modernist perspective is addressed very clearly by Ceruti, who states that in our century, we have moved from viewing knowledge as a cumulatively built edifice to one of context—an ecology of knowledge. This eliminates the possibility of the knower as outsider or "bystander" and reflects an awareness of how knowledge stands not outside our world, but in it, and all knowledge passes through problem formulations, categories, and disciplines. Knowledge from this perspective has no foundations, but it does have a history.

Ceruti (1986/1994) writes that knowledge is therefore beginning to study its own origins. In a shift triggered by Von Foerster's (1984) development of the cybernetics of cybernetics, we are studying not just observed systems but also the observing system, the context from which knowledge emerges. This is a shift from acquired knowledge (and the idea of possessing knowledge) to the roots and matrices of that knowledge in history, biology, anthropology, politics, and so forth (the historically constituted and constitutive nature of knowledge).

Ceruti (1986/1994) argues that the historical development of knowledge is by no means predetermined. Paths open up and close down and are not always followed. Paths are constructed by inquirers, whether as individuals or in teams, communities, or research groups. Ceruti goes on to argue that therefore an encyclopedia is more the acknowledgement of a series of paths, rather than an exposition of results. Every path of knowledge is idiosyncratic and contingent, but the heuristic and strategic nature of every grouping of problems and theories has historically been left out and replaced by a linear view of acquired knowledge. In Ceruti's view, we find different historical contexts, with different problems and questions, approaching knowledge in different ways and with different interests, as opposed to a univocal, homogeneous, developmental process of edifice building. With the loss of foundations, we find instead historical trajectories, a series of paths, routes, voyages, and adventures that may or may not be followed or continued. Ceruti states that this shows us an enormous plurality of perspectives and positions that are at the same time complementary, concurrent, and antagonistic and that the idea of a uniform, homogeneous knowledge with privileged ontological or linguistic access to reality is simply not plausible anymore.

One only has to think of the existing plurality of management theories or personality theories to grasp Ceruti's point. An attempt to homogenize these inevitably does violence to their complexity and the at times incommensurable nature of their basic assumptions. In this view, an observed system (or phenomenon we seek to study) does not exist "out there"; it is created by the observing system through an act of choice, of *system definition* (Bocchi & Ceruti, 1985). Enormous complexity of experience is reduced to a manageable description. A system is constructed, not just described. Boundaries are traced by the inquirer, establishing what is "in" the system and what is "out," and at what level of detail one is choosing to study the phenomenon in question. Ceruti (1986/1994) writes that the process of system definition is where the observer's operations are first apparent, because they trace the boundaries between system and environment and establish the relationship between system, subsystems, and suprasystems. Ceruti thus makes the case that depending on one's perspective, different worlds emerge as reflections of different positions. No longer is it possible to start with the assumption, as classical science did, of an ideal of omniscience, beyond *positions,* requiring an inquirer who had been external to the observation and whose presence was "neutralized" for maximum objectivity. Ceruti points out the significance of this:

> The radical integration of the observer into the fabric of knowledge necessitates the development of a new theory of the observer, the emergence of a new image of the subject, and the constitution of a new cognitive paradigm. The elaboration of a theory of the observer is outlined today as possible and paradoxically necessary only by foregoing

the view of the observer her/himself as a condition external to the domain being observed. This corresponds to the nonexistence of a fundamental observation point whose privilege corresponded, para-doxically, to both the project of an epistemology without a subject and to the ideal of a neutral language. (p. 107)

What we find in this position is the reintroduction of the inquirer—but also the environment—into the context of inquiry. Clearly, Ceruti and the other systems thinkers he discusses (Morin, Von Foerster, Atlan, Von Glasersfeld, Varela, Maturana, and so on) do not hold to a modernist epistemology. Indeed, Lyotard's critique of systems theory is in actuality a critique of Luhmann, who is not representative of systems theory as a whole (he is certainly not widely known in America, where he is mostly unreferenced in the systems literature). Indeed, given the fact that Lyotard's *The Postmodern Condition* was published in 1979, it is a critique of the "first" Luhmann; the German sociologist's work has undergone a considerable change, integrating the epistemo-logical shift of the second cybernetics of Von Foerster, which Luhmann developed most thoroughly in his book *Social Systems* (1984/1990). Our discussion of Ceruti also points to the fact that some systems theorists have in fact devoted an enormous amount of time to critiques of modernist epistemologies. The postmodernists' monolithic view of systems theorists is clearly untenable, as is their claim that (all?) "systems theorists" operate with a modernist epistemology.

EXPERTISM/MACHINE METAPHOR/LEARNING

For critics like Lyotard, systems theorists view a system, such as an organization, as a machine whose purpose is *performativity*. In the kind of machine system critiqued by postmodernists (but also, we should note, many systems theorists), problems are attacked through social engineering and the mentality of expertism. When the machine is broken, one calls the expert—the systems analyst. But unlike ma-chines, which are literally dumb, human beings can communicate about their own predicament and indeed occasionally change it. The expert mentality invalidates the knowledge of nonexperts, who are, in fact, considered dumb, whether explicitly or implicitly, literally or metaphorically.

More important, in such a machine view of organization, our direct perceptual experience of the natural environment and social field is invalidated by the primacy of conceptual or abstract knowledge, which compartmentalizes problems (whether they be organizational or environmental) as it abstracts them from the whole context. Such a perspective is linked to what Tulku (1987) refers to as the technological model of knowledge development, which requires specialized information processing by qualified experts with the "technical know-how" to find solutions to social and organizational problems. The main concern with technological knowledge is gaining power over our environment.

A telling example of how our dependence on scientific cognition is supplanting a more direct knowing of the natural environment is described by Mander's (1991) juxtaposition of wildlife biologists' models of resource management and the tradition, the Inuit Indians' intimate knowledge of caribou behavior. Mander argues that the intimate, personal knowledge of Inuit Indians is being replaced by complex computer print-outs that stress "a fast-paced, objective, abstract, quantitative kind of knowledge" (p. 257) and that this knowledge has in fact often proved disastrous.

For disqualifying the lived experience and knowledge of those who have been labeled nonexpert individuals and are viewed merely as interchangeable parts of a large machine, expertism has been severely critiqued by systems theorists such as Emery (1982). One of the problems with the mentality of social engineering and expertism is that, in keeping with the reductionist/disjunctive nature of modernist thought, it reduces the number of individuals who have any kind of authority to address a problem and then makes a strict (hierarchical) disjunction/division between those who can and those who cannot do this. This eliminates the possibility of systemic attempts at solutions by all stakeholders working collaboratively. In terms of research, the new postmodern/second cybernetic/systemic approach suggests the need to explore reflexivity and the "life-world" of organizations, with particular emphasis on actual practices and lived experiences (Gephart, 1993; Thatchenkery, 1992). Here we can find a potentially fruitful interaction of systems approaches with qualitative methodologies, such as existential phenomenology, hermeneutics, ethnography, and ethnomethodology, an effort already championed by Checkland (1981) and others.

The mentality of expertism does not merely invalidate, and therefore miss out on, the potentially vital lived knowledge of those actually working in organizations for the sake of technocratic expertism. It also invalidates the experience of those living in communities and larger ecosystems affected by organizations. It invalidates lived, historically developed alternative, and potentially very important nonscientific forms of knowledge of peoples who have in fact managed to live in relative harmony with Nature for perhaps thousands of years. Although the argument can be made that this closed-mindedness is an example of the scientistic machine paradigm of Western civilization, it also points us to the issue of knowledge/power: Who benefits from certain kinds of knowledge, certain interpretations of the human/Nature relationship? Most important, the question becomes: What are the alternatives to expertism?

SYSTEMS/POWER/DECONSTRUCTION

The issue of systemic thought's relationship to power is a theoretically interesting and practically important one. The criticisms leveled at systems theory have been, generally speaking, that it is a totalizing discourse, a grand narrative that opens itself up to the possibility of being employed by dominant groups to impose efficiency and performativity on the systems they seek to control. Lechte's (1994) summary of Lyotard's position is typical of the way systems theory and its practitioners are summarily dealt with in much postmodern discourse today:

> For the systems theorist, human beings are part of a homogeneous, stable, theoretically knowable, and therefore, predictable system. Knowledge is the means of controlling the system. Even if perfect knowledge does not yet exist, the equation: the greater the knowledge the greater the power over the system is, for the systems theorist, irrefutable. (p. 248)

Lechte's (1994) discussion is useful inasmuch as it isolates some of the assumptions of certain postmodernists regarding systems theorists:

that they describe systems (typically organizations) that are, or at any rate should be, homogeneous and stable, and therefore predictable (a critique that misses the entire chaos/complexity development, see Stacey, 1992) and that the systems theorists' knowledge is used solely for the purpose of gaining control over the system, which is viewed as being outside the theorist—in other words, it is really the observer/ theorist's environment.

We shall return to some of these criticisms as we go along, but we should first note that these postmodern criticisms of systems theory are nothing new and in fact seem woefully unaware of any developments in systems theory and cybernetics beyond the work done in sociology and political theory in the 1960s. McCarthy's (1991) critique of Habermas's flirtation with systems theory, for instance, uses the work of Buckley (1968) as its paradigmatic reference. This line of work was critiqued extremely well 20 years ago by sociologist Alvin Gouldner (1973). At that time, Gouldner criticized Parsons's systems-based functionalism because of its stress on interdependence, conformity, equilibrium, and "controlled power." Lyotard's (1979/1984) critique of systems theory likewise adds nothing new to Gouldner's thoughtful criticisms, apart from a discussion of recent developments in science that, in Lyotard's view, challenge the fundamental assumptions of systems theory. Lyotard uses the work of systems thinkers like Prigogine and Rapoport to stress the new emphasis in science on heterogeneity, disequilibrium, and complexity against equilibrium and homogeneity. This seems rather self-defeating if it is intended to discredit systems theory, because the work of these scholars, who are themselves systems thinkers and both former presidents of the International Society for Systems Sciences (ISSS), has been incorporated by many (although, of course, by no means all) systems thinkers. Lyotard is critiquing a functionalist, equilibrium-oriented form of systems thought that was popular in the 1960s but has lost favor in the 1980s and certainly the 1990s, suggesting that it is the foundation of all systems theory.

In other words, the postmodern "straw person" of an equilibrium-oriented systems theory is in fact a quite unsophisticated caricature of pioneering 1960s work by Parsons, Buckley, Easton, and others. The postmodern criticisms of this position add little if anything to Gouldner, apart from suggesting a profoundly misleading marginalization of systemic thought in the context of modern science.

Having disposed of the criticism that systems theory is somehow inherently, theoretically, biased toward maintenance of the status quo, we now turn to the issue of how power can be conceptualized in systems terms, and the potential cross-fertilization between systems theory and deconstructionism—in other words, the more vital questions of who benefits by a maintenance of the status quo, whose interests systems theorists are supposedly aiding and abetting, and what are the discourses and practices of domination.

An answer lies in the whole notion of system definition and the relationship between what is defined as system and what is defined as environment. Ackoff (1981) has argued that our view of organizations has largely been environment-free. The implications of this have been spelled out in numerous works outlining the deleterious effects of industrial society on the natural environment. When studying a subject of inquiry such as an organization, our thought essentially has been context-free, focusing only on that small part of the environment that we can directly identify as relevant to the organization—perhaps competition, perhaps consumer preferences, certainly the stock market.

A systemic/postmodern approach changes our concept of, and relationship with, the environment. Modernist epistemology and organizational discourse and practices can rightly be critiqued for being environment-free, as Ackoff (1981) suggests, in the sense that there was little or no awareness for the interconnectedness and mutually constitutive relationship between system and environment. However, a postmodern sensibility also draws our attention to the domination of the environment that was part and parcel of this so-called environment-free approach. What this tells us is that in context-free, mechanistic modernism (as opposed to the romantic aspect of modernism, which idealized Nature), the environment was not completely left out but was rather viewed solely in terms of a thing to be exploited and dominated (Code, 1991). The environment is therefore perceived as fundamentally "other" to the system, and the relationship to the other, whatever is at the bottom of disjunctive oppositions, is fundamentally one of domination. In other words, the systemic critique of environment-free reductionism has to be broadened to include the tendency for reductive/disjunctive thought to treat the context, the other, purely in terms of instrumental/power relations.

What we also see is that the term *environment* from a systemic perspective refers not just to the "natural" ecology but to the social ecology as well, with equally exploitative relations. In environment-free thinking, everything that was not part of the system definition was part of the environment and therefore other, and that includes people. Most obviously this includes minorities, women, and other nondominant groups.

The deconstructive approach championed by Derrida focuses on the hierarchical nature of oppositions so endemic in disjunctive thought, which appear at first to be horizontal: humans/Nature, subject/object, man/woman, and so on. Whereas these oppositions appear initially to just represent dichotomies, they in fact hide power relations that, from a systemic perspective, can be said to describe the choice of what is system and what is environment. In other words, we can see that historically modernity has favored one above the other (man over woman, humans over Nature, etc.), and that which is dominant depends on who was making the system/environment definition and who had the power to impose the dominant discourse. As an example, Wilden (1987) points out that woman has typically been viewed as environment to man and therefore as the object of domination, the inferior term.

From this perspective, we can see that systems theory can in fact benefit from a reading of deconstructionists and other postmodern thinkers (e.g., Foucault), in addressing the need for a greater understanding of the discourse and practices of power/domination. But systems thinking is in fact extremely amenable to aspects of this approach, as we have suggested, and in the work of Eisler (1987), Montuori (1989), and Wilden (1987), we already find discussions along these very lines. Likewise, Morin's (1994) effort to develop complex thought has captured the reductive/disjunctive nature of modern thought and extensively explored the relationship between disjunctive, dichotomous thought and domination.

By articulating the role of the inquirer in the system definition, we can begin to answer the questions "says who?" and "who benefits?" and begin to develop an understanding of the system-environment relationship. Clearly, more effort needs to be made by systems theorists to articulate the issue of power, but, as we have seen, far from being incompatible, there may be some important areas of cross-fertilization.

FURTHER CONSIDERATIONS

In summary, the critiques of systems theory by some postmodernists operate on many levels. (It should be pointed out that the systems theorist could here go on the offensive and argue that the postmodern criticisms of systems theory could be turned around and become systems critiques of much postmodern thought.)

1. The intrinsically holistic and therefore potentially totalizing nature of systemic thought. As we have seen, a systems epistemology that draws on the second cybernetics (Von Foerster, 1984) places the role of the inquirer at the forefront. Having disposed thus of claims to absolute knowledge, we address the interplay of values/intentions/ knowledge, taking a much more critical approach to knowledge generation and the politics of knowledge.

2. The "scientific" element in systems thought. Science has become an extremely questionable enterprise in the minds of many postmodern thinkers. Some postmodernists seem to want to dismiss any discussion of science as somehow a priori untenable on theoretical grounds and to dismiss systems theoretical and cybernetic approaches as pseudoscience and pseudo-social science. But particularly in the context of a discussion of ecology, this effort seems extremely ill-advised.

3. Following from the second point, much of present-day systems thinking, particularly in ecology, draws our attention to the biological and physiological nature of humanity (Laszlo, 1987; Morin, 1994) and its environment, rather than merely the semiotic component (the linguistic/semiotic "turn"). Again, we find much of postmodern thinking profoundly at odds with this notion. A fundamental reconceptualization of the environment as not merely the natural environment, or just the semiotic environment (simulations/hyperreality/information age/culture of images/TV as the "unreality industry," etc.), but as the whole socioecological or biopsychosocial system in which the participants live seems necessary to avoid extremely partial discussions.

The environment, from a systemic perspective, is not just an abstracted Nature, or abstracted signifiers without signifieds, but humans as part of Nature and Nature as part of humans. This requires an understanding of a perspective whereby the fundamental interconnection between humans and Nature is made clear and the physicality, the embodiment of human beings, is made apparent. Particularly in an age of so-called knowledge workers, when we are told that brains are replacing brawn as the arbiter of job worthiness, it becomes important not to leave our bodies at the door once we enter our organization and to remember that the mind/body disjunction is an equally pernicious correlate of the human/Nature disjunction.

4. Systems approaches in the social sciences generally address the need for action rather than merely interpretations of interpretations, particularly because they are applied in the much vilified domain of management. Indeed, the flirtation of organizational theory with post-modernist philosophy is not being reciprocated, and some postmodernists view organizational theorists' efforts toward integrating postmodern thought as merely another opportunistic attempt to misappropriate intellectual discourse for the sake of greater control and productivity (Rosenau, 1992). This raises a host of questions that cannot be addressed in this chapter. Although the postmodernists' suspicions may not be entirely unjustified, they are also in some respects related to the previously mentioned, rather limited notion and consequent totalizing (and profoundly suspicious) misrepresentation of organizational theory and systems theory by postmodernists like Lyotard.

5. Most important, perhaps the "real" issue here is power and control and the use of systems models to engage in precisely the kind of social engineering of whole systems so prevalent in Taylorist "scientific management" with its mentality of expertism. As we have suggested, this is a legitimate issue that needs much study and is being addressed to some extent by systems theorists.

Therefore, there appear to be signs that systems theoretical approaches are not entirely incompatible with postmodern critiques of modernity, and some form of postmodern systems theory—incomplete and even embryonic though it may be—is already emerging. In the next section, we will explore some of the implications of this development for ecological organizational theory.

Ecology/Postmodernism/Learning

What are the implications of the postmodernism/systems theory dialogue for organization theory? Let us try to summarize them here.

Postmodernists argue that linear progress, faith in technology, and our capacity for prediction are not only discredited but also dangerous. Nevertheless, ecologists argue, we need to think about the future, although not in the old way, with technological fixes or just lip service to "green slogans." Our suggestion is that this indicates the need for an ongoing process of learning that recognizes that we simply do not really know how to deal with the ecological crisis at present or how organizations may best address this problem, and that the search for *one* answer is part of the problem. We assume that "more of the same" will most likely not work, and we therefore need to engage in a process of collective, contextual discovery to see what might work in our situation (given our local resources, constraints, possibilities, etc.) and how that relates to the work of others. In other words, rather than calling in the experts, we are calling for the development of a participative learning process with members of organizations and their communities generating knowledge that may or may not involve bringing in experts who would, if called, take on a role more akin to expert witnesses or advisers.

Two things suggest themselves: (a) a curriculum to foster ongoing learning and the need to develop a theory base for such a curriculum and (b) ways in which this ongoing learning may be applied to real world organizational/ecological problems. For the curriculum of ongoing learning, we propose the development of a set of competencies that can best be described, in Morin's terms, as the development of complex thought. Montuori (1989, 1993; Montuori & Conti, 1992) has likewise argued that what is required is a shift toward a triad of systemic thinking/partnership-conjunctive thought/creative discourse and practices, as opposed to (modernist) reduction/domination-disjunctive thought/conforming (more of the same). These competencies would enhance the ability of organizational members to think together about problems in a way that much of present organizational discourse discourages. The ideal type of the modern organizations can be described as hierarchical, homogeneous, stable, fear-based, deviation reducing, stressing machinelike conformity, simple, emphasizing control and prediction, and fragmented in such a way that knowledge is parceled out on a "need to know" basis. The development of the competencies we are proposing would be a necessary but not sufficient step toward developing discourses and practices that might enable an organization to shift from such a postmodern-systemic organizational type. The alternative postmodern-systemic ideal type we are proposing would, while incorporating at some levels some of the characteristics of the former type, stress heterarchical organization, heterogeneity, process, alternating between simplicity and complexity, emphasizing understanding along with control, and a degree of scenario planning (recognizing the contingent, nondeterministic, creative nature of the future), with knowledge radically distributed throughout the organizaion (Montuori, 1989, 1993; Morgan, 1986; Purser & Montuori, 1995).

In other words, the competencies would stress the following:

1. The importance of a postmodern, complex systems thinking, which makes participants aware of the nature of open systems, embeddedness in larger ecosystems, the nature of interretroactive relations, and so forth. This way of thinking, in other words, is not reductive/disjunctive but contextual and realizes the inextricable connection between system and environment and the role of the inquirer in the process of system/environment definition—in sum, an awareness of the role of space (context/ecology/interconnectedness, etc.), time (evolution/history/process/genealogy), and knowledge (the role of paradigms/ mental models/mindscapes).

2. An ongoing process of learning about the nature of the system/ environment relation from a perspective such as that presented by Eisler's template of partnership/domination, which not only takes into account the deconstructionist critique of domination but also presents an alternative based on the potential for partnership. Who defines what is system and what is environment? What are the forces at play in the dominant discourse, in the system definition? Who imposes this order? What of the other alternative definitions?

3. A recognition of the fundamentally creative process involved in system/environment definition (i.e., the constructive, creative role of metaphor [Pepper, 1942] in system definition and the possibility of reframing) and in the possibility of generating a number of possible future scenarios for systems. This suggests the need for training in basic creativity awareness and for a training that is also systemic/partnership-oriented, which, in other words, focuses on creativity as a systemic process occurring in time and space within a context that includes other people, and that these people can be collaborated with in order to develop social creativity.

A form of social creativity (thinking and acting together in new ways), informed by the above curriculum, we would argue is what is needed to think about the future in a manner that is not likely to fall victim to the excesses of modernism (more of the same/technological fixes) and the apocalyptic nihilism of some postmodernists (e.g., Baudrillard, Vattimo). Although we are proposing this foundation for our curriculum in the context of learning about an organization's relation to its larger ecosystem, it is clear that we believe its applicability is in fact much greater than that. Learning to think beyond reduction/disjunction (i.e., in a complex or systemic manner), developing an understanding of the nature of partnership as opposed to domination as the central image of human relations, and nurturing our ability to think and act creatively are skills that we think have great general value and in fact turn the traditional organizational competencies (specialization/need to know; competition/domination; conformism/ obedience) upside down, at least in terms of the theory-in-use. We therefore believe that the context of this learning process is of great importance. The introduction of what might potentially be creative disorder into the existing organizational order can be channeled by focusing it on the development of positive, collective, attainable goals.

FROM PREDICTION TO PARTICIPATIVE SCENARIOS:
POSTMODERN ECOLOGICAL FUTURES

The modernist paradigm held a view of linear growth, bigger is better, and more of the same, imbued with a profound faith in technology and, as postmodernists like to remind us, a faith in control and prediction. Postmodernists and ecologists question the wisdom of this process and critique what is present organizational discourse and practices vis-à-vis the environment. Given the crisis of what is, the question often put is, What next—where to now? And the answer seems to be that we do not know, or at least, if we wish to be generous, that there are many different possible directions. It seems to us important to recognize also the need to understand what ought to be, particularly given the collapse of modernist manifest destinies, of modernist certainty and linear progress. Where should we go from here?

Again, we feel a systemic approach may be useful here. Along with the return of the inquirer in the second cybernetic/systems epistemology of observing, as opposed to observed systems (Von Foerster, 1984, 1990; Von Glasersfeld, 1987), and an appreciation of the active role of the knower, we also find a shift from a position of certainty and authority, so typical of much modernist discourse, to one of uncertainty and exploration—a recognition of ignorance that is in many ways very heartening. It suggests to us that instead of individual knowers, certain of our inexorable path, we might now consider ourselves cooperative learners, engaged in a search for new pathways, new trajectories, new possibilities.

If the modern project focused on the content of knowledge on which to build (organize) its edifice, then a postmodern-systemic, complex organization may develop the capacity for knowledge in a radically distributed network throughout the organization and its environment (Montuori, 1993). Clearly, this would entail a much greater degree of participation and representation on the part of everyone involved in an organization and its environs.

Given the irruption of fundamental uncertainty into organizational discourse, we cannot rely on a certain future in which, thanks to technology, every day in every way we are getting better and better. Living with uncertainty becomes necessary. Prediction fails us—and positive predictions seem missing entirely. Nevertheless, as the ecologists remind us, there is a need to take action to remedy environmental destruction. Furthermore, it can be argued that people need hope, the possibility of a better future (Ogilvy, 1992). What becomes necessary is developing the capacity to develop new forms of knowledge, and alternative futures, that go beyond the gloom and doom of many ecological predictions. Useful as they may be, the Club of Rome-style global predictions must be counterbalanced with the creation of hopeful, possible "little" (local) futures as well as "big" or global futures.

Scenario planning (Ogilvy, 1992) offers enormous opportunities to develop these alternative futures, while at the same time asking the fundamental questions: Where do we want to go, and what might happen if we decided to go there (Montuori, 1989). A host of new methodologies, from scenario planning (Ogilvy, 1992; Schwartz, 1991) to participative design (Emery, 1993) to interactive planning (Ackoff, 1981) to search conferences (Emery & Purser, in press), lend themselves to this process of uncovering values and figuring out where we want to go from here. In the process of scenario development, we also come to uncover many of our previously hidden assumptions about the present. Indeed, much of science fiction can be read as a linear extrapolation of the present into the future and proves highly instructive for that very reason.

What is particularly important about processes like scenario planning is that they stress collective learning—learning together about problems for which there is no one clear solution. In terms of the competencies we have suggested, scenario building and participative design ask participants to employ their creative abilities together (in partnership) within the larger context of their organization and ecosystem, to develop organization/environment/community and other intrasystemic partnerships. And, as we have argued elsewhere (Montuori & Purser, 1995), this opens up the possibility for a much needed social creativity in attempting to overcome societal/ecological problems. Particularly with the development of easy access to computer networks, one could imagine on-line scenario building and simulations (along the lines of such popular games as Sim-City and Sim-Earth) in which alternative futures are debated and discussed openly and applied within the context of organizations/communities/ecosystems.

Clearly, this points away from the need for experts to come in and plan one organizational trajectory, and ideally it suggests instead a democratizing process in which members of an organization and members of communities work together to develop scenarios that are contextually appropriate to their circumstances. Such a process would in and of itself represent training in systems thinking, in the creation of partnerships, and in creative thinking, training could benefit from outside resources for purposes of instruction and facilitation but would leave the ultimate directions and choices in the hands of participants.

Industry is in a remarkable position to develop what amounts to small laboratories in which ecological thinking could be nurtured within the inevitable real-time context of economic demands, and relative small-scale, community projects could be developed along the lines of Lyotard's (1979/1984) *little narratives* as opposed to one, dominant new ecological metanarrative (THE new paradigm). These small paradigms could be just that, in the original sense of the word, new models or examples of ways in which organizations learn to deal not just with the constraints of environmental realities but also with the possibilities of co-creating their relationship with the environment.

What we are proposing therefore is the development of small ecological learning communities within the context of organizations and their larger communities, in which participants can develop appropriate scenarios with appropriate technologies, based on the resources and needs of their community ecosystem. Companies like The Gap already have ecological task forces, a director of environmental services, and an organization, Gap Environmental Organization (GEO), that addresses such issues as minimizing pollution from dyes used in producing clothes and using organic cottons.

One of the important potentials in such a participative design/ scenario building/search conference approach to the future is the potential to bring together members of an organization with the hope of effecting positive change to their conditions and to envision an alternative future and leverage the existing initiatives of organizations like The Gap even further. In the process of working together in the microcosm of ongoing ecological learning, organizational members may:

1. Develop an ongoing process of learning transferable methodologies (scenario planning, participative design) that can be applied to other aspects of their work experience, such as job redesign
2. Engage in a process of uncovering values and assumptions, and develop a greater awareness of their "mental models" or paradigms, and their constraints and possibilities
3. Engage in systematic study of systems theory, partnership/collaboration development, and creative thinking as the theory base for the ongoing learning process and the ecological learning process
4. Develop a systemic understanding of their organization within its larger ecosystem, and therefore gain a better understanding of their organization as a whole, including financial, structural, and procedural constraints and possibilities

As with all democratic processes, but particularly the ones we are proposing, it is important that they not be seen merely as exercises but actually gain the support, active participation, and follow-through of top management. Nothing kills participation as quickly as the experience of it not making any difference in the eyes of management.

Conclusion

In this chapter we have attempted to show that the systems perspective that underlies much ecological thought is not incompatible with postmodern thought and that there is indeed a form of postmodern systems theory emerging. We have also argued that the postmodern and systems-theoretical perspectives can help us to think about the future—in this case, the future of the industry/ecology relationship—by (a) proposing the need for an ongoing process of learning that is systemic, based on partnership, and creative, and (b) suggesting that this process can be assisted through various projects of participative design, scenario planning, and search conferences in which members of organizations can apply their ongoing learning to the process of designing their organization's role within its larger ecosystem.

10

Simulacral Environments

Reflexivity and the Natural
Ecology of Organizations

ROBERT P. GEPHART, JR.

This chapter articulates a postmodern perspective on organizational environments that addresses Nature and ecology. First I discuss "Nature" and distinguish it from the human or built environment. Next, I discuss how reflection, endogenous reflexivity, and radical reflexivity can be used to integrate ecological issues into organization and management theories. The use of reflection is illustrated by discussion of *ecocentric management,* which integrates natural science variables into management and organization theory frameworks (Shrivastava, 1995). The advantages and limits of reflection and ecocentric management are explored from the view of postmodernism. Endogenous reflexivity is illustrated by (re)conceptualizing environment, ecology, and Nature as socially constructed phenomena. The radically reflexive investigation and postmodern reconceptualization of Nature, ecology, and environments are illustrated by using simulation and simulacra (Baudrillard, 1983, 1994) to uncover the paradox that, as a result of neglect of reflexivity, "factual" scientific and literary representations of the natural environment are simulations of the natural environment. Representations of environments feign to contain a true representation of the natural world independent of humans. Environment, ecology, and Nature are thus simulacra: copies of models representing a reality that does not exist apart from these representations. I explore the implications of reflexive, postmodern perspectives for investigation of the natural environment in management and organization theory.

The Environment in Organizational Analysis

The environment of organizations is generally conceived to exist as a spatiotemporal reality "outside" the boundaries of the organization (Bluedorn, 1993; Bluedorn, Johnson, Cartwright, & Barringer, 1994). Organizational theory's concern with the environment has been directed at human or socially constructed features of the world: the economy, the political system, technology, competitor organizations, and other social institutional spheres (Bluedorn et al., 1994; Gephart & Bowring, 1995; Shrivastava, 1995). For example, stakeholder theories of organization focus on human groups and actors politically able to influence organizational events (Donaldson & Preston, 1995, p. 69). Similarly, Daft's (1995) organization theory textbook represents the environment as 10 sectors or sets of human features of the world, such as markets, technology, and government. Raw materials is the one sector that potentially refers to nonhuman, natural aspects of the environment, which is provisionally defined here as consisting of nonhuman phenomena of the world, that is, the world prior to and exclusive of the impacts of industrialization and humans. This "natural environment" includes the earth and surrounding cosmos; geological features and land forms; biological organisms; and the biosphere itself, that is, the area of earth where ecosystems can operate (Odum, 1963). The natural environment is thus the nonhuman, nonbuilt context of human activities, which contrasts with the "built" or humanly constructed environment.

The neglect of the natural world produces a "denatured" view of organizations in management scholarship (Shrivastava, 1995, p. 125), giving precedence to the utilitarian use of Nature by humans and organizations. Other important assumptions of the denatured view are the following:

- A production and consumption bias that assumes that organizations are neutral and serve stakeholders largely through productivity

- A financial risk bias that preempts consideration of other forms of risk
- Anthropocentrism, the view that human welfare is the central purpose of social institutions (Shrivastava, 1995, pp. 125-127)

These assumptions work to deprivilege natural environmental concerns in organizational management. From this view "organizational exploitation of natural resources is legitimate, even desirable" (Shrivastava, 1995, p. 127).

An alternative to a denatured view of organizations is the ecocentric view, which aligns organizations with their natural environment (Shrivastava, 1995, p. 130). Development of a more ecocentric view is the task for much future work in the organizations and natural environment area (Shrivastava, 1995). How can this be accomplished? And is this the appropriate approach to adopt? I argue here that reflection and reflexivity (Pollner, 1991) offer strategies for integrating ecological issues into management and organization theories.

Reflection and Reflexivity

Social science reflection involves the exploration of human conduct so as to display the alternative and differential human processes at work in this conduct. Reflection opens new domains or courses of inquiry, which are then analyzed in terms of existent conceptual and empirical resources. Reflection attempts to "mirror" the social and/or natural world, that is, to reflect a true image of the world, one formed and constrained by "the outer rim" of established theoretical practice and processes (Pollner, 1991, p. 376). For example, one may reflect on rivers by conceiving them as riparian systems and use scientific knowledge of these systems to indicate processes disrupted by pollution.

Reflexivity differs from reflection by problematizing basic features of the phenomenon under consideration. Reflexivity takes two forms in social science. Endogenous reflexivity (Pollner, 1991) refers to the investigation of "how what members do about social reality constitutes that reality" (Pollner, 1991, p. 372). It is concerned with the local production of accounts and social order in settings where the very sense of the setting depends on the accounts given and vice versa (Leiter, 1980, p. 139). Endogenous reflexivity thus investigates the self-generating properties of settings and phenomena, the mutual elaboration of settings and accounts (Leiter, 1980; Mehan & Wood, 1975). For example, one might investigate the meetings of an environmental group by observing the group, producing descriptions of the accounts and stories told by the members of the group, and then examining how discussions of environment simultaneously composed the settings while being responsive to the setting as an environmental group meeting.

Radical reflexivity is a second form of reflexivity and involves an analyst who is self-referentially aware that analytical reflection occurs within an arena of assumptions that are themselves anterior to the process of reflection or the phenomenon on which one reflects (Pollner, 1991, p. 376). The tacit framework in which reflection occurs is invisible and yet it constitutes the basis of truth. Radical reflexivity recovers the hidden ontological practices that create the domain where reflection and endogenous reflexivity can occur. Radical reflexivity is thus an "abnormal discourse" (Pollner, 1991, p. 376), which disrupts normal inquiry and ordinary discourse, unsettles reality, and problematizes the features of discourse on which the sensibility of the discourse presumably rests. It addresses the bases and reproduction of the natural (Pollner, 1991, p. 377) and requires an appreciation of the accomplished character of all human meanings and actions (Pollner, 1991, p. 370). Radical reflexivity thus extends inquiry into regions beyond the "settled territory" of existing frameworks to generate insights about the bases and assumptions that underlie our knowledge and understanding.

Reflection in
Ecocentric Management Theory

The ecocentric management perspective (Shrivastava, 1995) is one primary approach to environmental issues in management and organization theory. The ecocentric model as outlined by Shrivastava (1995) and others (Buchholz, 1993; Stead & Stead, 1992) incorporates the logic and concepts of natural sciences into management and organization theory, particularly scientific knowledge about ecology. Ecocentric management presumes that natural science has identified objective features of the natural world subject to organizationally based degradation. To prevent such degradation, there is a need to integrate natural science knowledge and variables more directly into logical, positivist theories of organization, such as systems theory (Shrivastava, 1995; Stead & Stead, 1994). Ecocentric management thus seeks to establish a new domain for management theory—the environmental or ecological aspects of organizational activities. Here I argue that this domain is explored reflectively and not reflexively in ecocentric management.

Ecocentric management uses existent theoretical resources. For example, the proposed new view is one that "focuses centrally on technological and environmental risks, that is, one that does not treat risks as externalities but treats them as the core problems of management" (Shrivastava, 1995, p. 127). This merely relocates risk from the periphery of theorizing to the center, and hence the new perspective is largely delimited and constrained by preexistent concepts and concerns. Second, Shrivastava argues for use of a systems approach that closes "the loop of output and input processes" (p. 133; see also Stead & Stead, 1992). Systems analysis is a positivist perspective that has been used to compose the systems theory view of organizations, based on the organic metaphor (Morgan, 1986). The use of systems analysis thus serves to keep the new ecocentric management orientation well within the orbital or outer rim of conventional scientific theories and practices. Indeed, by emphasizing the need to "close the loop," Shrivastava ironically appeals to the closed systems model rejected in early organization theory (Katz & Kahn, 1966, pp. 26-28) in favor of open systems models (e.g., Katz & Kahn, 1966).

Furthermore, Shrivastava (1995) argues that we need to "adopt the perspective of the stakeholder that bears the most risks . . . Nature!" (p. 127). Although this extends stakeholder theory to a new stakeholder—Nature—it also preserves and uses the well-known framework of stakeholder theory, which is discussed by Donaldson and Preston (1995) in the same issue of *Academy of Management Review* that contained Shrivastava's (1995) article. In turn, the stakeholder framework is linked to the concept of industrial ecosystems, a metaphorical extension of the natural science concept of ecosystems. Industrial ecosystems, as conceived by Shrivastava, can emulate natural ecosystems. The organizations that are now contained within this new, more ecologically sensitive system are the same isolated, cellular organizations that degraded and polluted the environment before they were reconceptualized as components of industrial ecosystems. By virtue of reconceptualization into an industrial ecosystem, these same organizations are transformed into socially responsible entities. Furthermore, the industrial ecosystem itself exists as a representation in a line/word figure (Shrivastava, 1995, p. 129), which is a traditional and well-known tool of representation for modernist, cause-and-effect-oriented, organizational theories. Finally, Shrivastava calls for "new economic and industrial regulations" (p. 129), infrastructure, roles, and markets. Yet these new organizational features are simply extensions or elaborations of modernist organizational structures, albeit with potentially different contents.

Ecocentric management embraces a "mirror" view of science and Nature (Rorty, 1979) in which science is presumed to reflect a factual world. The task for ecocentric systems analysis is thus to determine the actual limits of sustainability of ecological and organizational systems, to set rules and policies that prevent one from exceeding these limits, and hence to more fully bureaucratize and modernize contemporary society. This perspective invokes a conservative vision (Jameson, 1991, p. xviii) of current and future society as "postindustrial modernization" (Shrivastava, 1995, p. 119) rather than postmodernism. It criticizes and excludes critical theories of society as a basis for theoretical reformulation (Shrivastava, 1995, p. 119). The ecocentric model thus overlooks social processes at work in organizations and society.

The ecocentric approach enlarges the domain of management theory to include the natural environment. The theoretical and metatheoretical bases of ecocentric management are consistent with prevailing positivist theories in both the organizational and natural sciences; thus, integration of the two sciences is facilitated by consistent ontological assumptions. There are also limits to the ecocentric management perspective. First, the perspective reproduces and privileges positivist versions of organization theory, particularly organizational systems theories that are metatheoretically compatible with systems views inherent in ecology. Second, ecocentric management fails to explicitly address human reasoning or sense-making practices or to contextualize these within a natural or ecological system. Similarly, ecology and environment are not addressed as human social

208 TECHNO-LOGY TO ECO-LOGY

constructions, but rather are treated nonreflexively as factual features of the world. Thus, the environment is reified and treated as ironically detached from human sense making and reasoning, even though human actions are argued to be the "cause" of environmental degradation. The perspective fails to offer to consider the role of sense making and discourse in the formation and change of worldviews, although it seems logically necessary for management and organization theory to address the constitutive features of worldviews if current views of organizations and the natural environment are to be modified so as to more appropriately incorporate concern for ecology. Finally, because ecocentric management embraces a positivist epistemology, the perspective fails to disrupt normal positivist science in organization and management theory and adds a new variable to management and organization theory—Nature. Thus, the ecocentric management perspective clarifies the silences about Nature in the modernist management literature, but it fails to open up space for new theories or postmodern alternatives to positivism.

Endogenous Reflexivity

Endogenous reflexivity (Pollner, 1991) provides a basis for opening up the concepts of environment and ecology. It encourages the analyst to view these concepts as sense-making resources or interpretive schemes (Gephart, 1993) that are created and used in everyday life discourses, textual productions, and social practices, including those of organizational theorists and ecologists. The use of endogenous reflexivity is based on a realist ontology that assumes a "real world" exists, but that this world can only be known to humans through interpretation and sense making. The world is differentially interpreted by social actors based on the differential cultural perspectives or worldviews actors use (Berger & Luckmann, 1966/1967; Gephart, 1984).[1]

Endogenous reflexivity thus relocates and de-reifies the environment, to investigate the social occasions and contexts where the environment and related concepts or phenomena are thematized in members' discourses and textual productions. From an ethnomethodological perspective, "environments exist by virtue of sense making because organizations and environments do not exist independently

of the sense-making practices which produce knowledge of them"
(Gephart, 1984, p. 212).

This view conceives of environments as socially constructed realities
produced in sense making (Gephart, 1984, p. 213). The search for the
true reality of the environment and ecology would thus be abandoned
and replaced with a search for the practices that sustain certain environmental realities or worldviews. Given differences among actors and
groups regarding their interests, motives, and knowledge, different
descriptions of environments will emerge (Molotch & Lester, 1975).
Environmental sense making is thus inherently political (Gephart,
1984, p. 213)—it involves the production of accounts as bases for
action in contexts where competing and divergent accounts exist.
Environmental crises and their resolution can thus be conceived in
terms of situationally enacted discourses and textual accounts wherein
divergent views of environment and social reality are produced and
used to warrant the interests and actions of participants.

Central to the use of endogenous reflexivity is the in situ investigation of the meanings and uses of *environment,* that is, the investigation
of the management of meanings of the environment (Gephart, 1988b)
in contexts where environmental issues arise as a concern. These issues
reflexively become constitutive of the social and organizational production of the environment.

Endogenous reflexivity has been used to investigate the textually
produced and embedded meaning of environmental disasters (Gephart,
1984, 1988a, 1993) and the in situ production and recognition of
expert status during discourse at public hearings concerning toxic
waste (Rifkin, 1994). For example, I used endogenous reflexivity to
demonstrate the importance and implications of sense making and
interpretation in the management of an environmental disaster—the
1968 Santa Barbara oil spill, as described in detail by Sethi (1977).
Different groups developed divergent views of the oil spill and its
impacts (Gephart, 1984, Table 3, pp. 215-216). These views were used
to warrant differential actions by the different groups. Accounts by
industry and government minimized the risks and environmental
impacts from the spill (Gephart, 1984, p. 214). These accounts claimed
there were no effects on the marine ecology and that withdrawal from
the drilling site would increase environmental risks more than would

continued drilling. This claim was challenged by critics who emphasized the pervasive impacts, risks, and long-term damage arising from the oil spill.

The factual claims of both groups can be problematized by endogenous reflexivity. The accounts of government and industry reflexively constitute the spill as a relatively modest event, thereby (re)producing and warranting the rationality of continued drilling and the appropriateness of responses to the spill. Endogenous reflexivity critically examines the constitutive features of these accounts and the alternative views of the spill that emerge in accounts by other actors and groups. The alternative accounts claimed the spill to be 5 to 10 times larger than government and industry assessments and asserted that "a dead sea is being created" (Sethi, 1977; p. 10 in Gephart, 1984). These accounts are reflexive: They warrant and constitute the critical responses made by environmental advocates. The demonstration that divergent accounts emerge thus problematizes each set of accounts, because the accounts produce alternative truths about the environmental disaster. Endogenous reflexivity demonstrates that different realities emerge from these different accounts and interpretations and shows how the accounts of the different groups and actors produce the realities they experience.

Furthermore, I found that critics lack access to control settings where differences in views are resolved; hence, they have difficulty in legitimately espousing their views in settings where the discursive production of these views can enact a dominant worldview or reality to be used as a basis for organizational action. The key question that emerges is "not the determination of the true reality: rather, it is the determination of how realities which routinely produce incidents viewed by others as environmentally disastrous are enacted and maintained" (Gephart, 1984, pp. 222-223). Endogenous reflexivity de-reifies organizations and environments as facts of the world, exposing the sense making and interpretive practices that produce organizations and environments as in situ contingent accomplishments of particular groups and actors. Endogenous reflexivity thus establishes conditions necessary to develop differential constructions of the environment consistent with privileging environmental issues in management research.

Endogenous reflexivity transforms the environment from the factual domain of the natural world into a socially constructed feature of society. It allows one to examine the environment as a first-order or naturally occurring concept of actors (Schutz, 1962) on which to base second-order or social scientific constructs that subsume members' first-order constructs and meanings. That is, it provides for the development of conceptions of the environment based in society and grounded in real human discourse. In particular, the perspective leads one to examine specific contexts where actual discourse and textual production occur and to base theorizing on the real-world data obtained from such contexts, including the meanings and interpretations of actors themselves. In addition, the perspective can be supported by specific methods including conversational analysis (Heritage, 1984) and textual analysis (Gephart, 1993). In general, endogenous reflexivity can be used to demonstrate how members' actions and sense making produce features of the environment as an aspect of the social world, to show the possibility of alternative accounts and interpretations and thus to de-reify interpretations that would otherwise be tacitly treated as factual.

The use of endogenous reflexivity in environmental management research challenges traditional, positivist theories by requiring a realist ontology that is radically different from positivist ontology. The perspective de-reifies Nature and does not allow the tacit acceptance of environmental features as facts immune from social construction. Indeed, the perspective breaches the taken-for-granted positivist view of Nature and thereby problematizes the ready importation of natural science variables into management and organization theory. By problematizing members' claims about the facticity of the natural world, the perspective enhances rather than reduces uncertainty about the important features of the natural environment; the importance of these features is itself socially produced through the interpretive practices and accounts of social members. There is no longer an "objective" point where the analyst can dispassionately observe facts unfolding. Finally, reflexivity challenges the production of a simple set of environmental variables to be manipulated in a cause/effect manner to resolve environmental problems. Indeed, the conception of the environment as constituted by variables is itself problematized. Human meanings are now viewed as constitutive of the environment, not merely artifacts emerging from passive encounters with an objective environment.

Radical Reflexivity
and the Simulacral Environment

Radical reflexivity (Pollner, 1991) seeks to probe and transcend the limits of reflection and endogenous reflexivity to indicate limits of human knowledge in general. It questions basic assumptions underlying all worldviews and even the possibility of worldviews as human means of conceptualizing the world. Here I outline simulation and simulacra (Baudrillard, 1983, 1994) as bases for postmodern radical reflexivity and illustrate their use in the study of scientific and naturalist texts concerning Nature, the environment, and ecology.

Simulacra emerge from simulation, "the generation of models of a real without origin or reality" (Baudrillard, 1983, p. 2). To simulate is to presume one has that which one does not have. Simulation traverses the phases of the image and envelops the entire edifice of representation. In the first phase of the image, representations are reflections of basic reality. Next, reality is masked or perverted in representation. Third, the image comes to mark the absence of any reality. Finally, the image bears no relation to reality (Baudrillard, 1983, p. 11)—it has become fully simulacral, a characteristic of signs in postmodernism. Simulacral simulation and postmodernity thus undermine "the reality principle" (Baudrillard, 1983, p. 43).

Simulation occurs where the model precedes reality. Facts thus have no independent trajectory: They arise only at the intersection of models (Baudrillard, 1983, p. 32). Illusion is not possible because the "real" is no longer possible. Simulation is basic to science, which increasingly uses models to dispense with its object; ultimately models displace their objects entirely (Baudrillard, 1983, p. 14).

The simulacrum is the object emerging through the process of simulation: "it is the truth which conceals that there is none" (*Ecclesiastes*, in Baudrillard, 1983, p. 1). Science is based on simulation because scientific ontology treats as real only that which is reproducible (Baudrillard, 1983, p. 146); hence, real scientific objects are not originals, but only those objects that can and have been reproduced, that is, copies of originals. Reality is thus displaced onto the copy. Science addresses only the copy, the simulated, the displaced, the reproduced: the simulacral.

There are three orders of simulacra. The first order are "natural simulacra" (Baudrillard, 1994, p. 121), counterfeit images founded on reality where a difference with reality is maintained. Second-order simulacra are "products" (Baudrillard, 1983, p. 83): mass-produced copies and reproductions that abandon a relationship of difference to the real. Second-order simulacra absorb appearances and liquidate the real (1983, pp. 94-95). The counterfeit is abandoned for the (re)production (1983, p. 90). Objects or signs no longer relate to castes or traditions but only to technique. Reproduction of the original requires obliteration of this original by the copy that absorbs and displaces it.

Models of simulation are third-order simulacra (Baudrillard, 1983, p. 83): objects entirely within simulation (p. 147). Every connection and contradiction between real and imaginary is effaced, and there is no more imaginary (p. 142). The real becomes the hyperreal: "that which is already reproduced" (p. 146).

The transition from one order to another displays a tendency toward reabsorption of "the gap" between the real and the imaginary, the gap wherein resides ideal or critical projection. In third-order simulacra, projection is implosively reabsorbed (Baudrillard, 1994, p. 122), and there is no longer either fiction or reality (p. 125). Third-order simulacra are the *circulation of the model;* they no longer transcend the real. They displace it, colonize it, and thereby anticipate the real (p. 122). It becomes impossible to "isolate the process of the real, or to prove the real" (Baudrillard, 1983, p. 41).

The concepts of simulation and simulacra can be used to develop a radically reflexive discourse on environment and ecology that disrupts our normal mundane and scientific discourses that conceive Nature as a real natural, universal feature of the world. The concepts of simulation and simulacrum lead us to investigate the origin, maintenance, and reproduction of the natural (Pollner, 1991, p. 377) and to contextualize the scientific observer and ourselves within the framework of simulated environments. Here I offer provisional insights into the use of simulation and simulacra as concepts that can be used to address and reconceptualize Nature and ecology from a radically reflexive perspective. The purpose here is to demonstrate possibilities. More extensive applications of these concepts constitutes part of the future agenda for postmodern environmental studies.

The Ecology Literature

Science and scientific literature transform Nature into the ecosystem—an interaction system between living things and the nonliving habitat (Evans, 1969, p. 56). The ecosystem concept embraces the structure and functioning of ecosystems (Odum, 1963, 1969) and uses a systems focus (Van Dyne, 1969) to address parameters controlling ecosystem cycles and dynamics. The ecosystem is thus a concept for viewing certain features of the world, and ecology is the branch of science that uses the concept of ecosystems (Buchholz, 1993; Cox, 1969; Howell, 1994; Odum, 1963, 1969) as a way of viewing the natural world. The ecosystem concept is a first-order or counterfeit image of Nature—an imperfect representation. The concept as representation differs from the actual living beings and habitats; hence, the ecosystem is a first-level simulacrum: an image founded on reality (Nature) where a difference with reality is maintained (Van Dyne, 1969). In particular, this natural simulacrum emerges precisely as a sign intended to represent Nature (Baudrillard, 1983, pp. 87-88).

The ecosystems concept represents Nature as an aggregation of systems constituted by systems dynamics that can be represented mathematically, statistically, and diagrammatically. Similarly, conceptual models of the organizational environment in organization theory—for example, as a set of sectors (Daft, 1995)—are first-order images and simulacra, that is, partial representations or imitations of the environment.

Models of the ecosystem compose a second-level image, for example, models of the transfer of energy across subsystems. Thus models of ecosystems simplify reality and mask or pervert it; they include only a limited number of possible features. That is, there is a tendency for ecosystem models to become reified as constituting "true descriptions" of the natural world, and in such instances, the scientific models and representations of Nature become constitutive of the ecosystem.

Scientific models of the ecosystem produced through scientific and mathematical reasoning are thus second-order scientific simulacra because the ecosystem as a detectable scientific phenomenon depends on techniques of scientific activity and observation as bases for its existence. This is illustrated conceptually by the definition of ecosystems. An ecosystem can be detected where Nature exhibits "recognizable unity both in function and structure" (Odum, 1963, p. 11). The ecosystem as such is thus visible only through evidence of this "recognizable unity," and this unity itself is only visible through scientific techniques and concepts. For example, comparing a pond with a simple terrestrial ecosystem reveals otherwise unknown relations between structure and function in ecosystems (Odum, 1963, p. 15). This comparison requires scientific "tools," such as scales used to measure biomass and insect respirometers (see photo of tools, Odum, 1963, p. 16). Therefore, the ecosystem features or recognizable unities in the real environment—now reconconstituted scientifically as the ecosystem—are visible features of the ecology only when and if scientific tools can be used to detect (socially construct and produce) these. Ecological facts and ecosystems themselves thus require scientific models to produce them. Scientific models refer to, are based on, and constitute reproducible phenomena. There is no longer any real Nature; rather, ecosystems displace and substitute for Nature. Similarly, in organizational analysis in general, there is the tendency of models or representations of the environment to become bases for organizing research into features of environments and also as bases for managerial actions. These representations pervert or distort environments by simplification, demarcating specific sectors, which thereby substitutes a false image—the model—for some real or more direct representation of the environment.

The third- and fourth-level of images mark the absence of reality. The simulacrum comes to bear no resemblance to reality, that is, it becomes a true simulacrum, one based in models of simulation. The emergence of true or third-order environmental simulacra is a topic for future research as it is an emerging feature of postmodernism. Hence, the points are provisional and are intended to suggest possible future lines of inquiry.

The reification of models occurs in science where the natural processes themselves are displaced by mathematical and other models of these processes. It is presumed that natural or ecological processes are composed in terms of mathematically representable phenomena;

hence, mathematics is the *language of Nature*. For example, in early discussions of ecology, it was assumed that Nature consists of "deterministic and stochastic phenomena" (Van Dyne, 1969, p. 40). These mathematical and statistical processes are represented scientifically as hypotheses and variables that become the objects of scientific inquiry. Indeed, reality is exhibited by the relationship of "observations" to the model rather than by the observations per se. Thus the ecologist

> will often have to guess at the fundamental cause-and-effect relationships in his system and may even have to guess about the basic variables. He will then test these hypotheses by comparing the quantitative and qualitative behavior of the real world with that predicted from his model. (Van Dyne, 1969, p. 41)

Indeed, when measurement of parameters of the system "is impossible without disruption of the system, perturbation of the system followed by measurements may still give new insight for the definition of a model" (Van Dyne, 1969, p. 41).

Thus, the reality of ecology is preconstituted by science and mathematics such that scientific reality exists only in theorizing and experimentation—reproducible knowledge—and this reality is endogenous to science and is not equivalent to the real world external to science. The model displaces Nature as the object of scientific inquiry, as the point where inquiry begins, and as the culmination or goal of inquiry. The ecosystem, as a model of the natural world, thus becomes simulacral.

Science-Based Naturalist Literature

The simulacralization of science as a basis for interpreting Nature is a common theme in science-based naturalist writing, a genre of natural science writing that provides detailed, in situ descriptions of species and their habitats and that seeks to interpret the descriptions in terms of scientific concepts and theories. This genre evidences the displacement of Nature by scientific theories. For example, white-throated swifts are a bird species that has been observed to copulate in the air. The basis of their copulatory behavior is explained as constituted by scientifically theorized processes (Alcock, 1985) of evolution, in particular, the theory-based tendency of male swifts to maximize their individual reproductive gain and hence promote their individual reproductive success (Alcock, 1985, p. 26). Evolutionary theory thus provides a simulated basis for explaining these facts, and this theory can be used to develop "a biological philosophy that can inform and guide an analysis of all living things" (p. 26).

This genre includes a critical perspective that addresses how the models of science can become reified and then the models drive analysis. For example, scientific models of wildlife biology and ecosystems have been used to determine the natural features of Yellowstone Park and to warrant interventions in the current biological state of the park intended to "restore" it to a more natural state. Because this natural state can only be known scientifically, the restored Nature is simulacral of true Nature, which has long since been displaced both by change in the natural world and by the scientific model that now drives conceptions of Nature (Chase, 1987). Yellowstone Park thus simulates an original Nature that no longer exists.

NATURALIST LITERATURE

Naturalist literature can be distinguished from scientific writing and from science-based Nature writing. Naturalist literature in general seeks to describe and interpret features of Nature without necessarily invoking scientific concepts and processes to explain the observed features of Nature. Essentially, this genre of naturalist writing uses the author's voice to represent the perspectives and worldviews of natural species and land forms. Here I use naturalist writing by Joseph Wood Krutch (1951) to illustrate the genre. Krutch, regarded as one of the premier modernist U.S. naturalist writers, addressed the desert in his writing. He said he lived in the desert to "listen to" (p. 11) the voices (p. 5) of Nature. After 12 years of living in the desert, he found that "I do not yet know what it is that this land, together with the plants and animals who found its strangeness normal, has been trying to say to me" (p. 9).

Krutch (1951) conceives metaphorically that the wildlife speak to him: "It is well, I think, that the road runner should greet me at the beginning" (p. 15), as does the desert itself: "Love me or hate me the

desert seems to say" (p. 20). Krutch discusses the reflective limits of
our species, which is likely to forget that "there are other creatures in
the world" besides us (p. 39). Nature is simulacral in these accounts or
texts because the voices of Nature in naturalist texts are human representations of Nature: Nature does not speak in human words and
voices. These voices are human simulations of Nature that produce
Nature as "the other" to society.

The transformation of natural into simulacral phenomena is also
addressed in naturalist texts. For example, Krutch (1951) rescued a
number of spadefoot toad tadpoles from a vanishing puddle of water,
in order to study them (pp. 101-119). The natural subjects became
artificial by this process, living in an artificial habitat and becoming
unnaturally large because of plentiful food and water. It is only in this
unnatural habitat that the natural aspects of the toad can be observed,
for in Nature, the toad is unobserved, difficult to find, and not well
understood at all.

Krutch (1951) is reflexively self-aware of the limits of scientific
knowledge and criticizes scientific descriptions of the desert, which
although "detected so fragmentarily" are privileged over the realities
of direct experience: "Why should one of these worlds be called realer
than the other; why, especially, should the one of which I can have the
least experience [science] be called the realest?" (p. 130). Krutch
(1951) argues for a pluralistic view of realities because every attempt
to escape pluralism "ends in the denial that one or the other reality is
real" (p. 131).

Nature as examined by Krutch and other naturalists is simulacral.
First, the writing itself implies that the surfaced voices are simulations
or simulacra of the first order: These are counterfeit representations
or copies of Nature that retain their difference with Nature. The
naturalist produces the textual descriptions of the features and voices
of Nature, and these textual descriptions are imperfect replicas of
Nature. Second, Nature is transformed, through this textualization,
from a reality out there into textualized descriptions and graphic
representations (e.g., drawings) that can be mass-produced and copied. Nature now resides in the second-order simulacrum, the mass-
produced and copied textual reproduction of Nature. Furthermore,
Krutch (1951) explicitly notes how this Nature is simulacrized, particularly when investigated scientifically, by transforming its objects into

unreal copies or replicas. For example, he notes that science studies "thanatology" and not biology because it begins "not with the observation of some living creature . . . but with the dissection of a preserved" specimen (p. 109). These dead, formaldehyde-saturated specimens used in biology education are mass "produced" on a large scale with an image of sameness. Nature becomes simulacral at the third order in science when the study of living frogs in Nature metamorphoses into its inverse, the study of dead frogs in laboratories (Krutch, 1951, p. 106). That is, the dead frog that the introductory biology student dissects is simulative of the living frog and displaces it because it is the biology of the dead frog that science observes and recovers. We know little about the living frog or the spadefoot toad. What does he or she eat? How long does she remain buried in sand? "On these questions, the books cover their silence with an air of not having the space to go for these sort of things" (Krutch, p. 104).

Discussion

This chapter has addressed three genres of modernist representations of the natural world—science writing, science-based naturalist writing, and naturalist literature. I have discussed how reflection and reflexivity can be used to address the meaning and ontological status of Nature, environment, and ecology in these literatures. In particular, I have discussed how one can use the concepts of simulations and simulacra to develop a more fully postmodern view of organizational environments. Conceiving of Nature and ecology as simulacra allows us to reconnoiter new terrain (Pollner, 1991) beyond the reality of traditional conceptions of the organizational environment. Here, the new terrain refers to the natural world conceived as orders and processions of ecological simulacra. By examining these as simulation, we are forced to call into question fundamental assumptions about the reality of Nature, ecology, and the natural environment and to examine how these assumptions shape the practices that produce Nature, ecology, and environments as humanly accessible features of reality relevant to organizational analysis.

Given that the "entire world" now bears the human "stamp" (Buchholz, 1993, p. 20), one might argue that there is no real Nature remaining in terms of phenomena not affected by human activities. Rather, the natural environment as we now conceive of it is simulacral (Baudrillard, 1983): a representation of a true natural environment that has somehow escaped us, a vision of a reality that vanished as we developed the temerity to examine it closely. Thus, our knowledge and representations of the natural environment—both scientific and literary— are composed in terms of simulations: representations of pure, hypothetical phenomena for which no original exists.

Summary and Conclusions

Management and organization theory have given extensive consideration to the built environment of organizations. Recent attempts to incorporate the natural environment or ecology into organization theory rely on positivist conceptions of science, employ systems theory, and hence use scientific reflection to detect and import natural science variables into variable analytic models of management and organization theory. Thus, scientific reflection on the environment explores the unaddressed or mistakenly interpreted features of the natural world, which itself is taken for granted as a nonreflexive fact. Reflection uncovers the lacunae within generally accepted frameworks and the points at which they require elaboration. However, reflection does not allow theorizing or analysis to transcend itself, and reflexivity is required for such transcendence.

Endogenous reflexivity begins with the limits of reflection and focuses on the social construction of scientific facts (Knorr-Cetina, 1981). It de-reifies the environment by providing insights into the environmental selections and choices that actors make in constituting features of an inherently social world. It reveals differential constructions and how the situational production of knowledge of the environment in turn produces the environment as a feature of social settings.

Radical reflexivity seeks to transcend the limits of reflection and endogenous reflexivity by addressing the very limits of human knowledge. That is, where endogenous reflexivity indicates possibilities for alternative environments, radical reflexivity seeks to demonstrate the limits to conceiving of a world composed of environments, that is, alternatives *to* environments. It questions the basic assumptions underlying both scientific and literary worldviews of environments, and even the possibility and implications of science and literature as ways of conceiving of worlds. Simulation and simulacra were thus offered as concepts that could help reformulate or reconceptualize the environment in radically reflexive terms, as a basis for a truly postmodern management perspective on Nature and ecology. From this view, Nature, environment, and ecology are radically de-reified, then reconceived as images or copies of Nature that displace Nature itself. Behind the simulacrum, nothing remains.

There are several implications of this view. First, by viewing Nature and ecology as simulacral social constructions, one becomes aware of the opportunity to construct and reconstruct a much greater variety of images of Nature than would be the case were Nature constituted of facts independent of humans. That is, reflexivity provides the awareness that humans have significant latitude in creating "the facts of Nature"—and hence greater responsibility for Nature and its desecration—than if Nature were in fact natural, that is, independent of humans. Second, the postmodern view incorporates reflection and positivist science as phenomena to be analyzed, rather than as tacit theoretical resources or variables to be added to management theory. Nature and ecology thus become endogenous to management theory and are subject to analysis from a postmodern perspective. In contrast, a positivist view treats Nature as a set of factual resources to be used, not explained, in management thought. Third, the chapter argues that although the science of ecology is one useful basis for launching a field of studies on organizations and the natural environment, it is an imperfect or incomplete basis, which must be supplemented by cultural studies of Nature. Furthermore, insofar as ecology is the theory of the system of systems, a postmodern theory of environments could become the social organizational theory of the limits of systems and theories.

To summarize, scientific and literary reflection on the environment seek to explore more fully the terrain or domain of Nature, which is bounded by existing knowledge, that is, to explore the unknown and make it known. Endogenous reflexivity seeks to problematize the limits of this knowledge of Nature or ecology and seeks new or alternative maps of the terrain, that is, to understand the boundaries of the known. Postmodern radical reflexivity seeks to transcend the terrain, to explore the unknown and to establish its limits—the spaces where the unknowable begins.

In conclusion, Baudrillard (1986) provides glimpses of a more fully postmodern or radically reflexive depiction of this terrain of natural environments. He explicitly uses the concepts of simulation and simulacra to explore human encounters with Nature and to locate this experience as simulacral. His analysis allows us to glimpse the limits of human signs and to develop an awareness of transcendent nonhuman signs that lie beyond: "an awareness of signs originating, long before man appeared. . . . Among this gigantic heap of signs—purely geological in essence—man will have had no significance" (p. xx). Behind human signs, there are only natural signs that themselves represent the nothingness beyond. The desert of natural signs thus becomes the critique of culture (Baudrillard, 1986, p. 5). Perhaps then, radical environmental reflexivity teaches us one simple lesson. As a species, we must learn to live in the desert and to develop organizations that thrive in a habitat of cataclysmic signs.

Note

1. This contrasts with positivist, objectivist ontologies, which assume a factual world where differential interpretations arise because of "flawed" interpretations and reasoning practices.

PART IV

Postmodern Pedagogy

11

Pedagogy for the
Postmodern Management Classroom
Greenback Company

GRACE ANN ROSILE

DAVID M. BOJE

> Caution: Discretion is advised. The following material may not
> be suitable for untenured or junior faculty. Do not try these
> pedagogies at home.

Teaching postmodern management and organization theory (PMOT)
can change your life. The personal experiences of the two authors,
Grace Ann and David, include academic acclaim along with reviling
reviews, Teacher of the Year awards as well as institutional reprimands,
collegial friendships and some alienation, incredible intellectual excitement and enthusiasm accompanied by some charges of fanaticism—all
in the same academic year, with David's proposal of marriage to Grace
Ann thrown in for good measure. It appears that teaching PMOT
somehow infuses one's life with the dynamism, chaos, and uncertainty
that characterizes the PMOT field itself.

The field of management and organization theory is awash with the
rhetoric of change, as demonstrated by the other chapters in this
volume. To keep pace with these changes, this chapter suggests the

need for critically questioning our classroom management approaches and pedagogical methods. Vance (1993) observes that "schools will face major problems if they believe they can continue effectively to pour these new potent wines of change into old curricular bottles of instructional content" (p. xi). Management education must abandon its primary role as panopticon (Boje, in press-a; Fineman & Gabriel, 1993; Fox, 1989) to mitigate the innovation-resisting academic "tyranny of the disciplines" (Aronowitz & Giroux, 1991, p. 149). Without attention to such issues, postmodern pedagogy risks being little more than "metatheoretical gesticulations" (Rogers, 1992, p. 231). As Bradford (1993) notes,

> We need to make sure that we don't send the wrong metamessage. If organization members of the future (present?) need to take initiative and ownership for their own work, are we doing them a service by the tight control (and ensuing passivity) that we demand in most of our classrooms? (p. x)

This chapter will describe premodern and modern pedagogy, demonstrating how each created totalizing combinations of power and knowledge to establish "regimes of truth" (Foucault, 1980b). Next are some postmodern challenges to the "stultifying bureaucratic nature" of modernist pedagogies (Best & Kellner, 1991, p. 23). A pedagogy reflective of postmodern concerns is characterized as self-reflexive, decentered, deconstructionist, and nontotalizing. Finally, the authors describe their strategy for incorporating these characteristics of postmodern pedagogies into their teaching of postmodern management by using the Greenback Company classroom-based organization. The discussion concludes with guidelines for putting postmodern pedagogy into your classrooms.

A premise of this chapter is that rather than there being some paradigm shift from premodern to modern to postmodern, all three discourses are alive and engaged in a struggle in the business school classroom. The following section draws on previous reviews by Boje (1992b, 1994a, 1994b, 1995, in press-a, in press-b) and Rosile (1995). For a summarized comparison of the three discourses, see Table 11.1.

PREMODERN EDUCATION

Premodern organization is a mythic and nomadic journey, defending preindustrial artisan craftsmanship, spirituality, family, and a strong sense of community over economic rationality. Pope Pius XI, for example, continued to resist the discourse of commodified labor and laissez-faire capitalism, and other economic activity "directed by the arbitrary will of owners without regard for the training and dignity of the workers" (Clune, 1943, pp. 254-255). In feudal Japan, Western-style capitalism was initially considered too threatening to premodern ethical heritages: Modern ideas could lure people away from old customs and make people egotistical (Hirschmeier & Yui, 1975, p. 201). Premodern Western discourse did not differentiate people from their social or religious roles: spouse, soldier, and so forth (Thatchenkery, 1992, p. 225). Premodern forms of organization include the military, the church, the university, guilds, and the crown. Each form has been imposed over university education. For example, in monastic education, there is the monastery (where the voice of religion speaks about idle time, the path to enlightenment through discipline, the solitude of cellular life, the sanctity of work, and a God who sees into your very soul, let alone your study). Foucault (1979) gives an account of early university education to reveal how the mass production model of education was slowly implemented across several centuries by borrowing from these varied forms of organization. The faculty that championed Aristotle and Copernicus in the face of the Inquisition, said no to Henry VIII's divorce, and demanded that the pope respect the freedom of its liberal arts inquiry has become too timid and too immobile—and far too financially dependent on sovereigns, princes, parliaments, trustees, and accrediting agencies—to threaten the powerful with mass migrations and lecture cessations. There have been spurts of lecture cessations, such as the McCarthy inquisitions, which saw scores of professors dismissed or denied tenure without much resistance (Boje, in press-a). In the Vietnam years, a tactical naiveté characterized the resistance movement. In the ancient university, the students' rhythmic march was into apprenticeship, able to become masters of their own small business, apprenticing others along their

TABLE 11.1 Comparison of Premodern, Modern, and Postmodern Pedagogies

	Premodern	Modern	Postmodern
Location of the learning	Sites; apprenticeship at the job site	Sequestering in classrooms	Series of locations; boundary crossing with internships, community-based learning sites, and simulations
Role of the instructor	Royalty; master craftsman	Robot; impersonal conduit of expert knowledge; role diminishing as computer-based instruction with concept/ example matching and video instruction replaces in-the-room instructor	Radical; expert at deconstruction; uses teaching materials that present many sides of a given story (including dominant and marginal sides)
Teaching in society	Roots; in the premodern discourse, stories dispatch, delegate, and monitor the customs and traditions of sovereignty and eldership	Rationale; business sets the curriculum and agenda of topics; stories dispatch and monitor the cult of efficiency and legitimate functional interpretations	Renewal; involves stories; dispatch, delegate, and monitor a diversity of voices: that is, the environment, communities
Methods of classroom control	Initiation; habits of discussion that included masters, craftspeople, and apprentices, control based on expert knowledge	Indoctrination; instructor dominates; reinforces privilege and hierarchy; instrumentation; goal displacement values control over learning	Inspiration; give up control and trust the process; postmodernization of returning students to the world; habits of discussion that include a great diversity of voices

Goals/values	Ideals; promote ideals of excellence and personal mastery; age stratification and respect for elder learning are stressed	Imitation; preserve the impersonal machine bureaucracy and "the system"; hierarchical stratification and respect for expert learning are stressed	Inquiry; question the dominant paradigm; overcome dichotomy of teacher/learner; wide inquiry networks of inclusion and respect for local learning are stressed
Evaluation of students	Personalized assessment by the master, elder, or guild	Standardized; multiple choice test banks created for the instructor	Negotiated format involving student, instructor, and other stakeholders
Evaluation of instructors	Acclaim; de facto acclaim by followership	Acceptance; rank and tenure; use of students as gazers with course evaluation instruments	Appeal to a local interest group; popularity
Questions	How many angels can dance on the head of a pin?	What is the optimum span of control?	Can any form of organized action be nonexploitive?

journey. In the old university, the examination was more visible, more of a joust among pupils pitched against each other in verbal combat, while the master controlled the battle. The Ph.D. oral examination remains the most direct and ritualized carryover from the Spanish Inquisition: a spectacular display of power potency, a manifest gaze of the sovereign, an inversion of visibility. As masters began to command more capital and to invest in more expensive tools and larger enterprises, it became increasingly difficult for craftsmen to become master entrepreneurs who became owners and could then teach their own apprentices. Guild membership also began to be passed by inheritance, instead of apprenticeship. It is ironic that management education is the puppet of big business, when most new jobs in many countries are coming from joining or starting a much smaller company.

MODERN EDUCATION

Modernist discourse sought to tame premodern pagan and mythical passion, contain the feudal corruption of absolute monarchy, and counteract the autocracy of the clergy. "Modernism is described as having elevated a faith in reason to a level at which it becomes equated with progress" (Parker, 1992, p. 3). Apprenticeship pedagogy did not fit with mass production, semesters or quarters, AACSB evaluation studies, and the needs of the curriculum committee. The management discipline, taken to include the university, the AACSB, the academy, and the business institution, constitutes a panoptic machine where probationary tenure functions as a period of disciplined obedience to the rules; where surveillance is everywhere; where academic freedom, transformed from the Middle Ages, now means intellectual subordination to the more or less plural professorial paradigms (Boje, 1992b, 1995). It is only very recently that the institution of the university has become organized upon much the same lines as mass production methods. Our curriculum materials and practices are prepackaged, and the pedagogical performance is thoroughly prescribed and Taylorized in ways that remove choice and deskill our face-to-face dialogue. The disciplinary time of a military organization has been imposed on pedagogy.

In our management education, everything is regulated by the clock. Time is broken down into 16-week intervals. Each discipline breaks its subject down into simple elements that can be arranged into interval steps to develop more difficult elements across the 16 weeks. The disciplinary space of a military organization has been imposed upon management pedagogy. Our students are spatially distributed and regimented into class programs as they sit in rows and columns during 50-minute time intervals. In each classroom cell, repetitive exercises are performed as the student body moves rhythmically in time and cellular-spatial segmentation. "Count off by seven; each group take their assigned space; we will begin with the spokesperson for group one." This is the ascetic life of management education.

POSTMODERN CRITIQUES OF MODERN EDUCATION

Modernist education itself has been a stimulus and a focal point for postmodern critique. The French university students' revolts of 1968 were key in shaping postmodern theory.

> The student revolts politicized the nature of education in the university system and criticized the production of knowledge as a means of power and domination. They attacked the university system for its stultifying bureaucratic nature, its enforced conformity, and its specialized and compartmentalized knowledges that were irrelevant to real existence. (Best & Kellner, 1991, p. 23)

Foucault (1980b) then began to focus on the link between power and knowledge, on how power determined and constituted knowledge. Fox (1989) characterizes Foucault's contribution as demonstrating "how the mutually reinforcing knowledge of the church and power of the monarchy [were] superseded by the mutually reinforcing knowledge of the techno-sciences." The power-knowledge connection is such that "disciplinary power is everywhere about us, hidden, obscured, taken for granted, built into the categories . . . which the disciplines have codified and taught us . . . to legitimately define our situation in terms of their expert discourses" (p. 726).

The expert discourses of typical modernist management education seek to ask and answer questions such as "What is the optimum span of control?" Such questions are now seeming as irrelevant as how many angels can dance on the head of a pin. Both of these questions make the positivist assumption that a discoverable best answer exists and that the job of the educational system is to transmit those empirically derived best answers. What is unquestioned, in the case of the angels, is the premise of a God who is the source of divine order in the universe. But as the postmodern philosophers have shown, the "regime" of truth based on logic and rationality is just as totalizing, terrorizing, and exploitative as the church-and-monarchy, knowledge-power configuration of premodern times. The relevant question for postmodernists might be "Can any form of organized action be nonexploitative?" The question for management education is "Can any best answer approach to knowledge be nonexploitative?" Power and knowledge combine to create answers in the form of dominant discourses. Some truths are privileged over others. Instead, postmodernist education favors a play of differences, seeing many truths and valuing paralogy, while hoping to avoid the dominance of singular and even taxonomic discourses.

Foucault (1979) has thoroughly excavated the disciplinary features of social organizations, work organizations, and even of the social sciences in *Discipline and Punish*. O'Neill (1986) demonstrates how these disciplinary aspects are rooted in the Weberian model of the rational legal bureaucracy. Management education mirrors the Weberian bureaucracy's disciplinary structure in both senses of the word discipline, as a field of study and as a means of control. As Fox (1989) explains,

> Management education has demonstrated . . . the panoptic hierarchical observation of inmates (students and junior faculty by senior faculty), normalizing judgment (the opinion of editorial boards over "proper" academic work and writings . . .) and, finally, the examination. (p. 729)

Extending Fox's argument, it seems that management classrooms further mirror these panoptic principles, creating what Boje (in press-a) calls the "nightmarish Weberian iron cage of pseudo-rationality" (p. 1). Although the panoptic features of management education serve to control the academic bureaucracy, they also serve to socialize and prepare students for the panoptic cage of work life. However, these disciplinary mechanisms have grown ever more subtle and internalized, spilling over corporate and ivy-covered walls into so-called "private" lives. The "internalized gaze" is overshadowing the panoptic tower. One example of this is Grey's (1994) study of the concept of "career." From this perspective, the self becomes objectified in a project of self-discipline guided by the concept of career. Proper attitude and enthusiasm are identified as key factors in achieving career success. Going beyond work life, social contacts (networking) and even marriage are assessed for their career-enhancing potential. Some people may view disciplinary measures (such as a reprimand) as helping them to develop the proper attitude and therefore aiding their careers.

The point of comparing the premodern, modern, and postmodern is not to judge these dynamics as good or bad but to indicate the subtle, complex, and pervasive nature of these various forms of discourse. The panoptic discipline of management education, professional organizations, and work organizations all contribute to the internalized control of the career concept. How great is the influence of management education in such processes? The extent of management education's influence is reflected in the more than 10-fold explosion of MBA degrees awarded in the United States alone, rising from 5,306 in 1962 to 67,137 in 1986 (Fox, 1989, p. 728). Given both the depth and breadth of the panoptic effects of modernist management education, Fox concludes that "across all institutions (formal and informal) of management learning, not only are these panoptic features to be found, but . . . they are on the whole unresearched" (p. 729).

Who is steering this great ship of management education, and where does academic freedom fit into this picture? From a postmodernist perspective, instructors as well as students are structured and otherwise controlled by the disciplinary discourse of management theory, of the university, and of business and capitalism. Derrida (1985) discusses Nietzsche's "On the Future of Our Educational Institutions" and elaborates on Nietzsche's image of the student as the "ear." As a student, note taking "links you, like a leash in the form of an umbilical cord, to the paternal belly of the State. Your pen is its pen . . . like one of those Bic ballpoints attached by a little chain in the post office" (p. 36). The speaker or teacher is little more than a mouth that transmits what the ear transcribes. Furthermore,

> The person emitting the discourse . . . does not himself produce it; he barely emits it. He reads it. Just as you are the ears that transcribe, the master is the mouth that reads, so what you transcribe is, in sum, what he deciphers of a text that precedes him. (p. 36)

From that text, he is suspended by a similar "umbilical cord" (p. 36).

Instructors are dead; they do not speak for themselves, they speak the discourse of management education, which is the discourse of conservative capitalism (Boje, 1994a). Instructors do not originate pedagogical action. Neither instructors nor students have a voice. The college classroom is a modernist machine.

Fortunately, postmodern critique is ideally suited to dismantling modernist machines. More difficult is the creation of a postmodern alternative. Below we provide some characteristics of postmodern pedagogies, along with guidelines for inventing your own. Next, we present the Greenback Company class-based organization as one approach we have used to teach management from a postmodern perspective. Finally, we conclude with cautions and encouragements for creating your own postmodern pedagogies.

Creating Postmodern Pedagogy

Who Are the Characters in
Our Story of the Postmodern Classroom?

With "dead" teachers and students, for whom is this pedagogy being created? Some recommend revitalizing the modernist subject or, alternatively, creating a "postmodern individual." This is a delicate task. Our challenge is to accomplish this "within an anti-humanist philosophy and without resurrecting the object, the alienating shadow that so burdens the modern subject" (Rosenau, 1992, p. 53).

Rosenau (1992) suggests that the decentered, postmodern individual has a multiplicity of fragmented identities with no distinct reference points, dispersed not concentrated, unrehearsed, not organized. He or she focuses on choice, autonomy, and personal liberation and does not need ideological consistency (p. 54).

> The postmodern individual is relaxed and flexible, oriented toward feelings and emotions, interiorization, and holding a "be-yourself" attitude . . . content with a "live and let live" (in the present) attitude . . . shying away from collective affiliation and personal development as a threat to privacy. . . . Modern community is . . . oppressive, it demands

intimacy, giving, self-sacrifice, and mutual service . . . domineering and humiliating. (pp. 53-54)

Our educational systems are so rooted in modernist assumptions about modernist subjects that "to question the most basic principles of modernity redefines the meaning of schooling" (Aronowitz & Giroux, 1991, p. 58). Although we have no pretensions of redefining schooling, it seems that constructing the educational process as a "learning community" would better suit postmodern individuals. However, postmodern community is a community without unity (Corlett, 1989, pp. 6-7). Thus, creating a postmodern learning community for postmodern individuals requires abandoning practices that reinforce hierarchy in favor of strategies that diffuse and decenter power.

How Do We Design a Pedagogy for Postmodern Individuals?

It is our challenge to (re)construct our images of instructor/student and teaching/learning in ways that overcome past dichotomies that privilege the teacher over the learner. The following list of five features of postmodernism provides a starting point for shaping a postmodern pedagogy for management and organization studies. This list is culled primarily from the bodies of work of Derrida, Foucault, and Lyotard, as well as from the excellent interpretations of postmodernism provided by Aronowitz and Giroux (1991), Best and Kellner (1991), Boje and Dennehy (1994), Hollinger (1994), and Rosenau (1992), among others. Readers are referred to these other works, as well as to the other chapters in this volume, for discussions of postmodernism. The list below is not exhaustive and the items are not mutually exclusive.

Five Features of Postmodern Pedagogy

1. Self-reflexive
2. Decentered
3. Deconstructionist
4. Nontotalitarian, nonuniversalist
5. Be postmodern and add your own

1. *Self-reflexive.* Hollinger (1994) describes postmodernism as "the rigorously self-reflexive clinical examination of modernity," which may incorporate a "radicalization" of many elements of modernity, but is "without nostalgia or regret for lost realist ideals of objectivity and truth" (p. 177) and "without utopian aspirations for what we create under conditions of postmodernity" (p. 170). This characteristic suggests that every element of pedagogy be subject to review, especially with regard to power-knowledge interactions (Fox, 1989). An excellent example of pedagogical self-reflexivity is Gilson's (1994) article. He examines critically the hoped for or espoused goal of fostering students' independent thinking and active learning, while simultaneously subjecting them to the hierarchical control and punishment of instructor-centered schemes to grade participation. This critique also is an excellent example of deconstruction. Without using postmodern terminology, Gilson reads between the lines, reinterprets, and tells another side of the story of grading classroom participation. (A more extensive discussion of deconstruction appears below.)

2. *Decentered.* Developing a postmodern learning community as a networked web requires eroding the power-knowledge hierarchy of traditional classrooms. Such hierarchies are challenged by the postmodern strategy of decentering. A more decentered model of the relationship between management students and their instructors may be patterned after Calton and Kurland's (1995) postmodern view of corporate stakeholder relationships. Viewing students as stakeholders has several advantages. First, it facilitates a shift from the model of teacher/expert as manager/agent who controls one-to-one interactions in a series of bilateral contractual relationships and moves more toward a model of creating a community of voices involving a web of mutually satisfactory contracts defining the learning community. Also, each participant must enter into a relationship with each other participant (not just with the expert/instructor), so the comments of those other than the expert become important. Finally, in addition to being decentered, such relationships and dialogues model the forms we are attempting to create in postmodern organizational settings between managers and stakeholders.

Attempts at decentering are not always effective. Spivak (1981) placed her students in a nonhierarchical circle during their first class period. At their second meeting, she found students had left vacant for her the same seat she had occupied in the previous meeting, imposing upon themselves the hierarchy she had explicitly attempted to remove. In proper postmodernist fashion, she initiated a self-reflexive discussion of the seating issue and succeeded in removing at least that one self-imposed barrier to decentering. Aronowitz and Giroux (1991) cite the persistent marginalization of the working class to contextualize our perspective on decentering. They observe that "the postmodern does not consist chiefly in decentering practices; these were already present in modernism" (p. 160).

One of Grace Ann Rosile's most successful experiences has been with the decentering strategy of sharing information and abandoning the privilege of "instructor manual" sorts of information. Before conducting the prisoners' dilemma-style, Win-As-Much-As-You-Can game, Grace Ann discusses previous research on "tit for tat" strategies and describes the full range of results of the game when played by "uninformed" subjects. Students are then given the choice to play or not. They always play, with similar results and postactivity processing discussions as obtained traditionally. However, there are almost no complaints about not understanding the rules, and there appears to be greater enthusiasm for the game.

3. *Deconstructionist.* Deconstruction is the dismantling or undoing of constructions. It "tears a text apart, reveals its contradictions and assumptions" (Rosenau, 1992, p. xi). Rosenau (1992, p. xiv) further notes that for postmodernists, everything is text. In Table 11.2, Boje and Dennehy (1994) provide a useful summary of seven deconstruction methods applicable to storytelling.

Mills and Simmons (1995) deconstruct an excerpt from Schein's (1985) book, *Organizational Culture and Leadership.* Schein describes some advantages of his consulting-based research activity, where the groups under study are clients. Mills and Simmons (1995) "read between the lines" and suggest that the word *clients* in effect refers to managers only, whereas the groups "will almost certainly be employees" (p. 19). One could further deconstruct Mills and Simmons's deconstruction by pointing out the management-employee duality or dichotomy they have just created.

4. *Nontotalizing, nonuniversalizing, nonessentializing.* Totalisms, universalism, and essentialisms all are aspects of the unitary "grand narrative" (Lyotard, 1979/1984) that distorts, suppresses, or ignores "local"

TABLE 11.2 Story Deconstruction Method

1. **Duality search** Make a list of any bipolar terms, any dichotomies that are used in the story. Include the term even if only one side is mentioned.

2. **Reinterpret** A story is one interpretation of an event from one point of view. Write out an alternative interpretation using the same story particulars.

3. **Rebel voices** Deny the authority of the one voice. What voices are not being expressed in this story? Which voices are subordinate or hierarchical to other voices?

4. **Other side of the story** Stories always have two sides. What is the side of the nonrepresented (usually a marginalized, underrepresented, or even silent) story character?

5. **Deny the plot** Stories have plots, scripts, scenarios, recipes, and morals. Turn these around.

6. **Find the exception** What is the exception that breaks the rule, that does not fit the recipe, that escapes the strictures of the principle? State the rule in a way that makes it seem extreme or absurd.

7. **State what is between the lines** What is not said? What is the writing on the wall? Fill in the blanks. Storytellers frequently use "you know that part of the story." What are you filling in? With what alternate way could you fill it in?

Source: Boje and Dennehy, 1994, Appendix A. *Managing in the postmodern world: America's revolution against exploitation.* Reprinted by permission of Kendall/Hunt Publishing Company.

differences, diverse perspectives, and alternative interpretations. Psychological instruments or any methods that categorize people or things may stereotype and essentialize. Postmodernists view such labeling as exploitative, giving power to those who administer the instruments or choose the theoretical frameworks.

It may not be possible or desirable to discard all theoretical constructs for categorizing and understanding human behavior. It is certainly not easy. Grace Ann Rosile stopped using one popular personality instrument in her classes. She discovered she could present the theory behind the typologies, let students self-select into homogeneous groups, and proceed as before, feeling very noble for avoiding those exploitative instruments and saving some paper. Then Robert Gephart pointed out that although the instrument was gone, the problematic categories still survived. Grace Ann's conclusion is that becoming postmodern is a continual consciousness-raising process.

Another laudable approach to counteracting the pernicious "isms" listed above is reported by Andre (1992). Attempting to teach students a healthy skepticism for "psychobabble," she gave students falsified psychological profiles. After students had a chance to discuss and accept these randomly imposed labels, she then debriefed them regarding the deception. Akin (1992) responded by suggesting that Andre's "inoculation" approach might be as controversial for the behavioral sciences as for the biological sciences. Is deception, even in the name of ultimate freedom, justifiable? Can we conduct most classroom exercises without any deception?

Greenback Company
Classroom-Based Organization

Greenback is based upon experiences of David Boje since fall 1993, Grace Ann Rosile at Indiana University of Pennsylvania since spring 1994, and Bruce Texley at Behany College since spring 1995. It is part of "greening the business curriculum" and "experiential teaching" movements (Albrecht, Bultena, Holberg, & Nowak, 1982; Dunlap & Van Liere, 1978; Shetzer, Stackman, & Moore, 1990). We modified Boje and Pondy's (1976) and Miller's (1991) "classroom as an organization" design to focus on postmodern concepts (Boje & Dennehy, 1994), and the new environmental paradigm was based upon input Boje received from Egri, Shrivastava, and Throop's (1993) session on environmental sustainability at the annual meeting of the Organizational Behavior Teaching Conference, as well as visits with John Miller and Gordon Meyer at the Bucknell University Business School. Miller and Boje have been treating their classrooms as learning organizations since the 1970s. The following is a brief description of Greenback Company. For more information on creating a Greenback Company in your classroom, please contract either of the authors.

The *Wall Street Journal* (Butler, 1994) discusses community service projects being incorporated into college classes to teach social responsibility. The article questions whether adequate effort is made to link such "real world" experience with traditional theoretical classroom concepts. The Greenback Company goes beyond classroom-as-organization pedagogies where the primary objective is to create a financially viable business complete with market dynamics, cash flows, and management/employee issues. Instead, Greenback limits the product/ service to a not-for-profit activity for a broadly defined concept of

community benefit. Within these parameters, Greenback employees/
students are compelled (by various structural mechanisms) to experience for themselves what it is like to be organized according to
premodern, modern, and postmodern concepts (Boje & Dennehy,
1994, Appendix A). Students are also taught deconstruction skills (see
Table 11.2). Thus students go beyond simply creating a business
organization to the more complex task of controlling their own evolution from the instructor-defined modernist organization to a group-
self-defined postmodern organization.

The instructor as "Guildmaster" begins the semester by creating a
fraternity- or sorority-like Guild composed of the entire class. The
motto of Greenback Company is "putting green back into Mother
Earth." Green is defined as money to help rebuild any community, as
well as the green environment of Mother Earth. All students are
"Greenies" who are initiated with oaths, candles, music, and guild
secrets. The Guildmaster/instructor and veteran students from previous semesters' Greenback companies volunteer to act as Guild Elders. These Elders present stories of their own experiences with
Greenback as the basis for answering Greenies' (students') questions
and offering "survival tips." This premodern guild, with some guidance
from the Elders, democratically chooses both a fund-raiser (to provide
capital) and a "postmodern campaign" project that is ecological and
community-service oriented. The project must involve some "sweat
equity" and some "giving back" to the community or the environment.
After brainstorming fund-raiser and project ideas, the Guild (class)
narrows the list to the most promising items. Self-selected teams
research and report back on the best ideas, and the whole Guild votes
on the final choice of fund-raiser and project. At this point, which is
usually 2 to 3 weeks into the semester, the Guild is officially ended and
the modernist organization is born with the class election of a chief
executive officer (CEO) and five functionally based executive vice
presidents. From two to four nominees are selected for each position.
Election day is one of the most exciting of the semester, with campaign
speeches, signs, supporters, and sometimes even candy treats (bribes?)
for the class. Election winners are announced on the spot. The instructor next presents an overview of the duties and responsibilities of each
department, and students are asked to self-select into departments by
reporting to their respective department heads. From this point, all

issues, such as maldistribution of employees (students), workloads, attendance policies, and so on, are delegated by the Chairman of the Board (the instructor) to the Executive Committee (the CEO and relevant vice presidents).

The major tasks of the modernist organization are to (a) manage themselves internally, (b) create and present a business plan for the fund-raiser and project that must be accepted by the "External Board" (composed of business executives, entrepreneurs, former Greenback CEOs, and anyone else the instructor wishes), and (c) conduct the fund-raiser. We devote at least one full class period and additional follow-up sessions to teaching goal setting, strategy implementation, team building, and other traditional management skills. Teams learn to identify and address problems of attendance, motivation, team spirit, work quality, authority, and accountability.

The new Greenback Company has only 2 to 3 weeks to present its project proposal to the External Board, a process that may include extensive modification and revision of the proposal. The modernist phase concludes with the completion of the fund-raiser. Traditional classroom issues like extending deadlines become management strategic decisions, controlled completely by the Executive Committee and based upon closer approximations of real-world constraints than the usual instructor-determined policies. For example, postponing fund-raiser deadlines may not allow sufficient time for completion of the project, and project delays reduce analysis and writing time available for the required annual report.

By the time the project is implemented, the instructor helps the students transform their very modern organization into something more postmodern. In the postmodern phase, students are asked to redesign Greenback Company to reflect postmodern concepts they have been reading during the semester. Students are invited to rehearse the transitions corporations all around them are making in this postmodern world (Boje & Dennehy, 1994; Clegg, 1990). Department heads must write how they plan to change their leadership style or policies to be more postmodern. Departments modify existing goals and add new ones to reflect the postmodern transition. One company eliminated some departments, then reinstituted them when chaos ensued. Similarly, several departments experienced excessive absenteeism when they abandoned their attendance policies, so they quickly reinstated them. Often, departments as well as their heads reported greater satisfaction when the department head became "just another employee" and decisions were made by the group.

This approach involves much more time and effort than students (or instructors) expect for a typical class. However, both authors, as well as many veteran students, have felt it was all "worth it." As instructors, we find our roles to be more like organizational consultants. We have found that the more we minimize our control of the process, the greater the learning experience. One defeated (male) candidate for CEO during one class pulled out a wad of cash and attempted to "buy out" the company when he did not like the way the (female) CEO was running things. The class rallied in support of the CEO and voted down the takeover bid. One head of the "Friends" department (human resources) who was a human resource management major decided she never wanted to work in the field. Departments have had to confront the problem of high-performing but burned-out department heads (and even one CEO) wanting to resign. They learn about their responsibility to nurture and support leaders as well as followers. Throughout the semester, but especially in the postmodern phase, we emphasize that no model, whether premodern, modern, or postmodern, is the ultimate answer. Our purpose is to create a management discourse based on critical self-reflexivity, with an awareness of the artificiality of premodern, modern, and postmodern discursive boundaries. After all, we do not know of any "purely" postmodern companies. At best, we are trying to encourage some postmodernity in a modern world.

The following section summarizes the main features of postmodern pedagogy. Each feature is followed by an example of how the authors have incorporated this feature into the Greenback Company classroom-based organization.

1. The Approach Presents Many Sides to a Given Story

Instead of cases, postmodernists use stories. Story assignments are turned in throughout the semester. Students are invited to reflect upon their own experiences inside and outside the classroom. They are taught how to deconstruct their stories (see Table 11.2). Instead of lectures, we do storytelling and storysharing. The difference is that the story is local knowledge, and the textbook and the cases are grand narrative(Lyotard) knowledge. By grand narrative, we mean that there is one dominant perspective, it is wrapped inside a logic that defies alternative perspectives, and the voice of the author is cloaked in pseudoscience jargon and rhetorical moves that make the author invisible to the reader.

> Hi, my name is Grace Ann. I am speaking here. Hello, this is David Boje, I am here too. We want to share our stories about our life with you. We want you to share your stories with us. We want to get Fred from Xerox to come in here to share his story. Finally, we want to send you to the hardware store to talk to Betty, who founded the business and cannot figure out how to pass it along to anyone in her family. They all hate the hardware business.

2. The Material Shows Several Interpretations, Including Alternatives to Dominant Interpretations

For example, in the Greenback Company department called Balance, the students are told that *balance* means more than financial profit; it also is to include spiritual profit. As an example of spiritual profit, Boje invited a Native American storyteller to present stories of creation, Mother Earth, and Nature. The stories represented challenges to the Western, science-based ideology that students grew up on. The stories attacked those views of creation and Nature that Western society has accepted as truth. The weapons that the storyteller used were not the conventional Western weapons of logic and experimental data. In contrast to the dominant interpretation of business goals—make money, increase profit, and climb to the top—the goal of Greenback Company is to prove that businesses need not be destructive to their surrounding communities, that businesses can be profitable while at the same time helping their communities and Mother Earth.

3. The Approach Brings Traditionally Marginalized People or Groups to the Center of Attention

Community action projects get students to interact with people not normally included in their protected university world. Projects to date have included working with the homeless, gang members, AIDS victims, battered women's shelters, Big Brother/Sister/Littles, and other communities. When students encounter the "other," they often say, "this has been the most valuable part of my university education." One student, after interacting with an AIDS victim, said, "I don't see anything the same anymore!"

4. The Lesson Plan Encourages Instructors
and Students to Discuss the Often Hidden,
Formal and Informal "Rules of the Game"

We let the students know what parts of this are modernist. For example, we systematically "gaze" student performance in written and oral work (to use the term coined by Foucault, 1979). We enroll students in a "performativity" machine (Lyotard, 1979/1984). The syllabus says: "You will be graded on your value-added performances." We purport to use new pedagogic practices, but we still use the written examination and in the end rank students using numerical grading practices. During the guild phase, the students interact with their instructor to change such areas as the syllabus (see next item).

5. Students Have Opportunities to
Change the "Rules of the Game"

During the guild phase, students use Robert's rules of order to make any changes they want in the syllabus, including voting out quizzes, changing deadlines, dropping assignments, changing the final into a nonevent, declaring days off (company flex days) in anticipation of their workload in the college, and so on. Students also nominate and vote on who they want as corporate officers. They select their own fund-raiser and community service campaign.

6. Instructors Encourage Students to Question
the Game Itself and Self-Reflexively Examine the
Tendency to View Everything as a Game

In one class, students canceled their "Lip Sync" fund-raiser when it became apparent that it would not make money. Repercussions, including morale problems, were felt throughout the semester. During a dramatic "town meeting" session, students reexamined the purpose of the semester project. They refocused on their common desire to help the homeless and thereby revitalized their morale. In the AIDS project, questioning the game became questioning the nature of university education when the Jesuit university kicked the AIDS-benefit dance off campus because students intended to distribute condoms and condom literature at the event. Self-reflexivity was demonstrated when in a town meeting, students had to decide how to react to the university's decisions: Are we going to give up on a cause that affects the lives of our classmates? There was also reflexivity when students went to the AIDS shelter to do their work and had to decide whether they would take off their work gloves when doing their work. These examples enabled students to rise above the conflict in question (i.e., the gaming behavior) to reflect upon their own values.

7. The Classroom Is Treated as the "Real World"

For example, one of the benefits of the Greenback Company design is real-world environmental turbulence and chaos that students must deal with directly. In the reforestation project, the students decided to work with the Santa Monica Mountains Conservancy Foundation in Temescal Gateway Park. The Conservancy is a nonprofit organization whose goals are to conserve land for scientific, historical, educational, and recreational purposes. Students did not plan on the November 1993 fire storm in Southern California. As one student reported,

> The Greenback Company community campaign is not an easy road to follow. It is a bumpy trail with many turns and unforeseen hazards, but it eventually arrives at a beautiful, placid spot snuggled in the Santa Monica Mountains.

Robert became the champion of the tree planting campaign. Before, during, and after the fire storms, he gave daily progress reports (we do not have the tree site yet; no one can talk to me because of the fires). The fire storm finally ended, and the students planted 15 oak and 20 California bay trees. There would have been more trees planted, but one of the tree farm trucks got caught in a Santa Ana windstorm, and all the leaves were blown off the trees, killing them. Replacement trees had to be ordered.

The best laid plans go astray. For example, one class contracted with an inner-city public school to repaint two classrooms and a kindergarten toilet. During the painting, the masking crew did not finish taping the second room. The bathroom was locked, so it did not get prepared with the two classrooms. Therefore, the bathroom did not receive a primer coat. The second classroom was a mess after the painting crews did their jobs. After all, it was not their job to mask. The cleanup crews had to spend twice the allocated time cleaning the paint off the floors. Everyone pitched in, and the results were quite remarkable. Despite all the screwups, the rooms looked almost professionally painted. The principal, teachers, and parents were all excited about the results. A lot of teachers have asked the author to get their rooms painted next semester.

When a cultural survival employee contacted the school to schedule a weekend to go into the school and paint, she was told: "We can open the school, but a janitor will have to be there and that will cost you $300 for the weekend." She complained to the principal, "We are volunteers. Can we get around the $300 charge?" Several teachers and an administrator volunteered their time, instead of paying the janitor overtime. Next, the students found out that parents and children could not come to the painting events. It was considered too dangerous to open the school up to the community on a weekend. The school had been closed for several days because of incidents of gang activity. This was no idle threat. One student reported a child he worked with had recently been shot, and the bullet passed through his body barely missing his heart. He was only 8 years old.

8. Student Peer Evaluations
Are Not Forced Into Hierarchical Patterns

Students get all the hierarchical patterns they can stomach during the modernist phase. This is when students (as in other courses) evaluate each other's group work. The department heads, for examples, as team leaders, evaluate members of their team using formal rating scales. Students usually object to their scores, and there is often quite heated debate. During the postmodern phase, we ask students to implement an evaluation system that compensates for the modernist shortcomings of the evaluation systems. Some sections have dismissed the whole idea of performance assessment as performativity. Others, taking a more enlightened (Jameson calls it "high" modernism) stance, try to reform the empirical scale to more equitably capture student performance. Students are invited to talk with human resources professors to solicit their ideas on how this can be done. Final grades, including project scores, are not be related to students' formal positions in the company but nevertheless reflect hierarchical patterns. The student's final project is evaluated by the board of directors, and there is a requirement for producing an annual report and turning in a final grade to the registrar of the university. In short, we can only be somewhat postmodern, in the context of a modernist university.

9. The Material Is Explicit About Underlying Values

For example, much of the Boje and Dennehy (1994) book asks students to challenge white male values in organizations. Gender becomes a topic for discussion. For example, almost identical statements were made by several male students regarding their female CEO in one case, and by males regarding a female department head (of an all-male department) in several other cases: Who does she think she is, telling us what to do? What is she going to do, sit around and watch us do the work? Another male complained: "I have a female department head and a female CEO. What am I supposed to do?"

10. The Methods Encourage Student Discourse and Critique

In one class, after 5 weeks of frustration, the male CEO told the class: "I want to resign. I am letting the Greenback Company down. I do not have time to do all the things that need to be done. I think someone other than me could do a better job." After limited critique, the class rallied to his support. There were cries of "How can we help?" "What can we say to make you change your mind?" In another class, students discussed absenteeism. Should attendance be required? In one section, requirements in the syllabus about attendance were voted out during a guild meeting. However, during the modernist phase, with fewer and fewer people coming to class, department heads complained that communications were getting "fouled up" and they were having to call missing members to keep them informed. Others complained that "morale was awful" and the "spirit and energy" of the class was at an all-time low. The executive committee responded by reimplementing the attendance requirement. When people still did not come to class, they began to deduct 10 points a day from their grade. The point is that when students control parts of their classroom context, they engage in lots of discourse and critique to get things under control. This raises a more fundamental issue: Do postmodern methods really work when we have to resort to modernist controls?

11. The Material Addresses Who Stands to Gain (or Lose) Politically and Economically From the Labels and Categories Being Espoused

Just the label of CEO creates interesting classroom dynamics. On her first day in office as CEO, Michele was confronted by a male who pulled out a wad of money and offered to buy the stock of the company from the class members for $300. He said: "I think I can do a better job of running this company. I am willing to put my money where my mouth is." The executive committee bolted to the front of the room and one by one opposed the takeover attempt. There was a lot of yelling, and author Boje had to step between the takeover artist and several female employees who said he was "just upset because you lost the election." He replied, "You are not letting me express myself. I have a voice in this." Boje had many class discussions about this incident. From this day on, the executive committee bonded as a team, having faced a major challenge to its authority. As with the Zimbardo Prison Experiment, the complaining individual was labeled a "trouble maker" and was isolated by the class. Boje worked with him to process his feelings and made several process observations to the class as a whole.

12. The Approach Reveals the Essentializing and Totalizing Effects of Labels and Categories

The course model itself has essentializing and totalizing labels and categories. The language-in-use, as adopted by the instructor and students, socially constructs the definitions of reality. During the guild phase, students respond to the labels of Greenie, Apprentice, Elder, and Guildmaster. They are challenged to confront their pre-Guild labels of professor and student. Students report

> This is so unstructured, compared to my other courses.

> It took me a while to get used to the lack of structure.

> Then, I realized, I had a vote and I could put the kind of structure I wanted into the class.

In the modern phase, there are the corporate-business labels students anticipate in a business course: CEO, department head, employee. During the postmodern phase, students often drop their stereotypes about the homeless, AIDS victims, and other groups. The real-world encounters with the "other" (as described above) are the best antidote to stereotypical labels.

> I didn't think a homeless person would be like that. He had many different jobs in his lifetime and traveled all over the world. Even now, he spends part of his day doing volunteer work. Next week he is expecting to start a new job.

Conclusion

Since deciding to postmodernize our classrooms, we have had some of the most exciting experiences of our careers. When Grace Ann's students decided to open one class with "Tarzan yells," five faculty complained to the dean of the college, and Grace Ann was nearly thrown out of the building. When David's students passed out condoms outside the Jesuit university lunchroom, he was summoned to the vice president's office. The story became an item in *The Chronicle of Higher Education* ("University Says," 1994, p. A6). We both have students from previous semesters who have come back to work as student mentors (consultants, Elders, board members) because they believe that this course can make a difference. Grace Ann's students, after the term had ended, created a "Greenback" student organization of their own to engage in community service projects ("but we will not be writing annual reports!"). One of David's students went to the placement office of the university and asked: "Do you have a listing of postmodern companies I could interview at?" This raises a final concern. By teaching students to critique modernism, we free them to create change. Who knows, maybe someday there will be a category of "postmodern companies" in the placement office.

12

Reconstructions of Choice

Advocating a Constructivist Approach to Postmodern Management Education

GHAZI F. BINZAGR

MICHAEL R. MANNING

Cooper and Burrell (1988) argue that modernism "is that moment when man invented himself" (p. 94). Postmodernism, we argue, is that moment when humanity discovered it can reinvent itself. Preparing managers for a future world that is capable of constant reinvention is quite a challenge. In this chapter, we wish to advocate a constructivist orientation to postmodern management education. By constructivist, we suggest that reality is what we make out of our experiences and observations via sense making. If we believe, as Berger and Luckmann (1966/1967) suggest, that social reality is our creation, then if we so choose, we may re-create our social reality. Effective postmodern management education should teach managers to be proactive creators of their work (social reality).

Our approach also proposes that what one creates (or constructs) is based on what one chooses to believe. If this is so, then both instructors and students must be more aware of the ontological and epistemological assumptions that underlie their realities. In fact, postmodern educators will strive to create a classroom where students can gain such an awareness. This will allow postmodernism a useful role in enabling educators to teach managers how to initiate and sustain the work realities of choice.

Shifting postmodernism more fully from the circles of academic debate to the hard utilitarian realities of management education is an underlying factor motivating this chapter. Our contribution is in advocating a constructivist approach to postmodernism that will begin to facilitate this shift. A new generation of educators is needed who can build on Berger and Luckmann's (1966/1967) work on the social construction of reality and what Gergen and Thatchenkery (1993) defined as the constructive dimension of postmodernism.

Some Beginning Assumptions

The greatest challenge to developing postmodern approaches to education is in defining what postmodern might mean. Is postmodern a word or a movement? There does not, as of yet, exist an agreed-upon definition of postmodernism (Hassard, 1993). In fact, as Hassard (1993) points out, it is not even certain if postmodernism is a phenomenon, a theoretical perspective, or both. Instructors desiring to teach postmodern organization theory face the dilemma of first establishing what postmodernism means to them in order to formulate a strategy or method of teaching. We encourage postmodern teachers to clarify and reflect on ontological (what is one's reality) and epistemological (how does one know such a reality) assumptions they hold regarding postmodernism. In a postmodern classroom, instructors strive to create teaching methods and approaches consistent with their philosophical assumptions. We find the work of Berger and Luckmann (1966/1967) most useful in grounding a constructivist strategy for postmodern education. Three assumptions are central to this position.

First, according to our understanding of Berger and Luckmann, habits are seen as the foundation of our social constructs. Habits lead to institutions that, once created, are reified and preserved by mechanisms of control, such as sedimentation and legitimation. Therefore, in our view, postmodern management education, to be successful, must be able to generate new social habits among organizational members.

Second, implied in Berger and Luckmann's (1966/1967) ideas about reification is "that man is capable of forgetting his own authorship of the human world, and further, that the dialectic between man, the producer, and his products is lost to consciousness" (p. 89). This fact has profound implications. It implies that postmodern education must have as a primary objective the restoration of people's ownership of the human reified world.

Third, according to Berger and Luckmann (1966/1967), all social constructs, because of societal mechanisms of control, are internalized in collective and shared mental symbolic universes that become the ultimate controllers of our institutional order. Symbolic universes are what are referred to in current day thinking as *paradigms* (e.g., see Barker, 1992, pp. 30-41; Guba & Lincoln, 1994, p. 107) or *schemas* (e.g., see Bartunek & Moch, 1987; Lord, 1985; Neisser, 1976). Symbolic universes ultimately hold our society together, but they also hold society back from new forms of innovation (physical or social). To teach the ways of creating new institutional orders, postmodern educators aim for paradigm shifts (Barker, 1992).

It is difficult to recommend specific techniques for postmodern instruction. We believe that these teaching methods must be born from the situation and cannot be clearly specified a priori. Of course, we do not advocate an attitude of anything goes because the methodological question will always be dependent upon ontological and epistemological dimensions that the instructor holds (Guba & Lincoln, 1994). Decisions regarding methods of teaching will be dependent upon these philosophical assumptions in relationship to the specific classroom dynamics.

This chapter is a beginning effort advocating ontological and epistemological assumptions that we believe can be useful to postmodern management education. One application using these assumptions is offered, using the classical functions of management (Fayol, 1937). These functions are first deconstructed and then reconstructed in light of our constructivist assumptions. We hope that this beginning discussion will invite and encourage others to expand on management education that leads to reconstructions of choice. Because this chapter is just a beginning, we leave it to others to share cases and methods that specify their experiences with postmodern management education.

Advocating a Connection Between
Postmodernism and Constructivism

To begin, let us first explore what we mean by postmodernism. Although there are many formulations to understanding postmodernism, we find the definition offered by Botwinick (1993) to be useful. We believe this definition encompasses many of the definitions appearing in the literature. According to Botwinick (1993), at the core of postmodernism lies an attitude of relativism and skepticism, leading to what may be best described as a state of generalized agnosticism. According to *Webster's Collegiate Dictionary* (1993), agnosticism means "holding the view that any ultimate reality is unknown and probably unknowable." This definition is useful in that it helps differentiate postmodernism from other paradigms of inquiry, such as contingency theory, which some have suggested it resembles (e.g., see Tsoukas, 1992).

Although relativism may be the essence of numerous philosophical orientations (for example, contingency theory), postmodernism remains unique in combining relativism with skepticism as the core of its essence. The combination of both views leads to a challenging philosophical position regarding the nature of knowledge, with important implications for postmodern management instruction. In our view, a combination of relativism and skepticism implies a state of inquiry that denies the existence of any universal truths. In addition, this combination imposes uncertainty regarding all matters, including the statement that no universal truths exist. To teach postmodernism, so defined, will in our opinion ultimately lead to a state of inaction within the classroom. Taken to a logical extreme, this philosophical orientation could be responsible for the creation of a world of total social despair.

Based on the foregoing discussion, why do we then advocate teaching management from a postmodern perspective? One could argue that relativism is a positive contribution to management education. For example, to know that nothing is fixed, nothing is total, and nothing is universal can be comforting, especially if change seems advantageous. However, to add to that a requirement of skepticism can be intellectually devastating. Skepticism, argues Botwinick (1993), "is a self-referentially unsustainable philosophical thesis, since to be consistently skeptical requires one to be skeptical of skepticism itself, as well of all competing and alternative philosophical theses" (p. xii). How would one teach postmodern organization theory under such an orientation and expect it to be useful? A manager operating under such assumptions of reality could never act. What would be the basis for action? Questions like these identify a dilemma for postmodern management education; we must find a way to teach that brings about practical and useful contributions to managers. If not, then what becomes the purpose of management education—is it philosophizing for philosophy's sake?

To maintain a sense of practicality as well as creating a new vitality in management education, we advocate a constructivist approach to postmodernism. A constructivist orientation allows for free will. Under such an orientation, meaning becomes central. It is not that we *internalize* different meanings of reality. It is that we *create* different meanings; thus, we create different realities. Under this conceptual orientation, the requirements of skepticism and relativism embedded in postmodernism no longer lead to inactivity and despair. On the contrary, a creative tension now exists that enables one to appreciate the uncertainty implied in postmodernism as a necessary precondition to creation. When constructivism is joined with skepticism and relativism, the three can be used to create meanings of choice, thus enabling the creation of realities of choice. Furthermore, the combination of these philosophies allows us to appreciate that what we fixate and make certain is what we want to fixate and make certain. When the reality we have created no longer is experienced with joy or value, we can return to skepticism and relativism, deconstruct this reality, and then reconstruct it again.

Postmodernism:
Epoch or Epistemology?

We stated earlier that one of the challenges facing postmodern teachers is to decide what postmodernism means. As Hollinger (1994) explains, "The literature on postmodernism is so vast, diverse, and unwieldy that even the initiated cannot keep up with it, let alone make coherent sense of it all" (p. xi). One of the most important and central

debates concerning postmodernism centers on whether we are in an
age of postmodernist social science or an age of the social sciences of
postmodernity. In other words, is postmodernism a way of looking at
reality or a reality per se? Hassard (1993) differentiates both by defining them in two different perspectives: epoch and epistemology. According to Hassard, the distinction is one "between postmodernism as
the signifier of a historical periodization, or as a theoretical perspective" (p. 2). He adds on the same page:

> In the first use, postmodernism as an epoch, the goal is to identify
> features of the external world that support the hypothesis that society
> is moving toward a new postmodern era. The practice is based on the
> realist notion that we simply need to find the right way of describing the
> world "out there."

To explain postmodernism as an epistemology, on the other hand,
Hassard (1993) adds,

> Postmodern epistemology suggests that the world is constituted by our
> shared language and that we can only "know the world" through the
> particular forms of discourse our language creates. It is argued, how-
> ever, that as our language-games are continually in flux, meaning is
> constantly slipping beyond our grasp and can thus never be lodged
> within one term. (p. 3)

While noting the above distinction between epoch and epistemology, we would like to emphasize the primary distinction between these
two approaches. What Hassard terms epoch simply implies that postmodernism is a real objective historical reality open for analysis and
investigation. On the other hand, what Hassard terms epistemology
views postmodernism as a philosophical lens through which to see the
world.

The foregoing differentiation suggests that adopting an epoch orientation to postmodernism leads to a strategy for postmodern education different from the strategy implied by an epistemological
orientation. In the first orientation, teachers would emphasize the
postmodern reality that is already in existence in society and prepare
students to effectively participate in such a world. We believe that the

highly innovative book by Boje and Dennehy (1993), which has made an invaluable contribution to postmodern management education, may be seen as an example of the epoch orientation to postmodernism. Although these authors attempt to remain neutral on the epoch-epistemology debate by characterizing postmodernism into era and deconstructive approaches, we characterize this valued work as primarily a contribution to epoch postmodernism. Boje and Dennehy (1993) view postmodernism as an actual (real) political movement revolting against the status quo and bringing new voices within society to power. In their view, the postmodern movement allows diverse, traditionally unaccounted for segments of society (such as women and other minorities) influence in organizations through "their voice." To the extent that this movement takes hold, it results in a postmodern world where the traditional functions of management (defined by Boje and Dennehy as planning, organizing, influencing, leading, and controlling) remain as central defining forces but are performed differently. Boje and Dennehy's (1993) work is ripe with postmodern thought presented in a clear innovative approach; however, we believe that their work can be extended further by employing Hassard's epistemological approach.

When using this philosophical approach to postmodernism, one does not start with the state of the organization (such as the classical functions of management), but with the state of mind that creates the classical functions of management through the language of discourse. If, under this approach, we speak of postmodern organization theory rather than postmodern organizations (Parker, 1992), then theory becomes the target of postmodern instruction, not reality. The reality of the organization becomes what we make of it as a result of our theorizing. Under this approach, we appreciate that the traditional functions of management, such as those identified by Boje and Dennehy (1993), should themselves be open to question. In fact, postmodern management education under Hassard's epistemological orientation emphasizes teaching students to critically deconstruct such categorization as the functions of management. By adding the constructivist philosophy, students will go even a step further; they will learn to reconstruct new categories and theories of organization based on their values and desired future outcomes.

Example of the Constructivist Orientation to Postmodern Education Using the Classical Functions of Management

It should be clear to the reader that we are strongly advocating a constructivist orientation to postmodern management education. To further elaborate our position, we will illustrate with a personal case one way of deconstructing and reconstructing the classical functions of management. Berger and Luckmann's (1966/1967) social construction theory and Hassard's (1993) epistemological orientation to postmodernism are pivotal sources for our constructivist approach.

Implied by Berger and Luckmann (1966/1967) is the assumption that how something looks depends on how we look at it. Adding Hassard's definition of epistemological postmodernism, even modern organizations look different when seen through the postmodern eye. Using this constructivist approach, the frozen reification of an entity called organization is no longer seen (Weick, 1979). Rather, the ongoing organizing processes of construction and destruction of meaning are visible (Gray, Bougon, & Donnellon, 1985). However, putting issues of perception aside, it is legitimate to ask: Will a constructivist postmodern perspective enable management students to generate new ways of theorizing about organizing? Will this approach allow students to become purposeful creators of future organizing processes that can be differentiated from organizing processes generated by the current modernistic perspective?

We believe that the answer to the above questions is yes. Let us use the classical functions of management as an example to illustrate this point. First, however, let us say a word on how we see organizations under our orientation toward postmodernism. Given our constructivist bent to postmodernism, we like to view the process of organizing differently. The process of organizing becomes one of philosophizing rather than engineering (Sackmann, 1989). In the latter view, managers are seen as the engineers of designs for their organizations. They do so by attempting to fit organizations to the laws of the universe. If the universe becomes postmodern, then members must design their organizations accordingly. The role of management under such a perspective will always be one of planning, organizing, influencing, leading, and controlling. However, in a postmodern universe, these functions will be engineered differently (à la Boje & Dennehy, 1993).

From the philosophizing perspective, on the other hand, managers are seen as the generators of philosophies for organizational members to guide their actions. Managers realize that the very categories they create to define their role in the organization will contribute to the creation of new unique organizing processes. Under such a perspective, managers do not take for granted or accept a predetermined theory of their role. Rather, they realize that the most important role they can play is to create new theories for themselves.

Under the philosophizing perspective, managers start by deconstructing their role and regaining authorship (à la Berger & Luckmann, 1966/1967) of the management functions they perform. It is our experience that when managers are asked to define their roles or what they do, they unknowingly generate Fayol's (1937) classical management functions. When asked where these functions come from, these same managers are not able to trace the historical roots of these concepts. We then introduce Fayol's classical roles to help the managers regain authorship and appreciate the world such roles have created. Then we suggest that because these roles were actually created for us by others some time ago, we might want to revisit whether this view of reality creates what we want in organizational settings. When they want to generate their own theories of their roles as managers, we facilitate strategies to contrast the classical roles with the kind of world they want to create. Then students propose theories of roles that would make such worlds possible.

According to Fayol (1937), the role of an executive in an organization is to plan, organize, command, coordinate, and control. These are the principles of administration that permeate most of our current organizing. In fact, the concepts are taught typically to all students of management in their introductory courses. In a constructivist postmodern class, management students will question the wisdom of Fayol and attempt to generate a new set of roles consistent with a desired postmodern future of their choosing. What may such roles look like? This is what we will illustrate in the following section.

Fayol Redefined

Here is another example of how we worked collaboratively with a group of students to redefine the role of management proposed by Fayol to create a postmodern world of choice where creation and free will are emphasized. Our work resulted in a redefinition of Fayol's classical functions into five new roles: invention, proactive reorganizing, persuading, co-creating, and co-validation. This example comes from a doctoral seminar; however, the idea remains the same for all students at all levels.

In this doctoral seminar, the students spent an entire semester reading the classical works of management (i.e., Fayol, Taylor, Follett, Barnard, McGregor, March and Simon, etc.). Individuals deconstructed these classical writings in terms of the original author's assumptions and implications for organizing. Then as a group, we reflected on how current organizations could be seen as manifestations of these ideas. And finally, the class identified a desired future for organizations and reconstructed Fayol's classical functions into the five roles listed above. This process took most of a semester in which we discussed, debated, and developed a new view. In this particular instance, the class met in a seminar fashion where we all sat in a circle, with the traditional distinction between teacher and student minimized. What is important to emphasize here is that the nature of our class sessions focused on philosophizing and creating a new view of reality. In addition, it is also important to realize that the method or class activities used in this postmodern classroom were of little relevance. What is important is to use whatever methods or devices are available to the instructor to shift the classroom focus from the traditional analysis and critique to a framework that fosters philosophical inquiry, thereby allowing for the creation of a new order or view of the world. In this instance, we shifted from viewing organizations as a reality to be analyzed and engineered to a social reification that can be renegotiated and re-created. We offer a short description of the outcome of this postmodern process, in this case redefining Fayol's five classical roles of management. These are described below.

Invention. To plan, according to Fayol (1937), "is to deduce the probabilities or possibilities of the future from a definite and complete knowledge of the past" (p. 103). It was clear to our doctoral students that Fayol's definition of planning is grounded in a deterministic view of the universe, in which the executive role is to engineer a map of the future based on the best knowledge of the past. In the postmodern world that was desired by our students, where creation is allowed, the future was not to be determined from the past, because new creations cannot be predicted from old creations. Under these conditions, a new role for the executive was proposed by the students. It was a role of invention, based on visioning and imagination. To invent under these new terms is to generate probabilities or possibilities of the future from a definite and complete knowledge of values and desires.

Proactive Organizing. To organize, according to Fayol (1937), "is to define and set up the general structure of the enterprise with reference to its objective, its means of operation, and its future course as determined by planning" (p. 103). In the postmodern world desired by our students, this role of organizing was not seen as sufficient. First, the very definition of the word had to change. Second, the role of organizing was no longer seen to be adequate. Instead, a role of proactive reorganizing was proposed.

In the postmodern world desired by our students, organizing was believed to be better defined by the words of Karl Weick (1979) in *The Social Psychology of Organizing*: "consensually validated grammar for reducing equivocality by means of sensible interlocked behaviors" (p. 3). Weick adds, "To organize is to *assemble* ongoing interdependent actions into *sensible* sequences that generate sensible outcomes" (p. 3, italics added). There is a postmodern emphasis in Weick's foregoing definition of organizing; however, those familiar with his work may accurately point to a strong modernistic flavor in Weick's methods of organizational analysis and investigation. For another illustration of what postmodern methods of analysis may look like, see Gephart (1993).

The students then defined proactive reorganizing as a form of organizing; it, too, was seen as a consensually validated grammar for reducing equivocality by means of sensible interlocked behavior. However, these students saw proactive reorganizing as more than organizing. It was recognized that to proactively reorganize is to conscientiously reassemble ongoing interdependent actions into sensible sequences that generate desirable outcomes.

Proactive reorganizing, according to the students, may be grounded in a deliberate process of consensual revalidation. Because consensual validation emerges as a result of people's commonsense apparatus and deeply common interpersonal experiences (Weick, 1979, p. 3), consensual revalidation could emerge only out of a new collective agreement caused by new commonsense and/or interpersonal experiences.

If organizing "is like grammar in the sense that it is a systematic account of some rules and conventions by which sets of interlocked behaviors are assembled to form social processes that are intelligible to actors" (Weick, 1979, p. 3), then proactive reorganizing was seen by the students as referring to the conscientious reassembling of such grammar. Proactive organizing takes place, according to our students, when managers actively change the rules for forming variables and causal linkages into new meaningful and desirable structures. In a sense, proactive reorganizing, in the view of our students, could be about the renegotiation of the social contract (Weick, 1979) that binds people together.

Persuading. According to Fayol (1937), the third role of the executive is commanding: "to set going the services defined by planning and established by organizing" (p. 103). In the postmodern world desired by our students, where inventing and proactive reorganizing set reality in motion, commanding was no longer seen as sufficient. Persuading now became the new role of the executive. To persuade is to argue for and legitimate the new realities defined by new inventions and established by reorganizing.

Co-Creating. As to the fourth role of executives, which according to Fayol is coordination, it too was changed in the postmodern world desired by our students. Fayol (1937) explains that to coordinate, among other things, "is to adapt the means to the end and to unify disconnected efforts and make them homogeneous" (p. 103). He adds that "it means establishing a close liaison among services specialized as to their operations, but having the same general objective." Coordination by Fayol's definition was seen as impossible in the postmodern world desired by our students. If reality is constantly being re-created by organizational members, then, our students suggested, a better role for the executive is to help others co-create. To help co-create is to help make what was imagined (envisioned/invented) possible by helping other organizational members realize that the whole of their reality is the creation of all of them. It was desired that this created reality be based on common ground generated from individual ownership and driven by a desired future.

Co-Validation. Finally, argues Fayol (1937), an executive must control: "to make sure that all operations at all times are carried out in accordance with the plan adopted" (p. 103). In the postmodern world of our students, plans are less important. If this is so, then a traditional view of control may also be unimportant (unless one redefines control in a more liberal way, as suggested by Mary Parker Follett, 1937). A new executive role was suggested, one in which executives facilitate co-validation. Consistent with Weick's definition of organizing and their definition of proactive reorganizing, consensual validation and revalidation were seen by the students as the essence of a manager's role. The students felt that this creates affirmation, a valued characteristic of their ideal workplace. Therefore, to co-validate is to ensure effectiveness of a process of consensual validation and revalidation over the new realities generated by organizational visioning (imagination/invention).

The contrast between the new postmodern views of organizing generated by our students and the traditional views of the literature is fascinating. It creates stimulating discussions and helps students begin to conceptualize what a postmodern organization of their choosing may look like. We believe this to be testimony to the great power embedded in the constructivist orientation to postmodern management education.

How to Stimulate Reconstructions of Choice in the Postmodern Classroom

In describing the difference between the traditional and postmodern textbook, Fineman and Gabriel (1994) explain,

The traditional textbook is designed to enable students to master a certain number of areas, even though they may be ignorant of all the others. The alternative text constitutes a sequence of visits into territory which becomes increasingly familiar, yet never quite transparent. The ultimate aim of these visits is self-evident: to enable the student to undertake future visits unaided; to learn without requiring textbook assistance. (p. 392)

How do we create an atmosphere in the postmodern classroom that can support and encourage this kind of learning and knowledge generation? We propose that this can best be done by designing an alternative classroom environment based on a constructivist paradigm of postmodernism. In essence, postmodern educators strive to create in their students the ability to be builders of knowledge and experience rather than be tenants of current buildings of knowledge structures. They do so by helping students experience what K. Gergen (1992) describes as the postmodern transformation, replacing the real by the representational and appreciating representation as a communal arti-fact. The criteria of success or progress for such a model of postmodern management education shifts from an emphasis on objective testing of objective facts based on predictability, to an emphasis on strength-ening the students' ability for creative sense making and sense giving. In the eyes of postmodern educators advocating a constructivist bent, success is measured by their students being able to collectively create a new sense of reality aligned with what they value and desire. If they can collectively enact such future choices, then that is truth. They would not have discovered it, they would have made it so.

To stimulate reconstructions of choice in a postmodern manage-ment classroom, we specifically focus on three philosophical shifts in thinking:

1. Education shifts from preaching calculated adaptation to facili-tating proactive creation. If reality is mostly our own creation, then why learn to adapt to it? Why master the art of adapting to the obstacles we create? Why not learn to be effective and active in the enactment of futures of choice? Why not learn to en-vision before we think and act?

2. The basis of education shifts from seeking certainty to celebrat-ing equivocality. Why lie to ourselves? We do not have all the answers and no one does. Therefore, management education should be based on an appreciation and love for the vagueness inherent in the universe.

It is what gives us the power to create meanings of choice. In basing education on certainty, we stifle creativity, kill initiative, and take away the passion of our humanness (Schneider, 1993).

3. The method of education shifts from indoctrination to exploration. We now realize that truth or understanding is in the heart of each one of us. We all bring a different angle of the truth to one another. Educators have no more right over the truth than does the peasant working in the fields. The more voices we incorporate in our construction of reality, the better our conception of truth will be.

Conclusions

In this chapter, we have advocated a constructivist orientation to postmodern management education. In our view, postmodern management education without constructivism leaves us only with relativism and skepticism. This can only lead to despair; yet with the addition of constructivism, hope emerges. In addition, we have favored an epistemological approach to postmodern management education. By advocating postmodernism as a constructivist philosophy, we promote ideals that can empower us to regain our authorship of the worlds we have created. A constructivist philosophy gives us the choice to re-create our world every time we so desire. And when the term *postmodern* is no longer trendy, we will have left our students with a far more important legacy, that of reconstructions of choice.

13

Modernism, Postmodernism,
and Managerial Competencies
A Multidiscourse Reading

ERIC H. NEILSEN

I understand the postmodern project as an attempt to delegitimize the grand narrative forms of social science (Lyotard, 1979/1984) and, concomitantly, to legitimize local narratives of multiple self-identified marginal groups, for example, by race, ethnicity, gender, and social class. Special attention is given to the heretofore ignored views of historically oppressed parties. Delegitimation is accomplished by showing how all knowledge claims are rooted in the unique histories and cultures of their proponents, rather than in representations of universally objective truth.

Proponents of the white male-dominated modern social sciences in particular are attacked for hiding the culture boundedness of their arguments behind claims of a value-free methodology, capable of presuppositionless representation and the development of "axial principles for explaining all manner of social phenomena" (Agger, 1991, p. 116); for using positivist methodology and abstract empiricism rhetorically to justify claims about what is true, when on the contrary, all truth claims are ultimately undecidable; and for using their political control over the social science professions to submerge other knowledges.

Alternatively, the acceptance of multiple local knowledges is rooted in the presupposition that the knowledge claims of different groups cannot be synthesized into overarching theories. Each local knowledge is unique and too rooted in its historical context to presume that such a synthesis is possible.

The result is a posture toward life that eschews attempts at grand syntheses of knowledge and, instead, embraces either an informed pessimism dedicated to debunking others' attempts at symbolic hegemony or an affirmative commitment to shape action in behalf of a more egalitarian, just, and humane society through inputs from multiple, unintegrated local knowledges (Rosenau, 1992). The latter posture acknowledges the impossibility of either perfectly shared dialogue across local knowledges or collaborative action that is equally satisfying to all interested parties. However, it does presume that conditions can be improved over the present through greater attempts at mutual affirmation and more balanced readings of the local knowledges interested in a given action.

The Problem

I began with the question of whether the field of managerial assessment and competence education could legitimately be characterized as a project of modernity and thus subject to postmodernist critique. Some of the more obvious features of the field certainly suggest this. Assessment center activities typically involve coding the verbal and nonverbal behaviors of managers as they engage in problem-solving exercises, assessing those behaviors against positive science-based standards, and providing feedback and instruction to promote conformity to those standards.

One is reminded of Foucault's (1979) discourse on the techniques for disciplining workers between the mid-18th and mid-19th centuries. The techniques were used to train workers to function efficiently as tools for developing industrial wealth. The peasantry, who heretofore had owed little to the nobility other than deference and tribute, were forced to learn how to arrange themselves in spatial matrices, work according to timetables, master consecutively more difficult exercises, and rapidly implement strategies combining space, time, and activity, all for the sake of fitting seamlessly into the mass production routines of the Industrial Revolution.

Could it be that modern-day management-assessment centers with their competence-building agendas are spreading such discipline even further into human thought and action within the management ranks? The imagery of aspiring executives having their thoughts and speech isolated, assessed, and recalibrated to fit the standardized subroutines of some great corporate brain would seem to be cause for concern. The fundamental question is, is this actually what is happening?

The Research Setting and Methodology

I found this question intriguing when my school began a new course entitled Managerial Assessment and Development, to be required of all incoming MBA students (see Boyatzis, Cowen, & Kolb, 1995). Although it was billed as an opportunity for incoming students to take charge of their own learning by assessing their skills and abilities as managers, and subsequently, designing a learning plan, the assessment center technology that would be central to it made me question who would actually be in charge.

My research methodology was participant observation. I served on the faculty design committee that eventually approved the course and as one of its instructors during the first two semesters it was offered. During the latter, I shared responsibility with another faculty member for a subset of about 100 students and for coordinating their interactions with nine Executive Advisers from the local business community. Although I did not interview any of the students, Executive Advisers, or fellow faculty explicitly on their modern or postmodern leanings, postmodern thinking was popular among a subset of our Ph.D. students, some of whom were assisting in the course. We maintained an ongoing dialogue regarding the extent to which the management assessment technology we were teaching was being employed in modern or postmodern ways, and in turn, how it might be improved so as to minimize symbolic oppression while maximizing individual development.

Overview and Conceptual Framework

I should warn the reader that my findings so far as postmodern critique is concerned were equivocal. There were indeed encounters

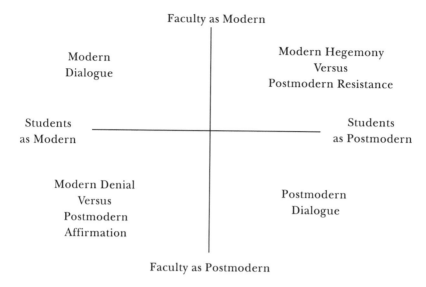

Figure 13.1. Dimensionalizing Modernism and Postmodernism by Role

among students and faculty that could be interpreted as evidence of modernist hegemony. But I witnessed other kinds of encounters as well. Two kinds of factors seemed relevant. First, there was wide variation among faculty and students with respect to their tendencies to take either a modern or a postmodern position toward the course material as they conversed with one another. Second, the quality of the conversation seemed to depend on which rank was taking which position. Figure 13.1 crosses the modern/postmodern dichotomy with rank (faculty/student) to suggest four types of encounters. It seemed to me that encounter type, defined in this way, acted as an important mediating variable between the course material and the students' actual experience of symbolic oppression or the lack thereof. Talk mattered more than words on paper, and who was agreeing or disagreeing with whom mattered more than private readings of the printed page.

The kind of symbolic oppression one might expect to see, based on a postmodern reading of the course material and procedures taken alone, was most evident when the faculty (be they professors, graduate instructors, or Executive Advisers) were taking a modern posture while the students were preoccupied with the local knowledges of their own life experiences. However, this was frequently not the case. There were many occasions when the students argued from a modernist posture as well, sometimes in ways that aligned with and at other times in ways that competed with the modern postures of the faculty. Likewise, there were occasions when the faculty adopted a postmodern position on some aspect of the course material while the students were treating it from a modernist perspective. And finally, there were still other occasions when both students and faculty took postmodern positions on the course material in their conversations with one another, sometimes conflicting and sometimes searching for common ground across their respective local knowledges.

Thus, what I have to report here is neither a documentation of unalloyed modernist oppression or a postmodern theoretical deconstruction of a particular competence assessment program. Rather, it is a case study of how and why such oppression was not significant in a particular pedagogical situation where a postmodern analysis of the course materials taken alone would have predicted this.

In the following sections, I will first summarize the content and structure of the course and then elaborate on the types of postmodern critique one might make of it. I will then juxtapose this against the kinds of behavior I observed that could be associated with each of the quadrants in Figure 13.1, providing historical data to suggest why particular encounters took one form rather than another. The chapter will conclude with a discussion of alternative scenarios and implications for management education and postmodern theory.

Managerial Assessment and Development

COURSE STRUCTURE

Managerial Assessment and Development is a 15-week course required of all incoming MBA students at the Weatherhead School of Management. Its stated goal is "to learn a method for assessing one's knowledge and abilities relevant to management and for developing and implementing plans for acquiring new management-related knowledge and abilities throughout one's career" (Boyatzis et al., 1995, p. 51).

The curriculum is designed around a particular taxonomy of managerial knowledge and abilities, elsewhere called managerial competencies (Boyatzis, 1982). The structure of the course allocates roughly equal periods of time to data gathering, assessment, and planning in terms of this taxonomy. The class is divided on the first day into 12-person Executive Action Teams designed to be roughly representative of the class as a whole in terms of learning styles (Kolb, 1985), gender, and race. Each team is assigned both a facilitator, usually a graduate student in the Organizational Behavior Ph.D. program, and a local executive who will act as their Executive Adviser over the next several months.

The facilitator meets with the team every week, serving as a resource for understanding and interpreting assignments, as well as for supporting the team's development as a safe and supportive learning group. The Executive Adviser acts as a resource regarding the world of management and, in particular, as a reality check on both the faculty's and the students' assumptions about executive thought and behavior. Meetings with this person usually take place outside the classroom and, beyond some basic commitments, are by mutual agreement.

Meeting weekly in 3-hour blocks and in varying formats (lecture, team, subgroups), as well as separately with an interviewer, the students spend the first third of the course taking a variety of assessment-center exercises, which are coded for evidence of management abilities. The students also fill out background questionnaires on their past careers and current knowledge capabilities. Once the exercises have been completed, the students are taught the assessment model's logic, so that they can assess themselves in terms of it using their subjective experience as their database. They also give a questionnaire, built around the model, to several close associates in their work or private lives, so that the latter can assess them in terms of the abilities model as well.

The middle 5 weeks of the course are devoted to accomplishing two objectives. One is to build the Executive Action Team as a supportive learning group where people can give and receive feedback productively and help one another interpret the data they have generated. This dovetails with the second objective, which is for each member to produce an integrated assessment of his/her management-related abilities and knowledge, using all three data sources (exercise ratings, self-ratings, and colleagues' ratings). Team activities vary from learning the coding scheme by applying it to the videotapes of some of the exercises, to discussing on a voluntary basis how various members were coded in the same or other exercises, to free-flowing discussions of people's concepts of management competence and its implications for their careers.

In the last third of the course, the students use their individual assessments as the basis for developing a learning plan for the future, using the group again as a discussion forum and reality check. The team also takes stock of its own capabilities and plans for further team learning events in subsequent semesters.

COURSE CONTENT

Although the students in this course are asked ultimately to develop learning plans that cover professional knowledge areas, for example, accounting and finance, as well as more behaviorally codifiable managerial abilities or competencies, the bulk of the course's instructional time is devoted to the latter. The competencies focused on are primarily those formulated by Boyatzis (1982; bolstered by the research of Campbell, Dunnette, Lawler, & Weick, 1970; Howard & Bray, 1988; Kotter, 1982; Thornton, & Byham, 1982; Luthans, Hodgetts, & Rosenkrantz, 1988).

The term *managerial competence* as used by Boyatzis refers to underlying characteristics of people that result in effective and/or superior job performance (Boyatzis, 1982, p. 21). Such competence is characterized as generic, manifest in many forms, and measurable in many ways. Different competencies may be more relevant in some settings than in others, but the general notion is that there is a core set of competencies that are relevant to the vast majority of contexts in which managers must operate. Therefore, all managers would do well to master them.

Even though most managerial competencies are measurable in a variety of ways, a core theme that runs through the assessment literature is that they can be identified most reliably through the content analysis of speech patterns, either taken alone or in the context of observed behavior. In the course under discussion, the students discuss their past management activities in a critical incident interview, give a speech on a management topic, and then conduct a discussion with the audience and participate in a group problem-solving session. These activities are either audiotaped or videotaped, and the participants' speech behaviors are content-analyzed for evidence of one or more of 22 distinct managerial abilities.

The content analysis coding procedure is quite rigorous from the viewpoint of the modern research paradigm. It is usually performed in the course by our Ph.D. students in organizational behavior, who must first take a coding course and pass a test at an acceptable level of reliability. The coding involves the assessor's application of both a general theme to the dialogue and the identification of particular behaviors, either reported or observed. For example, the following is the code for identifying the managerial ability, Efficiency Orientation:

Efficiency Orientation is the ability to perceive input/output relationships and includes the concern for increasing the efficiency of action (i.e., maximizing output per unit of input). This will often appear as a concern for doing something better, whether this comparison is with previous personal experience, others' performance, or a standard of excellence. It is indicated when a person:

a. Assesses inputs and outputs, or costs and benefits, with the expressed intent of maximizing efficiency (i.e., output/input)

b. Expresses a concern for doing something better or accomplishing something unique

c. Seeks to exceed or outperform a standard of excellence or goal, or

d. Uses resources (e.g., time, people, money, etc.) to maximize efficient progress toward goals (Faculty of Weatherhead, 1991)

The claim for the relevance of this ability and 21 others is based on research data from the sources noted above. In most cases, panels of managers identified by their organizational peers and superiors as highly effective performers were compared in various assessment-center activities with others who were rated by the same group as average or below-average performers. Those rated as more effective were more likely to display these abilities (or to describe themselves in critical incident interviews as having enacted them) than were their less effective counterparts.

The abilities focused on in the course cover a wide variety of themes, ranging from analysis to action and from abstract thought to interpersonal relations. They include planning, initiative, attention to detail, self-control, flexibility, empathy, persuasiveness, networking, negotiating, self-confidence, group management, developing others, oral communication, use of concepts, systems thinking, pattern recognition, theory building, using technology, quantitative analysis, social objectivity, written communication, and efficiency orientation.

Such an approach, I would argue, is thoroughly modern in outlook. It is based on the assumption of an underlying objective reality and the human capacity for the development of concepts that represent aspects of that reality. It also follows the spirit of the Enlightenment in presuming that there are laws of Nature guiding managerial behavior that can be discovered by systematic, positive research and assimilated by human actors to their benefit.

Although neither Boyatzis nor other writers offer an overarching theory or grand narrative to explain why these abilities are more important for managers to learn than others, the very technology for measuring them makes it easy to generate one with some face validity. For example, one might argue that people who code high on many of these abilities essentially think their organizational reasoning out loud and act in concert with that reasoning as if on stage. Were this not the case, an observing coder would have nothing to code. Such behaviors, when enacted in front of other organization members, can be seen as modeling potentially productive thought processes and actions for the less skilled, as well as increasing the opportunity for others to build on the content of their ideas and actions, thereby enhancing the quality of mutual collaboration and coordination. The imagery implied is that of the corporate world held together by a collective mind, with individual managers tied into it through a shared language of abilities and translating thought into action through their personal behaviors.

Postmodern Critique

The course as described above is ripe with opportunities for postmodern critique on two levels, first, with respect to numerous internal components that can be deconstructed, and, second, with respect to the course in its entirety as a force submerging other potentially relevant knowledges. Regarding deconstruction, and without going into detail, let me suggest several of the more obvious possibilities, using a sampling of categories from Boje (1995).

Voice. Privileged voice (Rosenau, 1992, p. xiv) is given to the standardized assessment instruments; witness the fact that the first third of the course is devoted to their administration and explanation. Although data are also gathered from each participant's colleagues and from the person's own life experiences, the message implicit in the distribution of classroom time is that the instrument results have primacy.

Marginalization. The database for the development of the codes was located for the most part in large, white, male-dominated corporate organizations, thereby potentially marginalizing managerial abilities that might be especially relevant to small enterprises, entrepreneurial endeavors, or enterprises staffed with a greater mix of marginalized social groups, for example, racial minorities and women.

Universalism. Although students are invited to add additional categories of abilities to their self-assessment papers, primary attention in the coding process is given to 22 specific abilities; this can be read as suggesting a universal taxonomy for describing effective managerial behavior, thus submerging any number of other categories of ability, as well as multiple local knowledges whose potency might be situation specific.

Essentialism. The coding process itself, with its mandate that one must be able to both observe a behavior and find evidence of a certain kind of intent to confirm the presence of a particular ability, suggests an essential principle that may also submerge more intuitive assessment strategies.

Panoptic Gaze. The continuous, disciplined, anonymous surveillance that facilitates monitoring of, evaluation of, control of, and experimentation with an organization's members (Foucault, 1977, pp. 175-180) is evident in the systematic way in which students are assessed, in the data they are obliged to provide in justifying their self-assessments, and in the detail with which they must articulate their learning plans. It is as if the essence of the course is to teach them how to make themselves into the objects of their own experimentation.

In general, the scientific basis of the codes and coding process and the legitimation of the abilities thus identified through reference to this basis can be interpreted as making it difficult for students to champion their own uniqueness, modify category definitions to fit their personal lexicons, add others of special relevance to their aspirations, and justify idiosyncratic interpretations based on personal experience, even though these options are formally encouraged.

Turning to the course as a whole, as a force submerging alternative knowledges, the emphasis on a particular science-based conceptualization of abilities may hide the possibility that the qualities leading to managerial success are yet to be measurable through current assessment-center methodologies and in fact may be embedded in a more subtle local knowledge of the management world. The scientific results supporting the course concepts may simply be spurious by-products of such deeper knowledge.

Bourdieu (1993), for example, has suggested that successful performance among professionals in the art world is based on their possession of a particular kind of *social habitus.*

> The habitus is sometimes described as a "feel for the game," a "practical sense" (*sens pratique*) that inclines agents to act and react in specific situations in a manner that is not always calculated and that is not simply a question of conscious obedience to rules. (p. 5)

Bourdieu uses the term to indicate something akin to the more subtle skills and perspectives related to a given social role, while avoiding the latter term because of its functionalist connotations. In Bourdieu's formulation, the habitus one acquires is a product of a long socialization process that begins in childhood, extends throughout one's adult years, and can be influenced greatly by one's social class and the cultural capital (p. 7) one is endowed with as a by-product of growing up in that class.

Bourdieu's writings have little to do with management and focus rather on the world of art. Nonetheless, a brief digression on his notion of habitus and its application to professional work in the art world suggests the possibilities of similar phenomena in the management professions. Museums, according to Bourdieu (1968), are both democratic and elitist. Anyone may enter, but only the educated elite can truly appreciate what is there. Their ability to do this is based on the possession of what Bourdieu calls art competence.

> Art competence can be provisionally defined as the preliminary knowledge of possible divisions into complementary classes of a universe of representations: A mastery of this kind of system classification enables each element of the universe to be placed in a class necessarily determined in relation to another class, constituted itself by all the art representations consciously or unconsciously taken into consideration which do not belong to the class in question. (p. 595)

Art competence, in turn, forms the basis of the social habitus of professionals in the art world, for example, art critics, buyers, sellers, exhibitors, and the artists themselves. Without the internalization of such competence, so that it pervades a person's habitus in ways that are far beyond the mere knowledge of textbook definitions, people are incapable of participating in the discourse that produces, maintains, enhances, changes, and reproduces the world of art. By contrast, the less educated public has relatively little understanding of the internal workings of this world and is encouraged to take the professionals' word as authoritative.

One might hypothesize that a similar formulation can be made regarding the practice of management, especially as it is found in large corporate organizations requiring key players to cope with complex patterns of technical and interpersonal interdependence. Specifically, within the corporate world of a given national culture or region, there might be a way of participating in management discourse that requires the possession of its own kind of habitus, which is, in turn, based on the possession of a particular form of management competence. Part of that competence might well be the knowledge base provided by most MBA programs and perhaps by Boyatzis's list of management abilities, but the possibility remains that the particular competencies that really count are more subtle, based in part on upbringing in executive families or association from the bottom up with a particular industry, and beyond the scope of assessment-center technology.

In turn, one might argue that managers who possess this habitus are rated as high performers. They can spot one another by the very way they talk and act in management settings, benefit from one another's transparency, build on one another's ideas, and develop cadres of enthusiasm and support for important decisions. Those who cannot join in these kinds of interactions are experienced as average or below par and, in any case, become the implementers of others' ideas, whereas the first group produces, reproduces, enhances, and changes the organizations in which they work.

Were there some grains of truth in the foregoing surmise, it would have interesting implications for the course's Executive Advisers. For example, the latter might give nominal credence to the course's concepts for social reasons while remaining uncertain at a more visceral level.

The implications for the students would be more serious. Suppose, for example, that two students took the course and subsequently concentrated in the same area, earned identical grades throughout the program, and applied for identical positions upon graduation. Suppose further that what was different about them was that one had come from a blue-collar background and the other from an executive family and that the work and social life the first one had before enrolling in the MBA program involved little interaction with the executive community, whereas the work and social life of the second individual had involved a lot of this. Were the internalization of social class-based viewpoints and habits a more important basis for being seen as having executive potential than the mastery of the course's managerial abilities, the second person might have gotten the job both students desired, while the first was ignored.

The foregoing hypothesis comes close to my own experience when I asked a recruiter why one of my former students had moved rapidly up the ranks upon entering his firm, whereas another former student who had entered at the same time had shown little progress during the same period. I had found both students similarly skilled from a cognitive viewpoint and equally as diligent, but I was also aware that they came from markedly different socioeconomic backgrounds. The recruiter's response had been to acknowledge that both had demonstrated similar technical skills, but the one who had progressed seemed to everyone to carry himself more as an executive, to "have a feel for the game," and frequently to be at the right place and time to take on new responsibilities. This incident occurred before the establishment of the assessment course, so that I could not tell whether the latter would have made a difference. Nonetheless, the possibility that it might not have is worth pondering.

Modern Hegemony
Versus Postmodern Resistance

Let us now turn to what I witnessed during my participation in the course. My observations are organized according to the quadrants in Figure 13.1. I will start with those observations that seemed the most consistent with the foregoing critique and might be characterized as modernist hegemony by faculty over the students.

The views of the faculty actually teaching the course ranged from fairly strong commitment to positive research on managerial competencies to considerable disenchantment with it. But neither the students in the course nor the Executive Advisers to the teams were unusually impressed with this discourse. Incidents of symbolic oppression seemed most evident when students and faculty disagreed on matters of principle over how to interpret the instrument results. In such cases, the abilities model seemed to defy what the students thought they knew about themselves, whereas the faculty were more inclined to believe that the students were refusing to face up to personal weaknesses.

Such disagreements occurred most frequently at two kinds of occasions. The first was when the students received the initial results of the instrumented exercises. The intended message was:

> Here are some useful data about your abilities based on these instruments. It is up to you to gather additional data from colleagues and explore your own experiences with respect to them, and then integrate your findings in a way that will help you pursue your chosen career.

However, especially in the first semester, the message did not come across as clearly as desired. The students seemed to interpret it more often as: Here is a scheme for evaluating managers and here is how you rate in terms of it. What are you going to do about it? This alternative interpretation, I believe, was probably due to the amount of time the faculty and staff spent on perfecting the administration and scoring of the instruments, compared to the time and effort put into developing a colleague-review questionnaire or helping the students understand the logic of the scheme sufficiently to apply it to themselves. Effort was put into these other tasks, but not until well after the students had received the bulk of their assessment-instrument data.

Moreover, much of the model had been perfected previously on already successful mid-career managers (Boyatzis, 1982), and the students scored well below that group. Although that outcome is not surprising, it did not help their egos. Also, in the rush to perfect the administration of the assessment exercises, some faculty (myself included) were not completely confident in interpreting the fine points of all of the codes. If anything, this made us less secure in deviating from the technical definitions of the abilities when interpreting data and perhaps even more dogmatic in the eyes of the students. Thus, many of the original feedback sessions were filled with silence, discomfort, and periodic attacks on the value of the scheme and/or the appropriateness of the scoring process.

Similar conflicts occurred later in the course when students and faculty disagreed over a student's claim, through reference to personal experience, that he or she had more of a particular ability than the instruments had indicated. In both cases, the claims of "science" were being pitted against the life-world of the individual.

Modern Dialogue

Except for a couple of weeks early in the course, classroom time was not spent exclusively on the assessment-center instruments. Students were also asked to review their prior cognitive learning relevant to the MBA—what they already knew about finance, marketing, accounting, and so on—in order to determine which courses they might want to take in subsequent semesters. Faculty from each of the departments in the school led discussions of the MBA course offerings, the Executive Action Teams were introduced to their Executive Advisers, and the team facilitators spent considerable time discussing the logic of the MBA curriculum and the possible career paths it might facilitate.

The discussions surrounding these topics involved considerable excitement and little conflict, but they were not what one might call postmodern in tone either. The students were intent on getting data from authoritative sources about the capitalist edifice they had chosen to enter, and in my view, they behaved quite consistently as fellow modernists with the faculty in exploring the metanarrative of 20th-century management. This appeared to be the case regardless of the students' gender, age, race, or national culture. Such conversations, I believe, helped considerably in establishing faculty/student rapport in spite of the tension over the assessment instruments.

Interestingly, the interaction between the faculty and the Executive Advisers was cordial and demonstrated a friendly accommodation between two metanarratives, positive science and modern management. For the Executive Advisers, I believe, the fact that the abilities seemed to make sense in terms of the realities of their day-to-day lives was far more important than the scientific procedures used to validate their relevance.

Some anecdotal evidence supports this argument. On two occasions, I attended gatherings for the school at which the course and its competency model were presented to groups of our MBA alumni, including many who would become Executive Advisers. In dinner conversations following both presentations, I found that the audience appreciated the scientific findings, but especially for the prospective Executive Advisers, the idea of mastering the coding scheme seemed to require more time and effort than they could afford to offer. What did make sense, however, was that the codes pointed to abilities that were figural in how they evaluated their own managers. Sometimes specific words in the codes had connotations that differed from what they were accustomed to using to define a particular ability. Nonetheless, the general sense of the categories felt right to them.

In turn, the advisers thought they could be helpful to their teams by confirming the general importance of the competencies, especially by stressing that these kinds of action-oriented skills were often just as important as the possession of specific kinds of content knowledge, for example, marketing principles, accounting rules, and so on. My subsequent experience as instructor bore this out, with the students reporting increased respect for the codes when the latter's pragmatic validity had been confirmed by their Executive Advisers.

Postmodern Dialogue

By the second semester in which the course was given, the faculty and staff had improved its administration, and an attractive questionnaire had been developed for obtaining assessments from the students' colleagues. More time was put into both teaching the students techniques for feedback and paying attention to each of the executive teams as emergent groups going through their own developmental processes. Faculty and staff were more comfortable with the logic of the course, more capable of dealing with various ambiguities in the scoring process, and more at ease in distinguishing between correct coding per se and giving the students free reign to draw conclusions about what the results implied.

In line with these improvements, as well as others of a similar nature in subsequent semesters, more students seemed to accept the notion that the course really was designed to assist them rather than reshape them. Most of my colleagues would agree, I believe, that the driving force behind these changes had little to do with our attitudes toward postmodernism. They were simply pragmatic attempts to improve the course so that students would find the model more useful in their personal development and career planning. Few changes were made in the actual design or scoring of the instruments or in the data provided to substantiate the scientific basis of these measures. What was added was a variety of activities designed to make the students feel more comfortable in dealing with personal data, more in charge of their learning process, and more affirmed in creating plans that made sense in terms of their unique personalities and life experiences.

In retrospect, however, one might argue that we achieved our objective essentially by transforming the modernist metanarrative surrounding the abilities model into a local knowledge. We did so in four ways. First, although the discourse represented by the abilities model was in a sense standardized and scientized, the students could see that its application was not expected to be hegemonic. For example, in the first round, the faculty were probably overcommitted to interpretations that gave priority to the instrument results over personal and collegial data, but now it was clear how important it was to acknowledge alternative interpretations, so long as students dealt with all three data sources in the context of their life plans.

Second, the group activities supported the surfacing of local knowledges in conjunction with the discussion of people's personal experiences. The teams, as representative of the class as a whole, were quite diverse and usually contained at least one third women, age ranges of up to 20 years, and representatives from two if not three races, several ethnic backgrounds, and multiple industries. Norms heightening interpersonal respect and sensitivity also facilitated the development of a mutual appreciation for the local knowledges stemming from each of these differences.

Third, the course was experienced as postmodern in the sense of being "past" modern, because although the scientific base of the assessment model was not overemphasized, it was not discarded or ignored either. Students were obliged to learn the logic of the codes before critiquing them and to ponder the research results supporting the codes before deciding whether they were relevant to their interests and objectives. Likewise, the reality base of the Executive Advisers' worlds was stressed as important to understand and appreciate. At the same time, it was up to the participants to draw their own conclusions about the relevance of these inputs to their own lives.

Finally, the experience of the students could be characterized as postmodern in the sense of its resurfacing something of the premodern in its liberal arts emphasis. The course was part of a larger redesign effort for the whole MBA program, the objectives of which included contributing to liberalization of student perspectives. Just what the term *liberalize* meant to the faculty was open to considerable debate, but a commonly discussed theme was that of inducing students to move beyond seeing their MBA studies as involving almost exclusively the mastery of functional specialties, to viewing the management profession more broadly as a humanly created phenomenon.

This definition echoes the classical definition of the liberal arts, the Latin root of liberal being *liber* (free) and that of arts being *ars* (skill). The liberal arts are the freely rendered creations of the mind, as opposed to the mechanical arts, which involve the creation of products using physical objects, where human creativity is subordinated to the world of things (Mcerny, 1983, pp. 252-253). In the early Middle Ages, students learned the seven liberal arts (grammar, rhetoric, dialectic, arithmetic, music, geometry, and astronomy) in order to influence their fellow human beings so as to achieve friends, patronage, power, wealth, and fame (Morrison, 1983, p. 35). We still speak today of the liberal arts as important for the development of leadership qualities and enlightened citizenship in a free society.

It is only a small leap to suggest that the competencies taught in the course contain important elements of the liberal arts related to the pursuit of enlightened citizenship both inside and outside the corporate world. Consider 17 of the 22 abilities in the course's model: self-control, flexibility, empathy, persuasiveness, networking, negotiating, self-confidence, group management, developing others, oral communication, use of concepts, systems thinking, pattern recognition, theory building, quantitative analysis, social objectivity, and written communication. All involve the creation of distinctly mental as opposed to physical products and thus involve liberal artistry.

Overall, then, the student-faculty interaction could be characterized as an exercise in postmodern analysis and planning. Students were architects of their own self-construction, the privileged readers and final arbiters among a variety of discourses, each with its own knowledge base: science, the local knowledge of executive life, the local knowledges of fellow students and the subgroups represented by them, the premodern logic of the liberal arts, and personal biography. The faculty provided access to some of these discourses and techniques for identifying common ground among all of them.

So as to avoid the impression that everything had been perfected after the first couple of semesters, it is important to identify one more type of interaction among students and faculty that in turn falls into the category yet to be covered in Figure 13.1.

Modern Denial
Versus Postmodern Affirmation

The student ratings of the course for its first two semesters were mixed, but the second round was better received than the first, and by the third semester the course was getting generally good ratings (about 4 on a scale of 5). Now, 2 years later, the ratings remain solid but rarely as high as the faculty would like, even though changes of the kind we have discussed continue to be made. One reason for this might be that the course is required of all entering students. Thus, some people who might be uninterested in self-assessment at this point in their lives still have to take it, and they may find themselves disenchanted, regardless of the faculty's efforts and their fellow students' enthusiasm.

This response, however, begs the question as to the causes of such lack of interest. On one hand, one could point to the inevitable discomforts of personal assessment, either because of lack of skill at doing so or brought on by the sheer potential of being unduly categorized, marginalized, and so on, as discussed earlier. On the other hand, I found that a small but noticeable minority of students took the tactic of passing the whole course off as irrelevant to their educational needs. As one student put it, "I am here for the content courses such as finance and accounting; this process stuff gets in the way."

In short, for these students, we were postmodernists with a local knowledge meriting dismissal in the face of their particular interpretations of the modern metanarrative of management education. Faced with the fact that they had to take the course in any case, they tended to behave politely in teamwork sessions and to go through the motions with respect to the assignments, barely deviating from the examples provided by the faculty for interpreting data or developing learning plans. Sadly, they would then rate the course poorly at the end of the term and dismiss its relevance to their MBA educations. We often could reach those who complained either about their own abilities to cope or the particulars of the assessment process, because such encounters created opportunities for constructive dialogue. We had no chance with those who were silent.

Implications for Management Education

I began this chapter with the question of whether the field of managerial competence education can legitimately be characterized as a project of modernity and therefore vulnerable to a postmodern critique. Through the preceding case analysis, I have tried to show that this is not necessarily so. The positive science-based methodology involved is clearly modern in its conceptualization, but this did not get in the way of implementing a successful program that was multidimensional, eclectic, and highly consistent with an affirmative postmodern mentality.

In fact, one might argue that the course would not have succeeded had its proponents stayed with a single grand narrative. Its multidiscourse nature was part and parcel of its success. The discourse of positive science was critical for formulating the course in the first place, for lending it legitimacy in the world of management training, and, incidentally, for getting the course approved by the school faculty. The Executive Advisers found meaningful ways to contribute because the competencies being taught fit intuitively and pragmatically with their day-to-day realities, but not necessarily because of their scientific base. The students found the course worthwhile when they realized they had permission and encouragement to select from both of these discourses and others in developing their self-assessments and learning plans.

It is important to remember that these findings are based on a single case. A variety of alternative situations can be imagined that might heighten the potential for a less affirmative outcome. Suppose, for instance, that Executive Advisers were not used in the course and that the faculty actually teaching the course (including the graduate student facilitators) were less inclined to help the students see themselves as in charge of their own learning. Under these conditions, the students might have been faced with a more uniform and potentially oppressive mandate to use the assessment codes dogmatically and without reference to alternative meanings and contexts. Suppose the socioeconomic backgrounds of the students and the Executive Advisers had been more consistently different. Social class issues might have become more salient to both parties. Suppose the students themselves were more similar in age, ethnicity, race, and gender. There might have been fewer opportunities for the teams to explore the variety of meanings that the codes could create in their members' experience.

I would argue, however, that the multidiscourse nature of the course was not a fluke, but rather that it stemmed from two conditions endemic to U.S. management culture. The first is that American business education has always contained an element of postmodernism, that is, competing and often noncommensurate discourses on reality. Although postmodern theorists point to positive science and capitalism as typically aligned hegemonies, positive science was only brought into U.S. industry about 100 years ago with the development of the first company research laboratories (Chandler, 1977). The dialogue between business and academia has often involved conflict between the pragmatist views of American business and the theory-driven strategies of positive science. Therefore, any school of management with students from industry, much less executives as advisers, has had to and must continue to deal with multiple versions of the truth.

The second factor is that, although one might decry the ethos of individualism in the United States as an inducement to narcissism (Lasch, 1979, pp. 71-75), it is consistent with some themes within the postmodern movement (Rosenau, 1992, p. 53), and its pragmatic elements can also be interpreted as hindering the hegemony of any one grand narrative, save that of individualism itself. U.S. educational systems make individuals responsible for shaping their own careers, and our economic system idealizes individual mobility. Bellah, Madsen, Sullivan, Swidler, and Tipton (1985) found that utilitarian individualism (the pursuit of personal fulfillment through contracted effort and the acquisition of wealth) and expressive individualism (the pursuit of personal fulfillment by doing what intuitively feels right) were fundamental anchors of meaning in the American psyche. One might add to this an emerging form of intellectual individualism, the pursuit of self-fulfillment through creating and acting in accordance with an aesthetically satisfying worldview.

In line with the foregoing, one can also hypothesize that educational activities such as the one discussed here, which are congruent with an individualist focus, will have a culturally induced advantage within the United States over those that do not.

Implications for Postmodern Theory

Clegg (1992) has made the distinction between modern and post-modern analysis, on one hand, and modern and postmodern organizations, on the other, thereby pointing to the possibility of doing postmodern analyses of modern organizations, postmodern analyses of postmodern organizations, modern analyses of modern organiza-

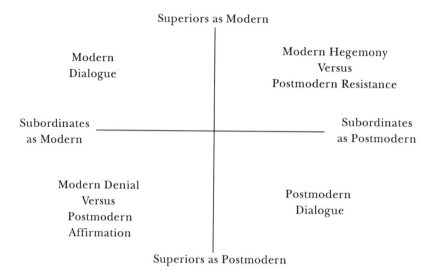

Figure 13.2. Dimensionalizing Modernism and Postmodernism by Rank

tions, and modern analyses of postmodern organizations. The fore-going case study suggests that two other useful distinctions can be made that involve integrating the analyzer into the organization itself, assuming that the preponderance of organizations over the next several decades will have some degree of hierarchy. Specifically, I would argue that

1. All members can be viewed as analysts of their organization's dynamics.
2. Their views on any given subject can be characterized as falling on either side of the modern-postmodern dichotomy.
3. The experiences members generate in themselves and one another with respect to postmodern concerns, and regardless of the written discourses they encounter, will depend at least in part on how their views coincide or conflict with those of their colleagues of higher or lower ranks.

Figure 13.2 dimensionalizes the modern/postmodern dichotomy by rank and is a generalization of Figure 13.1, substituting the superior/subordinate hierarchy for the roles of student and faculty. One qualification I would add in generalizing from the case study is that neither purely modern nor purely postmodern dialogue should be characterized as being as harmonious as it was in our examples. Modern dialogues over whose truths are more universal and postmodern dialogues over the feasibility of collaboration across noncommensurate discourses can be equally conflict ridden.

My hunch is that the presence of a mixture of postures and the kinds of encounters they generate is more often the norm than the pure cases of organizations being populated either by all modernists or by all postmodernists. We may be moving toward a postmodern world, but there is no reason to suggest that the transition will be either smooth or rapid. The findings of the present study suggest that the ecology of members' philosophies with respect to the modern-postmodern dichotomy within a given organization may have an important impact on how policy is implemented and thus invite further research.

PART V

Critical Issues in Global Organizational Studies

14

Metaphors of Globalization

STEWART R. CLEGG

JOHN T. GRAY

Frequently, after Kuhn (1962), it is argued that science emanates from underlying assumptions. Such differing assumptions, if strongly framed, may constitute alternative realities or paradigms. For Kuhn, their framing and its strength is a matter of historical linearity. Rarely do we see mutually exclusive and strong paradigmatic assumptions occupying the same chronological space.

Within paradigms, we construct metaphors. These function as the basis for schools of thought that employ consistent technologies to analyze and interpret data or to puzzle solve. While Morgan (1980, 1983) seems sanguine concerning the temporal co-presence of alternative realities as underlying assumptions to science, Kuhn's (1962) original explanation of a paradigm was as a dominant assumption accepted by a community. This dominant paradigm defined normal science. "Discovery commences with the awareness of anomaly, i.e., with the recognition that Nature has somehow violated the paradigm-induced expectations that govern normal science" (p. 65). Furthermore, he argues that such anomaly brings on scientific revolution. (Kuhn appears here to express a decidedly objectivist view of Nature although he is not consistent in that stance.) This explanation of scientific domination (see Phillips, 1973, pp. 13-17) seems to express the notion of a battle of paradigms, with only one declared victor at any time by the consensus of a scientific community.

Pinder and Bourgeois (1983) argue that poetic or metaphorical inexactitude causes the "reader . . . to analogise, . . . to gain an appreciation for the complexity and indeterminacy . . . in the process." Of course they do. That is a constitutive part of the purpose of metaphors. It is, one might say, their form of life. "Effective metaphor is a form of creative expression which relies upon constructive falsehood as a means of liberating the imagination" (Morgan, 1980, p. 612). Indeed, it does.

Recall the dichotomous views concerning the ontology of social reality that Morgan suggests. In the interpretative perspective, we can say that language is the phenomenon under investigation. Wittgenstein (1968) put it aptly, in one of those allusive aphorisms that made up his *Philosophical Investigations,* (cited in Phillips, 1973, p. 29):

> So you are saying that human agreement decides what is true and what is false?—It is what human beings say that is true and false: and they agree in the language they use. That is not agreement in opinions but in form of life.

The test of "truth" of interpretations is acceptance of a scientific community, which depends on ideological commitment learned within a culture of language. Therein metaphors are means of expression, liberation, and innovation. From the point of view of our region of the dismal sciences, they are part of that language game by which organizational analysts define what they do.

How do we use metaphors in organizational research? Metaphors are part of our means for forging experiences. It may be that they can be traced back to underlying assumptions or dominant paradigms or that the device can be used to switch analysis from one school of thought to another. Typically, however, we use them in explanation of phenomena we have experienced. We attach them to phenomena to shape and interpret. Researchers review their data and detect some patterns, and then they use metaphors to explain these patterns.

Most metaphors are attached to processes post hoc. A prime example of this behavior is represented by Bolman and Deal (1991) in their explanations of the different frames that one may use in conducting organizational research. They identify patterns of understanding organizational behavior and symbolism and attach metaphors to these patterns. Thus, the structuralist or determinist view of an organization is typified as the factory; the people management approach as the family; the political approach as the jungle; and the symbolic approach as theater. Bolman and Deal (1991) use the organization as their unit of analysis and do so in a reflexive attitude. These post hoc analytical formulae have found favor with practitioners. Dunford and Palmer (1995) have tested these analytical metaphors with practicing managers and report that the metaphors were easily understood, that managers were able to switch frames to reflect upon data; furthermore, the managers reported that this improved their decision making. Researchers might note the potential of such a scheme for their interpretation of data.

Other authors adopt a more individual focus. They investigate the use of metaphors in unraveling organizational dilemmas and as a means of interpreting the "mental chart" of the manager. Hampden-Turner (1990) is a prime example of such an approach. His work, rich with metaphors, portrays the manager as "Standing at the Helm" charting the organizational craft between the rock (Scylla) and the whirlpool (Charybdis). His research uses metaphors to explain phenomena described by respondents and iterated to others. As Hampden-Turner reminds us, Lévi-Strauss once described a metaphor as "the likeness of unlike categories" and goes on to explain that managers create a mental construct laden with metaphor to interpret organizational affairs. Managers thereby use metaphors in the process of managing organizational meaning, as artifacts in the culture of the organization.

The majority of authorities agree that metaphors enable the creation of mental constructs, either within a scientific community or among practicing managers or research respondents. Within the scientific community, certain metaphors seem to hold us captive, so that we use them ubiquitously, but in such a way that their very ubiquity occludes their metaphoric basis. Globalization is one such term. It has a certain intangible quality. We think we live it; we see the term in the newspapers on a daily basis; our leaders and politicians exhort us to be a part of it; we experience it through CNN, the BBC World Service,

and other media. Globalization is by now a staple of the promotion of
the international management literature (at the 1994 Australian and
New Zealand Academy of Management meetings in Wellington, New
Zealand, little foam squeeze stress balls, colored, contoured, and
shaped as representations of the globe, were used as promotional aids
for one book on Pacific Rim management). The metaphor is well and
truly lodged in the collective consciousness of people who, in general,
think of themselves as intellectually sophisticated: academics, politicians, journalists, and so on.

But what are the metaphors that have been applied with the advent
of globalization? How should we conceptualize it? Investigation of the
literature suggests that, overwhelmingly, we should think of it as an
economic object, through the metaphors of economic discourse (Dunning, 1993, is the paramount example). What would it be like, however,
to try and develop a different set of metaphors, a set of metaphors not
as beholden to the economics discipline and its neoclassical paradigm?

Adequately Conceptualizing Globalization

Globalization is a metaphor hard to trap solely in economics paradigms. For instance, as Robertson (1992, p. 8) so aptly puts it, "Globalization as a concept refers both to the compression of the world and
the intensification of consciousness in the world as a whole" (p. 8). Yet,
not surprisingly, the disciplines of the business academy view this
tendency to globalization almost one dimensionally, almost unreflec-
tively, as a one-way street in which more and more of the world becomes
sucked into the vortex of the global economy, based upon markets
controlled disproportionately by the leading 750 transnational corporations that dominate world trade, principally through their trade
within themselves and with each other.

In organization theory, riding on the back of the convergence
debate and its assumptions, a view of globalization gave rise to what
has elsewhere been called the TINA tendency (Clegg, 1990). Nearly all
societies were converging on the same point. The reason for this
convergence was the functional necessity for large-scale organizations
to make the transition to modernity. Modernity implied a mass society,
which in turn required large-scale organizations to deliver mass prod-

ucts and services to mass markets, consumers, and publics. In order to manage the complexities of scale that large-scale organization implied, given the available knowledge of management techniques, bureaucracy seemed the most appropriate tool (Perrow, 1986). Bureaucracy came to be seen as the essence of modern organizations and modern societies: At the time, it seemed that There Is No Alternative (TINA), what I have called elsewhere the TINA tendency (Clegg, 1990).

Well, this conception of globalization was patently wrong, for four reasons that have been elaborated at length elsewhere (see Clegg, 1990):

1. The narrative thrust that underlay this organization ontology was the imperative of efficiency. Large-scale organizations were a global phenomenon. Large-scale organizations in India or the former U.S.S.R. would be more like one another than would smaller organizations in their respective countries. Yet, in countries like the U.S.S.R., it was clearly the case that large scale had little to do with efficiency in any of the usually understood ways. Instead, scale had much to with politics, as the Korean case was to confirm, compared with other East Asian examples.

2. Efficient organizations emerged in parts of the globe that did not conform to the TINA tendency: Benetton, in Middle Italy; Chinese family business throughout the Pacific Rim; new form network organizations everywhere. Organizations emerged that were not big in numbers of employees, not less efficient than rivals who were bigger, and not markedly bureaucratic in their structure.

3. Organizations appeared to be diverging in some respects, converging in others, on the basis of global comparisons, or at least the terms of their analysis. Culture became identified as a major marker of difference. Its divergences became a major element of global explanation from Hofstede (1979) onward. Links between identity and authority relations became important in ways that the older globalization paradigm, of the universal rationalization of the world, derived from Weber (1978), could not comprehend.

4. The emergence of concerns with identity and difference signaled the recurrence of a number of critiques of large-scale organization in the name of various repressed and essentially encapsulated interests:

women, with Ferguson (1984); earlier the "wretched of the earth" with
Freire (1973); even earlier of course, those workers, who in Rousseau-
vian vein, had nothing to lose but their chains, whom Marx and Engels
(1848/1955) had identified. Such critiques, with their emphasis on the
wrongfully excluded and the rights of the repressed, seem in retrospect
peculiarly estranged from the experience of globalization as it unfolded subsequently. Globalization, rather than being the broadening,
all-inclusive process of inclusion that Marx and his epigones imagined,
was rather a ragged, uneven struggle to impose various exclusionary
ideologies of world order: fascism; communism, liberalism. Rather
than a single transition from an undifferentiated *Gemeinschaft* of community to a *Gesellschaft* of one model of society, conceived of in
universalistic terms by the founding fathers of the social sciences, the
internationalization of *society* became characterized by sharply contrasting models, in which globalization, conceived on the convergence
model, came to play a key polemical role. Within the convergence
perspective, all societies were seen as converging toward one model,
premised on the United States, driven by technological imperatives
and increasingly, after Aston, the imperatives of organization.

Resisting Convergence

The resistance to convergence has been multifaceted. From an
organizational point of view, the convergence hypothesis hardly begins
to account for the existence of the "born global" emergent export
firms that McKinsey (1993) studied in Australia, firms that became
microtic multinationals almost from their inception. These are high-
tech firms selling very specialized products and services in a global
market, but they are not large organizations converging to a model of
an existing multinational organization form. Indeed, many seem nearer
to postmodern organizations with their virtuality, networking, and
flattening of structure.

Not just practical organization developments undercut the TINA
paradigm of convergence. An intellectual shift against convergence
gathered momentum from the 1960s onward. Initially, it grew from
debates in development theory on the development of underdevelopment, particularly with respect to Latin America, which Wallerstein

(1974) took up in the "world systems" perspective. The success of East Asia in the 1970s, despite the nostrums of development theory, rather put "paid" to this literature, as Berger (1987) was not slow to realize in his book on *The Capitalist Revolution*.

Partly in light of this debate, and partly inspired by a broader debate about culture, a number of writers have suggested, more or less implicitly, that the strengths of indigenously embedded ways of doing things need reevaluation. In some respects, these attach to postmodern themes, where there is the implicit idea that stages may be jumped, that societies can move from premodernity to postmodernity (Clegg, 1990). In this phase of thought, which characterizes the current sociological thinking about globalization, there is a realization that convergence is neither necessary nor desirable; that individual identities differ greatly across national societies, as well as within them; that culture is critical; and that convergence is less likely and less productive than divergence. These themes become characteristic of postmodernism.

Theorizing Globalization

Globalization leads to complexity, relativity, compression, collision, and postmodern plurality, which Dicken (1992, pp. 1-2) reflects in stressing it as an advanced and complex form of internationalization, one that implies a degree of functional integration among internationally dispersed economic activities that have combined and uneven effects across space and time. These are our words, not his, but they do sum up the sense of what he is referring to, or so we think.

If the term has any resonance with the worlds that organizational theorists inhabit, principally it is through a heightened awareness that we live in an increasingly global economy. What is the global economy? Overwhelmingly, as far as the business disciplines are concerned, it is an object viewed through a form of fundamentalism that Robertson (1992) warned us about. Two forms of simplism, or reduction, are involved.

First, there is the reduction of societies to economies. This is most evident in standard and excellent texts, such as Dunning's (1993) *The Globalization of Business,* which, despite a rather strange introductory chapter (one that defines the study of international business and globalization almost entirely in terms of the representation of the interests of the practitioners of the study of international business), does advance the claim for the need to take into account a broader array of what is essentially social science knowledge. That the book rarely does so in the remainder of the text should be no surprise to anyone familiar with members of the economics tribe and its peculiar disciplines.

Second, there is the reduction of questions of identity centered on the relativism of self and humankind to the terms of problems: once the world has been reduced to the economic dimension alone, then people figure in it precisely as sources of failure for economic rationality. For instance, consider the key text, *Global Assignments,* by Black, Gregersen, and Mendenhall (1992) in which

> the authors present solutions to such key problems as how to help employees balance the demands of overseas assignments with family concerns; how to resolve conflicting loyalties in globally integrated, locally responsive companies; and how to ensure that the repatriate's knowledge is not lost upon return but applied to strengthen the parent organization's competitive position.

The relativisms of self and humankind gain consideration only in so far as they affect the balance sheet of the global company. In this respect, the analysis is unreflexive, characteristically of much of the discussion of global business. Unreflexive analysis, focused on the economic dimension considered only in relation to those selves whose profits are served by corporate power, leads to anthropocentrism, suggests Purser (1994), in relation to the global constituents of the firm's environment, including other selves, humankind, and the natural environment. Globalization of this reductionism is a "death threat to the environment." This will be the case particularly where there is a high degree of separation of the simulacraic from the real economy. Real economies root themselves in place; simulacra are free-floating signifiers. The free float of signification burns, wounds, scars, and mars aspects of place that it settles on, suggests Purser. Against this Purser proposes a new kind of search conference, a new kind of "community therapy" attuned to local issues. The conclusions that he reaches are unclear in their organizational implications; also, the prioritizing of localism occurs in the context of the compression of the world and the intensification of consciousness in the world as a whole. Although localism may be an appropriate point of intervention qua resistance, it is likely that more strategically pointed intervention oriented to the locus of calculation could be more efficacious. A great deal depends on what the practical correlates of the stress on localism are. Echoes of the radical humanist project of Bailey, Héon, and Steingard (1993) suggest themselves. The project that they endorse seeks not to intervene from the West into all those spaces that this signification constitutes as "other," but to enable these other ways of doing things to be recognized as authentic, useful, and exemplary. One risk that this project runs is that the other will simply learn the new, therapeutic, and mutualistic discourse that is proposed as another tutelary means, one where the subjects who embrace the process have, perhaps, a better grasp of disciplinary power than do ingenuous and unreflexive "postmodern experts."

Conceiving of the world system of states as societies, one can be hostage to a further form of economistic reductionism, one leading to a new respecification of convergence. Walck (1994) focuses on the Russian transition to a market economy. Transition; development: This is how U.S. business commentators represent the implosion, meltdown, and reaction of life in the new Russia, she suggests. Development in the Russian context meant a new lease on life for economistic simplisms and abstractions that disassembled economies and organizations from their societal context. Missionaries, managerialists, madmen: blind to culture, context, and the civilities and disciplines that sustain forms of life, both real, imagined, and invoked, as imperatives. If one definition of madness sees it as failure to relate to context, normative order, and tacit rules, then since 1989, Russia increasingly resembles a madhouse signified as a "cuckoo's nest" that the saner inmates seek to fly away from.

The postmodern concern with globalization is with the problematic and creative conjunction of different forms of life (Robertson, 1992): "In an increasingly globalized world there is a heightening of civilizational, societal, ethnic, regional, and, indeed, individual, self-consciousness" (p. 27). Robertson proposes capturing this through a model that relates national societies, the world system of societies, selves, and humankind.

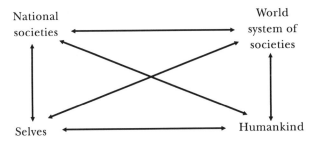

Figure 14.1. Robertson's (1992) Model of Globalization

The key aspect linking all of these together is relativization. According to Robertson (1992), globalization, expressed through Figure 14.1, produces a profound relativization of experiences.

- On the top, linking national societies and the world system, is the relativization of societies.
- Along the bottom, linking selves with humankind, there is the relativization of self-identities.
- Linking national societies to selves, there is the relativization of the problematic of the relation of individuals to society.
- Linking the world system of societies to humankind, there is the relativization of the relationship between the Realpolitik of the world system and the rights of humankind within that world system.
- Linking national societies to humankind, there is the relativization of citizenship.
- Linking the world system to selves, there is the relativization of societal relevance.

Globalization, then, rather than foreclosing these questions of identity in convergence on one form, opens them all up in a thoroughly postmodern way. Failure to appreciate this, or the tendency to focus on one aspect of this relativism, the virtual exclusion of relativity, is a form of theoretical fundamentalism that fails to reflect the current global conjuncture as one that is postmodern. The postmodern global world is simultaneously one of compression of space and time and, consequent upon this, an exacerbation of relativities between narratives of self, society, the globalizing world, and the increasingly transparent ways of being human, one to the other, that this complex of compression and relativization presents.

Some of the empirical tendencies hastening this simultaneous compression and relativization include the following: the increasing separation of the "real" economy of production and its simulacra in the "symbol economy" of financial flows and transactions; the emergence of a new international division of labor and a new international financial system, the latter centered on London, New York, and Tokyo; and a new international division of labor that is truly global, compressing and fragmenting both space and distance. Not only the sphere of production but also the sphere of circulation, such as the various business service industries, may be said to be globalizing; these new divisions restructure geographic space in ways that introduce both relativism and tension to the settlement of space through nation-state forms. In the value sphere, there is the rise of postmaterialism and the emergence of more complex notions of personal identity attendant upon the revolution in gender, sexual, ethnic, and racial mores. The interpenetration of culture and economy produces new markets of microtization, increasingly premised on the differentiation of identity. The emergence of the world's first postmodern society occurs in Australia, with its formal policies of multiculturalism and its multiethnic ways of being Australian, forms of being that exist without an overarching ideological commitment to being anything else in a formal sense. The demise of the Cold War and the globalization of the problems of "rights" in a world no longer bipolar introduces a plurality of considerations relativizing relations between states. There are also the emergence of global communication through E-mail, faxes, satellite TV, CNN, and so on; the rise of a global ecological consciousness, manifested through phenomena such as the Rio Earth Summit and the appreciation of the global warming threat posed by the thinning of the ozone layer; and the reemergence of old questions of identity whose energies had been contained in the modern era through state socialist hegemony, principally in the Balkans, but globally through the assertion of religious identity, notably Islam. All of these tendencies—and many more—may be said to simultaneously compress and relativize experience in the world.

Robertson (1992) is the appropriate starting point for an analysis of these tendencies toward compression and relativization precisely because his systemic model includes consideration of the reflexive autonomy of selves and humankind, as well as world systems and societies.

Robertson requires synthesis with concerns similar to those that Dicken (1992) raises. What is lacking from both frameworks, however, is a conception of the organization circuits or conduits through which reflexive autonomy is intermediated (Clegg, 1989).

These organizational circuits may take many shapes, many forms. However, a limited architectrony characterizes their structuration. Much of the changing shape of this global circuitry is sculptured by transnational corporations (TNCs). Such organizations have significant control over both production and consumption; they have this control in more than one country; they have an ability to take advantage of geopolitical differences between countries; they dominate world trade through their internal trade, amounting to about 25% of world trade; a single center of calculation dominates them; and they have a geographical flexibility that enables them to shift resources and operations among global locations.

Yet there are a plurality of TNCs. They do not necessarily dominate national industrial sectors in all markets; they operate across more or less sovereign states; and the world system of both states and TNCs involves relations that are not only concertative but also competitive. Only a small number of TNCs are truly global, and not all TNCs are necessarily large in conventional definitions of that term. Global patterns of transnationalization differ markedly according to the national origin of the transnationalizing firm. New supplies and sources of TNCs evolve as the world economy evolves, so that we now have the case of emergent NIC (newly industrialized countries) TNCs. New forms of disciplinary power emerge as changes in generic technology systems develop, often in relation to "long wave" phenomena, such as the emergence of information technology. Product development stages destabilize existing nodal points of production and market strategies, and particularly in embryonic industries, flexible organizations of a putatively postmodern form emerge, displaying characteristics of virtuality, networking, and dedifferentiation, all in an uneven distribution.

In part, the distribution is uneven because we are dealing with strategic calculation, and calculation implies choice. Some transnationalization is driven by the choices of firms that are up- or downstream in the chain that links organizations. Yet, make, sell, or lease decisions hardly exhaust the limits of possibility for network and virtual organizations. Expectations of profits are notoriously unreliable and

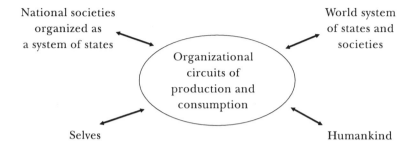

National societies
organized as
a system of states

World system
of states and
societies

Organizational
circuits of
production and
consumption

Selves

Humankind

Figure 14.2. A Proposed Revision of the Model of Globalization

are hardly a sufficient basis for all direct foreign investment decisions. National centers of calculation are of diminishing importance for TNCs choosing globally integrated competitive strategies in a world system marked by extensive differentiation in national societies, states, and selves. An internal tension exists between globalization forces, on one hand, and pressures to localization, on the other (Dicken, 1992, p. 144). Although Robertson (1992) captures this tension, his actors include nations, selves, humankind, and world systems: There are no organizations. Yet, how is any global reach possible, any conquest of space and time achievable, whether by nations or by firms, without some concept of the centrality of organization and organizations as the media through which globalization occurs? In the past, global reach occurred through warfare; however, as a form of global, rather than local, societal interaction in the postmodern conjuncture, warfare is a form of sociability in decreasing frequency. Organizations are the media of global reach.

What is missing, then, from Robertson is a strong sense of the centrality of circuits of production and consumption through which relations between selves, humankind, nations, and world systems route. Increasingly this intermediation occurs through circuits of production and consumption. With this premise, one can reconfigure the model that Robertson (1992) provides so that it is of greater value for organization theory, by making organization central to its design. We propose the relationships shown in Figure 14.2.

Is it possible to attempt some provisional guidelines accounting for globalization/localization tendencies, using the revised framework suggested above? To do so, it will help to focus on further issues for management with respect to globalization, conceived within an empirically ethical context: empirical, because it alerts us to a range of specific issue areas in which business has an impact, and ethical, because the nature of that impact depends greatly on the strategic choices that we choose to make with respect to these areas.

Some indicative issues areas for further research, drawing focus from the perspective of selves and humankind, may be suggested as major arenas for ethical consideration:

- Individual selves: key questions for selves in the TNCs
  □ Problems of adaptation and readaptation
  □ Cultural relativism or universalism
  □ Salience of individualism or familialism as TNC employee
- Selves in states receiving TNC investment: key questions
  □ Integrity of the life-worlds of the peoples of the states
  □ Implications of the integration of their life-worlds into modernity and postmodernity
  □ The salience of their life-worlds as a sphere of both TNC production and consumption
  □ Process of becoming proletarianized and consumerized, which might lead to resistance to TNCs
  □ Cultures of the life-worlds, such as those of ethnicity, tribe, gender, age, and their degree of impermeability/permeability to the new forms of consciousness that TNCs transmit
  □ Preservation of selves in the face of pressure on the immediate natural resource, cultural and material life environments
- Humankind: key questions
  □ The ecological threat to survival, both globally (global warming) and locally (specific habitats or resources)
  □ Transformations in the reflexive consciousness of what being human entails as forms of life increasingly tie in with changing forms of consumption and consciousness of these

The lacunae of the globalization debate in business are evident through comparing the contents of any of its key texts with the list of possible questions presented above. Think of them as a grid for future research. An ethical postmodern business practice will have to consider each of these issues in the future.

Conclusion

Without conceptual innovation, organization theory withers as a metaphorical branch of the tree of knowledge, unwatered and uncared for. The sap that flows through the tree that we would tend is unashamedly sociological, but it is management, and it is organization theory as well. If left to wither on a tree of knowledge watered only from the economic subsoil, globalization will be a poor, impoverished thing.

We see globalization as perhaps the most significant analytical and conceptual challenge for management and organization theory. We are caught up in its drama, but, like Plato's slaves, seem frequently to catch only the flickering representation of its appearance. Globalization, rather than foreclosing questions of identity in convergence on one form, opens them all up in a thoroughly postmodern way. Yet it is simultaneously a process of compression of space and time and, consequent upon this, an exacerbation of relativities between narratives of self, society, the globalizing world, and the increasingly transparent ways of being human, one to the other, that this complex of compression and relativization presents. And these are not free-floating signifiers of equal weight in dreamtime stories that imagine futures now rather than pasts. They are stories that lodge in different forms of consciousness, encoded in the lore of the elders, the wisdom of the tribe, the news on the airwaves, the sights and sounds that come down the tube, and the transmissions through the satellites, optical cables, and microwaves.

Power is never absent from knowledge. Some global significations route more global imagination than others. The Murdoch News Corporation satellite now spreads its footprint all over the Asian region: Australian iconic events such as the Rugby League Grand Final and rock singer Tina Turner, each a successful commercialization of a once spurned, marginalized, and despised culture, meet in a spectacular union that now competes with Hindi soap operas for the attention of a subcontinent. Certainly, there is considerable fixity to the messages that the media transmit but, recalling the error with which McLuhan (1964) started the whole globalization debate, there is also considerable diversity in the way in which they are interpreted, instantiated, and used. Fixity in forms of production and distribution does not mean closure in forms of cultural consumption.

15

Organizations as a Play of
Multiple and Dynamic Discourses
An Example From a
Global Social Change Organization

TOJO JOSEPH THATCHENKERY

PUNYA UPADHYAYA

T his chapter is an attempt to theorize organizations in a way that is
evocative, multiplicitous, and generative. We offer theoretical narratives of dynamic and multiple discourses, narratives that could ground
our explorations and inquiries into organizational life. And we ground
this in the experience of a transformative global organization that has
explored some of these dynamics. Let us begin with an exploration of
multiplicity.

On Multiplicity

In "Stories of the Storytelling Organization," David Boje (1995)
shares his experience of watching Los Angeles's longest-running play,
Tamara.[1] It is an interactive, multidimensional play and is structured
for dynamic multiplicity. A dozen characters unfold their stories before
a walking (sometimes running) audience. In the play, the audience
splits into small groups that chase characters from room to room and

from floor to floor in order to co-create the stories that interest them the most. Assuming a dozen stages and a dozen characters, the number of story lines an audience could trace chasing the "wandering discourses" of *Tamara* is significant (726 to be exact). For example, Boje (1995) followed the chauffeur from the kitchen to the maid's bedroom; there she met the butler who had just entered from the drawing room. Later, they each moved on to different rooms, leaving Boje and the audience to choose whom to follow. As the audience decides to follow different characters through different spaces, each of them experiences a different story. No one in the audience can follow all the stories, because the action is simultaneous, involving different characters in different rooms on different floors. As a result, *Tamara* cannot be understood in one visit, even if a group of friends split off into six different directions and share their stories.

> One can even be in one room with one's best friend and if they both came to this room by way of different rooms and character sequence, each friend can walk away from the same conversation event with entirely different stories. (Boje, 1995, p. 4)

Thus, although the audience can trace innumerable wandering discourses in this play, its members cannot find one story to hold it all together; each member experiences a different story depending on his or her choices of character and stage.

Tamara can be a discursive metaphor to underscore the plurivocal interpretations of organizational stories in a distributed and historically contextualized meaning network (Boje, 1995). (As Gephart, 1991, would argue, stories may be seen as tool or program for making sense of events.) We develop this idea a notch deeper by describing how an organization can be understood as multiple discourses operating simultaneously.

The multiple discourses create a pluralistic construction of innumerable stories realized differently by participants in an organization. This chapter attempts to show that, contrary to the commonly held view, the multiple discourses are not necessarily integrated by a grand logic or common purpose. They are simply discourses of various types coexisting simultaneously, like those in *Tamara*.

The Nature of Discourses

The concept of discourse is most closely identified with the writings of Foucault (e.g., 1976). In general terms, a discourse may be conceived of as

> a set of ideas and practices which condition our ways of relating to, and acting upon, particular phenomena. Because a discourse is always embedded in social practice, it cannot be reduced to its ideational content any more than be seen as devoid of theory. (Knights & Morgan, 1991, p. 253)

For example, in Foucault's analysis of madness, the concept is constructed in particular social contexts. Once they are recognizable as such, that is, when actors come to understand the world in these terms, then social practices develop that reproduce this perception as "truth." This occurs not least as a result of a combination of the power-knowledge relations represented by political activists and "experts" generating a convincing discourse that entails physically segregating the mad and the insane from "normal" society through a system of institutional incarceration. Such an exercise of power clearly institutionalizes the knowledge that sustains and reproduces these dividing practices and the truth of the distinction between the subjectivity of normality and insanity. The discourse, in this sense, produces its own truth effects through elaborating a view of the world in which problems are defined that the discourse can "solve." "A discourse is not then simply a way of seeing; it is always embedded in social practices which reproduce that way of seeing as the truth of discourse" (Knights & Morgan, 1991, p. 253).

Discourses are changeable. In this postmodern world, there is a plurality of discourse that actors can draw upon. According to Foucault, the power effects of discourses are always subject to resistance, making discourse a very dynamic concept. Social order is typically achieved through the skilled actions of actors who coordinate their relationships with others through various tactics that establish or confirm the grounds of the communicative exchange. Discourse changes as actors adapt and change conditions of the process of reproduction. If that was not the case, we would not have talked about the emergence of new discourses, which are the genesis of new ways of accomplishing social relations. At the same time, discourses are internal to the subject, creating the foundation on which subjectivity itself is constructed. Thus, to understand actors and social relations, one needs to comprehend the discourses within which they routinely embed their own self-understandings (Knights & Morgan, 1991).

In summary, discourses may be a "shorthand for a whole set of power/ knowledge relations which are written, spoken, communicated, and embedded in social practices" (Foucault, 1976, p. 255). However, much of this understanding has flowed from a flawed assumption that only one discourse can be valid at a given time. This further assumes that if multiple discourses are present, it is a temporary condition, until one of them wins and "reduces equivocality." This chapter demonstrates, through its stories and theories, that multiplicity is a compelling and celebratory reality that can realize much of the potential of hermeneutics and discourses for emancipation and transformation.

This exploration has two aspects. For one, we will show that multiple valid and powerful discourses exist simultaneously in organizations. Second, we will describe the different dynamics of some discourses. This challenges the binary assumption about the nature of discourses (either they are present or they are absent) and instead points to a richness and subtlety that can inform our theories and change efforts. We perform these tasks simultaneously by sharing the stories of four discourses that flowed through the Institute of Cultural Affairs (ICA), a global organization extensively studied in this chapter. These four are not the only discourses that formed this organization, but they have been chosen to demonstrate four different dynamics of discourses. The richness of exploration and poesis that is possible in researching a complex transformative organization is not exhausted in one chapter. The present offering is but an introduction to multiple and dynamic discourses, not a complete exposition.

The rest of the chapter will begin with a brief description of an Indian metaphor that inspired us to reconceptualize the data: the ancient notion of *maya-leela*. This is followed by a brief mention of our methodology. The bulk of the chapter is based on stories of the ICA. Four discourses are described here. The first is the continuous discourse of *participation*, in many ways a thread that pulls the entire organization together from its inception. This is the type of discourse that is commonly theorized as never ending and slightly essentialist.

The second is an introduced discourse of *global social change organization,* which describes a process of incorporating new ideas into an organization. This is very crucial as it is linked to the praxis of many organizational consultants. The third is a cyclical discourse of *intense reflexivity,* which started by being privileged, became deprivileged, and was reprivileged. This will be familiar to many of us, as old ideas rarely die, they just keep coming back in newer forms. Last, we describe a transformed discourse of *spirituality,* where a central theme of the organization changes over time into an entirely new form. This dissolves most notions of a single, essentialist identity for a discourse and offers the possibility for transformation that many organizations experience.

Maya-leela:
A Metaphor for Multiple Discourses

Like *Tamara,* maya-leela is the evocation of the play of multiplicities. It is rooted in one sophisticated millennia-old philosophy of the *sanathana dharma.*[2] *Maya* is a Sanskrit signifier for the multiplicity of forms and processes that we encounter in this world. *Leela* describes the cosmic play that expresses the universe as a byplay of ontological exuberance. Maya-leela thus evokes a sense of the world as a playful extravagance that generates abundance and multiplicities. It expresses a mode of being that responds from generosity to any invitation, seeing all as equals and experiencing reality as fecund and joyful. It is a metaphysical construct that offers a generative space to be with plurivocities.

In the realm of organizations, maya-leela is the context for theorizing how multiple discourses simultaneously engage many people. This is crucial if we choose not to reify organizations into specific constructs. Our offering is that organizations are the interplay of multiple discourses with the life-worlds of those who participate in them. These discourses are the many knowledge-power shapers of the social reality of organizational life. These would include many diverse discourses, some effective, some ineffective, some inspirational, others dysfunctional. For our current appreciation, we have chosen some of the important and influential discourses that exhibited change over time in the ICA, a large global nongovernmental organization.

This chapter is built on a core construct that seeks to understand organizing as the play and weave of discourses. This is facilitated by our celebration of the end of metanarratives (Lyotard, 1979/1984). As we experience the proliferation of discourses, it becomes possible to appreciate the multiplicity of evocations in organizations. Indeed, it behooves us to understand organizations as these multiple evocations, as the forms taken by the resonance and engagements of these discourses. However, this is not enough. For all the success and power of the postmodern offerings on discourses, we must also acknowledge their dystopic failure and move beyond them.

A crucial intervention in the conversation around discourses that the construct of maya-leela offers us is a reconceptualization of power. Most (post)modern discourse analysis falters and loses energy as it is focused solely on power based on violence, scarcity, and greed. The call to revolution is located in similar violence, changing nothing. The abundance and generosity evoked by maya-leela calls for a vaster, postcognitive sense of power. This is what gives us the strength to move beyond the lack of utopian energy in modern high-consumption societies. This lack can compel derision, individualism, or re-creation. We suggest re-creation by locating ourselves in a nondual location, one that celebrates the simultaneity of multiplicity and does not split discourse and experience. We believe that this simultaneity of discourse and experience is the creativity that can inspire risk, life, and transformation. We will describe how a multiplicity of discourses can create organizations alive in both continuity and change, using a detailed illustration from the ICA.

Methodology

Grounding is crucial for any discussion of discourses. The temptation to textualize realities must be eschewed by organizational theorists because of the impact that our work can have on the lives of people. We propose to show how the end of the grand narrative and the presence of multiple, complementary, and competitive discourses plays out in a real organization. This is crucial because pronouncements on the need for such work are not enough. This is also partially an epistemic limit of Western social science. As Garg and Parikh (1993), thinkers on

Indian management, point out, this may be a result of the absence of metaphors of simultaneity in Western theorizing. (The already discussed metaphor of *Tamara*, described in Boje, 1995, is one of the rare exceptions.) This chapter offers a description of how multiple discourses trace organizational realities, cohering into vital experiences and transformations for people and societies.

The chapter is grounded in stories of the ICA, which describes itself in a 1990 brochure as a "research, training and demonstration group concerned with the human factor in world development." It is a nonprofit organization, and at its peak, was active at over 100 sites in 35 countries. It has a holistic developmental orientation that makes it difficult to generalize about tasks, structures, and policies. The ICA participated in a 3-year inquiry project with a team of scholars from the Department of Organizational Behavior at Case Western Reserve University. The research team was partly based in Cleveland (at the university) and at the ICA centers in Chicago and the Midwest, although one of the authors also made a trip to Brussels to meet with organizational participants from all over the world.

In exploring the narratives, we are using an affirmative (Weick, 1982) or appreciative (Cooperrider & Srivastva, 1987) approach. Our aim is to celebrate and learn from the ICA through a sharing of stories, ideas, and perspectives. As will be described later, there has been a mutual learning process throughout the research. In this case, we will narrate the stories of four discourses important in shaping the life of the ICA, and theoretically important for the dynamics they exemplify. The central link we draw is the temporal nature of the interplay between discourses and life-worlds through appreciative narratives of the dynamics of these discourses and their interplay with the life-worlds of the participants of the organization. A key aspect of this will be the use of quotations from the participants to highlight the interplay between discourse and life-world. In the narratives, as mentioned earlier, we will share the dynamics of four types of discourses: a continuous discourse, an introduced discourse, a cyclical discourse, and a transformed discourse. A continuous discourse is a discourse that has enjoyed a privileged status all through the life of the organization. An introduced discourse is one that comes into use as a result of a significant event in the organization or as a result of some reconceptualization of the core activity of the organization. A cyclical discourse is one that gets privileged, deprivileged, and reprivileged over time. Finally, a transformed discourse is one that changes dramatically in form, while preserving some critical elements of its earlier identity.

These dynamics of discourses were mutually read into the ICA's stories. We are tempted to think that we could read similar dynamics in other organizations as well. Continuous discourses must exist in most organizations to offer some linear history.

Introduced discourses are seen when massive restructuring or mergers take place. In a smaller way, most organizational change projects attempt to introduce new discourses into organizations. Cyclical discourses are observed when an organization is studied longitudinally. Transformed discourses are seen when the core constructs of organizations change dramatically (e.g., when a new chief executive officer tries to change the culture of an organization, while building on its history). Other dynamics of discourses could also be observed—dialectical, spiral, mosaic, and so on—depending on the dynamics of each organization. We hope that these are generative for the imaginative possibilities of our ways of being with organizations as the interplay of multiple discourses and life-worlds.

This is the first of four stories we will share about the ICA. As the stories stretch your imagination on what is possible in an organization, the narratives stretch the possibilities of linearity. The four stories are quasi-independent, related intimately, yet not following one another.

The Continuous Discourses

Participation is a discourse that has consistently characterized the ICA. The institute started its work with a technology of participation it has developed for over 35 years. Participation was one of the five presuppositions that informed the first social impact project of the ICA:

> Everyone needs to find a way to participate and make a contribution unique to their position in the community. Throughout the development of the project, it became increasingly important to have community members as the leaders of the project. (from a 1965 ICA document, quoted in Joseph, 1994, p. 21)

Again, participation is one of the seven "nonnegotiable values" that the ICA identified in 1992. The draft of statement said that

> we value face-to-face participative processes because no one of us is as good as all of us. We believe everyone has a voice and everyone should be heard. We trust what is going on in a group. We believe that the something that is going on (especially conflict and change) is good and beneficial to a group. (quoted in Joseph, 1994, p. 148)

The discourse of participation has been very evocative for the life-worlds of the ICA members. It has imbued this organization with a compelling call, asserting that a global mind-set would only be created if people participated in it. Holding that "all the gifts of humanity belong to all the peoples" (from the 1971 Summer Research Assembly, quoted in Joseph, 1994, p. 32), ICA developed decision-making structures that enacted this discourse. These can be expressed in the ICA's emphasis on consensus and community, which leads to—and from—an emphasis on affirmation and enrichment of the people. As a result, the ICA's emphasis on the personal flowering of all participants fosters the growth of participative structures.

Community is reflected in the emphasis on cultural diversity and representation from multiple social strata. Here the family and the community become one, as if the community is an extended family, a concept expressed clearly in the ways in which discourses on shared living spaces constantly recur. Thus, their description of *corporateness* (shared body) has three aspects: team building, community life, and family roles. Strong interpersonal relationships among the members, through an emphasis on camaraderie, social support, and intense group experiences, are crucial for developing live participative processes. Globally, this also applies to work with multiple constituencies; as a member of the ICA said, "I can sit with executives and I can sit with peasants" (in Joseph, 1994, p. 121). In a deeper sense, the life of the ICA itself comes from its participation in the lives of the poor, dispossessed, and marginalized in many societies.

Consensual decision making is the dominant form of sharing in the ICA, supported by a bureaucratic structure for implementing the consensus and by symbolic functions for inspiring and evoking the collectivity. Decision making coheres around the notion that "power is at the center of the table" (quoted in Joseph, 1994, pp. 50, 134). The consensus is supported by methods that ensure that all voices at the table are heard. This takes into account the diverse styles of people and the different relationships among the people at the table. Structurally, the high point of such a discourse was in 1984, when local ICAs all over the world became completely autonomous and financially independent. This was accompanied by a process of intense soul searching to create alternate forms of organizing that would live out these values. This included the development of strong norms of accountability, secularism, leadership through spirit life rather than formal authority, and the celebration of new emerging structures. By being constantly open to all who want to participate, affirming the gifts that everyone brings to a situation, and celebrating their quotidian realities, the ICA has been reinvigorated and reinvented many times through the discourse of participation.

One of the clearest examples of reinvention through participative style became evident when one of the authors interviewed a representative sample of ICA members at a global gathering in 1989. A thematic analysis of the interview data clearly pointed toward the existence of nonnegotiable values, participation being one of the most fundamental. The manner in which the 5-day global gathering was held bore a vivid testimony to the participative values that are fundamental to the ICA. All decisions were made by consensus, because consensus decision making was yet another core value closely tied to the participative value. It also demonstrates the incredible flexibility it takes for a discourse to be live in organizing, as well as the power of a discourse to shape organizing compellingly.

The Introduced Discourses

This discourse differs from the others described here, as it was explicitly introduced by outside researchers. Unlike the others, this was not endogenous to the organizational space, or even invited by the organization. Instead, this concept was the spur that evoked the research team, which characterized the ICA as a global social change organization (GSCO). The description here will start by describing the context for the development of this discourse, show how it was introduced to the ICA, and outline its adoption.

The GSCO was the key conceptual focus of the first part of a 10-year research program into social innovations in global management started at Case Western Reserve University. This program focused on organizations that were—or created—social innovations for the global good. The ICA, along with the Latin American Division of the Nature Conservancy, Ohio in the World, International Physicians for the Prevention of Nuclear War, and the Hunger Project, was intensively studied, and detailed ethnographies were prepared. In the course of this inquiry, the concept of the GSCO was refined by sharing experiences and concepts with these organizations, as well as by additional research and inquiry (see Cooperrider & Thatchenkery, 1991; Johnson & Cooperrider, 1991).

Easily one of the most transformative global forces in the last 50 years has been the rise of grassroots organizations that support the indigenous transformations of society. Boulding (1988) considers GSCOs one of the most prominent social innovations of contemporary times. GSCOs provide society with (a) a longer-term time horizon and vision, (b) educational forums of the world's citizenship, and (c) an integrative knowledge vehicle providing data and conceptual innovation in the areas between disciplines. Above all, the GSCO is one of the most effective vehicles for "going to school," whereby we can all be active learners of the 10,000 societies that inhabit our planet in today's axial period of *heterogeneous universalism*.

The ICA as GSCO is important, as it was an introduced discourse affecting the ICA. This was based on readings of their dispersed organizing, social change orientation, missions of universal compassion, holistic growth orientation, moral and value rationalities, egalitarian and participatory authority structures, and holographic organizational knowledge and learning (Joseph, 1994, pp. 35-36). This description proved resonant with diverse elements of the ICA's self-descriptions. A document corporately written by the participants in the 1971 Summer Research Assembly, titled "All the Earth Belongs to All the People," is an instance of this orientation. The 40-page booklet opens with the following statement:

Never before have the world and its societies been faced with such incredible options. . . . It is now clear that the forces of revolution and reform have had but one vision: that human sociality means all the earth belongs to all the people; all the goods of Nature belong to all the people; all decisions of history belong to all the people; and all the gifts of humanness belong to all the people. These revolutionary principles grounded in a wider consciousness can create global brotherhood and the possibility of a human future. For it has been disclosed to us that this commonness has always been at the heart of society. It is the sharing of life which creates society; and in these times of our self-consciousness of that reality gives us the possibility of choosing a free and fertile future.

The ICA also showed other characteristics that were relevant in creating a good description of GSCOs. For example, if we look at how leadership was organized at the global level, the egalitarian nature of the ICA as a GSCO becomes evident. This may be located in the *Panchayat Trek Reflections* (ICA, 1988). *Panchayat* is a concept the ICA borrowed from the Indian village governance system. In essence, it is an elected leadership team consisting of five village elders. In the ICA, five members from its worldwide operations were chosen by consensus to act as symbolic leaders. A quote from their reflections reveals the following:

From mid-November 1987 to May 1988, the Global Panchayat along with selected members of the Global Priory traveled to 7 continents and visited some 35 locations. . . . It was our good fortune to meet a variety of people who represent the vast spectrum of our body. . . . Every location is involved in inventing inclusive metaphors and functional forms to nurture this expansive identity. . . . Culturally, economically, and socially appropriate indigenous organizations are being shaped. . . . A new story of planetary unity is emerging . . . one planet-wide community committed to co-creating and sustaining the planet. (p. 2)

As the excerpts from its documents show, the ICA expressed many of the elements of the researcher's discourse on GSCOs. This facilitated the process of sharing this discourse with the ICA in a friendly and mutual manner, over a 3-year research period, as part of a collegial, co-inquiring process. Both the existing resonance and the process of sharing made it easy for the ICA to own the discourses of a GSCO. As Joseph (1994, p. 32) said,

The stakeholders of the ICA find the GSCO characterization very appropriate and befitting of who they are. The term GSCO has gradually been assimilated into the discourses of the organization. For example, several newsletters that have come out of the ICA during the last 3 years have used the notion that the ICA is a GSCO. The ICA found the characterization so appealing that one of the researchers was invited to give a speech on GSCOs at one of the ICA's annual international gatherings in Prague, Czechoslovakia, in September 1992.

Such a discourse helps to reframe the ICA from being one among many international nongovernmental organizations to being a GSCO with specific and desirable qualities and a direct connection to the global civic culture it is helping to create.

The Cyclical Discourses

An important dynamic of discourses is a cycle of privileging, deprivileging, and reprivileging (Joseph, 1994). This cycle is read into the flux of a discourse crucial to the ICA, which we call intense reflexivity. This is a descriptor for the simultaneous acts of analysis and meta-analysis. It connotes the simultaneity of an act and reflections on the act. The relation to theories of learning (given their emphasis on reflection) is immediate and compelling. For example, linking it to Bateson's (1972) theory of single-loop and double-loop learning, intense reflexivity is the simultaneity of both. Thus, it is not just an analytic act, or a reflection on the analysis, but the simultaneous engagement in both.

Intense reflexivity is a discourse of simultaneously affirming and transforming social constructions. The analytic act starts this process, as it is always an incomplete mimesis of the object of reflection. Following Derrida (1981), the likelihood of imperfection in mimesis makes potentially infinite reflections possible. For example, while the ICA was reflecting on the decentralization of 1984-1985, each reflection was an imaginary construction of some event. Each reflection had some aspects that coincided with other reflections and some that did not. The aspects that coincided with the reflections of others help in the process of affirmation. Those points that did not coincide are undecidable by the person who is reflecting, thus preventing reflection from being only a solipsistic process of self-adequation and offering possibilities for transformation. A closure is possible at this juncture only by joining with others who also experience incomplete mimesis in dialogue about the discrepancies.

This dialogical process need not lead only to closure; it can lead to many variations of processes of affirmation and transformation. These processes are partly infinite because of the indeterminacy of any construction. As Platt (1989) put it, "the consistent application of any theory, or of any interpretation, includes claims that the theory's 'axiomatic formulations' cannot be used to decide . . . [i.e.] theories generate propositions which are not definable in their own terms" (p. 653). The importance of a discourse of intense reflexivity is that it can help people defer their need for closure by offering ways to respond to and play with an infinite range of interpretations of actions and processes in a social space (e.g., an organization).

The ICA was born out of dialogues that were intensely reflective in nature. During the period from 1952 to roughly 1973, intense reflexivity was a privileged discourse, articulated by practices and structures facilitating organizational dialogue. The formation of the Christian Faith and Life Community (CFC) in 1952 focused on experimentation with a lifestyle focused on research and study. The goal at that time was to create a curriculum of social and religious studies, again an intensely reflective practice. Finally, the expected outcome of the project also reveals a strongly reflective mission: "to awaken the university community, and later the church, to the fundamental issues people faced in their lives" (ICA, 1988, p. 6). This process continued until the early 1970s.

Although most theories of organizational learning processes emphasize the introduction of reflexive practices, particularly that of double-loop learning, few pay attention to the possibilities of changing from such an obviously desirable state. Given the ICA's formation through a discourse of intense reflexivity, it was surprising that this discourse came to be deprivileged, a process that began in the early 1970s. By deprivileging, it is not implied that reflexivity abruptly disappeared from the ICA. However, this discourse became peripheral, as the ICA focused more on putting into practice what had been learned rather than on learning more. The successes of the early projects were so powerful for the ICA that a strong need to replicate them was felt, leading to a strategy of maximum accomplishments in the most efficient manner.

The formation of the ICA in 1973 reflected this new emphasis, as its stated purpose was to further the application of methods of human development to communities and organizations all around the world based on a secular philosophy. The deprivileging of discourses of intense reflectivity peaked in 1984, at the International Exposition of Rural Development (IERD), a 3-year program (1982-1984) in sharing successful rural development approaches. Held in New Delhi, India, the IERD brought global publicity to more than 300 successful, locally managed projects from 55 countries, to promote their efficient replication.

Paradoxically, the IERD triggered the ICA's transition to reprivileging a discourse of intense reflexivity. Although successful in its own terms, the IERD drained the financial and social resources of the ICA significantly. In addition, disillusionment with the performativity mode of the organization became apparent through the intense questioning of the methods of the ICA by participants at the IERD. The consensus was that "we need to talk" regarding where the organization was heading.

The reprivileging of intense reflexivity could be seen in an ICA research effort that began in 1985, to explore the "trends, values, ideas, and approaches that will help people face the future" (ICA, 1988, p. 1). One of the best examples of the reprivileging of the discourses of intense reflexivity in the ICA is the *Panchayat Trek Reflections,* based on visits to 35 locations on seven continents (ICA, 1988). As the ICA decided to give up its "Global Order" identity in favor of a new one called the "Planetary Spirit Association," the reflective processes flowered in intensity and poesis.

> The evolutionary task of these times is to co-create the healthy emergence of the planetary stage of earth history. This requires the embodiment of a breadth and depth of the planetary ethic that is being birthed. This ethic nurtures a healthy ecology of cultures and styles, fosters a partnership mode with life forces, and embraces the assumption that reality is alive. . . . We participate in this sacred dance with the wisdom of ancestors and the genius of the modern age. This spirit of unification and integration, calls us to continue to grow in depth as a human species. (ICA, 1988, p. 2)

These collective transformations were evoked and spurred by individual reflexivity on the possibilities and terrors of this process. One of the tools used for facilitating this reflexivity was poetry, as many examples from the Panchayat documents illustrate. One is shared here to show the intensity and beauty of the processes.

> *The Moon threw off her dark cloak and shimmered*
> *in the inner sky of each self.*
> *The Sun no longer grasped the soul of man*
> *but formed new growth . . . verdant, rich.*
> *Now dancing together,*
> *The Moon and the Sun were in balance.*
> *One enriching the global community with*
> *knowledge and organization of curiosity,*
> *the other gifting with compassion and intuition.*
> *Such a community!*
> *Who could decline such a dance?*
> *Shall we?*
> *How can we not?* (ICA, *Panchayat Documents,* 1988, p. 4)

Since 1988, the ICA has been experimenting with an Earthwise Learning Series and new images of learning, which are a reprivileging of the imaginal education imperative of the ICA in the 1960s. This learning and reflective orientation was evident in the 1992 ICA international gathering held in Prague, Czechoslovakia. The theme of the gathering was "Making the great transition: Our new world," with a strong focus on multidisciplinary learning.

The reprivileging of intense reflexivity has produced tangible results in many areas of the ICA. The organization is experiencing another worldwide resurgence and growth as it is enlivened appropriately.

The Transformed Discourses

This dynamic is a tricky one to describe. It bucks a long-standing tendency in modern social science to construe identity in fundamentally static terms. Transformation then is usually seen as problematic, as there are no adequate frames to understand it. However, there are ways in which collectivities remain the same, even as they change dramatically. This, we believe, is facilitated by the presence of transformed discourses, ways for the organization to carry continuity into radical change. The story we have from the ICA is a particularly poignant example that explores some issues at the core of many lives.

The ICA, like many transnational relief and development organizations, started with a strong Christian background. The religious discourses of Christianity, with an emphasis on charity and service, inspire, create, and support many organizations (and social movements) around the world. These organizations are often the first to respond to social and ecological disasters such as earthquakes and floods with much-needed relief support. In recent years, many of them have expanded their mandate to include social change efforts on a more sustained basis. At this point, many have had to engage with the dynamics of a (possibly) exclusivist faith in a world with many faiths. The ICA, like many other organizations, has also confronted such issues. In this case, the engagements of the life-world with existing discourses have shown dramatic forms.

The discourse of Christianity was formative at the inception of the ICA. The ICA started in 1952 as the Christian Life and Faith Community (CFC). In 1956, Joseph Mathews, a charismatic teacher, joined the CFC and helped found a curriculum of studies called Religious Studies-I, which framed a continuing inquiry into the form and meaning of contemporary Christian community. In 1962, Mathews was asked to become the Dean of the Institute for Ecumenical Studies (set up by the World Council of Churches to facilitate dialogue among different types of churches in the United States). In 1963, the IES moved to Chicago, where it started working with local communities on processes of social and spiritual creativity. Spurred by the success of its domestic efforts, the IES made its first global forays. In 1967, members made trips to Africa, Latin America, the Middle East, and Asia. In 1968, another global foray was made as a group traveled to 12 countries in 1 month. The IES soon expanded globally, seeking to vitalize churches all over the world and in different parts of the United States. The hope was that a revitalized church would help bring about a revitalized world. As the IES expanded its efforts over the world, it found that its mandate had to expand far beyond the church.

During the early 1970s, the institute gradually started grappling with the issue of secularism. The exposure to different cultures catalyzed this reexamination of its secular roots. A dialogue titled *Reflections on a Trek* expressed this "turn to the world" (secularism) more clearly. Arising out of intense reflexivity, it showed a remarkable appreciation for other societies and their spirtualities:

> It is clear that more and more colleagues are needed. . . . Where do you send potential colleagues? One suggestion might be to send them to ITIs [International Training Institutes run by the ICA]. That raises the question of sending Hindus and Muslims and others to an ITI. The ITI construct presupposes an understanding of the Christian symbol system before the participant arrives. (ICA, *Reflections on a Trek*, 1986, p. 5)

The transformation of the IES to the ICA in 1973 was a response to the discourse of Christianity being experienced as a barrier. *Ecumenical* was an inadequate word to express the quality of interfaith engagement the ICA saw as its nature and future. It chose to focus on *culture* instead, to reflect the intuition that the world was in the middle of a massive cultural revolution. This change, from a Christian faith and mission to a secular one, was extremely painful for many, who had to reinterpret the philosophical basis of their lives so that it made sense to stay in the ICA. Although it was not easy, this move did bear fruit. One person later said,

> We started as a Christian group and because we were working in non-Christian countries, we worked with Hindus and Muslims who were a part of us, we became something different. We experienced that we are a people of faith—one human family grounded in different places. We were a microcosm of the world. (quoted in Joseph, 1994, p. 49)

It is important to understand the transformed nature of this discourse. The shift from Christianity to secularism was still located in a sacred context. Even today spirituality shapes the mission of the organization in a way that has more impact than any other life-giving force. The ICA uses it to describe a stance of equal respect and valuing of all faiths. As reflected in the quotation above, the multiplicity of faiths invigorated the ICA and created something new that had not existed before. And ICA documents now offer a more inclusive metaphor of spirituality as part of their discourse of secularism. Thus the Panchayat document speaks to it when it says that the ICA "is spiritual in the sense that at the center, it is based on a spirit of integration and unification, guided by a consciousness that we are inextricably linked to all that is" (Joseph, 1994, p. 78).

This prompts us to reflect on the importance of ineffability in organizational realities. There is a sense of the sacred that is invoked here, one that transcends all discourses. It is the unseen, the unknown, the untouched, the unheard, and the nonpresent of organizing. It is the sense of mystery that the Lakota celebrate in their prayers to Wakan Takan. It is Gabriel Marcel's evocations of mystery in his Christianity. It is the challenge of Nagarjuna as he invites us to recognize radical interdependence, which spirals into a profound unknowing (in Madhyamika Buddhism). This invocation of the sacred can offer profound ways of being, with potential transformations in different aspects of organizing. When the call to change is an upswelling of life and flowering, all collectivities can find the energy and resources to transform.

Ineffability also reflects the inadequacy of words to understand some of the constructs. Thus, words such as *secular* and *sacred* are not very helpful if we come to them loaded with assumptions. We should not confuse the transformation of the discourse of Christianity into the discourse of valuing secularism as a loss of faith. Rather, it is another expression of the mystical beauty that informs this world and all that lives. This is a profound reminder also of the fallibility and transience of discourses in the face of a reality beyond and within all discourse and experience.

This is what inspires the continuity in the ICA's basic assumption that the collective realization of a better future through spiritually driven service is not only possible but necessary. In their words, "it has to do with being a people who cared in a structured and spiritual way so that the future for generations to come would be improved" (Joseph, 1994, p. 49).

This sense is carried into their futures. Two of the visions for a desired future that the ICA developed are examples of the ways in which this transformed discourse shapes their reality in enabling and profound ways (from Joseph, 1994):

We value awakening people to the sacredness of who they are.

We release our spirit energy to the world through our common story that All is Good, We are Accepted, The Past is Approved, and The Future is Open. This enables all of us to live in any situation with a stance of possibility. (pp. 141-142)

This celebration is an appropriate space to end these stories on the creation and enlivening of organizations through the interplay of discourse and life-world. It is time to explore how the senses of illusion and play are the freeing spaces of our societies and our organizations.

On Multiplicity, Play, and Illusions

Spiraling to a close of the narratives, we are with the many stories we have not shared. There are many other discourses, some that could have expressed the issues we described as clearly. Other discourses could have highlighted a different type of issue (as against temporal dynamics). And there is the play of discourses with the life-worlds of participants other than formal organizational members. How do farmers or indigenous people experience the ICA and its discourses? How does the building in Chicago reflect the reality of the ICA's attitudes and tasks? Do the corporations that the ICA works with experience them differently from other consultants? and so on. There are many such questions, and as we pointed out earlier, this chapter is only a beginning. And yet, part of the dilemma of any research narrative is the might-have-beens. As reflexive narrators, we feel it is important to bring this to the center as we come to closure. Holding this sense of absence and missing pieces, let us reflect on what we have been with, using the metaphor of maya-leela to guide us.

Being with and describing the discourses that form and shape organizing is a powerful way to inquire into the multiplicity of meaning in organizations. Many conventional methods of organizational inquiries are partial and monolithic, like the six blind people describing an elephant. The process of discourse descriptions that we have used in this chapter has the benefit of appreciating multiplicity and dynamics and of recognizing the limits of any one description. Thus, the many

stories, values, visions, and histories that shape organizations over time
can all be celebrated. This is a method for inclusion, creativity, and
generosity in knowledge building inspired by maya-leela.

Maya-leela reminds us of the multiple expressions of cosmic exuberance. Although the profligacy of the universe inspires us to many tasks,
challenges, and celebrations, it also offers many resources for this task.
This play of multiple discourses and life-worlds points to ways in which
people and organizations can reshape this world to create more just,
equitable, and humane societies. It is also a statement of the multiple
possibilities for reshaping organizations through an appreciation of
parts of the organizations, while transforming others. Without a discourse of participation, the discourse of GSCOs would not have been
appropriate or creative. Similarly, once the life-worlds of the participants could not sustain a discourse of Christianity, discourses of participation and intense reflexivity supported a transformation to
discourses of secularism. Each time the play of discourses and life-
worlds helped the ICA be a truer context for its spiritual and social
tasks, while helping individual members be congruent in their lives.
This worked even in the counterintuitive move of deprivileging intense
reflexivity, where many benefits flowed for societies and people from
the ICA's efforts.

Maya-leela is also the play of multiplicity. This reminds us to be more
inclusive in our theoretical/practical engagements with organizations.
One rather obvious point to remember is not to get caught up with a
single discourse of performativity. In for-profits, performativity is often
expressed by the dominance of the bottom line. In a GSCO, the
temptation is to ask, "So how much of the world did you save today?"
In many ways, the temptation to performativity in GSCOs may be far
greater than in corporations. For most people, it is easier to be extraor-
dinarily concerned with ending world hunger than with selling tooth-
paste. Exploring the multiple discourses of organizing playfully can be
a way for all organizations, and the people and other species in
interaction, to learn how to be healthier and more alive.

Maya-leela calls us to remember the intricacies of our relatedness as
we move through the world. In telling the stories, we have emphasized
the independent and nonlinear nature of the narratives. And yet, as
the explorations unfolded, we have seen several instances of how the
different discourses have supported one another in calling forth the

best possibilities for the future of the organization. The transformation of the discourse of Christianity to the discourse of valuing secularism could never have been as compelling if it were not for the discourse of intense reflexivity. And the cycle of intense reflexivity could never have been possible were it not for the enlivened and creative engagements of the participants' life-worlds with the discourse of participation.

There is one important point related to the choice of subject. It is possible that the types of questions asked could have found poetry in an investment bank or spirituality in a computer superstore. And yet, some organizations are more meaningful and fun than others. As we go through the universe, there is a need to reflect on what it is that we do and for what purpose. In modern social science, there has often been the assumption of a moral homogeneity, where all aspects of reality are equally moral. Most of us then subsume our professional decisions under the plea of value neutrality. If postmodern social science is to be transformatively different and emancipatory, it has to develop moral vocabularies of its own. As this chapter shows, we are not advocating one monolithic standard morality but are calling for processes to inquire into our mutual moralities.

There is also an issue about the global dimensions of postmodernism. As several scholars have pointed out (Radhakrishnan, 1994; Sardar, 1993) in a global context, postmodernism is severely limited. Rather than critique this propensity, we have offered several ways to expand the metier of scholars in this realm. Two that we could highlight are the inclusion of metaphors from an Indian metaphysical system and our efforts to supplement the knowledge-power aspects of discourses with the enlivening and evocative aspects of stories. Many possibilities are available for the transformation of parochial postmodernism, and we hope to see more of them in the future (cf. Upadhyaya, 1995).

We end with a final note on a powerful implication of our guiding metaphor. Maya-leela literally means the play of illusions. In Vedanta (the root philosophy for this construct), this world is known to be illusory, not the illusions of stage magicians, where cards are really hidden up a sleeve, but a sense of ontological illusion. This is a step to unknowns, indeed the unknowable. In this metaphysics, the play of illusions is not a social game but has a deictic function of pointing us to ultimate reality. Learning from the ICA and many other spiritually grounded social change organizations, we would suggest that this is part of the imperative of all organizations—a serious concern with the path and process of moral development of all who participate. This play of discourses and life-worlds helps us realize the insubstantiality of the reifications with which we are habitually concerned. This disillusionment has a deictic function, pointing us to paths of the sacred and to transformations of being and becoming in lives and organizations. This is crucial to developing a metaphysics of organizing, located in a nondual context of being, knowledge, and love.[3]

Notes

1. *Tamara* is a production of Tamara International, 2035 N. Highland Avenue, Los Angeles, CA 90068.

2. The term *sanathana dharma* is the self-designation of the primordial traditions of India. Hindu is the more commonly recognized term, but it is an artifact of outside constructions. There are approximately 13 fully developed philosophical systems in these traditions (Bhattacharya, 1965), of which we have chosen a simple and popular one to anchor this exploration.

3. This is an unfolding of the traditional ontological statement of Vedanta. That statement is of *sat-chit-ananda,* that is, existence-consciousness-bliss is the ontological assumption. Seyyed Hosein Nasr (1981, p. 49) sees its association with the Sufi assumption of *quadrah-hikmah-rahmah.* This fans out to the ontological simultaneity of Knower-Known-Knowledge as well as Lover-Beloved-Love. This is the unfolding expressed here as a metaphysics of being, knowledge, and love.

16

Technologies of Representation
in the Global Corporation
Power and Polyphony

KENNETH J. GERGEN

DIANA WHITNEY

The postmodernizing of the organization is virtually synonymous with the thrust toward globalization. However, it is the globalized corporation that is most often viewed with suspicion. In their competitive telos, global corporations threaten to destroy the modes of life, value systems, ecological balance, and political autonomy of all cultures they invade. In this chapter, we shall propose not only that this critique is overdrawn but also that such organizations may indeed open a way toward a polyphonic or multivoiced world. Our thesis places an important emphasis on technologies of communication. As organizations expand to global proportion, they place increasing weight on representations from a distance. Face-to-face representation is gradually replaced by visual or graphic constructions of organizational reality and by electronically disseminated discourses. This shift is accompanied by profound losses in management's capacity to direct or compel forms of everyday activity. These losses in the monologic control of representation undermine the power of top management and singularity of organizational strategy.

AUTHORS' NOTE: We are indebted to the editors of this volume for their outstanding editorial assistance.

331

There are strong forces at work, then, to disrupt the spread of any particular set of values, ideals, or goals of a globalizing institution. And these same forces lend increasing weight to voices otherwise suppressed. As the technologies of constructing the organization change, we thus confront the potentials of postmodern, or polyphonic, organization.

The Threat of Globalized Organizing

The transformation from local or regional companies to multinational networks is now well documented. The availability of various communication and transportation technologies has made possible a dramatic expansion in frontiers. Local hopes for increased profit, a more satisfactory ecology, population control, scientific knowledge, or religious revival are spurred by fantasies of universal application. There is broad agreement among business leaders that, indeed, the continued viability of the corporation depends on global expansion. And so it is that, relying on a bevy of new technologies,

> large multinational organizations have been able . . . to increase their economic efficiencies by learning about and then obtaining inputs of material, human power, and capital from more cost-effective sources around the globe. Further, these new information and communication technologies have enabled multinational organizations to market their outputs internationally, thus expanding the domain in which these organizations take action and thereby enhancing their economic efficiency through scale. (Doktor, Tung, & Glinow, 1991, p. 259)

Every 10 years, the average multinational enterprise has added subsidiaries in seven new countries (Tehranian et al., 1977). Organizations devoted to social change—to reducing hunger, improving health, preventing nuclear war—have shown similar spurts. Since 1950, more than 20,000 transnational humanitarian organizations have sprung to life (Cooperrider & Pasmore, 1991).

Yet at the same time that corporate leaders exhort their colleagues to "go global" and other organizations extend their perimeters outward, there is a less audible but no less intense cry of despair. It is a despair that adopts several forms. But common to them is the concern with the colonizing threat of the globalizing organization, with the multinational corporation featured as the chief villain. As organizations extend globally, so do they absorb others into their orbit. As individuals in other cultures are co-opted into the organization, so must they adopt alien beliefs, values, and practices. And as the by-products of the organization—goods, information, advertising, services, and the like—are diffused into the indigenous culture, its traditions are slowly undermined. As some critics hold, the entry of a foreign business into a local culture is little short of an invasion.

Deetz's (1992) *Democracy in an Age of Corporate Colonization* argues that many organizations, business enterprises in particular, are not established on principles of democracy. They neither admit to processes of open communication within their confines nor answer to their various publics: the family, the schools, the state, and so on. Worse, such organizations colonize the perceptions, attitudes, and actions of these various publics.

> With the growth of (corporate) systems, the potential of corporations to represent their various stakeholds and contribute to the general welfare must be questioned. With the growth of corporate influence outside of the corporate site and the reduction of political questions to economic ones, the public becomes fragmented, recollected only by temporary images, and the possibility of meaningful public decision making appears progressively less likely. (Deetz, 1992, p. 2)

The present offering grows from a concern with this intensifying antimony between what may in its broadest form be viewed as thrust toward universal dominion on one side, as opposed to the value of maintaining local autonomy and integrity on the other. The relevant issues are many and complex, and our attempt here is to unwrap but a single enigma. However, the argument is one closely tied to issues of technology and representation. Our initial focus is on the process of social construction within the organization, and particularly the functions and efficacy of official representations of reality in sustaining organizational goals. Here we shall outline certain transitions in the communication process accompanying the process of globalization. Then we explore the functions of organizational constructions as current technologies enable broad-scale expansion. As we shall venture, with global expansion of the organization, traditional forms of representation lose their functional capacity. This argument will be illustrated with materials from recent casework. What we hope to demonstrate is that the globalization process is accompanied by a dissolution of organizational power and, thus, of its colonizing potential. As we find, new forms of social construction are increasingly required, forms that lend to local realities far greater potency than heretofore.

Power and Self-Representation

There are multiple sites for organizational representation. The organization is portrayed in the media, managers converse about the nature of their companies, commentators explore the foibles of organizational policy, consultants describe the organization's ills, and scholars provide endless accounts of organizational systems. In all cases, we are speaking of discursive (and sometimes graphic) objectifications; that is, representations without clear referential coordinates. We may speak of General Mills as a "financially solid structure," or organizational communication as a "cybernetic system," but in either case the precise referents of such accounts remain principally underdetermined. (Does, for example, an employee of General Mills remain an employee when she is not at work, or if she is in the office but speaking to a baby-sitter? Is the building in which she works part of the company if it is owned by the local bank?) The organizational account, then, is a representation, a situated simulacrum of a reality that is forever beyond its reach, an abstraction without obvious referent. This is not to say that the representation is either mythic or fictitious; rather, the representation stands as a discursive or pictorial resource that may be employed at any time in an act of objectification. It is a conversational implement that may be variously and momentarily rendered concrete (as well as abstract or irrelevant) in the process of social interchange.

Let us consider organizational self-representations in particular—that is, attempts by participants within what is taken to be an organization to represent their collectivity. Such self-representations take many forms, from informal conversations about "our crummy benefits package" to boardroom discussions of "the company's market situation." Our primary concern, however, is with those representations originated within the top management stratum: statements of purpose, 5-year plans, human resource policies, organizational diagrams, training manuals for new employees, annual reports to the stockholders in the firm, and so on. In general, these various artifacts are constructed for one important purpose: to enhance the major goals of the organization: economic prosperity in the case of the corporation, or effective government, education, and so on in various nonprofit spheres.[1] They are, then, essential resources for "making sense" within the organizational culture (Gephart, 1991).

Organizational representations function to achieve these goals in two major ways: They strive toward establishing first a local ontology and second a code of values, both the *is* and *ought* of organizational life. The policy statement, diagram, report, or credo furnishes what is taken to be a picture of the organization, setting forth its hierarchical structure, lines of communication, phases of production, or its telos in general. In constructing the organization as one thing as opposed to another, certain lines of action are invited and others discouraged. Those who are defined as "senior" in the structure require deference, for example, and are expected to give orders. In effect, within the definition of the organization are implied illocutionary imperatives. Standards of ought derive not only from ontological premises but also from additional forms of self-representation such as corporate statements of mission, internal codes of value, and the like. In such representations, standards of honor and abomination, as well as conditions for heroics and villainy, are all contained. To summarize in Bourdieu's (1990) terms, representation contributes to

> the production of a common-sense world, whose immediate self-evidence is accompanied by the objectivity provided by consensus on the meaning of practices and the world, in other words the harmonization of the agent's experiences and the constant reinforcement each of them receives from expression—individual or collective . . . of similar or identical experiences. (p. 58)

For Cooper (1992), it is through organizational representation that "the affairs of the world are made pliable, wieldable and therefore amenable to human use" (p. 257). Without these localized creations of meaning, organizational viability is placed in jeopardy.

The dark side of this constructionist sketch is adumbrated in Foucault's (1979, 1980a) roughly parallel account of discourse and power. For Foucault, the shift from what he sees as a feudal form of juridicodiscursive power to disciplinary power relations is essentially a movement from repression to internalization. In the juridicodiscursive case, specific rule systems, backed by the equivalent of a police force, demanded obedience; however, in the disciplinary context of the Panopticon, techniques were developed that led to the incorporation of belief systems within subjected populations. The aggregate essentially became self-managing, but as surrogates for those in power. Chief among the disciplinary techniques is discourse, for it is through discursive practices that those in power relations are furnished with a rationality for their own activities. In effect, the exercise of power is achieved through a regime of discourse. As the regime of truth or knowledge becomes the argot of everyday activity, seeping into the capillaries of daily relations (in company relationships, educational systems, the home), so does the aggregate become complicit in its own subjugation. In Foucault's view, the organizing process is simultaneously a form of self-imprisonment.

This view essentially reiterates the pervasive concern with the tyrannical effects of globalizing organizations. As an organization increases its internal capacities to fulfill its goals, relying significantly on representational procedures, its potential for transforming or subjugating its constituents is also enhanced. The effects are not only internal, altering the life trajectories of employees, but external as well, carrying into the family and community. The greater the power of management to organize the employees' efforts behind organizational ends, the greater the power of the organization to alter its surrounding environment. If employees produce, market, distribute, and so on, as planned by top management, the organization will ingest more resources from the environment (e.g., raw materials, energy, human resources) and have a greater impact on the environment in terms of the absorption of its products and the ramifications of this absorption for communal life. To the extent that processes of disciplinary power are effective, the global organization can subjugate local culture.

Technology and Representational Form

Before exploring further the problem of power in the globalized organization, we must consider variations in communication practices, or more formally, modes of representation and their metamorphosis over time. The efficacy of a given representation or construction to organize activity within the organization is, after all, dependent on its particular characteristics. The capacity of a given representation (policy, directive, explanation, etc.) to mobilize, direct, and control activity will depend importantly on the context of relationship. Let us consider, in particular, modes of organizational representation as they are related to organizational expansion. It is our proposal that as organizations expand their reach, they are forced to shift their primary modes of representation from the face-to-face conversation to print media and finally to electronic interaction. Each of these modalities, in turn, can be related to dominant metaphors of the organization itself. These shifts in modes of representation (and accompanying metaphors) are accompanied by a diminution in the capacity for top-down organizing. We are not suggesting that these stages are inevitable or fully general or that there are not myriad complexifying factors; rather, we offer here a template for appreciating the problems of a globally expanding organization in sustaining control.

Consider first, the small, face-to-face organization. Here conversational representation serves as the major mode in which the realities of the organization are developed and sustained. The proverbial boss can initiate disciplinary power through direct descriptions: Our products are of the highest quality, You are the floor manager, and it is your job to . . . , We treat our customers with special care, and so on. The reliance on conversational representation has distinct advantages in the face-to-face organization. It is wedded to a particular context or course of action, it is authored by a specific individual and directed to a specific other, it is accompanied by nonverbal signals and personal history, it is potentially sensitive to feedback by the recipient, and it can be directly monitored. In effect, the conversational mode is perhaps ideally suited to the generation of disciplinary power.

But now consider the effects of technologies that have facilitated organizational expansion during the late 19th and early 20th century. Here we refer especially to technologies of physical and electronic engineering (e.g., steel, concrete construction, and electricity), along with technologies enabling markets to expand (for example, steamships and the railroad). With the aid of these technologies, organizations could grow large and small physical plants could expand dramatically in size. Many companies of the period came to occupy a single, impressive or imposing structure. One could identify, for example, the Schlitz Brewery, the Minneapolis *Star* and *Tribune*, the Fidelity Bank Building, Harrods, and so on. Under these conditions, the conversational process could no longer serve as the major vehicle for organizational representation. Face-to-face interaction between management and employees is spatiotemporally precluded as a major mode of organizing. In the expanded organization, increasing reliance is placed on printed representations: policies, orders, plans, warnings, congratulations, and so on. Printed media can be standardized, produced at low cost, and circulated both broadly and rapidly.

In the case of print, the major options for organizational representation are linguistic, on one hand, and graphic, on the other. Directives, statements of mission or purpose, and operating philosophies illustrate the former option, and diagrams, charts, and photographs the latter. It is interesting to consider several differences between them. In certain respects, for purposes of sustaining disciplinary power, graphic representations are more effective. Graphics are to be favored primarily for their greater mimetic capacity, their closer visual association with the structures, actions, and implements of daily life. The sounds and markings that constitute linguistic discourse cannot be sensually compared to the phenomena of daily life in the way that visual representations can. The matching process in the discursive case relies on an existing social consensus, whereas in the case of visual images, there is strong reliance on immediate sensation.

Because of their match with "eyeball" reality, graphic representations also have greater rhetorical potential: the difference between being told in words and virtually seeing it for oneself. In this respect, the choice depicting organizational power arrangements in terms of a physical structure is highly propitious. In the typification of the organizational "structure" (see Figure 16.1) are found iconic reverberations with the large corporate building. The structural graphics of authority resonate with the major cityscapes, marked by the dominating images of single companies such as Chrysler, Rockefeller, Seagrams, and so on. Given the existence of the structures, once can scarcely doubt the palpability of the power arrangements. In addition, lurking within all such structural graphics lurk traces of the pyramid, the symbol of the pharaohs' dominion.

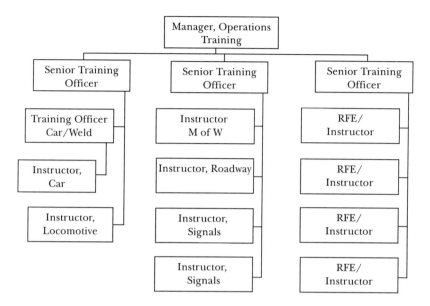

Figure 16.1. Organization as Structure

As technologies of production, transportation, and communication continue to develop, so can the organization continue to expand. The effective organization need not be constrained by a single physical structure. Building complexes are favored, often in separate geographic locations. Regional offices are often required, connected by mail and telephone. Under these conditions, the single, pyramidal metaphor ceases to be a compelling representation of the organization. The organizational diagram bears little mimetic relationship to physical structure. Rather, the way is opened for a metaphorical shift from the structure to the flow diagram (see Figure 16.2). In this case, the primary emphasis is on directions of communication and the function they are to fulfill. The dominant image is that of the telephone connection, with the diagram directing its desired movement over time.

Within recent decades, however, as the technologies of communication have become increasingly powerful and sophisticated—for example, jet transportation, direct overseas dialing, computer, fax, satellite transmission—organizational perimeters again have expanded. In effect,

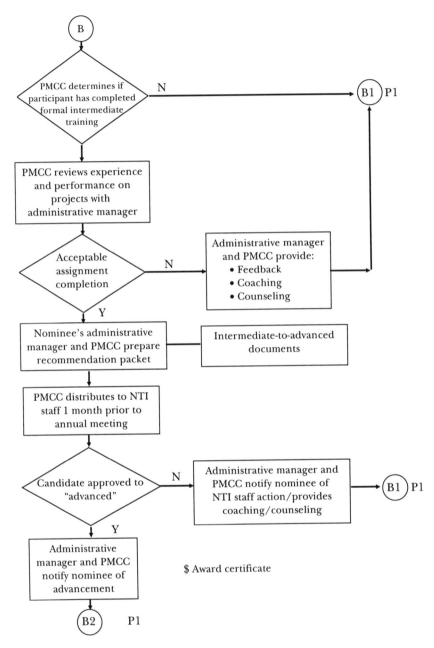

Figure 16.2. Organization as Process

the available technologies permit even the small to moderate-size organization to go global. As organizational expansion takes place, the flow diagram, as a form of self-representation, becomes increasingly unwieldy. The number of linkages, their function, and the possibilities for feedback render unmanageable virtually any attempt to trace lines of authority, information transmission, and functional interdependency. With graphics thus receding as a representational form, what other possibilities exist for representing the complex practices making up the organization?

In our view, with the impasse of the visual medium of management (and related organizational theories), the representational process reverts again to the prototype: namely, to the conversation. This is seldom, however, the conversation of the small firm, wedded closely to the context of operations. Rather, it is the electronically transmitted conversation, carried through telephone, E-mail, fax, and video conferencing. Of course, these conversations are seldom limited to the electronic medium. The print medium retains a strong function, and periodically both print and electronic communication are supplemented with face-to-face interaction (as in the occasional visit from the home office, team meetings, training programs, etc.).

With the electronic medium dominant, how is the organization to be portrayed? What forms of representation can organize disparate groups into a unified whole? Whatever the forms, it is important that they be abstracted from the particulars of daily life. Their meaning cannot be exhausted in the unique, concrete case; rather, the discourse must be sufficiently general that all can find it applicable. Consider two prevalent forms of this abstracted mode of sustaining power favored by electronic conversations (and their supporting technologies). Highly popular in the last decade have been attempts to formulate strategic goals for the organization. This project resonates with the strategic management formulations popular within management theory (Lawrence & Lorsch, 1969; Locke, 1968; Miles & Snow, 1978). By establishing goals and strategies, management moves above the myriad details of daily activity to establish an overarching telos, a direction that should unite and direct movement in many variegated localities. Statements of strategy typically provide an account of how these goals will be reached and where the emphasis of action should be placed. They indirectly serve as motivational devices, demonstrating the ways and means to a successful future, regardless of the particular conditions of application.

More recently, the emphasis on strategies has been joined by a values clarification movement. Here the attempt is to generate a statement of overall values or aspirations that typify and define the organizational ethos. Articulations of value are often accompanied by group meetings and workshops in which their significance is stressed, implications demonstrated, and a sense of group identity and commitment instilled. This movement is noteworthy, as it represents a major shift from a physical to a human resource as the major metaphor for self-representation. Building structures, communication systems, and organizational products are replaced by human beings—and more significant, the psychological states of human beings—as the dominant metaphor of organizational essence. The emphasis on the values of organizational participants resonates as well with a spate of literature on organizational culture (Frost, Moore, Louis, Lundberg, & Martin, 1991; Schein, 1990) in the academic domain. And, although this literature places a strong emphasis on relationships and interdependency, its power-producing purposes in the organization should not be underestimated. To the extent that upper management can succeed in "capturing the minds and hearts" of the employees, disciplinary power is sustained.[2]

To summarize, we are suggesting that with the growth of organizations from the local and self-contained to the global and multiplex, the path of self-representation typically moves from the conversational modality to the printed, and then the electronically based, interchange. It is our central contention that this shift is accompanied by a loss of centralized power. To use Deetz's (in press) terms, "Power is present in the attempt to hold one sign value or articulation as preferable over others. Domination occurs when one articulation is systematically, but arbitrarily, privileged through practices suppressing alternatives" (p. 10). In these terms, it will be proposed, the power relations through which central management hopes to maintain control over its extended system, and which for them is considered essential to the execution of rational strategies, become progressively ineffectual.

However, to make good on this argument, further detailing is required. Let us first consider a case in which establishing central control is essential for an organization, and then some of the major reasons for the comparative inefficacy of the processes by which this control is sought.

Instituting Values in a Global Organization[3]

Sloan-Becker, as we shall call them, is an organization formed by the merger of Sloan, Inc., an American company with extended offices across the United States and Canada, and Becker, Ltd., a British-based firm whose products and services are sold throughout the United Kingdom and the Continent. Both companies were already extended geographically, and with the merger, a highly globalized organization took form. However, in planning for the integration of the corporations, top management fully realized that it faced difficulties in exerting the kind of power that would organize the two unwieldy complexes into a single, effective unit.

The problems were exacerbated by distinct differences in management style and cultural ethos within the two companies. Sloan, the American company, was strongly oriented toward interpersonal skills. A strong sense of traditional ethics was maintained, and management relationships were marked by a sense of restraint, respect, and an abiding emphasis on personal integrity. Managers were carefully recruited to fit the customs of the "old boy network" that formed the basis of the management process. In contrast, Becker was market driven. The strong emphasis was on increasing profits. Managers were motivated by bottom-line results, and strategic planning was a dominant form of decision making. As a result, top managers from the respective firms worked together, and with their colleagues in human resources, to generate a corporate code of values, a set of principles and aspirations to which employees at all levels could commit. This code was not only to be disseminated through printed material and supported through conversation, but a plan was hatched to instill these values in a face-to-face setting. As announced to the employees,

We are all about to begin a very special undertaking: the planned and conscious effort to develop our own unique organizational culture; a *Simply Better* way of doing things at Sloan-Becker on a day-to-day basis.

Simply Better

Simply Better, (f. SIMPLY adv. +
BETTER adj.) Phrase belonging to,
or associated with the company
_____ Denotes a way
of working that encourages continual
improvement by each individual.
Simply (si·mpli), adv. ME **1.** With
simplicity; not complicated, efficient
and effective; **2.** With sincerity; in an
honest or straightforward manner. **3.**
Without exception; absolutely.
Better (be·t ə.ɪ), adj. **1.** Constantly
improving. The comparative of good.
2. Never satisfied. **3.** Of persons and
things; more profitable, useful, or
suitable for a purpose; more
desirable;

  1. To be S.B.: To be, do and act better, to
build a healthcare company that is "Simply
Better" than the competition . . . in products, in
people and in performance.

Figure 16.3. Cover of the *Simply Better* Booklet

It is these daily actions which cumulatively will help us to realize the
Promise of Sloan-Becker.

Simply Better, then, was the overall slogan for a composite of values
that, when extended in implication, should seep into every capillary
of the organization. A booklet distributed to all employees of the

organization featured the cover shown in Figure 16.3. The dominant stress, we find, is on continuously improving performance by each individual employee, coupling the sincerity, honesty, and authenticity of the Sloan manager with the Becker eye on profits, products, and utility.

The dissemination of the booklet was accompanied by a series of management training workshops. At these events, some 50 managers from North America and Europe met for a period of several days. The workshops were used to explain and illustrate in greater detail the new, integrative value slate, a related set of leadership practices, and a list of common expectations for employees of Sloan-Becker. The dominant rallying cry of these lively meetings was "walk the truth," a phrase that exhorted employees to live out the overarching values in the daily performance of their jobs. Spirits were high, lively camaraderie prevailed, and dedicated song even erupted from the group. As they chorused:

> *Paradigms need to shift and we can do it now*
> *And since we'll do it right we'll be a real cash cow.*
> *We can really improve our systems by TQM*
> *We'll take it to our people and encourage them.*
> *A message to our Victory on this final day*
> *Remember to use our talents in the SB way.*
> *We feel a little sorrow cause we're at the end*
> *But we're feelin' pretty good 'bout our newfound friends.*

Globalization and the
Limits of Centralized Power

Here is a case in which an impressive initiative is put forward to create a unified corporate culture, a culture that will operate in synchrony with the vision of top management. We are not proposing that these efforts are in vain. However, there are important limitations to this kind of initiative, along with all similar efforts to organize through an appeal to abstracted representations. The following problems are particularly noteworthy.

THE ALTERED CONTEXT

As made clear by much semiotic and literary theory, along with recent turns in pragmatic linguistics, word meaning is derived neither from the capacity of language to map reality nor from the capacity of the interlocutor to make cognitive contents manifest.[4] In the first instance, because language cannot serve the mimetic functions often ascribed to it by positivists and semanticists, accounts of "the way things are" do not in themselves possess revelatory capacities. And in the second, because there is no viable hermeneutic for moving logically from manifest to latent or cognitive content, ambiguities in such accounts cannot be clarified by recourse to "speaker intention." Rather, word meaning depends primarily on its contextual embedding, or essentially, its social use within a material context (or in a Wittgensteinian frame, its use within a language game, embedded within a particular form of life). This is to say that any proposition concerning the way things are depends largely for its meaning on how it is treated by a group of interlocutors within a particular context. Stripped of its sociopragmatic and physical setting, its capacity for coordinating relations is diminished (or altered).

Let us first consider the implications of the vanishing context for the representations of an organization's values. Abstract values, such as integrity, determination, or excellence, cannot be derived from any particular set of actions; the terms have no unambiguous spatiotemporal coordinates. Thus, if such terms are to carry management aims into the fiber of organizational life, their meaning must be socially negotiated within the context of particular, concrete activities: this particular way of speaking as opposed to that; this kind of report, research, contact making, design, marketing program, assembly line performance, and so on, as opposed to some other. Without ongoing processes of anchoring, such terms lose their capacities for organizing activity. It is precisely this disadvantage that electronically disseminated discourse (and its ancillaries) suffers in comparison to face-to-face discourse.

Consider as an example the Sloan-Becker attempt to fill out the value structure that would enable them to be "simply better." Managers and workers throughout the extended company were supplied with an account of the values to be pursued by Sloan-Becker participants

We at (SB) will succeed in our competitive aspirations by concentrating our activities around the following values:

Performance

SB is performance driven. We continuously aim to improve performance in all that we do.

Customers

SB is customer-oriented. We strive to provide products and services of superior value to meet the expectations of our internal and external customers.

Innovation

SB constantly strives to be creative and innovative in all its endeavors. All SB employees are encouraged to bring forth new and better ideas for improved performance, whatever their responsibilities.

People

SB employees are all partners, working together in the pursuit of the SB mission and strategy. We strongly value teamwork, and we want every employee to be motivated to succeed.

Integrity

SB demands openness and honesty throughout its operations to engender trust, and integrity underscores everything that we do. We believe that every activity must be able to pass the test of public and internal scrutiny at all times.

Figure 16.4. The Values of Sloan-Becker

(Figure 16.4). These include continuously improving performance, sensitivity to customer expectations, continuous innovation, teamwork, honesty, and trust. Yet to what specific activities and in what specific conditions do such terms apply?

To what does the term *performance* apply, to what movements of the arms and legs, the hands or tongue? Does it apply to the speed of one's gait, to the rapidity of speech, to the quantity or the quality of one's reports? And if one is performing more rapidly than the resulting products can be absorbed, should performance increases still be sought? Or if one's performance is creating tensions among one's

peers (as in rate busting), should one strive for continued incre-
ments? Clearly, what is meant by "improving performance" is action-
and context-specific, and it is precisely this information that cannot
be communicated in this fashion.

THE VANISHING AUTHOR

It is not simply the loss of physical context that places the disseminated language at a disadvantage. Also absent are aspects of social
interchange that lend to language its illocutionary power. Consider
first the loss of authorship. In many instances, the author bears the
name of a distant individual (e.g., the chief executive officer) or a
committee or board of nameless individuals; in many other cases, the
representation is cut away entirely from an author. The diagrams of
organizational structure, or information flow, for example, are "representations from nowhere," operating as if they were God's-eye tem-
plates of organizational life. As authorship is diminished or obscured,
the directive capacity of a communication again suffers. The recipient
is, for one, cut away from collateral information about the author,
specifically of the kind that can elaborate or clarify the communication. We know nothing of the author's personal life or character,
manner of treating others, record of accomplishments, and so on,
essentially the sorts of information that enable us to judge the way in
which the communication is to be understood. The author's role is also
obscured; is he or she (or are they) communicating in an avuncular
capacity as a boss or as equal colleagues? Each role may nuance the
communiqué in different ways.

Consider again the Sloan-Becker menu of values. Who is the "we"
who will succeed in "our" competitive aspirations? The recipients of this
communique have had no hand in its creation; are they then included
in the we? And if they are not, then is this we (a "they") legislating the
values and then, subtly and misleadingly, extending the term we to
seduce employees into believing they share the authorship? And if this
is so, who is the we who will succeed in "our competitive aspirations"?
Are these *my* aspirations, it may be asked, or am I being co-opted to
achieve someone else's aspirations? But then again, the authorship still
remains opaque. Perhaps the entire slate of values is drawn up by the
personnel department, with little but formal approval by top manage-

ment; perhaps it represents the views of top management but is disregarded by middle management. All remains clouded.

THE LOSS OF SPEECH ACT POTENTIAL

When a communication is abstracted from normal contexts of interchange, it also loses its speech act potential, that is, its capacity to function as a definitive performative, an action in itself. The performative capacity of a given communiqué is often signaled at the nonverbal level by tone of voice, gestures, and facial expression. One knows the difference between a command and a suggestion, for example, not necessarily by the content of a communiqué but by the imperious tone of voice accompanying the former but not the latter. It is not that disseminated representations lose all speech act potential; however, such potential is severely truncated and made ambiguous. For example, how is the employee of Sloan-Becker to treat the table of values? Are these a set of marching orders, suggestions, hopes, or something else? Are they truly intended to direct or organize activity at the local level, or are they simply being used to generate a sense of overall cohesiveness, a vision of one large, homogeneous team? Or is this perhaps window dressing to impress investors or the board of directors? None of the necessary markers are present in the document.

THE AMBIGUITY OF IDENTITY

Disseminated representation is not only cut away from the author, but often from the recipient as well. Typically the recipient is addressed in only a vague way (as a member of the organization, or one of its divisions), or not at all. In effect, the recipient is left unable to know in what sense—if any—the representation is intended for him or her. Is this charge addressed to me, one might ask, and if so, in what capacity? Is it addressed to me as a dependent worker, a member of a powerful union, a minority representative, a colleague, or something else? Or am I truly the proper recipient of the communiqué? Perhaps it is intended to impress the stockholders, other companies, or the press. In this sense, the values outlined by Sloan-Becker make up a message from no one in particular to no one in particular: a message in free-floating space.

THE RECEDING VOICE OF THE RECIPIENT

Although differences in structural power have always operated to suppress the voices of those in the lower echelons, variations do exist in the sensitivity of organizations to employee voices. A critical site for openness to such voices is in the assertion of authority. As directives, advisories, goal setting, and the like are formulated and communicated, sensitivity to employee voice can be critical. At such points, employee reactions—their interpretations, attitudes, reservations, and puzzlements—may do much to modify the organizing process. Important fine tuning—elaboration, modification, clarification, and even withdrawal—may ensue. The result, in any case, can be a more inclusive form of management, which should yield more effective coordination of action. Yet, as management moves from direct interchange to print and electronically disseminated languages, the possibilities for employee expression are simultaneously diminished. Important backchannel information, available in the face-to-face context, is lost when information is disseminated from afar. The directive arrives as a fait accompli, with no reflection of local concerns, dissent, or alternative views.

Consider again the Sloan-Becker values. There is first a range of internal tensions left unresolved. How is the demand for continuously higher performance to be reconciled with the ideal of teamwork? Am I to outstrip my colleagues, one may ask, demonstrating their inferiority, and thus jeopardizing our relationship as a team? Will not the demand for innovation often conflict with teamwork in the same way, disrupting smooth flowing coordination of action? Likewise, if I remain true to my own values—a mark of integrity—will I be able to cooperate with a group committed to antithetical values? And if we do not produce products of "superior value" (as we promise our customers), and if we pollute the environment (contrary to their expectations), should I as an individual with integrity speak out publicly on such matters? In addition to these internal tensions, there are also alternative values that go unmentioned, values that may be far dearer to the hearts of many workers. Nothing is said here about the personal well-being, self-realization, or sense of fulfillment of the individual employee; the firm is silent on matters of sexism and racism, the well-being of employee families; the well-being of the communities or

TABLE 16.1 Evolution of Objectives

	1990 Plan	*1991 Plan*	*1992 Plan*
Sales growth	10%	12%	14.5%
Margin improvement (points)	1.0	0.8	0.8
Profit growth	@20%	>18%	>20%
DSO	<50	<48	42
Capital expenses (as percentage of sales)	<5%	<5%	<5%
ROTA	42%	>50%	60%

the countries in which it operates; and so on. Are these not valued by the organization?

These tensions and silences are all the more threatening in many companies because of broad evidence of double- or triple-speak on the part of top management, evidence that management creates a different reality for different audiences. That is, the self-representations disseminated throughout the ranks of the organization are not necessarily, or scarcely ever, those shared either within top management or between top management and the investors, the press, the government, and so on. In many cases these alternative or semioccluded representations seem to be "the true" or authentic ones—the stories told offstage, revealing basic motives. In the Sloan-Becker case, for example, meetings between top management and human resources representatives yielded a chart of company objectives (see Table 16.1). These objectives were exclusively financial: sales growth, improvement of market share, profit growth and the like. As this information is made available in annual reports, newspaper coverage, and so on, employees are left again to ponder the commitment to the Sloan-Becker values. Is the commitment of the company to a set of values sui generis, or is it not to values as mere implements to profit? The company, then, is essentially motivated by profit and not essentially invested in employee, family, community, or national welfare. The expressions of value are in this sense disingenuous.

Centralized Power in Jeopardy

As we find, the printed and electronic dissemination of organizational representations is accompanied by multiple losses: of context, author's identity, speech act potential, recipient identity, and recipient voice. At the same time, this deterioration of centralized authority is accompanied by two additional factors related to communication technology. First, the technological conditions of the global organization further militate against the kinds of monitoring that might offset these deteriorations in control. Removed from the panoptical gaze, employees' actions are not easily correctable by high-level management. Representatives of top management may set up shop in far-flung regions of the world, but even they are isolated in a hermeneutical jungle, uncertain as to how the disseminated languages are to be applied in the local setting. This is not to say that with new electronic means of collecting and evaluating large masses of data, the possibilities for centralized surveillance are not omnipresent. As Poster (1990) has warned, the "circuits of communication and the databases they generate constitute a Superpanopticon, a system of surveillance without walls, windows, towers or guards" (p. 93).

However, there are also countervailing resistances to database control. As Zuboff (1988) demonstrates, it is frequently the lower-level employees who serve as the technicians and users of the data files and on whom upper-level management must rely for their information. Lower-echelon employees are thus privy to the information (including reports on upper-echelon management) and mediate its representation. Nor can upper-level management gain full control over the representations that make their way into the data bank. In the case of employee evaluations, for example, there is also an inevitable gap between an action and its representation, between a particular form of behavior and its appearance as an integer in a data bank. This translation is quite frequently a local process of reality construction that is itself without monitoring. Thus, whether an employee is evaluated well or poorly in terms of his or her realization of company values is largely left to local negotiations.

Coupled with a certain loss of monitoring capacities[5] at the level of top management, the conditions of employee self-organization at the local level are enhanced. Both face-to-face accessibility and electronic technologies (phone, E-mail networks) enable employees at the local level to conceptualize themselves as a common unit, with specific values, needs, and visions of equity. Furthermore, this local unit may derive its definition from its very alterity, locating an "us" that gains its character by a contrast with "them." This sense of us may also function as an energizing source, from which members derive a sense of pride, purpose, and identity. Furthermore, because the self-representations at the local level can often be accompanied by face-to-face interchange, they can be contextualized, their authorship made apparent, their speech act implications made transparent, the identity of the recipient clear, and the recipient's voice available. In effect, communication within the local setting becomes action specific.[6]

On a more general level, this is to elaborate the possibilities for a resistance to "descending" power relations. Foucault (1978, 1979) himself is ambivalent on the issue of circumventing disciplinary power, the possibilities for "ascending" power relations. In both *Discipline and Punish* and *The History of Sexuality,* the primary emphasis is on the hegemonic process, the effects of dominant, knowledge-generating institutions on the sphere of individual action. Resistance to power, in these terms, "is never in a position of exteriority in relation to power" (Foucault, 1978, p. 95).

And yet, in other writings, particularly those stressing the genealogical method, Foucault speaks of the "insurrection of subjugated knowledges," forms of knowledge or experience that "have been disqualified as inadequate to their task, or insufficiently elaborated: naive knowledges, located low down in the hierarchy, beneath the required level of cognition or scientificity" (Foucault, 1980a, p. 208). It is in this "particular, local, regional knowledge, a differential knowledge incapable of unanimity" that the potential for authentic—rather than substantiating—resistance may be located. In present terms, these are the argots of the local employees in the globalizing organization.[7]

Does this analysis resonate with other accounts of life in the global organization? Consider a recent summary of the efficacy of expanding American businesses:

Many Americans do not succeed in their overseas assignments. Between 16 and 40 percent of all American employees sent overseas return from their assignments early, and each premature return costs a firm roughly

$100,000. . . . In addition to these costs, approximately 30 to 50 percent of American expatriates, whose average compensations package is $250,000 per year, stay at their international assignments but are considered ineffective or marginally effective by their firms. (Black, Mendenhall, & Oddou, 1991, p. 291)

Kanter's (1991) recent survey of some 11,000 business managers from 25 countries showed that the major worry in their relations with suppliers and customers was the conflict in corporate cultures. Robert Reich (1991) has spoken of the fading significance of world head-quarters in the globalizing process. All suggest the inadequacy of centralized control in the global organization. This is scarcely to argue for an across-the-board erosion of top-down authority. Companies may take initiatives to counteract such tendencies: training programs, audits, frequent reports, teleconferencing, and personal visits. How-ever, without such actions, the dissolution of monologic power may be anticipated.

The Emergence of
the Polyphonic Organization

In our view, we are poised for another iteration in the quest for organizational representation. Required is a new metaphor for orga-nizational life, one that is congenial with the shift toward electronic conversation and that may continue to serve an organizing function— but without the presumption of strong centralized control.[8] We must opt for a metaphor that enables local languages to be placed in a mutually benefiting relationship with the centralized powers, such that the very concept of organizational efficacy is continuously negotiable. There are tendencies in this direction beginning to emerge in the postmodern organizational literature. Boje (1995) notes the wide-spread sensitivity to organizational metaphors based on language (e.g., text, novel, discourse, conversation). We, too, are moved in this direc-tion. However, we find ourselves particularly drawn in this case to the work of the literary theorist Mikhail Bakhtin (1984). For Bakhtin, the language of any culture is invariably a polyglot, a patchwork of sundry dialects, traditions, and interpolations. This heteroglossial composition is in a state of continuous transformation as various traditions interact, combine, and mutate over time. In his literary work, Bakhtin identifies what he views as a major creative turn in the form of the novel, from the traditional novel, in which the singular view of the author prevailed, to that of the multivoiced, or polyphonic, novel. In the polyphonic novel, such as Dostoevsky's *The Brothers Karamazov*, there is no singular vantage point, dominated by the author. Rather, there are multiple voices of enchantment, a plurality of characters, each given the space to make his/her actions and beliefs intelligible; the ultimate reality of the novel is that which issues from the interchange. In effect, one moves from a monologic determination of the truth of the novel to a dialogic process, a fuller expression of the polyglot.

We may fruitfully employ such concepts in considering new forms of organizational representation, for does the traditional, top-down organization not form a convenient parallel to the monologic novel? And, as globalization takes place and the force of the monologue is weakened, we are positioned for a shift to a dialogic mode of organizational life. In the polyphonic organization, then, monologue is replaced by a dialogue among the voices of the constitutive cultures and subcultures. In the polyphonic organization, we can replace the language of the system—with its logic of reliable interdependencies among elements and its demand for centrally controlled consensus— with that of the systase (Gebser, 1985, pp. 309-310). The systase, unlike the system, is a conception of the organization with no central voice or pivot around which order is established, because whatever order is achieved results from a "patchwork of language pragmatics that vibrate at all times" (Lyotard & Thébaud, 1985, p. 94). Or we might say systasis is a form of collective praxis in continuous process.

Can an elaboration of the polyphonic process yield new forms of organizing, ones that are more viable in the globalized context? Many would argue against possibility. For one, is the polyphonic organization not one in which chaos prevails? After all, if everyone has a voice, self-organization is impeded; conflict and confusion may become rampant. Yet as organizational theorists have begun to see the parallels between organizational change and chaos models in the biological sciences (see, e.g., M. Gergen, 1992), they have also become sensitized to the possibility of a unifying disorder, abstract goals that may encompass contradictory particulars. Or, as Bakhtin (1984) has said of the polyphonic novel, it admits to "a unity of a higher order."[9]

Surely there is substantial reason to press toward a viable articulation of the polyphonic organization. As Cooperrider and Bilmoria (in press) put the case to the management field,

> High on the list of the "global agenda for change" is an appreciative search for new organizational arrangements that allow for a closing of what can be called the institutional gap—the dichotomy between organizations born of the modern bureaucratic world of the last several centuries and the new demands of a post-modern, supranational globally linked world system of change.

Yet if the representational resources for such a challenge are to emerge, the conversation must be substantially extended. Dialogue must ensue with theorists such as Beck (1992) and Giddens (1991a), who conceive of postmodern existence as riven with both risk and opportunity, and Handy (1992), who has outlined a new form of federationism for the organization. Social theorists concerned with the interpenetration of universalization and particularism (see, e.g., Robertson, 1992) must be added to the discussion, along with scholars concerned with the varied contribution to organizational life carried by differing cultures (see, e.g., Franke, Hofstede, & Bond, 1991; C. H. Turner, 1991); with intercultural coordination and the means by which it may be managed (Lobel, 1990; Tung, 1991); and with management potentials in a postmodern world (Clegg, 1990).

These scholarly explorations also must be conjoined with the experiences of organizations attempting to implement more polyphonic forms of management. What can be gained, for example, from the Whirlpool International experience of generating a management committee made up of six individuals from six different nations? And does the attempt by the Institute of Cultural Affairs to bring managers from across the globe together to share their independent narratives (Srivastva, Cooperrider, & Thatchenkery, 1992) not have something to say about polyphonic integration?

In effect, the most promising means of achieving effective representational resources is through the process of polyphonic dialogue itself. In the end, it may be this form of dialogue—interactive interchange rather than crystallized representation—that serves as the most effective technology of postmodern organization. It is not to face-to-face encounters between management and employees that the organizing function will thus return. Rather, the representational function may be optimally carried by myriad, capillary conversations. And these conversations may ideally erode the artificial boundaries between upper and lower echelons, inside and outside the organization. In this way we might move toward a viable form of global organization.

Notes

1. See Boje (1995) for an extended illustration of the way in which the Disney corporation crafts and commodifies an official story of Disney.

2. See Clegg (1975) for an extensive account of the discursive generation of power.

3. The case materials described in this section are the results of the on-site work of Diana Whitney.

4. For a more extensive treatment of these arguments and their scientific and social implications, see Gergen (1994).

5. For an account of increasing top-down power through electronic monitoring, see Poster (1990).

6. See also K. Gergen (1992) for an account of power within organizations as self-destructive.

7. See also Wardell's (1992) discussion of "the practical autonomy of labor" and processes of "bottom up" organizing.

8. New metaphors such as the global network, web, or latticework are already commonly used. However, these concepts are far too structural, as opposed to processual, for the outcomes now envisioned.

9. See also Lash and Urry's (1987) discussion of "the disorganizing dynamic," which views disorganization as a systematic process of disaggregation and restructuration.

Conclusion

Reconstructing Organizations for Future Survival

ROBERT P. GEPHART, JR.

TOJO JOSEPH THATCHENKERY

DAVID M. BOJE

We are living in a simulacral society (Baudrillard, 1983), a neocapitalist cybernetic order constructed from signs and simulations, from models that are inherently self-referential. Reality is continuously overtaken by its images (Baudrillard, 1975) and ruled by indeterminacy. When reality is increasingly simulated for people, hyperreality emerges. This hyperreality is currently constructed by powerful media and other cultural sources. As a consequence, managers and other citizens lose the ability to distinguish between simulations and reality; yet this ability to distinguish imaginary from real is a precondition of all social criticism and hence for any attempts to reconstruct and legitimate the state and organizations, and thus to achieve a brighter future. But if images are all that are left, what would be the nature of reconstructions and legitimacy for organizations for the future? How can organizations survive and thrive in the postmodern condition?

The chapters in this volume lead us to pose these questions. The chapters have also outlined many of the features and challenges in the transition from modernism to postmodernism, features that are relevant to answering such questions, yet the answers to these questions are still unclear.

The practical importance of these issues is underscored by popular management texts that have addressed the postmodern challenges to organizations and the need for reconstruction. Such texts often approach these issues more positively than many academic works. For example, *Thriving on Chaos* (Peters, 1987) argues that the organizational world is not neatly organized according to principles but is full of contradictions, uncertainties, and ambiguities. Peters thus attempts to offer prescriptions for dealing with this chaos in the context of accepting it rather than attempting to vanquish it.

The prevailing modernist paradigm also tries to investigate the emergent forms of this chaos to find clear cause-and-effect relationship to guide action. Yet, as we have argued, this is an attempt to impose generalized rationality on phenomena which, if subject to rationality, are subject only to a local rationality of which there are multiple forms.

The postmodern paradigm we have presented, on the other hand, does not seek universal truths or organizing principles but rather seeks local knowledge and insights from which to develop the capacity for reflection and reflexivity in managers and citizens so that chaos can be addressed, accepted, and, when possible, controlled or managed. Thus, an important part of the reconstructive effort in organization theory is developing new concepts and elaborating postmodern perspectives, as indicated in this book. Concepts of deconstruction, reflexivity, simulacrum, and polyphony are basic to this new or postmodern theoretical framework, and these have been discussed in some detail in the essays in this volume.

A related approach to reconstruction is to address organizational "enactment" (Daft & Weick, 1984). Enacting organizations believe that the environment is unanalyzable, but instead of becoming passive, they are actively intrusive in the markets, by experimenting and learning by doing, on some form of anticipatory (Cooperrider, 1990) and relational (Gergen, 1994) reality. By studying the enactment of organizational images, one can get a sense of where the organization is going. A focus on enactment, however, challenges organizational scientists to interrogate their own taken-for-granted self-exemption from the sullying interests of perspective, passion, polemic, and politics. The enactment perspective implies that organizations and organizational science are based on discursive and literary practices and that enactment could thus be done differently, more dramatically and less technically.

One example of doing organizational inquiry differently is *appreciative inquiry* (Cooperrider & Srivastva, 1987). In appreciative inquiry, the researcher begins the inquiry with the presupposition that the process is not value free. Observers and participants in organizational life ought to be more cognizant of the power of images and expectations. What we need therefore are good images, or as Morgan (1993) would put it, "imaginization." Instead of looking at organizations as problem-solving entities, appreciative inquiry encourages others to look at what is there instead of what is not there. The focus is on affirmation of positivities, and this is deliberate, because it frequently produces positive outcomes (see Joseph, 1994; Srivastva et al., 1989, for examples).

A third approach to reconstruction of organizations involves the use of a discourse of intense reflexivity. Joseph (1994) studied one such case, involving the Institute of Cultural Affairs (ICA), an international private voluntary organization. A discourse of intense reflexivity has always been a strong part of this organization. Intense reflexivity is a descriptor for the conscious and simultaneous acts of analysis and metaanalysis (analysis of the analysis). It is the simultaneity of the act and the reflecting on the act, for example, the simultaneous differentiation from and identification with the thought and its object. To link this to Bateson's (1972) notions of single-loop and double-loop learning, intense reflexivity is the simultaneous act of single- and double-loop learning. Thus, it is not just the analytic act, or the reflection on the analysis, but the simultaneous engagement in both that characterizes intense reflexivity.

Analysis of the ICA suggested that what made it survive many drastic environmental changes was its ability to selectively privilege, deprivilege, and reprivilege a discourse of intense reflexivity. In the early years of the life of this organization, intense reflexivity was a privileged discourse because it allowed it to stay focused on its core values and mission. However, as the organization expanded, members got deeply engaged in the instrumental aspect of managing growth, which necessitated a deprivileging of intense reflexivity. Many years later, when the growth led to fundamental transformations in the organization, it was time to return to the roots, resulting in the reprivileging of intense reflexivity. The outcome was a worldwide renewal of the organization and a clear resurgence and growth. In each stage, the reflexivity has enabled the ICA to reinterpret many events and developments as indicative of positive transformations rather than decline. This proactive capacity of organizations to create a meaning system to respond to changes from both inside and outside is what we consider to be the most distinctive character of the postmodern organization.

A fourth approach to reconstructing organizations involves the reconstruction of traditional organization theories and concepts in postmodern form: structure, technology, environment, and effectiveness. For postmodern theory, organizations are discursively produced and socially constructed, that is, they are sense-making resources. The postmodern view closes the gap between the substantialist, reified conception of organization and the analytically reflexive or relationalist view of organizations as locally contingent interpretations that constitute and reflect the intersection of local forces. The gap is problematized; that is, it is made a topic of analysis. In a sense the gap remains, but it is no longer an empty space, but rather the space where analysis is accomplished.

Structure can be reconceptualized in these terms by addressing the interpretive flexibility of structure—the different views of what it means, and the different uses of structure as a category of explanation—as well as the possibilities for flexibly interpreting structure, that is, offering alternatives or different structures. The recently proclaimed "virtual" organization demonstrates that this sense of interpretive flexibility is now a feature of social actors' worldview, as well as part of an analytical perspective, because virtuality refers to a spatially independent form of organization—one existing through interpretive practices. The new spatial context of structure is an electronic presence or medium.

Technology must also be reconsidered. As we move from verbal and written information to communication technologies that transmit digitized information, the spatial context of organizational structure becomes a technology, that is, the technological media that harness and direct the flow of electrons.

Reconceptualizing structure and technology thus requires that we focus more on human interpretive acts and discourse and hence decenter human artifacts that were privileged in previous reified conceptions of these phenomena. This has important if unclear implications. For example, in modernism, corporations were concerned to accumulate sufficient money (currency, dollars, etc.) to avoid insolvency. Money as an artifact (based on the gold standard) has retreated from primacy in economic institutions and is being replaced by credits, that is, digitized representations of accumulated wealth and worth. The recent failure of Barings PLC illustrates how the rapid transmission and flow of credits can quickly produce financial insolvency. The interesting postmodern organization theory issues here relate to the ways in which credits are more amorphous images of wealth than actual "dollars in the bank," the interpretive flexibility this allowed, and how this interpretive flexibility both produced and constituted the Barings collapse. Now we must view credits as "information" transmitted digitally; that is, money is no longer an artifact but a simulacral image.

Similar reconstructive issues arise regarding the environment. The environment is inseparable from organizations, and yet it is separated in modernist theory. Postmodern organization theory must investigate this gap, dissolve it, and yet allow its continued existence as a common reification in mundane reasoning. The task for postmodern organization theory is to investigate representations and images of environments and to understand the practical features and implications these have for—and as—organization actions.

Finally, organizational effectiveness is an ideological tool of management control in modernism. It is derived from and is reflexively constitutive of the organizational imperative, despite attempts and claims to found it on a "scientific" basis that discloses objective elements required for organizational survival. We argue that there is no solid scientific basis on which to develop a conception of organizational effectiveness. Rather, effectiveness can be reconceptualized as an evaluation made by social actors of the relevance of organizations to their images of personal, social, and organizational needs. Different groups and people will inevitably develop different conceptions of effectiveness, so long as there is some ideological variation among the groups. Whereas modernist organization theory tends to seek a singular or best model of effectiveness based in science, postmodern organization theory seeks a practical and ecologically viable set of images of effectiveness that incorporate a range of views and concerns of different groups. These groups have been conceptualized as stakeholders. In the essays in this book, we have attempted to show the important nature of the stakeholder concept, as well as the need to elaborate the concept in postmodern terms.

This task requires that organization theory become concerned with cultural critique and analysis so as to recognize the features and limits of the various views and to allow actors themselves to use radical reflexivity to appreciate the limits and implications of their views. If there is no objective basis for defining effectiveness, then there is no longer any single best set of needs or functional imperatives for organization. What is required is thus the development of a process of effectiveness theorizing among both social actors and scholarly theorists, a process that is sensitive to the multiple and diverse claims of social actors, to the silent voices of nonhuman stakeholders, and to inherent incompleteness of these views. The task thus again becomes that of investigating the precessions and processions of images of effectiveness and of the development of possibilities for alternatives.

Conclusion

The book has called for the deconstruction of organizations and management, that is, for making elements of organization work against one another to reveal gaps, silences, and contradictions in the textual and discursive appearances of organization. We have argued that the next step is a positive reconstruction of organizations, one that we hope will build on emergent local logics to fashion organizational images and schemes that establish bases for future organizational survival. A positive reconstruction necessarily focuses on the underlying assumptions made by social actors when they construct organizations and other features of society. The focus should be on examination of assumptions, presentation of alternatives, and consideration of choices.

The reconstruction of organizations for future survival thus means the deconstruction of modernist features of organization and reconceptualization of these organizational phenomena from a postmodern perspective. These reconceptualizations must be reconstituted in the images of organizational members, particularly the concretized, artifactual images or signs that modernists conceive as constitutive of organizations.

This requires that rationality be decentered but not abandoned. Rationality is pluralized in postmodernism, but it is not extinct. Rather, rationality must take its role alongside other human capabilities, such as love, fear, pain, and hope. Postmodern management and organization theory thus seeks to reconstruct organizations by restoring a sense of harmony and balance in our species, our institutions, and our theories.

References

Ackoff, R. (1981). *Creating the corporate future.* New York: John Wiley.

Ackoff, R. L. (1989). The circular organization: An update. *The Academy of Management Executive, 3,* 11-16.

Agger, B. (1991). Critical theory, poststructuralism, postmodernism: Their sociological relevance. *Annual Review of Sociology, 17,* 105-131.

Akin, G. (1992). Reflections on the AF managerial assessment exercise. *Journal of Management Education, 16*(2), 243-245.

Albrecht, D., Bultena, G., Holberg, E., & Nowak, P. (1982). The new environmental paradigm scale. *Journal of Environmental Education, 13*(3), 39-43.

Alchian, A. A., & Demsetz, H. (1972). Production, information costs, and economic organization. *American Economic Review, 62*(5), 777-795.

Alcock, J. (1985). *Sonoran desert spring.* Chicago: University of Chicago Press.

Allison, G. (1971). *Essence of decision: Explaining the Cuban missile crisis.* Boston: Little, Brown.

Alvesson, M. (1987). *Organization theory and technocratic consciousness.* Berlin: De Gruyter.

Alvesson, M., & Willmott, H. (1990). Critical theory and the sciences of management. In Ph. v. Engeldorp Gastelaars Si. Magala, O. Preub (Eds.), *Critical theory and the science of management* (pp. 23-74). Rotterdam, The Hague, The Netherlands: University Press.

Alvesson, M., & Willmott, H. (1992). *Critical management studies.* London: Sage.

Andre, R. (1992). The AF managerial assessment: Experiencing the pitfalls of psychobabble and the emotional aspects of organizational socialization. *Journal of Management Education, 16*(2), 231-242.

Andrews, K. R. (1971). *The concept of corporate strategy.* Homewood, IL: Irwin.

Ansoff, H. I. (1965a). *Corporate strategy.* New York: McGraw-Hill.

Ansoff, H. I. (1965b). *Strategic management.* New York: John Wiley.

Aronowitz, S., & Giroux, H. (1991). *Postmodern education: Politics, culture, and social criticism.* Minneapolis: University of Minnesota Press.

Astley, G. (1985). Administrative science as social constructed truth. *Administrative Science Quarterly, 30,* 497-513.

Astley, G., & Van de Ven, A. (1983). Central perspectives and debates in organization theory. *Administrative Science Quarterly, 28,* 245-273.

Austrom, D., & Lad, L. (1989). Issues management alliances: New responses, new values, and new logics. In J. Post (Ed.), *Research in corporate social performance and policy* (pp. 233-255). Greenwich, CT: JAI Press.

Axelrod, R. (1984). *The evolution of cooperation.* New York: Basic Books.

Bailey, D., Héon, F., & Steingard, D. (1993). Post-modern international development: Intervelopment and global interbeing. *Journal of Organizational Change Management, 6*(3), 43-63.

Bakhtin, M. (1984). *Problems of Dostoevsky's poetics* (C. Emerson, Trans., Ed.). Minneapolis: University of Minnesota Press.

Baldwin, F. (1984). *Conflicting interests: Corporate-governance controversies.* Lexington, MA: Lexington Books.

Barker, J. (1992). *Future edge: Discovering the new paradigms of success.* New York: William Morrow.

Barker, J. (1993). Tightening the iron cage: Concertive control in self-managing teams. *Administrative Science Quarterly, 38,* 408-437.

Barley, S. R. (1983). Semiotics and the study of occupational and organizational cultures. *Administrative Science Quarterly, 28,* 393-413.

Barley, S. R. (1990). The alignment of technology and structure through roles and networks. *Administrative Science Quarterly, 35,* 61-103.

Barley, S. R., & Kunda, G. (1992). Design and devotion: Surges of rational and normative ideologies of control in managerial discourse. *Administrative Science Quarterly, 37,* 363-399.

Barley, S. R., Meyer, G. W., & Gash, D. C. (1988). Culture of cultures: Academics, practitioners, and the pragmatics of normative control. *Administrative Science Quarterly, 33,* 24-60.

Barry, D. (1991, Spring). Managing the bossless team: Lessons in distributed leadership. *Organizational Dynamics,* 31-47.

Barry, D. (1994). Making the invisible visible: Using analogically based methods to surface the organizational unconscious. In D. P. Moore (Ed.), *The Academy of Management best paper proceedings* (pp. 192-196). Madison, WI: Omnipress.

Bartunek, J. M., & Moch, M. K. (1987). First-order, second-order, and third-order change and organization development interventions: A cognitive approach. *The Journal of Applied Behavioral Science, 23*(4), 483-500.

Bass, B. M., & Avolio, B. J. (1994). *Improving organizational effectiveness through transformational leadership.* Thousand Oaks, CA: Sage.

Bateson, G. (1972). *Steps to an ecology of mind.* New York: Ballantine.

Baudrillard, J. (1975). *The mirror of production.* St. Louis: Telos.

Baudrillard, J. (1983). *Simulations.* New York: Semiotext(e), Inc.

Baudrillard, J. (1986). *America.* London and New York: Verso.

Baudrillard, J. (1994). *Simulacra and simulation.* Ann Arbor: University of Michigan Press.

Bauman, Z. (1988a). Is there a postmodern sociology? *Theory, Culture, and Society, 5*(2), 217-237.

Bauman, Z. (1988b). Viewpoint: Sociology and postmodernity. *Sociological Review, 36*(6), 790-813.

Beck, U. (1992). *The risk society.* London: Sage.

Belenky, M. F., Clinchy, B. M., Goldberger, N. R., & Tarule, J. M. (1986). *Women's ways of knowing: The development of self, voice, and mind.* New York: Basic Books.

Bell, D. (1973). *The coming of post-industrial society.* New York: Basic Books.

Bellah, R. N., Madsen, R., Sullivan, W. M., Swidler, A., & Tipton, S. M. (1985). *Habits of the heart: Individualism and commitment in American life.* New York: Harper & Row.

Bendix, R. (1960). *Max Weber: An intellectual portrait.* Garden City, NY: Anchor Books, Doubleday.

Bensimon, H. F. (1994, January). Violence in the workplace. *Training and Development,* pp. 26-32.

Benson, J. K. (1977). Organizations: A dialectical view. *Administrative Science Quarterly, 22*(1), 1-22.

Berger, P. (1987). *The capitalist revolution.* London: Wildwood.

Berger, P. L., & Luckmann, T. (1967). *The social construction of reality: A treatise in the sociology of knowledge.* Garden City, NY: Anchor Books. (Original work published 1966)

Best, S., & Kellner, D. (1991). *Postmodern theory: Critical interrogations.* New York: Guilford.

Bettman, J. R., & Weitz, B. A. (1983). Attributions in the board room: Causal reasoning in corporate annual reports. *Administrative Science Quarterly, 28,* 165-183.

Beyer, J. M. (1982). Part I: The utilization of organizational research. *Administrative Science Quarterly, 27,* 588-590.

Bhattacharya, K. (1965). *Philosophy, logic, and language.* Bombay: Allied Publishers.

Bittner, E. (1974). The concept of organization. In R. Turner (Ed.), *Ethnomethodology* (pp. 69-81). Markham, Ontario: Penguin.

Bixler, S. (1984). *The professional image: The total program for marketing yourself visually.* New York: Putnam.

Black, J. S., Gregersen, H. B., & Mendenhall, M. (1992). *Global assignments: Successfully expatriating and repatriating international managers.* San Francisco: Jossey-Bass.

Black, J. S., Mendenhall, M., & Oddou, G. (1991). Toward a comprehensive model of international adjustment: An integration of multiple theoretical perspectives. *Academy of Management Review, 16,* 291-317.

Block, P. (1987). *The empowered manager.* San Francisco: Jossey-Bass.

Bluedorn, A. (1993). Pilgrim's progress: Trends and convergence in research on organizational size and environment. *Journal of Management, 19*(2), 163-192.

Bluedorn, A., Johnson, R., Cartwright, D., & Barringer, B. (1994). The interface and convergence of the strategic management and organizational environment domains. *Journal of Management, 20*(2), 201-262.

Bocchi, G., & Ceruti, M. (Eds.). (1985). *La sfida della complessità* [The challenge of complexity]. Milano: Feltrinelli.

Boje, D. M. (1991). The storytelling organization: A study of story performance in an office-supply firm. *Administrative Science Quarterly, 36*(1), 106-126.

Boje, D. (Ed.). (1992a). Postmodern discourse and change: Part II. *Journal of Organization Change Management, 5*(2), 3-69.

Boje, D. M. (1992b). *The university is a panoptic cage: The disciplining of the student and faculty body.* Paper presented at Postmodern Management: Diversity and Change Showcase Session for OT, RM, and OD Divisions of National Academy of Management Meetings in Las Vegas, Nevada.

Boje, D. (Ed.). (1993). Anti-total quality management debate [Special issue]. *Journal of Organization Change Management, 6*(4), 2-57.

Boje, D. M. (1994a). Organizational storytelling: The struggles of pre-modern, modern, and postmodern organizational learning discourses. *Management Learning Journal, 25*(3), 433-461.

Boje, D. M. (1994b, August 14-17). *Resistance and the Greenback Company model.* Paper presented at the Academy of Management Meetings, Dallas.

Boje, D. (Ed.). (1994c). Spirituality and organizational change [Special issue]. *Journal of Organization Change Management, 7*(1), 2-57.

Boje, D. M. (1995). Stories of the storytelling organization: A postmodern analysis of Disney as "Tamara-land." *Academy of Management Journal, 38*(4), 997-1035.

Boje, D. M. (in press-a). Management education is a panoptic cage: Disciplining the student and faculty bodies. In C. Grey & R. French (Eds.), *Critical perspectives on management education.* London: Sage.

Boje, D. M. (in press-b). Premodern, modern, and postmodern: Which way is up. In G. Palmer & S. Clegg (Eds.), *Constituting management: Markets, meanings, and identities.* London: Sage.

Boje, D. M., & Dennehy, R. (1992). Postmodern management principles: Just the opposite of modernist-bureaucratic principles. In *Proceedings of International Academy of Business Disciplines* (pp. 442-448). Washington, DC: International Academy of Business Disciplines.

Boje, D. M., & Dennehy, R. F. (1993). *Managing in the postmodern world: America's revolution against exploitation.* Dubuque, IA: Kendall/Hunt.

Boje, D. M., & Dennehy, R. F. (1994). *Managing in the postmodern world: America's revolution against exploitation* (2nd ed.). Dubuque, IA: Kendall/Hunt.

Boje, D. M., & Pondy, L. (1976). The experiential learning organization: An alternative way to teach and learn about management and organization. In D. M. Boje, D. J. Brass, & L. R. Pondy (Eds.), *Managing II* (pp. 467-521). New York: Ginn.

Boje, D. M., & Winsor, R. (1993). The resurrection of Taylorism: Total quality management's hidden agenda. *Journal of Organizational Change Management, 6*(4), 57-70.

Boje, D. M., & Winsor, R. (1994). The globalization and rediscovery of the American system. *Business Research Yearbook: Global Business Perspectives, 1*, 688-694.

Boje, D., & Wolfe, T. J. (1987). Transorganizational development: Contributions to theory and practice. In H. J. Leavitt, L. R. Pondy, & D. M. Boje (Eds.), *Readings in managerial psychology* (pp. 733-754). Chicago: University of Chicago Press.

Bolman, L., & Deal, T. (1991). *Reframing organizations.* San Francisco: Jossey-Bass.

Botwinick, A. (1993). *Postmodernism and democratic theory.* Philadelphia: Temple University Press.

Boulding, E. (1988). *Building a global civic culture: Education for an interdependent world.* New York: Teachers College Press.

Boulding, K. E. (1956, April). General systems theory. *Management Science, 2*, 197-206.

Boulding, K. E. (1958). Evidences for an administrative science: A review of the *Administrative Science Quarterly,* Volumes 1 and 2. *Administrative Science Quarterly, 3*(1), 1-22.

Boulding, K. (1968). General systems theory—the skeleton of science. In W. Buckley (Ed.), *Modern systems research for the behavioral scientist* (pp. 3-10). Chicago: Aldine.

Bourdieu, P. (1968). Outline of a sociological theory of art perception. *International Social Science Journal, 20*(4), 589-612.

Bourdieu, P. (1990). *The logic of practice* (R. Nice, Trans.). Stanford, CA: Stanford University Press.

Bourdieu, P. (1993). *The field of cultural production: Essays on art and literature* (R. A. Johnson, Ed.). New York: Columbia University Press.

Boyatzis, R. E. (1982). *The competent manager: A model for effective performance.* New York: John Wiley.

Boyatzis, R. E., Cowen, S. S., & Kolb, D. A. (1995). *Innovation in learning.* San Francisco: Jossey-Bass.

Bradford, D. (1993). Foreword. In C. Vance (Ed.), *Mastering management education: Innovations in teaching effectiveness* (pp. ix-x). Newbury Park, CA: Sage.

Bradshaw, P., Murray, V., & Wolpin, J. (in press). Women on nonprofit boards: Do they make a difference? *Nonprofit Management and Leadership.*

Bradshaw-Camball, P. (1990). *Women on Canadian boards: Excellence in a box.* Working Paper, York University.

Brenner, S., & Cochran, P. (1991). A stakeholder theory of the firm: Implications for business and society theory and research. In *Proceedings of the second annual meeting of the International Association for Business and Society* (pp. 449-467), Sundance, UT.

Brown, R. H. (1990). Rhetoric, textuality, and the postmodern turn in sociological theory. *Sociological Theory, 8*(2), 188-197.

Brown, R. (Ed.). (1992). *Writing the social text: Poetics and politics in social science discourse.* New York: Aldine de Gruyter.

Buchholz, R. (1993). *Principles of environmental management: The greening of management.* Englewood Cliffs, NJ: Prentice Hall.

Buckley, W. (1968). *Modern systems research for the behavioral scientist.* New York: Aldine.

Burke, P. (1987). *The renaissance.* Basingstoke, UK: Macmillan.

Burke, R. (1994). Women on corporate boards of directors. In J. de Bruijn & E. Cyba (Eds.), *Gender and organizations—Changing perspectives* (pp. 191-222). Amsterdam: VU Press.

Burrell, G. (1980). Radical organization theory. In D. Dunkerley & G. Salaman (Eds.), *The international yearbook of organization studies.* London: Routledge & Kegan Paul.

Burrell, G. (1988). Modernism, postmodernism, and organizational analysis 2: The contribution of Michael Foucault. *Organization Studies, 9*(2), 221-235.

Burrell, G., & Morgan, G. (1979). *Sociological paradigms and organisational analysis: Elements of the sociology of corporate life.* London: Heinemann.

Butler, S. (1994, December 30). Service courses teach students some lessons in the real world. *Wall Street Journal,* pp. B1, B4.

Calas, M. (1987). *Organizational science/fiction: The postmodern in the management disciplines.* Unpublished Ph.D. Dissertation, University of Massachusetts, Amherst.

Calas, M., & Smircich, L. (1991). Voicing seduction to silence leadership. *Organization Studies, 12*(4), 567-602.

Calas, M., & Smircich, L. (1992). Rewriting gender into organisational theorizing: Directions from feminist theorizing. In M. Reed & M. Hughes (Eds.), *Rethinking organisation: New directions in organisation theory and analysis.* London: Sage.

Callinicos, A. (1989). *Against postmodernism.* Cambridge: Polity Press.

Calton, J. M. (1991). The dark side of commitment. Is the literature on organizational commitment an ideological black hole? In K. Paul (Ed.), *Contemporary issues in business ethics and politics* (pp. 69-99). Lewiston, NY: Edwin Mellen Press.

Calton, J. M., & Lad, L. (1993). Collaborative governance: The firm, the interorganizational field, and "negotiated order." In J. Pasquero & D. Collins (Eds.), *Proceedings of the fourth annual meeting of the International Association for Business & Society* (pp. 84-89). Madison: University of Wisconsin School of Business.

Calton, J. M., & Lad, L. (1995). Social contracting as a trust-building process of network governance. *Business Ethics Quarterly, 5*(2), 271-295.

Campbell, J. P., Dunnette, M. D., Lawler, E. E., III, & Weick, K. E., Jr. (1970). *Managerial behavior, performance, and effectiveness.* New York: McGraw-Hill.

Casey, C. (1995). *Work, self, and society after industrialism.* London: Routledge.

Ceruti, M. (1994). *Constraints and possibilities. The evolution of knowledge and knowledge of evolution.* New York: Gordon & Breach. (Original work, *Il vincolo e la possibilità* [Constraint and possibility], published 1986, Milano, Feltrinelli)

Chandler, A. D., Jr. (1977). *The visible hand: The managerial revolution in American business.* Cambridge, MA: Harvard University Press.

Chase, A. (1987). *Playing God in Yellowstone: The destruction of America's first national park.* San Diego: Harcourt Brace Jovanovich.

Cheal, D. (1990). Authority and incredulity: Sociology between modernism and post-modernism. *Canadian Journal of Sociology 15*(2), 129-146.

Checkland, P. (1981). *Systems thinking, systems practice.* New York: John Wiley.

Chen, C. C., & Meindl, J. R. (1991). The construction of leadership images in the popular press: The case of Donald Burr and People Express. *Administrative Science Quarterly, 36,* 521-551.

Cheng, C. (Ed.). (1994). Recognizing authors' voices in diversity stories [Special issue]. *Journal of Organization Change Management, 7*(1), 2-57.

Clegg, S. (1975). *Power, rule, and domination: A critical and empirical understanding of power in sociological theory and organisational life.* London: Routledge & Kegan Paul.

Clegg, S. (1979). *The theory of power and organization.* London: Routledge & Kegan Paul.

Clegg, S. (1989). *Frameworks of power.* London: Sage.

Clegg, S. (1990). *Modern organisations: Organisation studies in the postmodern world.* London: Sage.

Clegg, S. (1992, August). *Postmodern management?* Paper presented at the showcase session on postmodern theory at the Academy of Management, Las Vegas, NV.

Clegg, S. R. (1994a). Foreword: Managing in the postmodern world: America's revolution against exploitation. In D. Boje & R. Dennehy (Eds.), *Managing in the postmodern world: America's revolution against exploitation* (2nd ed., pp. vii-x). Dubuque, IA: Kendall/Hunt.

Clegg, S. (1994b). Weber and Foucault: Social theory for the study of organizations. *Organization, 1*(1), 149-178.

Clegg, S. R., & Dunkerley, D. (Eds.). (1980a). *Critical issues in organisations.* London: Routledge & Kegan Paul.

Clegg, S. R., & Dunkerley, D. (1980b). *Organisation, class, and control.* London: Routledge & Kegan Paul.

Clegg, S. R., & Rouleau, L. (1992). Postmodernism and postmodernity in organizational analysis. *Journal of Organizational Change Management, 5*(1), 8-25.

Clifford, J., & Marcus, G. E. (1986). *Writing culture: The poetics and politics of ethnography.* Berkeley: University of California Press.

Clough, P. (1992). *The end(s) of ethnography: From realism to social criticism.* Newbury Park, CA: Sage.

Clune, G. (1943). *The medieval guild system.* Dublin: Browne & Nolan.

Code, L. (1991). *What can she know? Feminist theory and the construction of knowledge.* Ithaca, NY: Cornell University Press.

Concise Oxford Dictionary (J. Sykes, Ed.). (1983). Oxford: Clarendon.

Conquerwood, D. (1991). Rethinking ethnography: Towards a critical cultural politics. *Communication Monographs, 58,* 179-194.

Contractor, F., & Lorange, P. (1988). *Cooperative strategies in international business.* Lexington, MA: D. C. Heath.

Cooper, D. (1992). Formal organization as representation. In M. Reed & M. Hughes (Eds.), *Rethinking organisation* (pp. 254-272). London: Sage.

Cooper, R. (1983). The other: A model of human structuring. In G. Morgan (Ed.), *Beyond method* (pp. 202-218). Beverly Hills, CA: Sage.

Cooper, R. (1987). Information, communication, and organization: A post-structural revision. *Journal of Mind and Behaviour, 8*(3), 395-416.

Cooper, R. (1989). Modernism, postmodernism, and organizational analysis 3: The contribution of Jacques Derrida. *Organization Studies, 10*(4), 479-502.

Cooper, R. (1990). Organization/disorganization. In J. Hassard & D. Pym (Eds.), *The theory and philosophy of organizations: Critical issues and new perspectives* (pp. 167-197). London: Routledge.

Cooper, R., & Burrell, G. (1988). Modernism, postmodernism, and organizational analysis: An introduction. *Organization Studies, 9*(1), 91-112.

Cooperrider, D. L. (1990). Positive image, positive action: The affirmative basis of organizing. In S. Srivastva et al. (Eds.), *Appreciative management and leadership* (pp. 91-125). San Francisco: Jossey-Bass.

Cooperrider, D. L., & Bilimoria, D. (in press). The challenge of global change for strategic management: Opportunities for charting a new course. In P. Shrivastva & L. Dutton (Eds.), *Advances in strategic management* (Vol. 9). Greenwich, CT: JAI Press.

Cooperrider, D. L., & Pasmore, W. A. (1991). The organization dimension of global change [Special issue]. *Human Relations, 44.*

Cooperrider, D., & Srivastva, S. (1987). Appreciative inquiry in organizational life. *Research in Organizational Change and Development, 1,* 129-169.

Cooperrider, D., & Thatchenkery, T. (1991). Building the global civic culture: Making our lives count. In P. F. Sorensen et al. (Eds.), *International organization development* (pp. 250-274). Champaign, IL: Stipes.

Corlett, W. (1989). *Community without unity: A politics of Derridian extravagance.* Durham, NC: Duke University Press.

Coser, L. (1977). *Masters of sociological thought: Ideas in historical and social context* (2nd ed.). New York: Harcourt Brace.

Cox, G. (Ed.). (1969). *Readings in conservation ecology.* New York: Meredith.

Culler, J. (1981). *The pursuit of signs: Semiotics, literature, deconstruction.* New York: Cornell University Press.

Culler, J. (1982). *On deconstruction: Theory and criticism after structuralism.* Ithaca, NY: Cornell University Press.

Cyert, R. M., & March, J. G. (1963). *A behavioral theory of the firm.* Englewood Cliffs, NJ: Prentice Hall.

Daft, R. L. (1980). The evolution of organization analysis in ASQ, 1959-1979. *Administrative Science Quarterly, 25*(4), 623-637.

Daft, R. (1995). *Organization theory and design.* St. Paul, MN: West.

Daft, R., & Lewin, A. Y. (1993). Where are the theories for the "new" organizational forms: An editorial essay. *Organization Science, 4*(4), i-vi.

Daft, R. L., & Weick, K. E. (1984). Towards a model of organizations as interpretation systems. *Academy of Management Review, 9*(2), 284-295.

Davidow, W., & Malone, M. (1992). *The virtual corporation: Structuring and revitalizing the corporation for the 21st century*. New York: HarperCollins.

Deal, T. E., & Kennedy, A. A. (1982). *Corporate cultures: The rites and rituals of corporate life*. New York: Addison-Wesley.

Debate on postmodernism [Special issue]. (1992). *Sociological Theory, 10*(2).

Deetz, S. (1992). *Democracy in an age of corporate colonization*. Albany: State University of New York Press.

Deetz, S. (1995). *Transforming communication, transforming business: Building responsive and responsible workplaces*. Cresskill, NJ: Hampton Press.

Deetz, S. A. (in press). Studying the corporate simulacra: A communication analysis of representational practices in corporations. In B. Kovacic (Ed.), *Organizational communication: New perspectives*. Albany: State University of New York Press.

Delany, W. (1961). Some fieldnotes on the problem of access in organizational research. *Administrative Science Quarterly, 5*(3), 448-457.

Demb, A., & Neubauer, F. (1992). *The corporate board: Confronting the paradoxes*. New York: Oxford University Press.

Denzin, N. K. (1986, Fall). Postmodern social theory. *Sociological Theory, 4*, 194-204.

Derrida, J. (1976). *Speech and phenomena*. Evanston, IL: Northwestern University Press.

Derrida, J. (1978). *Writing and difference* (A. Bass, Trans.). London: Routledge & Kegan Paul.

Derrida, J. (1981). *Dissemination* (B. Johnson, Trans.). London: Athlone.

Derrida, J. (1982). *Margins of philosophy* (A. Bass, Trans.). Chicago: University of Chicago Press.

Derrida, J. (1983). The principles of reason: The university in the eyes of its pupils. *Diacritics, 19*(3), 3-20.

Derrida, J. (1985). *The ear of the other* (P. Kamuf, Trans.). Lincoln: University of Nebraska Press.

Devall, B., & Sessions, G. (1985). *Deep ecology: Living as if nature mattered*. Salt Lake City, UT: Peregrine Smith.

Dicken, P. (1992). *Global shift: The internationalisation of economic activity*. London: PCP.

Di Stefano, C. (1990). Dilemmas of difference: Feminism, modernity, and postmodernism. In L. Nicholson (Ed.), *Feminism/postmodernism* (pp. 63-82). New York: Routledge.

Doktor, R., Tung, R., & Glinow, M. A. (1991). Interpreting international dimensions in management theory building. *Academy of Management Review, 16*, 259-261.

Donaldson, L. (1985). *In defence of organisation theory: A reply to the critics*. Cambridge: Cambridge University Press.

Donaldson, L. (1987). Strategy and structural adjustment to regain fit and performance: In defence of contingency theory. *Journal of Management Studies, 24*(1), 1-24.

Donaldson, L. (1988). In successful defence of organizational theory: A routing of the critics. *Organization Studies, 9*(1), 28-32.

Donaldson, T., & Dunfee, T. (1994). Toward a unified conception of business ethics: Integrative social contracts theory. *Academy of Management Review, 19*(2), 252-284.

Donaldson, T., & Preston, L. (1995). The stakeholder theory of the corporation: Concepts, evidence, and implications. *Academy of Management Review, 20*(1), 65-91.

Dore, R. (1983). Goodwill and the spirit of modern capitalism. *British Journal of Sociology, 34*, 359-382.

Douglas, M. (1970). *Natural symbols: Explorations in cosmology*. New York: Pantheon.

Douglas, M. (1973). *Natural symbols: Explorations in cosmology.* Harmondsworth, UK: Penguin.

Drucker, P. (1957). Introduction: This post-modern world. In *Landmarks of tomorrow.* New York: Harper.

Drucker, P. (1990, May/June). The emerging theory of manufacturing. *Harvard Business Review,* pp. 94-102.

Drucker, P. (1992). *Managing for the future: The 1990s and beyond.* New York: Truman Talley Books/Dutton.

Dunford, R., & Palmer, I. (1995). Claims about frames: Practitioners' assessment of the utility of reframing. *Journal of Management Education.*

Dunlap, R. E., & Van Liere, K. (1978, February). Environmental sociology: A new paradigm. *The American Sociologist, 13,* 41-49.

Dunn, D. (1987, March 16). Directors aren't doing their jobs. *Fortune,* pp. 117-119.

Dunning, J. H. (1993). *The globalisation of business.* London: Routledge.

Eagleton, T. (1976). *Marxism and literary criticism.* Berkeley: University of California Press.

Earle, A. (1990). *Compensation for chief executive officers—Test of corporate governance.* London, Ontario, Canada: National Center for Management Research and Development.

Egri, C., Shrivastava, P., & Throop, G. (1993). *Greening business education.* Post-conference workshop, Organizational Behavior Teaching Conference, Bucknell University.

Eisler, R. (1987). *The chalice and the blade: Our history, our future.* San Francisco: Harper & Row.

Elsea, J. (1985). *First impression, best impression.* New York: Simon & Schuster.

Emery, E. (1993). *Participative design for participative democracy.* Canberra: Australian National University.

Emery, M. (1982). *Searching: In new ways, for new directions, in new times.* Canberra: Australian National University Press.

Emery, M., & Purser, R. (in press). *Search conferences in action.* San Francisco: Jossey-Bass.

Evan, W. M. (1993). *Organization theory: Research and design.* New York: Macmillan.

Evan, W. M., & Freeman, R. E. (1988). A stakeholder theory of the modern corporation: Kantian capitalism. In T. L. Beauchamp & N. E. Bowie (Eds.), *Ethical theory and business* (3rd ed., pp. 97-106). Englewood Cliffs, NJ: Prentice Hall.

Evans, F. C. (1969). Ecosystem as the basic unit in ecology. In G. Cox (Ed.), *Readings in conservation ecology* (pp. 3-5). New York: Merideth.

Faculty of the Weatherhead School of Management. (1991). *Management 403: Management assessment and development* (Codebook). Cleveland, OH: Case Western Reserve University.

Farganis, S. (1994). *Situating feminism: From thought to action* (Sage Series on Contemporary Social Theory, Vol. 2). Thousand Oaks, CA: Sage.

Fayol, H. (1937). The administrative theory in the state. In L. Gulick & L. Urwick, *Papers on the science of administration* (pp. 101-104). New York: Columbia University Press.

Fayol, H. (1949). *Industrial and general administration.* London: Pitman.

Featherstone, M. (1988). In pursuit of the postmodern: An introduction. *Theory, Culture, and Society, 5*(2-3), 195-215.

Featherstone, M., Hepworth, M., & Turner, B. (1991). *The body: Social process and cultural theory.* Newbury Park, CA: Sage.

Feldman, R. (Ed.). (1992). *Applications of nonverbal behavioral theories and research.* Hillsdale, NJ: Lawrence Erlbaum.

Ferguson, K. (1984). *The feminist case against bureaucracy*. Philadelphia: Temple University Press.

Ferguson, K. (1994). On bringing more theory, more voices, and more politics to the study of organization. *Organization, 1*(1), 81-99.

Fetterley, J. (1978). *The resisting reader: A feminist approach to American fiction*. Bloomington: Indiana University Press.

Fineman, S., & Gabriel, Y. (1993, July). *Changing rhetorics: The case of the introductory OB textbook*. Paper presented at the 11th EGOC Colloquium, Paris, France.

Fineman, S., & Gabriel, Y. (1994). Paradigms of organizations: An exploration in textbook rhetorics. *Organization, 1*(2), 375-399.

Fiol, C. M. (1989). A semiotic analysis of corporate language: Organizational boundaries and joint venturing. *Administrative Science Quarterly, 34*(2), 277-303.

Fisher, A. (1993, August 23). Sexual harassment: What to do. *Fortune*, pp. 84-86.

Fitzgibbons, D., Steingard, D., & Boje, D. (1993). *Rethinking the backlash to postmodern administrative science*. Unpublished manuscript.

Flax, J. (1990). *Thinking fragments: Psychoanalysis, feminism, and postmodernism in the contemporary West*. Berkeley: University of California Press.

Fleischer, A., Hazard, G., & Klipper, M. (1988). *Board games: The changing shape of corporate power*. Toronto: Little, Brown.

Follett, M. P. (1937). The process of control. In L. Gulick & L. Urwick (Eds.) *Papers on the science of administration*. New York: Columbia University Press.

Foucault, M. (1965). *Madness and civilization*. New York: Random House.

Foucault, M. (1970a). The order of discourse. In R. Young (Ed.), *Untying the text: A poststructuralist reader* (pp. 48-78). Boston: Routledge & Kegan Paul.

Foucault, M. (1970b). *The order of things*. New York: Vintage.

Foucault, M. (1973). *The birth of the clinic*. New York: Pantheon.

Foucault, M. (1976). *The archaeology of knowledge and the discourse on language*. New York: Harper & Row.

Foucault, M. (1977). *Surveiller et punir: Naissance de la prison* [Discipline and punish]. Paris: Gallimard.

Foucault, M. (1978). *The history of sexuality, Vol. 1* (R. Hurley, Trans.). New York: Pantheon.

Foucault, M. (1979). *Discipline and punish: The birth of the prison* (A. Sheridan, Trans.). New York: Vintage.

Foucault, M. (1980a). *Introduction to Herculin Barbin: Being the recently discovered memoirs of a nineteenth century French hermaphrodite*. New York: Pantheon.

Foucault, M. (1980b). *Power/knowledge*. New York: Pantheon.

Foucault, M. (1982). The subject and power. In H. Dreyfus & P. Rabinow (Eds.), *Michel Foucault: Beyond structuralism and hermeneutics* (pp. 208-226). Chicago: University of Chicago Press.

Foucault, M. (1984). The body of the condemned. In P. Rabinow (Ed.), *The Foucault reader* (pp. 170-178). New York: Pantheon.

Fox, S. (1989). The Panopticon: From Bentham's obsession to the revolution in management learning. *Human Relations, 42*(8), 717-739.

Frank, A. W. (1991). For a sociology of the body: An analytical review. In M. Featherstone, M. Hepworth, & B. S. Turner (Eds.), *The body: Social process and cultural theory* (pp. 36-104). London: Sage.

Frank, R. H. (1988). *Passions within reason: The strategic role of the emotions*. New York: Norton.

Franke, R. H., Hofstede, G., & Bond, M. (1991). Cultural roots of economic performance: A research note. *Strategic Management Journal, 12,* 165-173.

Frederick, W. C. (1995). *Values, nature, and culture in the American corporation.* New York and Oxford: Oxford University Press.

Freeman, J. H. (1986). Data quality and the development of organizational social science: An editorial essay. *Administrative Science Quarterly, 31*(2), 298-303.

Freeman, R. E. (1984). *Strategic management: A stakeholder approach.* Boston: Pitman.

Freeman, R. E. (1994). The politics of stakeholder theory: Some future directions. *Business Ethics Quarterly, 4*(4), 409-421.

Freeman, R. E., & Evan, W. (1990). Corporate governance: A stakeholder interpretation. *Journal of Behavioral Economics, 19*(4), 337-359.

Freeman, R. E., & Gilbert, D. R. (1988). *Corporate strategy and the search for ethics.* Englewood Cliffs, NJ: Prentice Hall.

Freeman R. E., & Gilbert, D. R. (1992). Business ethics and society: A critical agenda. *Business & Society, 31,* 9-17.

Freire, P. (1973). *The wretched of the earth.* Harmondsworth, UK: Penguin.

Froiland, P. (1993, December). What curse job stress? *Training,* pp. 32-36.

Frost, P. (1980). Toward a radical framework for practicing organizational science. *Academy of Management Review, 5,* 581-587.

Frost, P., Moore, L. F., Louis, M. R., Lundberg, C. C., & Martin, J. (1991). *Reframing organizational culture.* Newbury Park, CA: Sage.

Frost, P. J., & Taylor, R. N. (1985). Partisan perspective: A multiple level interpretation of the manuscript review process in social science journals. In L. L. Cummings & P. J. Frost (Eds.), *Publishing in the organizational sciences* (pp. 35-62). Burr Ridge, IL: Irwin.

Gadamer, H. (1975). *Truth and method* (G. Barden & J. Cumming, Eds. and Trans.). New York: Seabury.

Garfinkel, H. (1967). *Studies in ethnomethodology.* Englewood Cliffs, NJ: Prentice Hall.

Garg, P. K., & Parikh, I. J. (Eds.). (1993). *Transience and transitions in organisations. Vol. 4: Organisation theories, issues, and applications.* Ahmedbad, India: Indian Society for Individual and Social Development.

Geber, B. (1992, June). Saturn's grand experiment. *Training, 29*(6), 27-35.

Gebser, J. (1985). *The ever-present origin.* Athens: Ohio University Press.

Geertz, C. (1973). *The interpretation of cultures.* New York: Basic Books.

Geneen, H. (1984, September 17). Why directors can't protect the shareholder. *Fortune,* pp. 28-32.

Gephart, R. (1978). Status degradation and organizational succession: An ethnomethodological approach. *Administrative Science Quarterly, 23,* 553-581.

Gephart, R. P. (1984). Making sense of organizationally based environmental disasters. *Journal of Management, 10,* 205-225.

Gephart, R. (1986). Deconstructing the defense for quantification in social science: A content analysis of journal articles on the parametric strategy. *Qualitative Sociology, 9*(2), 126-144.

Gephart, R. P. (1988a). *Ethnostatistics: Qualitative foundations for quantitative research* (Qualitative Research Methods, Vol. 12). Newbury Park, CA: Sage.

Gephart, R. P. (1988b). Managing the meaning of a sour gas well blowout: The public culture of organizational disaster. *Industrial Crisis Quarterly, 2,* 17-32.

Gephart, R. P. (1991). Succession, sense making, and organizational change: A story of a deviant college president. *Journal of Organizational Change Management, 4,* 35-44.

Gephart, R. P., Jr. (1993). The textual approach: Risk and blame in disaster sense making. *Academy of Management Journal, 36*(2), 1465-1514.

Gephart, R. P., & Bowring, M. (1995). Silent stories: Excluded stakeholders and the natural environment. In A. F. Alkhafaji (Ed.), *Business research yearbook* (Vol. 2, pp. 723-727). Lanham, MD: University Press of America.

Gephart, R. P., & Pitter, R. (1993). The organizational basis of industrial accidents in Canada. *Journal of Management Inquiry, 3*, 238-252.

Gergen, K. (1982). *Toward transformation in social knowledge.* New York: Springer-Verlag.

Gergen, K. (1991). *The saturated self: Dilemmas of identity in contemporary life.* New York: Basic Books.

Gergen, K. (1992). Organisation theory in the postmodern era. In M. Reed & M. Hughes (Eds.), *Rethinking organisations: New directions in organisation theory and analysis* (pp. 209-226). London: Sage.

Gergen, K. (1994). *Realities and relationships: Soundings in social construction.* Cambridge, MA: Harvard University Press.

Gergen, K., & Thatchenkery, T. (in press). Organizational science in a postmodern context. *Journal of Applied Behavioral Science.*

Gergen, M. (1992). Metaphors for chaos, stories of continuity: Building a new organizational theory. In S. Srivastva & R. E. Fry (Eds.), *Executive and organizational continuity* (pp. 207-226). San Francisco: Jossey-Bass.

Gerlach, M., & Lincoln, J. (1992). The organization of business networks in the United States and Japan. In N. Nohria & R. Eccles (Eds.), *Networks and organizations: Structure, form, and action* (pp. 491-520). Boston: Harvard Business School Press.

Gibson, W. (1984). *Neuromancer.* New York: Ace.

Gibson, W. (1986). *Count Zero.* New York: Ace.

Gibson, W. (1988). *Mona Lisa overdrive.* New York: Bantam.

Gibson, W. (1993). *Virtual light.* Toronto: Bantam.

Giddens, A. (1990). *The consequences of modernity.* Stanford, CA: Stanford University Press.

Giddens, A. (1991a). *Modernity and self-identity: Self and society in the late modern age.* Stanford, CA: Stanford University Press.

Giddens, A. (1991b). A reply to my critics. In D. Held & J. B. Thompson (Eds.), *Social theory of modern societies.* Cambridge: Cambridge University Press.

Gilbert, D. (1992). *The twilight of corporate strategy: A comparative ethical critique.* New York: Oxford University Press.

Gilbreth, F. B. (1911). *Motion study, a method for increasing the efficiency of the workman.* New York: D. Van Nostrand.

Gillies, J. (1992). *Boardroom renaissance: Power, morality, and performance in the modern corporation.* Toronto: McGraw-Hill Ryerson.

Gilligan, C. (1982). *In a different voice: Psychological theory and women's development.* Cambridge, MA: Harvard University Press.

Gilligan, C. (1988). Remapping the moral domain: New images of self in relationship. In C. Gilligan, J. Ward, & J. Taylor, with B. Bardige (Eds.), *Mapping the moral domain: A contribution of women's thinking to psychological theory and education* (pp. 3-19). Cambridge, MA: Harvard University Press.

Gilson, C. (1994). Of dinosaurs and sacred cows: The grading of classroom participation. *Journal of Management Education, 18*(2), 227-236.

Glaberson, W., & Powell, W. (1985, March 18). A landmark ruling that puts board members in peril. *Business Week,* pp. 56-57.

Goffman, E. (1959). *The presentation of self in everyday life.* New York: Doubleday Anchor.

Goffman, E. (1961). *Asylums.* New York: Anchor.

Goldman, P., & Van Houten, D. (1977). Managerial strategies and the worker. *Sociological Quarterly, 18*(1), 108-125.

Goodpaster, K. E. (1991). Business ethics and stakeholder analysis. *Business Ethics Quarterly, 1*(1), 53-73.

Gouldner, A. (1973). *The coming crisis of Western sociology.* London: Heinemann.

Gray, B. (1989). *Collaborating: Finding common ground for multi-party problems.* San Francisco: Jossey-Bass.

Gray, B., Bougon, M. G., & Donnellon, A. (1985). Organizations as constructions and destructions of meaning. *Journal of Management, 11*(2), 83-98.

Grey, C. (1994). Career as a project of self and labour process discipline. *Sociology, 28*(2), 479-497.

Griffin, A. (1985, August). Business forum. *Canadian Business,* pp. 73-77.

Grint, K. (1991). *The sociology of work.* Cambridge: Polity Press.

Guba, E. G., & Lincoln, Y. S. (1994). Competing paradigms in qualitative research. In N. K. Denzin & Y. S. Lincoln (Eds.), *Handbook of qualitative research* (pp. 105-117). Thousand Oaks, CA: Sage.

Habermas, J. (1973). *Legitimation crisis.* Boston: Beacon.

Habermas, J. (1981, Winter). Modernity versus postmodernity. *New German Critique, 22,* 3-14.

Habermas, J. (1987). *The philosophical discourse of modernity: Twelve lectures* (F. G. Lawrence, Trans.). Cambridge: MIT Press.

Habermas, J. (1990). *Moral consciousness and communicative action* (C. Lenhardt & S. W. Nicholsen, Trans.). Cambridge: MIT Press.

Hall, S. (1986). On postmodernism and articulation: An interview with Stuart Hall (L. Grossberg, Ed.). *Journal of Communication Inquiry, 10,* 45-60.

Hall, S. (1992). Cultural studies and its theoretical legacies. In C. N. Grossberg & P. Treichler (Eds.), *Cultural studies* (pp. 274-294). London: Routledge.

Hampden-Turner, C. (1990). *Charting the corporate mind.* Oxford: Blackwell.

Handy, C. (1992, November-December). Balancing corporate power: A new federalist paper. *Harvard Business Review,* pp. 59-72.

Hannan, M. T., & Freeman, J. (1989). *Organizational ecology.* Cambridge, MA: Harvard University Press.

Harland, P. (1987). *Superstructuralism.* London: Methuen.

Harvey, D. (1989). *The condition of postmodernity.* Cambridge, MA: Basil Blackwell.

Hassard, J. (1993). Postmodernism and organisational analysis: An overview. In J. Hassard & M. Parker (Eds.), *Postmodernism and organisations* (pp. 1-23). London: Sage.

Hassard, J., & Pym, D. (Eds.). (1990). *The theory and philosophy of organisations: Critical issues and new perspectives.* London: Routledge.

Hatton, M. J. (1990). *Corporations & directors: Comparing the profit and not-for-profit sectors.* Toronto: Thompson.

Hazen, M. A. (1993). Toward polyphonic organization. *Journal of Organizational Change Management, 6*(5), 15-2.

Hazen, M. A. (1994). Multiplicity and change in persons and organizations. *Journal of Organizational Change Management, 7*(5), 72-81.

Hazen, M. A., & Isbey, J. (1994, August). *Giving voice to the spirit: Soul making and organizational change*. Paper presented at the annual meeting of the Academy of Management, Organizational Development and Change Division, Dallas, TX.

Heckscher, C. (1994). Defining the post-bureaucratic type. In C. Heckscher & A. Donnellon (Eds.), *The post-bureaucratic organization: New perspectives on organizational change* (pp. 14-62). Thousand Oaks, CA: Sage.

Heifitz, R. A., & Sinder, R. M. (1988). Political leadership: Managing the public's problem solving. In R. Reich (Ed.), *The power of public ideas*. Cambridge, MA: Ballinger.

Heimer, C. (1992). Doing your job and helping your friends: Universalistic norms about obligations to particular others in networks. In N. Nohria & R. Eccles (Eds.), *Networks and organizations: Structure, form, and action* (pp. 143-164). Boston: Harvard Business School Press.

Heritage, J. (1984). *Garfinkel and ethnomethodology*. Cambridge, MA: Polity.

Hetrick, W. P., & Boje, D. M. (1992). Organization and the body: Post-Fordist dimensions. *Journal of Organizational Change Management, 5*(1), 48-57.

Hetrick, W., & Lozada, H. (Eds.). (1992). Postmodernism and organizational change. *Journal of Organizational Change Management, 5*(1).

Heydebrand, W. (1989). New organizational forms. *Work and Occupations, 16*(3), 323-357.

Hickson, D. J., Hinings, C. R., Lee, C. A., Schneck. R. E., & Pennings, J. M. (1971). A strategic-contingencies theory of intra-organizational power. *Administrative Science Quarterly, 16,* 216-229.

Hillman, J. (1983). *Healing fiction*. Barrytown, NY: Station Hill Press.

Hinings, C. R. (1988). Defending organization theory: A British view from North America. *Organization Studies, 9*(1), 2-7.

Hinings, C. R., Hickson, D. J., Pennings, J. M., & Schneck, R. E. (1974). Structural conditions of intra-organizational power. *Administrative Science Quarterly, 9*(1), 22-44.

Hirschmeier, J., & Yui, T. (1975). *The development of Japanese business 1600-1973*. Cambridge, MA: Harvard University Press.

Hirst, P., & Zeitlin, J. (1991). Flexible specialisation versus post-Fordism: Theory, evidence, and policy implications. *Economy and Society, 20*(1), 1-56.

Hochschild, A. R. (1983). *The managed heart: Commercialization of human feeling*. Berkeley: University of California Press.

Hofstede, G. (1979). *Culture's consequences*. Beverly Hills, CA: Sage.

Hollinger, R. (1994). *Postmodernism and the social sciences: A thematic approach* (Contemporary Social Theory, Vol. 4). Thousand Oaks, CA: Sage.

Holvino, E. (1993, August). *The Chicana worker meets OD: A deconstructive reading of productive workplaces*. Handout for the Academy of Management symposium, Unbounding organizational analysis: Questioning "globalization" through Third World women's voices.

Hosseini, J. C., & Brenner, S. N. (1992). The stakeholder theory of the firm: A methodology to generate value matrix weights. *Business Ethics Quarterly, 2*(2), 99-119.

Howard, A., & Bray, D. (1988). *Managerial lives in transition: Advancing age and changing times*. New York: Guilford.

Howell, D. (1994). *Ecology for environmental professionals*. Westport, CT: Quorum.

Huber, G. P. (1991). Organizational learning: The contributing processes and literatures. *Organization Science, 2,* 88-115.

Hussard, J. (1993, July). *Postmodern epistemology and organizational knowledge: Toward a conceptual framework.* Paper presented to the 11th EGOS Colloquium, Paris.

Iannello, K. (1992). *Decisions without hierarchy: Feminist interventions in organization theory and practice.* New York: Routledge.

Institute of Cultural Affairs (ICA). (1986). *Reflections on a trek.* Chicago: Author.

Institute of Cultural Affairs (ICA). (1988). *Panchayat trek reflections.* Chicago: Author.

Irigaray, L. (1985). *The sex which is not one* (C. Porter with C. Burke, Trans.). Ithaca and New York: Cornell University Press.

Irigaray, L. (1991). The power of discourse and the subordination of the feminine. In M. Whitford (Ed.), *The Irigaray reader.* Oxford, UK: Blackwell.

Jackall, R. (1988). *Moral mazes: The world of corporate managers.* New York: Oxford University Press.

Jameson, F. (1991). *Postmodernism, or, the cultural logic of late capitalism.* Durham, NC: Duke University Press.

Janis, I. (1971, November). Groupthink. *Psychology Today,* pp. 43-76.

Jensen, M., & Meckling, W. (1976). Theory of the firm: Managerial behavior, agency costs and ownership structure. *Journal of Financial Economics, 3,* 305-360.

Johnson, B. (1980). *The critical difference.* Baltimore: Johns Hopkins University Press.

Johnson, P. C., & Cooperrider, D. L. (1991). Finding a path with heart: Global social change organizations and their challenge for the field of organizational development. *Research in Organization Change and Development, 5,* 223-284.

Jones, T. (1995). Instrumental stakeholder theory: A synthesis of ethics and economics. *Academy of Management Review.*

Joseph, T. (1994). *Hermeneutic processes in organizations: A study in relationship between observers and observed.* Unpublished doctoral dissertation, Department of Organizational Behavior, Case Western Reserve University, Cleveland, OH.

Jung, C. G. (1965). *Memories, dreams, reflections* (A. Jaffe, Ed.). New York: Vintage.

Kanter, R. M. (1991, May-June). Transcending business boundaries: 12,000 world managers view change. *Harvard Business Review,* pp. 151-164.

Katz, D., & Kahn, R. L. (1966). *The social psychology of organizations.* New York: John Wiley.

Kegan, R. (1982). *The evolving self: Problem and process in human development.* Cambridge, MA: Harvard University Press.

Kegan, R. (1994). *In over our heads: The mental demands of modern life.* Cambridge, MA: Harvard University Press.

Keidel, R. W. (1994). Rethinking organizational design. *Academy of Management Executive, 4*(4), 12-27.

Kesner, I., & Johnson, R. (1990). Crisis in the boardroom: Fact and fiction. *Academy of Management Executive, 4*(1), 23-35.

Kets de Vries, M. (Ed). (1991). *Organizations on the couch: Clinical perspectives on organizational behavior and change.* San Francisco: Jossey-Bass.

Kieser, A. (1989). Organizational, institutional, and societal evolution: Medieval craft guilds and the genesis of formal organizations. *Administrative Science Quarterly, 34,* 540-564.

Kilduff, M. (1993). Deconstructing organization. *Academy of Management Review, 18*(1), 13-31.

Knights, D., & Morgan, G. (1991). Corporate strategy, organizations, and subjectivity: A critique. *Organization Studies, 12,* 251-273.

Knorr-Cetina, K. (1981). *The manufacture of knowledge.* Oxford, UK: Polity.

Kolb, D. (1985). *Learning style inventory.* Boston: McBer.

Kotter, J. P. (1982). *The general manager.* New York: Free Press.

Krasa, E. (1987, February). Being a corporate director can be risky. *Financial Times,* p. 22.

Kreiner, K. (1989, September). *The postmodern challenge to organization theory.* Paper presented at Postmodern Management: The Implications for Learning Conference, Barcelona.

Kristeva, J. (1980). Postmodernism. *Bucknell Review, 25,* 136-141.

Krutch, J. (1951). *The desert year.* Tucson: University of Arizona Press.

Kuhn, T. S. (1962). *The structure of scientific revolutions.* Chicago: University of Chicago Press.

Laing, R. D. (1965). *The divided self.* Baltimore, MD: Penguin.

Lakoff, G., & Johnson, M. (1980). *Metaphors we live by.* Chicago: University of Chicago Press.

Larson, A. (1992). Network dyad study. *Administrative Science Quarterly, 37*(1), 76-104.

Lasch, C. (1979). *The culture of narcissism.* New York: Warner.

Lash, S. (1988). Discourse or figure? Postmodernism as a "regime of signification." *Theory, Culture, and Society, 5*(2-3), 311-335.

Lash, S., & Urry, J. (1987). *The end of organised capitalism.* London: Polity.

Laszlo, E. (1987). *Evolution: The grand synthesis.* Boston: New Science.

Lawler, E. E., III. (1986). *High involvement management.* San Francisco: Jossey-Bass.

Lawrence, P. R., & Lorsch, J. W. (1969). *Organization and environment.* Homewood, IL: Irwin.

Lawson, H. (1985). *Reflexivity: The postmodern predicament.* London: Hutchinson.

Lechte, J. (1994). *50 key contemporary thinkers.* New York: Routledge.

Lee, C. (1992, March). Sexual harassment: After the headlines. *Training,* pp. 23-31.

Leighton, D. (1993, November/December). How can women access boards? *Women in Management, 4,* 2.

Leiter, K. (1980). *A primer in ethnomethodology.* New York: Oxford University Press.

Lévi-Strauss, C. (1950). Introduction. In M. Mauss (Ed.), *Sociologie et anthropologie* (pp. 1-18). Paris: Presses Universitaires de France.

Lévi-Strauss, C. (1978). *The raw and the crooked.* London: Routledge & Kegan Paul.

Lewicki, R. J., & Bunker, B. B. (1994). *Developing and maintaining trust in work relationships* (Working Paper Series 94-49). Akron: Max M. Fisher College of Business, The Ohio State University.

Linstead, S., & Grafton-Small, R. (1991). *On reading organisational culture* (Working paper). Lancaster, UK: University of Lancaster.

Litchfield, E. H. (1956). Notes on a general theory of administration. *Administrative Science Quarterly, 1*(1), 1-30.

Lobel, S. A. (1990). Global leadership competencies: Managing to a different drumbeat. *Human Resource Management, 29,* 157-189.

Locke, E. A. (1968). Toward a theory of task motivation and incentives. *Organizational Behavior and Human Performance, 3,* 157-189.

Lodahl, T. M. (1965). Editor's note. *Administrative Science Quarterly, 10*(4), iv.

Lodahl, T. M. (1976). Editor's note. *Administrative Science Quarterly, 21*(4), 715.

Longair, J. (1990). *Canadian directorship practices: A profile* (Report No. 51-90). Ottawa, Ontario, Canada: Conference Board of Canada.

Lord, R. G. (1985). An information processing approach to social perceptions, leadership, and behavioral measurement in organizations. *Research in Organizational Behavior, 7,* 87-128.

Lorsch, J., with MacIver, E. (1989). *Pawns or potentates: The reality of America's corporate boards.* Boston: Harvard Business School Press.

Lowen, A. (1958). *Physical dynamics of character structure.* New York: Grune & Stratton.

Lowen, A. (1967). *The betrayal of the body.* New York: Collier.

Lowen, A. (1985). *Narcissism: Denial of the true self.* New York: Collier.

Lowen, A. (1990). *The spirituality of the body: Bioenergetics for grace and harmony.* New York: Macmillan.

Luhmann, N. (1990). *Sistemi sociali: Fondamenti di una teoria generale* [Social systems: Foundations of a general theory]. Bologna: Il Mulino. (Original work published 1984)

Luthans, F., Hodgetts, R. M., & Rosenkrantz, S. A. (1988). *Real managers.* New York: Ballinger.

Lyons, N. P. (1988). Two perspectives: On self, relationships, and morality. In C. Gilligan, J. Ward, & J. Taylor, with B. Bardige (Eds.), *Mapping the moral domain: A contribution of women's thinking to psychological theory and education* (pp. 21-48). Cambridge, MA: Harvard University Press.

Lyotard, J.-F. (1984). *The postmodern condition: A report on knowledge* (G. Bennington & B. Massouri, Trans.). Minneapolis: University of Minnesota Press. (Original work published 1979)

Lyotard, J.-F., & Thébaud, J.-L. (1985). *Just gaming.* Manchester, UK: Manchester University Press.

MacDonald, G. (1990, November 19). Board seat a hotter place to sit. *The Financial Post,* p. 36.

Macneil, I. (1981). Economic analysis of contractual relations: Its shortfalls and the need for a "rich" classificatory apparatus. *Northwestern University Law Review, 75,* 1018-1063.

Mander, J. (1991). *In the absence of the sacred.* San Francisco: Sierra Club Books.

March, J. G. (1991). Exploration and exploitation in organizational learning. *Organization Science, 2,* 71-87.

March, J. G., & Simon, H. A. (1958). *Organizations.* New York: John Wiley.

Marcus, G., & Fischer, M. (1986). *Anthropology as cultural critique: An experimental moment in the human sciences.* Chicago: University of Chicago Press.

Marsden, R. (1993). The politics of organizational analysis. *Organization Studies 14*(1), 93-124.

Martin, J. (1990). Deconstructing organizational taboos: The suppression of gender conflict in organizations. *Organization Science, 1*(4), 339-359.

Martin, J. (1992). *Cultures in organisations: Three perspectives.* London: Oxford University Press.

Marx, K., & Engels, F. (1955). The manifesto of the Communist Party. In T. B. Bottomore & M. Rubel (Eds.), *Karl Marx: Selected writings in sociology and social philosophy.* Harmondsworth, UK: Pelican. (Original work published 1848)

Mason, R., & Mitroff, I. (1982). *Challenge strategic planning assumptions.* New York: John Wiley.

Mattis, M. (1993, Summer). Women directors: Progress and opportunities for the future. *Business and the Contemporary World, 5*(3), 140-156.

Mauws, M. (1995, June). *Relationality*. Paper presented at the annual meeting of the Organization Theory Division, Administrative Sciences Association of Canada, Windsor, Ontario.

Mayo, E. (1933). *The human problems of an industrial civilization*. New York: Macmillan.

McCarthy, T. (1991). *Ideals and illusions*. Cambridge: MIT Press.

McCloskey, D. (1983, June). The rhetoric of economics. *Journal of Economic Literature, 21*, 481-517.

Mcerny, R. (1983). Beyond the liberal arts. In D. L. Wagner (Ed.), *The seven liberal arts in the middle ages* (pp. 252-253). Bloomington: Indiana University Press.

McKinsey & Co. Inc. (1993). *Emerging exporters: Australia's high value-added manufacturing exporters*. Melbourne: Australian Manufacturing Council.

McLuhan, M. (1964). *Understanding media*. London: Routledge & Kegan Paul.

McNichol, P. (1995, May). Life of a liveaboard: Attorney casts aside landlubber ways to eat, sleep, and work on her cabin cruiser. *Detroit Monthly*, pp. 65-66.

Mehan, H., & Wood, H. (1975). *The reality of ethnomethodology*. New York: John Wiley.

Merton, R. K. (1975). Structural analysis in sociology. In P. M. Blau (Ed.), *Approaches to the study of social structures* (pp. 166-185). New York: Free Press.

Miles, R. E., & Snow, C. C. (1978). *Organizational strategy, structure, and process*. New York: McGraw-Hill.

Miller, J. A. (1991). Experiencing management: A comprehensive, "hands-on" model for the introductory undergraduate management course. *Journal of Management Education, 15*(2), 151-169.

Miller, J. G. (1972). Living systems: The organisation. *Behavioral Science, 17*, 1-182.

Mills, A. J., & Simmons, T. (1995). *Reading organization theory: A critical approach*. Toronto: Garamond.

Mimick, R. (1985, Winter). The "new age" board of directors. *Business Quarterly*, pp. 48-55.

Mintzberg, H. (1979). *The structuring of organizations*. Englewood Cliffs, NJ: Prentice Hall.

Mintzberg, H. (1983). *Power in and around organizations*. Englewood Cliffs, NJ: Prentice Hall.

Mitroff, I., & Emshoff, J. (1979). On strategic assumption-making. *Academy of Management Review, 4*(1), 1-12.

Molotch, H., & Lester, M. (1975). Accidental news: The great oil spill. *American Journal of Sociology, 81*, 235-260.

Montuori, A. (1989). *Evolutionary competence*. Amsterdam: Gleben.

Montuori, A. (1993). Evolutionary learning for a postindustrial society: Knowledge, creativity, and social ecology. *World Futures, the Journal of General Evolution, 36*, 181-202.

Montuori, A., & Conti, I. (1992). *From power to partnership*. San Francisco: HarperCollins.

Montuori, A., & Purser, R. (1995). Deconstructing the lone genius myth: A contextual view of creativity. *Journal of Humanistic Psychology, 35*(3), 69-112.

Moore, T. (1992). *Care of the soul: A guide for cultivating depth and sacredness in everyday life*. New York: HarperCollins.

Morgan, G. (1980). Paradigms, metaphors, and puzzle-solving in organization theory. *Administrative Science Quarterly, 25*(2), 605-622.

Morgan, G. (1983). Move on metaphor: Why we cannot control tropes in administrative science. *Administrative Science Quarterly*, pp. 601-607.

Morgan, G. (1986). *Images of organization*. Newbury Park, CA: Sage.

Morgan, G. (1993). *Imaginization: The art of creative management*. Newbury Park, CA: Sage.

Morin, E. (1994). *La complexité humaine* [Human complexity]. Paris: Flammarion.

Morrison, K. F. (1983). Incentives for studying the liberal arts. In D. L. Wagner (Ed.), *The seven liberal arts in the middle ages* (pp. 32-57). Bloomington: Indiana University Press.

Morrow, R. A. (with D. Brown). (1994). *Critical theory and methodology* (Contemporary Social Theory, Vol. 4). Thousand Oaks, CA: Sage.

Mumby, D., & Putman, L. (1992). The politics of emotion: A feminist reading of bounded rationality. *Academy of Management Review, 17*(3), 465-486.

Nasr, S. H. (1981). *Knowledge and the sacred.* New York: Crossroad.

Nathan, M. L., & Mitroff, I. I. (1991). The use of negotiated order theory as a tool for the analysis and development of an interorganizational field. *Journal of Applied Behavioral Science, 27*(2), 163-180.

Neisser, U. (1976). *Cognition and reality.* San Francisco: W. H. Freeman.

Nielsen, R. P. (1993). Organization ethic from a perspective of praxis. *Business Ethic Quarterly, 2*(2), 131-151.

Norris, C. (1991). *Deconstruction: Theory and practice* (Rev. ed.). London: Routledge.

Northcraft, G., Griffith, T., & Shelley, C. (1992). Building top management muscle in a slow growth environment: How different is better at Greyhound Financial Corporation. *The Executive, 6*(1), 32-43.

Nye, A. (1989). The voice of the serpent: French feminism and philosophy of language. In A. Garry & M. Pearsall (Eds.), *Women, knowledge, and reality* (pp. 233-249). Boston: Unwin Hyman.

Odum, E. (1963). *Ecology.* New York: Holt, Rinehart & Winston.

Odum, E. (1969). Relationships between structure and function in the ecosystem. In G. Cox (Ed.), *Readings in conservation ecology* (pp. 6-20). New York: Meredith.

Offe, C. (1976). *Industry and inequality.* London: Edward Arnold.

Offe, C. (1984). *Contradictions of the welfare state.* Cambridge: MIT Press.

Ogilvy, J. (1992). Future studies and the human sciences: The case for normative scenarios. *Futures Research Quarterly, 8*(2), 5-66.

O'Neill, H. M. (1994). Restructuring, re-engineering, and rightsizing: Do the metaphors make sense? *Academy of Management Executive, 4*(4), 9-11.

O'Neill, J. (1986). The disciplinary society: From Weber to Foucault. *The British Journal of Sociology, 37*(1), 42-60.

Paine, F. T., & Anderson, C. R. (1983). *Strategic management.* Chicago: Dryden.

Parker, M. (1992). Post-modern organizations or postmodern organization theory? *Organization Studies, 13*(1), 1-17.

Parker, M. (1993). Life after Jean-Francois. In J. Hassard & M. Parker (Eds.), *Postmodernism and organisations* (pp. 204-212). London: Sage.

Parsons, T. (1956a). Suggestions for a sociological approach to the theory of organizations (Part 1). *Administrative Science Quarterly, 1*(1).

Parsons, T. (1956b). Suggestions for a sociological approach to the theory of organizations (Part 2). *Administrative Science Quarterly 1*(2).

Parsons, T. (1960). *Structure and process in modern societies.* Glencoe, IL: Free Press.

Pearson, A. E. (1987). Muscle build the organization. *Harvard Business Review, 65*(4), 49-55.

Pepper, S. C. (1942). *World hypotheses.* Berkeley: University of California Press.

Perkins, R. (1986, May/June). Avoiding director liability. *Harvard Business Review,* pp. 8-14.

Perls, F., Hefferline, R. F., & Goodman, P. (1951). *Gestalt therapy: Excitement and growth in the human personality.* New York: Delta.

Perrow, C. (1986). *Complex organizations: A critical essay* (3rd ed.). New York: Random House.

Peters, T. (1986). *Thriving on chaos: Handbook for a management revolution.* New York: Free Press.

Peters, T. (1987). *Thriving on chaos: Handbook for management revolution.* New York: Knopf.

Peukert, D. (1989). *The Weimar Republic.* New York: Hill & Wang. (Original work published 1987)

Pfeffer, J., & Salancik, G. R. (1978). *The external control of organizations: A resource dependence perspective.* New York: Harper & Row.

Phillips, D. L. (1973). Paradigms, falsification, and sociology. *Acta Sociologica, 16*(1).

Pinder, C. C., & Bourgeois, W. (1983). Contrasting philosophiocal perspectives in administrative science: A reply to Morgan. *Administrative Science Quarterly,* 608-613.

Piore, M. J., & Sabel, C. F. (1984). *The second industrial divide: Possibilities for prosperity.* New York: Basic Books.

Platt, R. (1989). Reflexivity, recursion, and social life: Elements for a postmodern sociology. *Sociological Review, 37*(4), 636-667.

Pollert, A. (1988). Dismantling flexibility. *Capital and Class, 34*(1), 42-75.

Pollner, M. (1991). Left of ethnomethodology: The rise and decline of radical reflexivity. *American Sociological Review, 56,* 370-380.

Polster, E., & Polster, M. (1973). *Gestalt therapy integrated: Contours of theory and practice.* New York: Brunner/Mazel.

Pondy, L. (1976). *Beyond open system models of organization.* Unpublished manuscript, Organizational Behavior Group, Department of Business Administration, University of Illinois-Urbana.

Pondy, L. (1978). Leadership is a language game. In M. McCall & M. Lomardo (Eds.), *Leadership: Where else can we go?* (pp. 87-99). Durham, NC: Duke University Press.

Pondy, L., & Boje, D. M. (1980). Bringing mind back in: Paradigm development as a frontier problem in organization theory. In W. Evan (Ed.), *Frontiers in organization and management* (pp. 83-101). New York: Praeger.

Pondy, L., & Mitroff, I. (1979). Beyond open system models of organization. *Research in Organization Behavior, 1,* 3-39.

Porter, M. (1980). *Competitive strategy: Techniques for analyzing industries and competitors.* New York: Free Press.

Poster, M. (1990). *The mode of information.* Chicago: University of Chicago Press.

Potter, R. (1975). *The English morality play: Origins, history, and influence of a dramatic tradition.* Boston: Routledge & Kegan Paul.

Powell, W. (1991). Neither market nor hierarchy: Network forms of organization. *Research in Organizational Behavior, 12,* 295-336.

Power, M. (1992). Modernism, postmodernism, and organisation. In J. Hassard & D. Pym (Eds.), *The theory and philosophy of organisations: Critical issues and new perspectives.* London: Routledge & Kegan Paul.

Presthus, R. V. (1959). Editor's commentary. *Administrative Science Quarterly, 4*(1), iv.

Price, J. L. (1966). Design of proof in organizational research. *Administrative Science Quarterly, 13*(1), 121-134.

Progoff, I. (1975). *At a journal workshop.* New York: Dialogue House.

Pugh, D. S., Hickson, D. J., Hinings, C. R., Macdonald, K. M., Turner, C., & Lupton, T. (1963). A conceptual scheme for organizational analysis. *Administrative Science Quarterly, 8*(3), 289-315.

Purser, R. (Ed.). (1994). Greening in organizations [Special issue]. *Journal of Organizational Change Management, 7*(4), 4-92.

Purser, R., & Montuori, A. (1995). Knowledge development and epistemologies of practice: A systems theoretic analysis. In M. Beyerlein (Ed.), *Advances in interdisciplinary studies of work teams* (pp. 117-161). Greenwich, CT: JAI Press.

Quinn, B. P. (1977). Coping with cupid: The formation, impact, and management of romantic relationships in organizations. *Administrative Science Quarterly, 22*(1), 30-45.

Quinn, R., Faerman, S., Thompson, M., & McGrath, M. (1990). *Becoming a master manager: A competency framework.* New York: John Wiley.

Rabinow, P. (Ed.). (1984). *The Foucault reader.* New York: Pantheon.

Radcliffe-Brown, A. R. (1952). *Structure and function in primitive society.* London: Cohen & West.

Radhakrishnan, R. (1994). Postmodernism and the rest of the world. *Organization, 1*(2), 305-340.

Rawls, J. (1971). *A theory of justice.* Cambridge, MA: Belknap.

Reed, M. (1985). *Redirections in organisational analysis.* London: Tavistock.

Reed, M. (1992). *The sociology of organisations: Themes, perspectives, and prospects.* London: Harvester Wheatsheaf.

Reich, R. B. (1991, March-April). Who is them? *Harvard Business Review,* pp. 77-88.

Reich, W. (1949). *Character analysis* (T. P. Wolfe, Trans.). New York: Farrar, Straus & Giroux.

Rex, J. (1961). *Key problems in sociological theory.* London: Routledge & Kegan Paul.

Richardson, L. (1988). The collective story: Postmodernism and the writing of sociology. *Sociological Focus, 22*(3), 199-208.

Richters, A. (1991). Fighting symbols and structures: Postmodernism, feminism, and women's health. In L. Nencels & P. Pels (Eds.), *Constructing knowledge: Authority and critique in social science* (pp. 123-144). London: Sage.

Rifkin, W. (1994). Who need not be heard: Deciding who is not an expert. *Technology Studies, 1,* 60-96.

Ring, P. S. (1994). Fragile and resilient trust and their roles in cooperative interorganizational relationships. In S. Wartick & D. Collins (Eds.), *Proceedings of the fifth annual meeting of the International Association for Business and Society* (pp. 107-113). Madison: University of Wisconsin School of Business.

Robertson, R. (1992). *Globalisation, social theory, and global culture.* London: Sage.

Roethlisberger, F. J., & Dickson, W. J. (1939). *Management and the worker.* Cambridge, MA: Harvard University Press.

Rogers, M. F. (1992). Teaching, theorizing, storytelling: Postmodern rhetoric and modern dreams. *Sociological Theory, 10*(2), 231-248.

Rorty, R. (1979). *Philosophy and the mirror of nature.* Princeton, NJ: Princeton University Press.

Rorty, R. (1989). *Contingency, irony, and solidarity.* New York: Cambridge University Press.

Rosenau, P. M. (1992). *Post-modernism and the social sciences: Insights, inroads, and intrusions.* Princeton, NJ: Princeton University Press.

Rosile, G. A. (1995, April). *Greenback Company: Beyond simulation, the postmodern virtual corporation.* Paper presented at the International Academy of Business Disciplines Meetings, Postmodern Organization Track, Redondo Beach, CA.

Rossi, P. (1987). Idola della modernita [Idols of modernity]. In G. Mari (Ed.), *Moderno postmoderno* [Modern postmodern] (pp. 14-30). Milano: Feltrinelli.

Ryan, L. V., & Scott, W. G. (1995). Ethics and organizational reflection: The Rockefeller Foundation and postwar "moral deficits," 1942-1954. *Academy of Management Review, 20*(2), 438-461.

Sackmann, S. (1989). The role of metaphors in organization transformation. *Human Relations, 42*(6), 463-485.

Sackmann, S. (1992). Culture and subcultures: An analysis of organizational knowledge. *Administrative Science Quarterly, 37*(1), 140-161.

Salancik, G. R., & Meinl, J. R. (1984). Corporate attributions as illusions of management control. *Administrative Science Quarterly, 29*, 238-254.

Sardar, Z. (1993). Do not adjust your mind: Postmodernism, reality, and the other. *Futures, 24*(9), 858-866.

Saussure, F. de (1974). *Course in general linguistics*. London: Fontana/Collins.

Schein, E. (1985). *Organisational culture and leadership*. London: Jossey-Bass.

Schneider, S. H. (1993, April). A better way to learn. *World Monitor*, pp. 31-36.

Schein, E. H.(1990). Organizational culture. *American Psychologist, 45*, 109-119.

Schonberger, R. (1992). Total quality management cuts a broad swath through manufacturing and beyond. *Organizational Dynamics, 20*(4), 16-27.

Schutz, A. (1962). *Collected essays, I: The problem of social reality*. The Hague: Martinus Nijhoff.

Schwartz, H. S. (1985). The usefulness of myth and the myth of usefulness: A dilemma for the applied organizational scientist. *Journal of Management, 11*(1), 31-42.

Schwartz, H. (1995). Book review of "The postmodern organization: Mastering the art of irreversible change," by W. Bergquist, and "Managing in the postmodern world: America's revolution against exploitation," by D. Boje & R. F. Dennehy. *Academy of Management Review, 20*(1), 215-221.

Schwartz, P. (1991). *The art of the long view*. New York: Doubleday Currency.

Scott, W. G. (1974). Organization theory: A reassessment. *Academy of Management Journal, 17*, 242-254.

Scott, W. G., & Hart, D. K. (1989). *Organizational values in America*. New Brunswick, NJ: Transaction.

Sethi, S. P. (1977). The Santa Barbara oil spill. In S. P. Sethi (Ed.), *Up against the corporate wall* (2nd ed., pp. 2-32). Englewood Cliffs, NJ: Prentice Hall.

Shetzer, L., Stackman, R. W., & Moore, L. F. (1990). Business-environment attitudes and the new environmental paradigm. *Journal of Environmental Education, 22*(4), 14-21.

Shrivastava, P. (1995). Ecocentric management for a risk society. *Academy of Management Review, 20*(1), 118-137.

Silverman, D. (1970). *The theory of organisations*. London: Heinemann.

Simmel, G. (1968). *The conflict in modern culture and other essays*. New York: Teachers College Press.

Simmel, G. (1980). *Essays on interpretation in social science*. Manchester, UK: Manchester University Press.

Smart, B. (1990). On the disorder of things: Sociology, postmodernity, and the "end of the social." *Sociology, 24*(3), 397-416.

Smart, C. (1986). Feminism and the law: Some problems of analysis and strategy. *International Journal of the Sociology of Law, 14*, 109-123.

Smircich, L., Calas, M., & Morgan, G. (Eds.). (1992). New intellectual currents in organization and management theory. *Academy of Management Review, 17*(3).

Smith, C. (1989). Flexible specialisation, automation, and mass production. *Work, Employment, and Society, 3*(2), 203-220.

Snow, C., Miles, R., & Coleman, H. (1992). Managing 21st century network organizations. *Organizational Dynamics, 20*(3), 5-19.

Solomon, C. (1991, June). Behind the wheel at Saturn. *Personnel Journal,* pp. 72-74.

Sonenclar, R. J. (1990, July). Corporate sanity: A strategy for stress. *TWA Ambassador,* pp. 61-63.

Sonnenstuhl, W. J. (1986). *Inside an emotional health program: A field study of workplace assistance for troubled employees.* Ithaca, NY: Cornell University, NYSSILR Press.

Sorge, M. (1995, January). Ford shakes up its supplier base: It's working to globalize suppliers and create common parts. *Ward's Auto World,* pp. 51-53.

Spivak, G. C. (1981). Reading the world: Literary studies in the 80s. *College English, 43*(7), 671-679.

Spradley, J. (1979). *The ethnographic interview.* New York: Holt, Rinehart & Winston.

Srivastva, S., Cooperrider, D. L., Thatchenkery, T., Tian, X., et al. (1989, November). *Wonder and affirmation in discovery and transformation: A case study of the Institute of Cultural Affairs.* Paper presented at the Social Innovations in Global Management conference, Case Western University, Cleveland, OH.

Srivastva, S., Cooperrider, D., & Thatchenkery, T. (1992). *Wonder and affirmation in discovery and transformation: A case study of the Institute of Cultural Affairs (ICA).* Unpublished manuscript, Weatherhead School of Management, Case Western Reserve University.

Stablein, R. (1993, July). *Research residue: An analysis of organizational and managerial journal publications and authorships.* Paper presented to the 11th EGOS Colloquium, Paris.

Stacey, R. (1992). *Managing the unknowable.* San Francisco, CA: Jossey-Bass.

Starbuck, W. (1966). Some comments, observations, and objections stimulated by "design of proof in organizational research." *Administrative Science Quarterly, 12*(2).

Stead, W. E., & Stead, J. G. (1992). *Management for a small planet: Strategic decision making and the environment.* Newbury Park, CA: Sage.

Stead, W. E., & Stead, J. G. (1994). Can humankind change the economic myth? Paradigm shifts necessary for ecologically sustainable business. *Journal of Organizational Change Management, 7*(4), 15-31.

Sterling, B. (1988). *Islands in the net.* New York: Ace.

Stinchcombe, A. (1985). Contracts as hierarchical documents. In A. Stinchcombe & C. Heimer (Eds.), *Organization theory and project management: Administering uncertainty in Norwegian offshore oil* (pp. 121-171). Norway: Universitetsforlaget.

Stone, C. (1985). Public interest representation: Economic and social policy inside the enterprise. In K. Hopt & G. Teubner (Eds.), *Corporate governance and director's liabilities* (pp. 122-146). Berlin: Walter de Gruyter.

Strati, A. (1992). Aesthetic understanding of organizational life. *Academy of Management Review, 17*(3), 568-581.

Sutton, R. (1991). Maintaining organizational norms about expressed emotions: The case of bill collectors. *Administrative Science Quarterly, 36*(2), 245-268.

Symposium on postmodernism [Special issue]. (1991). *Sociological Theory, 9*(2).

Taylor, F. W. (1911). *Principles of scientific management.* New York: Harper & Row.

Tehranian, M. F., et al. (1977). *Communications policy for national development: A comparative project.* London: Routledge & Kegan Paul.

Terpstra, D. E., & Baker, D. D. (1992). Outcomes of federal court decisions on sexual harassment. *Academy of Management Journal, 35*(1), 181-190.

Thatchenkery, T. (1992). Organizations as "texts": Hermeneutics as a model for understanding organizational change. In W. A. Pasmore & R. W. Woodman (Eds.), *Research in organization development and change* (Vol. 6, pp. 197-233). Greenwich, CT: JAI Press.

Thatchenkery, T., & Pasmore, W. (1992). *Postmodernism and the learning organization: Implications for the academy*. Symposium presentation at the National Academy of Management Annual Meeting, Las Vegas, NV.

Thain, D., & Leighton, D. (1988, Spring). The board of directors: Key to effective governance. *Business Quarterly*, pp. 77-80.

Thompson, J. D. (1956). On building an administrative science. *Administrative Science Quarterly 1*(1), 102-111.

Thompson, J. D. (1967). *Organizations in action*. New York: McGraw-Hill.

Thompson, P. (1993). Postmodernism: Fatal distraction. In J. Hassard & M. Parker (Eds.), *Postmodernism and organizations* (pp. 183-203). Newbury Park, CA: Sage.

Thornton, G. C., III, & Byham, W. C. (1982). *Assessment centers and managerial performance*. New York: Academic Press.

Toffler, A. (1970). *Future shock*. New York: Bantam.

Toffler, A. (1980). *The third wave*. New York: Bantam.

Toffler, A. (1990). *Powershift: Knowledge, wealth, and violence at the edge of the 21st century*. New York: Bantam.

Townley, B. (1993). Foucault, power/knowledge, and its relevance for human resource management. *Academy of Management Review, 18*(3), 518-545.

Tricker, R. (1984). *Corporate governance*. Vermont: Gower.

Tsoukas, H. (1992). Postmodernism, reflexive rationalism, and organizational studies: A reply to Martin Parker. *Organization Studies, 13*(4), 643-649.

Tulku, T. (1987). *Love of knowledge*. Berkeley, CA: Dharma.

Tung, R. (1991). Handshakes across the sea! Cross-cultural negotiating for business success. *Organizational Dynamics, 19*, 30-39.

Turner, B. (Ed.). (1990). *Theories of modernity and postmodernity*. London: Sage.

Turner, B. S. (1991). Recent developments in the theory of the body. In M. Featherstone, M. Hepworth, & B. S. Turner (Eds.), *The body: Social process and cultural theory* (pp. 1-35). London: Sage.

Turner, C. H. (1991, September-October). The boundaries of business: The cross-cultural quagmire. *Harvard Business Review*, pp. 94-96.

University says no to condom distribution. (1994, April 27). *The Chronicle of Higher Education, 40*(34), p. A6.

Upadhyaya, P. (1995). The sacred, the erotic, and the ecological: Towards transformative politics of globalization discourses. *Journal of Organizational Change Management*.

Vance, C. (1993). Preface. In C. Vance (Ed.), *Mastering management education: Innovations in teaching effectiveness* (pp. xi-xiv). Newbury Park, CA: Sage.

van Dijk, T. (1993). Principles of critical discourse analysis. *Discourse and Society, 4*(2), 249-283.

Van Dyne, G. (1969). Ecosystems, systems ecology, and systems ecologists. In G. Cox (Ed.), *Readings in conservation ecology* (pp. 21-50). New York: Meredith.

Van Maanen, J. (1988). *Tales of the field*. Chicago: University of Chicago Press.

Von Foerster, H. (1984). *Observing systems*. Seaside, CA: Intersystems.

Von Foerster, H. (1990, October 4-6). *Ethics and second order cybernetics.* Paper presented at Systèmes & thérapie familiale: Ethique, Idéologie, Nouvelles Méthodes, Congrès International, Paris.

Von Glasersfeld, E. (1987). *The construction of knowledge.* Salinas, CA: Intersystems.

Walck, C. L. (1994, April). *Russia as other: The violence of development and missionary management.* Paper delivered at the International Association of Business Disciplines Annual Meeting, Pittsburgh.

Wallerstein, I. (1974). *The modern world system.* New York: Harcourt Brace Johanovich.

Walton, C. C. (1993). Business ethics and postmodernism: A dangerous dalliance. *Business Ethics Quarterly, 3*(3), 285-305.

Wardell, M. (1992). Changing organizational forms: From the bottom up. In M. Reed & M. Hughes (Eds.), *Rethinking organisation.* London: Sage.

Weber, M. (1946). *From Max Weber: Essays in sociology* (H. Gerth & C. W. Mills, Eds.). New York: Oxford University Press.

Weber, M. (1947). *The theory of social and economic organization.* New York: Free Press.

Weber, M. (1958). *The Protestant ethic and the spirit of capitalism.*

Weber, M. (1978). *Economy and society.* Berkeley: University of California Press.

Webster's collegiate dictionary (10th ed.). (1993). Springfield, MA: Merriam-Webster.

Weedon, C. (1987). Feminist practice and poststructuralist theory. In *Principles of poststructuralism* (pp. 12-42). Oxford, UK: Basil Blackwell.

Weick, K. E. (1977). Editorial note. *Administrative Science Quarterly, 22*(1), 138-139.

Weick, K. E. (1979). *The social psychology of organizing* (2nd ed.). Reading, MA: Addison-Wesley.

Weick, K. E. (1982). Affirmation as inquiry. *Small Group Behavior, 13,* 441-442.

Wheatley, M. J. (1992). Searching for order in an orderly world: A poetic for post-machine-age managers. *Journal of Management Inquiry, 1*(4), 337-342.

Wheatley, M. J. (1994). *Leadership and the new science: Learning about organizations from an orderly universe.* San Francisco: Berrett-Koehler.

Whitford, M. (1988). Luce Irigaray's critique of rationality. In M. Griffiths & M. Whitford (Eds.), *Feminine perspectives in philosophy* (pp. 109-130). London: Macmillan.

Wicks, A. C., Gilbert, D. R., & Freeman, R. E. (1994). A feminist reinterpretation of the stakeholder concept. *Business Ethics Quarterly, 4*(4), 475-497.

Wilden, A. (1980). *System and structure: Essays in communication and exchange.* London: Tavistock.

Wilden, A. (1987). *Man and woman, war and peace.* New York: Routledge.

Williamson, O. E. (1985). *The economic institutions of capitalism: Firms, markets, and relational contracting.* New York: Free Press.

Williamson, O. E. (1991). Comparative economic organization: The analysis of discrete structural alternatives. *Administrative Science Quarterly, 36,* 269-296.

Willmott, H. (1992). Postmodernism and excellence: The de-differentiation of economy and culture. *Journal of Organizational Change Management, 5*(1), 58-68.

Winsor, R. D. (1992). Post-industrial, post-Fordist, or post-prosperity: Talking the post-Fordist talk, doing the post-industrial walk. *Journal of Organizational Change Management, 5*(2), 61-69.

Winter, D., & Sorge, M. (1995, January). Sophisticated seats: They no longer reflect "golden" seat-of-the-pants design. *Ward's Auto World,* p. 49.

Wittgenstein, L. (1968). *Philosophical investigations.* Oxford, UK: Basil Blackwell.

Wood, D. J., & Gray, B. (1991). Toward a comprehensive theory of collaboration. *Journal of Applied Behavioral Sciences, 27*(2), 139-162.

Woodruff, D. (1991, December 2). Saturn, what workers want is . . . fewer defects. *Business Week,* p. 117.

Woodward, J. (1965). *Industrial organisation.* London: Oxford University Press.

Yang, C. (1995, February 6). Flamed with a lawsuit: Will courts set limits on the freedom of cyberspeech? *Business Week,* pp. 70-75.

Young, I. M. (1984). Justice and hazardous waste. In M. Bradie (Ed.), *The applied turn in contemporary philosophy* (pp. 171-182). Bowling Green, OH: Applied Philosophy Program, Bowling Green State University.

Zuboff, D. (1988). *In the age of the smart machine.* New York: Basic Books.

Zucker, L. G. (1986). Production of trust: Institutional sources of economic structure, 1840-1920. *Research in Organizational Behavior, 8,* 53-111.

Index

Environment. *See* Ecology
Epps, R., 169
Ethics:
  and capitalism, 24-25
  and globalization, 331-332, 342,
    343-345, 346-347, 348-349, 350-351
  bureaucratic, 29-31
Ethnography, 41-42
Ethnomethodology, 42
Evan, W., 160-161

Fair contracting, 161-162
Fayol, H., 145, 259, 260-263
Featherstone, M., 46, 48
Feminism. *See* Constituent directors;
    Radical separatism; Stakeholders
Ferguson, K., 297-298
Fetterley, J., 99
Fineman, S., 263-264
Fleischer, A., 95, 102-103, 113, 116-121
Flexible specialization, 54, 56, 168
Foucault, M., 35, 63, 100, 116, 142-143,
    227, 231, 232, 235, 267, 310,
    335-336, 353
Fox, S., 87, 231, 232
Frank, A., 146
Frank, R., 160
Freeman, J., 82-83
Freeman, R., 155, 158, 160-161, 165
Freire, F., 297-298
Freud, S., 131-132
Frost, P., 63, 67

Gabriel, Y., 263-264
Garg, P., 313-314
Gender, 80-81. *See also* Constituent
    directors; Radical separatism;
    Stakeholders
Gephart, R., 61, 86, 238, 261
Gergen, K., 49, 57-58, 64, 252, 264
Gibson, W., 36-38
Giddens, A., 62, 356
Gilbert, D., 165
Gilbreth, F., 144
Gillies, J., 95, 102-103, 107-113,
    114-115(table), 120-121, 122
Gilligan, C., 165
Gilson, C., 236
Giroux, H., 88, 235, 237

Global Assignments
    (Black/Gregersen/Mendenhall),
    300
Globalization, 17-18
  and analytical metaphors, 293-296
  and centralized authority, 331-332,
    345-354
  and communications technology,
    17-18, 331-332, 336-343, 352-354,
    361-362
  and economics, 299-306
  and ethics, 331-332, 342, 343-345,
    346-347, 348-349, 350-351
  and organizational representation,
    331-332, 334-343
  and polyphonic organization, 331-332,
    354-357
  and TINA tendency, 296-297
  and transnational corporations
    (TNCs), 304-306
  conceptualization of, 296-298
  convergence theory of, 298-299
  model revision for, 305-307
  relativism model of, 300-305, 307
  threat of, 331-334
  See also Institute of Cultural Affairs
    (ICA)
Globalization of Business, The (Dunning),
    299-300
Global social change organization
    (GSCO), 312, 315, 317-320
Goldberger, N., 165
Goodpaster, K., 156, 157-158
Gouldner, A., 190
Grafton-Small, R., 53
Gray, B., 172, 173, 174
Greenback Company (classroom-based),
    239-250
Gregersen, H. B., 300
Grey, C., 232-233
GSCO. *See* Global social change
    organization

Habermas, J., 3, 4, 62, 88, 167, 190
Hampden-Turner, C., 295
Handy, C., 356
Hart, D., 32
Hassard, J., 252, 256, 257, 258
Hazard, G., 95, 102-103, 113, 116-121

About the Editors

David M. Boje is Professor of Management at Loyola Marymount University. He edits *Journal of Organizational Change Management* with a focus on postmodern organizational change. He is on the editorial board of *Management Communication Journal* and has published in numerous journals, including *Administrative Science Quarterly, Management Science,* and *Academy of Management Journal.* His current books include *Readings in Managerial Psychology* with Hal Leavitt and Louis Pondy and *Managing in the Postmodern World* with Robert Dennehy. His current research interests include deconstructing reengineering, organizational storytelling, and developing a postmodern organizational behavior book with Grace Ann Rosile, Deborah Summers, and Robert Dennehy.

Robert P. Gephart, Jr., is Professor of Organizational Analysis in the Faculty of Business at the University of Alberta. He received his Ph.D. from the University of British Columbia. He is the author of *Ethnostatistics: Qualitative Foundations for Quantitative Research* (Sage, 1988), as well as more than 20 academic papers that have appeared in a number of scholarly proceedings and journals, including *Academy of Management Journal, Administrative Science Quarterly, Journal of Management,* and *Sociological Perspectives.* He is Associate Editor of the international journal *Technology Studies* and serves on the editorial boards of the *Journal of Management,* the *Journal of Management Inquiry,* and the

402   POSTMODERN MANAGEMENT

Journal of Organizational Change Management. He is a past Chair of the Organizational Behavior Division of the Administrative Sciences Association of Canada and a previous Program Chair of the Research Methods Division, Academy of Management. He is presently interested in technology risk, cultural transformation, and the role of qualitative research in organizational inquiry.

Tojo Joseph Thatchenkery is Assistant Professor of Organizational Learning in the Program on Social and Organizational Learning at George Mason University, Fairfax, Virginia. His seminars cater to a diverse group of students engaged in organization design, change, and development studies. His research interests include hermeneutics, critical social theory, and postmodern organizational analysis. He holds a Ph.D. in organizational behavior from Weatherhead School of Management, Case Western Reserve University, Cleveland, Ohio. He has published in *Research in Organizational Change and Development* and *International Organization Development* and is a reviewer for journals such as *Human Relations; Accounting, Management, and Information Technologies;* and *Information Systems Research.*

About the Contributors

Ian Atkin is Lecturer in Organization Behavior and Theory at Bolton Business School. He is a board member of the Standing Conference on Organizational Symbolism. His research interests focus on antiorganization theory and the visual representation of work.

David Barry is Senior Lecturer in Organizational Psychology at the University of Auckland, New Zealand. He has published in several leading journals, including *Organizational Behavior* and *Journal of Management Education*. His research focuses on interpretive and symbolic processes in organizations, particularly unconscious aspects of work life. As a sometime artist and yoga teacher, he is also interested in finding ways to apprehend organizations aesthetically and arationally. He earned his Ph.D. in organizational behavior and strategic management at the University of Maryland.

Ghazi F. Binzagr is a doctoral student at New Mexico State University. His research interests include organizational transformation and proactive reorganizing, contructivist inquiry, and the broadening of applications of management theory to non-Western countries. He holds a B.S. in physics from the University of California, Santa Barbara, and a master's degree in international management from Thunderbird.

Patricia Bradshaw is Associate Professor in Organization Behavior at York University in Toronto, where she completed her Ph.D. Her work has been published in journals including *Organization Science, Journal of Applied Behavioral Science,* and *Nonprofit Management and Leadership.* Her research interests include power, change, corporate and not-for-profit governance, and women in management.

Jerry M. Calton is Assistant Professor of Management at the University of Hawaii at Hilo. He has recently contributed to *Business and Society in a Changing World Order* (1993) and *Business Ethics Quarterly.* He is active in the Social Issues in Management Division of the Academy of Management and in the International Association for Business and Society. His research focuses on the role of ethics, values, trust, and trust-building processes in the management of collaborative network organizations. He earned dual Ph.D.s in history and management from the University of Washington.

Stewart R. Clegg is Foundation Professor of Management at The University of Western Sydney, Macarthur. He has held chairs at the Universities of St. Andrews, Scotland, and New England, Australia. English by birth, Australia has been his adopted home since he completed his postdoctoral European Group for Organization Studies Research fellowship in 1976. He is the author of many book and articles, including *Frameworks of Power* (1989) and *Modern Organizations* (1990), and recently has completed work in preparing *The Handbook of Organization Studies* (1996) with Cynthia Hardy and Sue Jones. Besides being an academic, he is a jazz announcer on Brisbane Radio Station 4ZZZ, a Joiner's Labourer for Dowsett's in northern England, and a researcher for the Australian government's task force into "Leadership and Management in the Twenty-First Century." In his spare time he likes to make tables out of old timber and strip and restore old furniture, preferably while listening to some favorite jazz.

Dale E. Fitzgibbons is Associate Professor of Management at Illinois State University, where he uses a critical theory approach and postmodern orientation in the classroom. Scores of students testify that his "postmodern case study" approach to pedagogy has been their most significant learning experience. He is Assistant Editor of the

Journal of Management Education and has published in many leading journals. His research interests include postmodern management, critical theory, feminist/alternative ethnographies, new paradigm organizations, and philosophy of science.

Kenneth J. Gergen is the Mustin Professor of Psychology at Swarthmore College. He is a pioneer in the development of social constructionist theory and its applications to the conception of science, as well as in the practices of organizational development, education, and psychotherapy. Recent works include *Realities and Relationships, Soundings in Social Construction* (1994) and *Toward Transformation in Social Knowledge* (2nd ed., 1992). He is cofounder of the Taos Institute, a forum for cutting-edge inquiry and dialogue about global leadership and organizational change. With Mary Gergen, a Professor of psychology at Pennsylvania State University, he works as an organizational consultant.

John T. Gray is the Director of the MBA program at the University of Western Sydney, Macarthur, which emphasizes the international and cultural aspects of strategic management education. He contributed to *The Inquiry Into Australia's Leadership and Management Needs Into the 21st Century*. His research interests include the implementation of change and the relationships between organizing modes and professional innovation. Previously, he was Managing Director of The Management Skills Company, a firm he founded in 1976 to consult in the implementation of organizational change.

John Hassard is Head of the School of Management and Professor of Organizational Behavior at the University of Keele, England. He has taught at the London Business School and Cardiff University. His publications include *Postmodernism and Organisations* (1993) and *Towards a New Theory of Organisations* (1994), as well as articles in *Human Relations, Human Resource Management Journal, Journal of Management Studies,* and *Organisation Studies*. His research focuses on organizational theory, and he has studied organizational and technical change at large-scale manufacturers.

Mary Ann Hazen is Associate Professor of Management at the University of Detroit, Mercy College of Business Administration. She has published on dialogue in organizations in *Human Relations* and the *Journal of Organizational Change Management.* Her research interests include postmodern organizational change theory and practice, as well as the application of Gestalt and Jungian theory to organizations. Her teaching interests include holistic management development.

Nancy B. Kurland is Assistant Professor of Management and Organization in the School of Business Administration at the University of Southern California. She has published in *Business and Society, Human Relations, Journal of Business Ethics,* and the *Journal of Applied Social Psychology.* Besides her interest in alternative conceptualizations of stakeholder theory, her research focuses on social impacts of the Internet, telecommuting, and commuter marriages. She earned a Ph.D. from the University of Pittsburgh's Katz Graduate School of Business and previously worked in investment sales.

Michael R. Manning is Professor of Management at New Mexico State University and has previously served on the faculty of Case Western Reserve University and the State University of New York at Binghamton. He has published numerous articles on organizational stress and individual well-being. His research interests include how large-scale organizational interventions can create opportunities for collective organizing. He received his Ph.D. in administrative sciences from the Krannert Graduate School of Management at Purdue University.

Alfonso Montuori is affiliated with the California Institute of Integral Studies in San Francisco and also serves on the faculty of the College of Notre Dame and the Saybrook Institute Graduate School. The author of numerous articles and books, he serves as the General Editor of a book series on system or complexity theory and is the Associate Editor of *World Futures, The Journal of General Evolution.* He is a member of the General Evolution Research Group, American Psychological Association, and the International Society for Systems Science. He consults on creativity and innovation with large corporations.

Eric H. Neilsen is Professor and Chair of Organizational Behavior at the Weatherhead School of Management, Case Western Reserve University. He is active as an organization development consultant and writer, and his articles have appeared in journals, including the *Academy of Management Review* and *Administrative Science Quarterly*. His research interests include management of organizational change and the impact of national culture on managers' receptivity to organizational improvement strategies. He earned his M.A. and Ph.D. degrees from Harvard University and his B.A. from Princeton University.

Ronald E. Purser is Assistant Professor of organization development at Loyola University of Chicago. He has published in books and journals and is a reviewer for the *Academy of Management Review* and other journals. Every year since 1986, he has presented papers and symposia in the Organizational Development and Change Division of the Academy of Management. His research/teaching interests include democratic organizational design, large-group interventions, epistemology, social creativity, and social ecology issues. He earned his Ph.D. in organizational behavior from Case Western University.

Grace Ann Rosile is Assistant Professor of Management at Indiana University of Pennsylvania. She has designed and presented her own management classroom exercises at regional and national conferences, with sponsors including the Organizational Behavior Teaching Society and the Academy of Management. In addition to her interest in pedagogy for management education, her recent research focuses on applying postmodern perspectives to management, organizational behavior, and leadership. She is currently developing a postmodern organizational behavior book with David Boje, Robert Dennehy, and Deborah Summers.

David S. Steingard is a doctoral candidate in organizational behavior at Case Western Reserve University. He has published in journals, including the *Journal of Organizational Change Management* and the *Journal of Management Education*. His research interests include spirituality in business and science; ecological forms of organizing; feminist and alternative epistemologies; holistic philosophies; organizational poetics, and the meaning of life. His dissertation will build a bridge between sacred and profane aspects of organizing, based on an internship with The Body Shop.

Punya Upadhyaya is a doctoral candidate in organizational behavior at Case Western Reserve University, and he was previously educated in India. He has published in the *Journal of Management Inquiry* and the *Journal of Organizational Change Management*. His research interests include spirituality (in organizing and elsewhere), global social change organizing, and postcolonial theory.

Diana Whitney is an international speaker and consultant in the fields of organizational communication, culture, and strategic change. She works with business, government, and nonprofit leaders to help their organizations meet the challenges of the 21st century. She believes that organization excellence means both profitability and prosperity and that working should be fun. She is cofounder of the Taos Institute and an adjunct faculty member at Cornell University. She is past President of the Philadelphia Human Resource Planning Society. She holds a Ph.D. in Organizational Communication from Temple University.